International Exposure

International Exposure

PERSPECTIVES ON MODERN EUROPEAN PORNOGRAPHY, 1800–2000

EDITED BY

LISA Z. SIGEL

Rutgers University Press
New Brunswick, New Jersey, and London

363.47
I61
2005

Library of Congress Cataloging-in-Publication Data

International exposure : perspectives on modern European pornography, 1800–2000 / edited by Lisa Z. Sigel.
    p. cm.
    Includes bibliographical references and index.
    ISBN 0–8135–3518–2 (hardcover : alk. paper) — ISBN 0–8135–3519–0 (pbk. : alk. paper)
    1. Pornography—Europe. 2. Pornography—Europe—History. I. Sigel, Lisa Z., 1965–
    HQ472.E85I57 2005
    363.4'7'094—dc22

                                    2004008243

A British Cataloging-in-Publication record for this book is available from the British Library.

This collection copyright © 2005 by Rutgers, The State University
Individual chapters copyright © 2005 in the names of their authors
All rights reserved
No part of this book may be reproduced or utilized in any form or by any means, electronic or mechanical, or by any information storage and retrieval system, without written permission from the publisher. Please contact Rutgers University Press, 100 Joyce Kilmer Avenue, Piscataway, NJ 08854–8099. The only exception to this prohibition is "fair use" as defined by U.S. copyright law.

Manufactured in the United States of America

CONTENTS

Acknowledgments   *vii*

*Introduction: Issues and Problems in the History
of Pornography*   *1*
LISA Z. SIGEL

*Wanderers, Entertainers, and Seducers: Making Sense of
Obscenity Law in the German States, 1830–1851*   *27*
SARAH LEONARD

*Censorship in Republican Times: Censorship and
Pornographic Novels Located in L'Enfer de la
Bibliothèque Nationale, 1800–1900*   *48*
ANNIE STORA-LAMARRE

*Anti-Abolition Writes Obscenity: The English Vice,
Transatlantic Slavery, and England's Obscene
Print Culture*   *67*
COLETTE COLLIGAN

*The Rise of the Overly Affectionate Family: Incestuous
Pornography and Displaced Desire among the
Edwardian Middle Class*   *100*
LISA Z. SIGEL

*Old Wine in New Bottles? Literary Pornography
in Twentieth-Century France*   *125*
JOHN PHILLIPS

*A Perfectly British Business: Stagnation, Continuities,
and Change on the Top Shelf*   *146*
CLARISSA SMITH

v

METHODIST COLLEGE LIBRARY
FAYETTEVILLE, NC

Global Traffic in Pornography: The Hungarian Example   *173*
KATALIN SZOVERFY MILTER AND JOSEPH W. SLADE

*Ideologies of the Second Coming in the Ukrainian
Postcolonial Playground*   *205*
MARYNA ROMANETS

*Stripping the Nation Bare: Russian Pornography
and the Insistence on Meaning*   *232*
ELIOT BORENSTEIN

*Walking on the Wild Side: Shemale Internet
Pornography*   *255*
JOHN PHILLIPS

Contributors   *275*
Index   *279*

ACKNOWLEDGMENTS

Edited volumes are labors of love. This volume has taken the time and energy of many people, and in the process it has demonstrated the mutuality and intellectual engagement that make scholarly endeavors worthwhile. First and foremost, I would like to recognize the efforts of my contributors. Their work made this volume possible, their insights made it a pleasure to create, and their good nature made the endeavor easy. Furthermore, this project called on the expertise of people across the academy both in the United States and Europe, and scholars responded with great generosity to my unsolicited queries about who was working on this or that area. In doing so, they demonstrated that intellectuals form a community whose degree of separation would make Kevin Bacon jealous.

Olivier Lessman, my polymath of choice, not only took time out of his busy research schedule to translate but did so with an acumen and a sense of nuance rarely matched among mathematicians or professional translators. Andre Berthiaume assisted in smoothing out confusions arising from the international transit in language and documents. I have been lucky to have as my technical assistant a doctorate in computer science whose talents are matched by his generosity. Finally, Ljubomir Perkovic solved many a program and translation incongruity; he was always on call and almost always a delight.

The people at Rutgers University Press treat their authors with professionalism and respect, and I would like to thank them for their efforts on this book's behalf. In particular, Leslie Mitchner, Brendan O'Malley, and Melanie Halkias have shown a commitment to scholarship, an attention to detail, and an understanding of the complexities of putting together such a project. They have walked me through the process of publication in all its stages with good humor and kindness.

The reviewers of this volume deserve praise. Peter Stearns reviewed the project for the press and, as always, offered gracious and useful advice on how to improve the project. Lesley Hall offered timely, thoughtful, and thorough feedback. In donating her time and intellect, she has demonstrated that she is a preeminent authority on the history of sexuality not only because of her impeccable scholarship but also because of her generosity. Any failures reflect on my abilities, not their advice.

My colleagues Colleen Doody, Valentina Tikoff, Chris Gaggero, and Ben Williams have set the bar and demanded that I jump it. For that and for their continuing support and encouragement, I am grateful. As always, I would like to thank Kris Straub for her ever tactical advice. Joe Spillane gave me sound advise on publishing, and Jennifer Trost and Jim Longhurst provided counsel on all aspects of professional development.

My students in History 330 at DePaul University served as guinea pigs for many of the ideas and materials in this volume. For their insights and enthusiasm, I would like to thank Teresa Alting, Melissa Avila, Paul Becker, Joy Coppoletta, Jenny Demetrio, Andy Harmon, Ryan Kawa, Elizabeth Mergen, Sarah Nedrow, Valerie Olson, Prerna Patel, Michael Valesco, and Glen Wellman.

Tim Haggerty has been my editor, collaborator, and evil genius for this project and others. For the title alone he deserves acknowledgment. For his insistence on eloquence he deserves recognition, and for his realistic assessments of life he deserves more than I can pay or repay. If all academics turned to him for editorial and life advice, academic writing would make people laugh, dinner parties would all be delicious, and the everyday would have far more verve.

Finally, I would like to thank my family for their continued support and encouragement.

International Exposure

Introduction

Issues and Problems in the History of Pornography

Lisa Z. Sigel

Like it or not, many of us come across pornography on a regular basis: naughty pictures wink from the seaside postcard rack, dirty magazines beckon from behind the convenience store counter, and scrambled images moan over cable TV. Full-length pornographic films can be ordered by mail, picked up in video stores, or downloaded over personal computers. One paradoxical effect of this saturation is that many people have come to ignore it altogether: to make a bad play on words, pornography is overexposed. Although cultural crises around sexuality and child pornography panics awaken the issue periodically, relatively few people spend their lives thinking about pornography. Consumers use it, but its production lies outside of public purview. Dirty literature, nude photography, and blue film production form the basis of their own industries but ones rarely highlighted in business school casebooks, the tabloid press, or the pages of the *Wall Street Journal.* In Western culture pornography's ubiquity is relatively new; the lack of state intervention is a product of contemporary society. Indeed, most previous work in the field of pornography has charted the history of legalization as a First Amendment or free speech issue in an extensive body of legal and activist works. While this volume necessarily touches on the processes of legalization, it is more concerned with the cultural impact of pornography, whether legal or not. For, if legal sanctions no longer apply to most pornography, if consumers use it as a matter of course, if an industry has emerged to meet that need, and if the general public has become so inured to pornography as to render it invisible, then why should scholars concern themselves with it?

One answer may be that academics engage the world of pornography to fulfill a basic function of scholarship: to provide a reservoir of information on a topic. If academics want to help answer those questions that the public periodically asks about sexuality and about pornography as a cultural form, then there is a need to study pornography. The emblematic "girlie magazine," for example, is a relatively new invention; nothing preordained its existence. At a material and technological level the developments of the Western printing press (1436–1437), photography (1827), and photolithography (1890s) made such a magazine possible. Even beyond these technical transformations, however, the iconic display of the naked woman is a relatively late invention and by no means the only one possible. Earlier erotic images certainly featured nude women, but they also featured nude men, couples, clerics, and humans and animals in compromising positions. Furthermore, Western European culture eroticizes certain aspects of the female form—such as breasts—while other cultures do not.[1] The girlie magazine is the result of alignments around issues of gender, consumer culture, technology, and class politics. Charting this emergence is no small task, but it remains necessary if we want to understand what such magazines might ultimately mean. To make a case about the recent saturation of such images, academics need to study such phenomena. Pornography's very presence justifies extended inquiry.

Truisms and generalizations have long stood in for clear studies of pornography; as a result, public policies are based on flawed and faulty information at best and a dearth of information at worst. Pornography, like sexuality itself, is an issue with deep symbolic importance. Pornography became a national problem in the nineteenth century, an international issue by World War I, and more recently, with recent debates about child pornography on the Internet, a transnational concern. Since the nineteenth century those concerned with the growing immorality of the general populace have viewed the spread of pornography as a litmus test. By focusing on the immorality of the masses and the vulnerabilities of the weak, European states reconciled an increasing intervention into private lives at the same time that they guaranteed greater freedoms through an expanding liberalism. Panics about cultural decay, whether at the end of the nineteenth century, between the wars, or during the 1980s, looked at pornography as evidence of and culprit in the problems of modern life.

Joan Hoff has connected the dearth of historical studies on pornography with the proliferation of policies against pornography in the United States. Hoff points out that, although both the Johnson Commission (1970) and the Meese Commission (1986) acknowledged that the historical work needed to be done, neither commission would sponsor the work. Instead, both commissions issued recommendations based on fictional, historical projections. Hoff argues that detailed histories of pornography would interfere with the underlying political agenda of social control.[2] Pornography became a focal point for concerns about the problems of modernity.

No matter how culturally or politically problematic, pornography remains an important economic enterprise. Sex sells; pornography proves the point. Pornography is a growth industry, and to understand the economics of modern society, particularly the economics of consumer culture, scholars need to engage pornography. The combination of relaxed legislation and rising consumer desires has made pornography a particularly viable industry. Because pornography encompasses shoddy and elegant literature—images that include postcards and photographs, cinema, videos, and even Web-based products—the study of pornography as an economic enterprise explains the selling of sex in the world market. Pornographers need relatively little capital to start an enterprise, allowing it to be a cottage industry at the petty level and a consequently inexpensive export. Production and distribution of pornography provide a blueprint for both illegal and legal entrepreneurial endeavors in the consumer age.

At the same time, pornography became a very private affair, integral to the formation of personal, sexual identities. The dearth of legitimate conduits for information about sexuality in the past has guaranteed that information and titillation overlapped. This is especially true for information regarding sexual deviance. Although novels, plays, philosophy, and medicine provide models and meanings for the budding and inquisitive heterosexual, even that heterosexual could find few guides to sex before the sexual revolutions of the 1920s and 1960s, notwithstanding a few popular works. Pornography provided detailed information on topics as varied as the genital kiss, anal intercourse, and multiple partners that legitimate works refused to acknowledge. This type of information, of no small importance to the "normal" male or female, became even more important for those whose desires deviated from the norm. The circulation of texts that acknowledged lesbian, gay, and rampant desires of all kinds helped create communities of deviants, whether existing purely in the minds of users or actually formed through the circulation of texts. The formation of subversive sexual identities and communities can no longer be written off as mere individual deviance, given recent work in feminist and queer studies. Following Michel Foucault's insights, scholars have shown that sexual identity has been central to the formation of disciplinary regimes. Rather than being irrelevant to the modern state, deviance is one of the central foci of state action and pornography became an avenue to challenge that relationship.

Sexuality constitutes a large part of modern people's sense of self. Identities, dreams, and fears can be grounded in sexuality, and pornography allows for the examination of these issues. Laura Kipnis argues that "it exposes the culture to itself. Pornography is the royal road to the cultural psyche (as for Freud, dreams were the route to the unconscious)."[3] In her model we need to confront pornography and come to terms with the entangled desires it documents in order to understand our society and its relationship to sexuality. Unconscious, subconscious, and occasionally conscious desires are articulated through pornography. In his masterly study of gay male erotica Thomas Waugh argues that the history of gay pornography provides an "acknowledgment of the erotic as a driving force in the gay imaginary." It is because of this imaginary that the gay community has been pilloried, and the recovery of it remains central to historicizing the gay experience.[4] If this is true, then recovering desires remain central to the understanding of identity and the individual's place in the broader society. Understanding either the gay or straight imaginary is an important project if we understand ourselves as beings driven by sexuality. Waugh's study provides a model of how to uncover the range of desires in a given community, but the diversity of desires makes this a momentous task. The emergence of multiple, overlapping sexual identities speaks to a new orientation between sexuality, the individual, and society.

The simple binaries of male and female, straight and gay, and rich and poor lose their analytical cogency when placed within the context of European culture. The perseverance of peasant beliefs, the formation of a working-class culture, the refinement of middle-class tastes, and the persistence of aristocratic attitudes not only overlapped, for example, but formed an extended argument around issues of sexuality that complicates any simple binary reading. When members of the middle class spoke about workers as sexually debased and dirty (as they frequently did in the nineteenth century) and when workers parried with allegations about hypocrisy (as they did less frequently but with equal vigor), both sides were taking part in a long-term deliberation about sexual behaviors, attitudes, and meanings. As Annie Stora-Lamarre demonstrates in her essay on the l'Enfer collection of pornography in France, these cross-class dialogues formed the backdrop of obscenity debates. The issue of access to ideas about sexuality remained embroiled in the class-based conversation about civic rights and virtues. The development of a broad-based democracy in France's Third Republic rested upon civic virtues that often amounted to the state's assessment of people's abilities to replicate bourgeois patterns of morality. This assessment occurred within the context of the formation of regional and national identities, which in turn happened in the context of international alignments. French pornographers, for example, used ideas about Russian court life to create fantasies about decadence, while Russian pornography developed against allegations of French decadence even while trying to copy French sophistication on sexual matters.[5] The clamor created by innumerable, simultaneous conversations about sexuality presents the basic stuff of scholarly dreams; documenting these conversations and then understanding what was at stake in them is central to the historian's task.

While pornography provides a scholarly topic like many others in one sense, it remains distinct in part because of the long-term illegality of the sources and in part because conversations about the topic are new and quickly evolving. Few archives collect pornography, and those that do are often subject to political pressures. While states designated many acts in the past, such as smuggling or prostitution, as illegal the articles relating to those acts were not immolated or subjected to a symbolic auto-da-fé, often complete with a sacrificial effigy. Tea drinkers in the eighteenth-century used that product openly despite its smuggled origins; prostitutes took part in broader community life even when their trade was outlawed. Pornography, on the other hand, remained illegal as a product even after the taint of illegal production dissipated and even though institutions such as the British Museum and the Bibliothèque Nationale developed collections as did prominent individuals who stood above the law.

The long-term illegality of pornography has stifled generations of scholarship. A wish list for scholarship in this volume would make this embarrassingly clear; Yugoslavia deserves its own article as being nonaligned in pornography as it was on much else; Swedish and Danish pornography still carries a subversive authority that deserves recognition in scholarship; little has been written about modern Italy, despite its designation as the birthplace of both modernity and pornography. Just working across the map of Europe can provide inspiration for future work. Furthermore, certain types of pornography have fallen between disciplinary gaps. Historians deal best with print sources, and only recently have scholars embraced the study of film either as a teaching enterprise or as a technical topic. Pornographic film has suffered even more than mainstream film by this omission. Visual culture in all its forms deserves a greater focus than it has received; as the world turns toward multimedia, scholars need to follow. The interwar years, as one can see in this volume, deserve more attention than they get. It is easy to understand why other issues such as the emergence of fascism or Stalinism might command attention to the exclusion of concerns such as sexuality, but we should not overlook sexuality or pornography during the period. Sexual dissidents were targets of liberal and radical regimes alike; pornography circulated throughout Europe and its empires and prompted extended discussion at the League of Nations; much of modernism as a cultural movement emerged from the recognition of sexual tensions in society. Thus, while other concerns have dominated scholarship of the period, sexuality remains so embedded that to overlook it seems willfully obtuse, but, with a few important exceptions, such temporal gaps in this volume echo larger gaps in the scholarship.

It is understandable that scholars might shy away from such a risky venture; it remains impossible to speak of complete collections, individual responses, or social attitudes with any solid assurance. Few other historical sources can so quickly get scholars arrested at customs; work on cinematic pornography remains retarded by current legal restrictions on sources, notwithstanding such works as Linda Williams's *Hardcore*.[6] Scholars who examine pornography do so at their own risk. Grants, funding, promotions—the bread and butter of academic life—are generally not supportive of the study of pornography.[7] And few other topics are at once so nebulous and heated: the so-called porn wars of the 1980s made pornography a lightning rod for divisions in the feminist community around the issues of sexuality and state intervention in the United States. The academic clamor from these debates remains ongoing. Only since legalization has the study of pornography been separated from political activism, and only since the relative quiescence over the porn wars has there been room for painstaking historical work.

Nevertheless, a number of remarkable works have appeared. Robert Darnton's *Literary Underground of the Old Regime,* Iain McCalman's *Radical Underworld,* and Lynn Hunt's *Invention of Pornography* each focus on the emergence of premodern pornography and place it within the mainstream of emerging Western society.[8] Darnton established the overlap between Enlightenment philosophers and erotic pamphleteers. McCalman argued that English revolutionaries used pornography as a way to delegitimize the British monarchy, and Hunt demonstrated the centrality of pornography to the political and cultural formation of modern Europe. These studies legitimized pornography as a serious topic, but the methods, approaches, and even subject matter remain open to further debate. Darnton's approach, for example, which centers on the history of the book, has done much to illuminate the parameters of publication and distribution but offers little insight into the cultural meanings of sexuality. McCalman's history of revolutionary movements demonstrates tangible links between political movements and pornography, but the meanings and uses of those erotic publications remain open. In many ways this generation of scholars legitimized the study of pornography because they were not pornography scholars but, rather, scholars of "serious" issues whose rigor led them to the topic. They established the importance of the topic, but the subject itself remains underexamined, as do questions about whether these early approaches constitute the best way to continue.

Basic analytical approaches vary as widely as methods and foci in the social sciences and humanities. An archaeological approach, established by Michel Foucault and represented here by Colette Colligan, takes a constellation of ideas and traces them backward in time to get at the cluster of associations that they contain at their root. In doing so, archaeological studies of ideas examine often hidden meanings as they circulate in the culture. A traditional, historical approach, as taken by Sarah Leonard, Annie Stora-Lamarre, and me, tends to move forward in time to explore the accretion of ideas and sources. Whereas the emphasis on archaeological examinations is on an encrusted present, the emphasis in historical deliberations is on the past in its own right. A more classical literary approach, used by John Phillips in his article on French literary fiction, examines new literary forms as aesthetic and cultural products. In doing so, Phillips weighs the strengths of such works in aesthetic, rather than political, terms, even as he acknowledges that some of the most important gains made by authors during this period were in the expansion of sexual expression. Katalin Milter and Joseph Slade's essay and Clarissa Smith's work examine cultural products through an economic lens. This approach highlights the business aspects of pornographic production and distribution to see the influence of the economy on fantasy. Eliot Borenstein and Maryna Romanets, in looking at Eastern European pornography, foreground the political aspects of pornography that emerged with the dissolution of the Soviet state: Romanets uses a postcolonial approach, while Borenstein uses a more traditional politics of culture approach. Finally, John Phillips uses a queer studies approach grounded in psychoanalytical theory to explore the meaning of gender transmutation. While economic and postcolonial approaches focus on the ways in which politics and economics create sexual options, the psychoanalytical approach explores the meanings of those options.

Clearly, these orientations provide only a beginning to styles and methods of study—for example, the anthropological and philosophical go unrepresented—and each has its own strengths and limitations. Nonetheless, what one can learn from the variety of approaches is the ensuing range of factors that influence sexual fantasy and the variety of effects that emerge from such dreams. Whether one highlights the political, aesthetic, economic, social, or psychological as the purpose of study clearly influences the outcome of analysis. This panoply of approaches can help the study of pornography emerge from the contentious legacy left by previous debates over free speech, social morality, and social protection.

These debates still affect scholarship, however; they have no more disappeared than have the early reasons for studying pornography. Basic definitions of *erotica, pornography,* and *obscenity,* for example, remain heavily theorized and heavily contested. To label a source "pornographic" is, in itself, to take a stand. Some scholars, such as Thomas Waugh, use the word *erotica* to avoid the stigma that the term *pornography* places on people's desires.[9] Others, such as Joseph Slade, use the term *pornography* to challenge the same stigmas. In their examinations of early modern sexuality Paula Findlen discusses Pietro Aretino and other Renaissance writers as pornographic, while David Frantz places the same writers within the rubric of erotica.[10] These scholars have all produced lucid, thoughtful, and thorough scholarship; more is going on here than shoddy word choice or slipshod editing. The distinction between pornography and erotica might look like semantic nitpicking, but the labels have important consequences that continue to affect policy and perceptions.

While the word *pornography* might have a certain risqué ring, it only emerged during the mid-nineteenth century, when *pornographos,* to write about prostitutes, became *pornography,* salacious art and literature.[11] As the new meaning developed, so did distinct ways of dealing with the phenomenon. Obscene art often had a historical legitimacy that saved it from immolation. Instead of destruction, these artifacts were preserved in the oddly evocative "Secretum," or "secret museum," where access was limited to erudite men.[12] Thus, it is anachronistic to use the term *pornography* before the nineteenth century; even during that period, states did not designate the materials as pornographic. A more precise way of discussing such writings and images might be to say that they had erotic elements that the state or church deemed obscene, though this phrase would be misleading, too. When the papacy referred to Aretino's writings as obscene in the sixteenth century, it meant to stigmatize them, much as someone would pejoratively use the term *pornography* today. The word does not need to exist for the category to be meaningful; scholars have shown that an illegal class of materials that promoted sexual arousal preceded the syllogism. Moreover, the use of the phrase "erotic elements deemed obscene" lends itself to an even more important anachronism of schematizing sexual artifacts into distinct categories. The line between what functioned as pornography and what did not has been historically ambiguous.

If the definition of *pornography* remains frustratingly unclear, its implications and effects are even more problematic. Pornography encompasses a wide variety of subjects, from "straight" procreative sex to incestuous unions, it comments upon a wide variety of human endeavors, from masturbation to revolution, and it communicates through a wide variety of mediums, from high literature to mass-produced videos. Some scholars try to establish that pornography serves a social good and thereby save the entire category from the censor's fires; others seek to delineate erotica from pornography and vilify the latter as the root of modern society's decay.[13] Essays in this volume provide an important counterweight by focusing on those items in which a rough accord was reached. Despite the different approaches to scholarship, the essays take on the task of exploring the production and consumption of desires and grounding these desires in a historic framework. As the authors argue, sexual representations and sexuality itself function in relation to the broader culture. To understand pornography, one must move beyond universalizing definitions or analyses to locate sexuality within complex frameworks that hinge upon changing definitions of obscenity, emerging forms of representations, and shifting cultural contexts. The task of excavating the factors that contribute to the "pornographic imaginary" demonstrates the complex relationships of sexuality to society during the critical period when sexuality became a focus of state concern.

In her earlier edited volume on the invention of pornography, Lynn Hunt argued that pornography "was almost always an adjunct to something else until the middle or end of the eighteenth century."[14] Pornography, rather than merely engaging in the libidinal, emerged from the very movements that defined the modern world: humanism, the scientific revolution, and the Enlightenment. Hunt argued that after that crucial point, the balance shifted and the erotic became a main focus of pornography; nevertheless, that does not mean that pornography did only sexual work. Science, imperialism, nationalism, race relations, and familial patterns developed through pornographic discourse; pornography remained enmeshed in the larger contradictions and problems of European society. At the same time, however, pornography had its own hidden history, one that it often wryly self-acknowledged. To understand modern pornography, whether literary, visual, or cinematic, one must acknowledge its debts and the ways it carries with it vestiges of its premodern inheritance.

Early modern pornography developed alongside the introduction of the printing press and the rise of print culture; the establishment of a commerce in learning; a new urban concentration of men, clubs, and societies; and an appreciation of satire and political subversion. The rediscovery of ancient works about sexuality encouraged Renaissance writers and painters to redefine erotic expression. Elite writers such as Ferrante Pallavicino adopted styles from the ancient world and immersed themselves in pre-Christian perspectives on sexuality. Ancient Greek and Roman writers had engaged topics such as priapism, prostitution, and same-sex love; the Renaissance rediscovery of these themes created room for the exploration of sexuality in opposition to ecclesiastical mandates at the same time that writers created works that circulated within and outside the ecclesiastical community. A heightened interest in the human form produced erotic as well as anatomical drawings of the body, and a voyeuristic gaze was incorporated into graphic and literary materials.

At a more popular level writers saw themselves as analogous to prostitutes; they used the trope of the whore to make the wheezing, farting, sexually protean body central to the human comedy, and they welded satire to sexuality. In doing so, they provided entertainment and political commentary by criticizing rivals, religious orders, and social rigidity. Their writings combined erudition and sophistication with the carnivalesque. Pornography also allowed those writers possessing rhetorical prowess to achieve patronage and a literary reputation. The most famous writer of this sort was Pietro Aretino, who deliberately violated religious and social taboos and who consciously commented upon the power of the word to arouse and sometimes deflate the body; he recognized the pornographic even as he created it.[15] Pornography thus emerged at two levels simultaneously, one that served the elites and one that filtered ever downward in opposition to elite hypocrisy.

The adoption of the mechanical printing press contributed to the dispersal of obscene texts. Renaissance pornography became so popular that the papacy explicitly outlawed recent erotic writings at the Council of Trent (1563), although classical texts remained exempt.[16] In spite of this ban, the Italian style of bawdy writing spread across the Continent. Taken as a whole, Italian pornography combined an attention to ribald and vernacular folk culture with pandering to the tastes of the urbane and wealthy. This combination of bottom-up impulses and top-down access paradoxically made pornography at once politically subversive and socially conservative by simultaneously scrutinizing the links between political and sexual order and limiting the extent of the conversation.

By the seventeenth century an international traffic in sexual ideas linked the intellectual centers of Europe. Because Italy had become the spiritual homeland of obscenity, other European authors paid homage by laying their fictional scenarios there. Italy was more than a geographical expression; it became a style, an orientation, and an erotic Utopia. Thomas Nashe, the English author of "Choice of Valentines," bluntly stated that he imitated the Aretines.[17] Such tributes suggest the breadth of bawdy learning across the Continent. Although publishers routinely falsified information about locations, authorship, and dates, the fictitious and real information signaled the arrival of a self-aware cosmopolitan sexuality. For example, Nicolas Chorier of Vienna wrote *Aloisiae Sigaeae Toletanae Satyra Sotadica de arcanis Amoris et Veneris* (commonly called *The Dialogues of Luisa Sigea*) and published it in Grenoble (or Lyon) in 1659 (or 1660). To further confuse matters, he attributed the work to a Spanish woman and the translation to a Dutchman. The text, first published in Latin, was then translated into English and French by the 1680s.[18] Between the fictive and real information, the work touched on the major and minor centers of education, literacy, and wealth and demonstrated the overlap between the realm of pornography and the arrival of a broad sense of European sophistication that was tilting toward Western Europe.

During the eighteenth century pornography spread across the Continent. Not every nation developed an indigenous pornographic tradition—indeed, most countries lacked one at least until the nineteenth century—but each nevertheless had a small pool of pornography that circulated among the wealthy. Establishing the non-existence of a tradition is always dicey, but it appears that little pornography was produced in Germany, Spain, Russia, or Finland; even the Netherlands had only an abortive pornographic tradition.[19] Even in these countries, however, translations and republications continued to appear. David Stevenson's work on Scottish Clubs during the Enlightenment demonstrates that the circulation of pornography reached from the backwaters of the Scottish countryside to Russia through the links of convivial societies, free trade, and informal ambassadors.[20] Pornography linked centers of learning, seeping into the fabric of eighteenth-century society.

Enlightenment ideals such as rationality and natural rights could be validly applied to sexuality. The ongoing rejection of tradition piqued pornographers into considering a sexuality freed from contemporary restraints; free-thinking politics overlapped with free-thinking sexuality.[21] A legal overlap between philosophy and pornography also emerged from patterns of censorship. By outlawing the works of the *philosophes* and pornographers in tandem, for example, the French government solidified the relationship between the two genres and between the writers and publishing houses that engaged in illicit trade.[22] Like philosophers, pornographers chiseled away at the corrupt foundations of society, including those built around sexuality. They accused the Church of perversity and insisted that it had little right to restrict more mundane sexual practices. Just to stay on everyone's good side, pornographers also made allegations of sexual perversity about the monarchy and argued against a familial (and thus implicitly sexual) rule of succession and for a new social contract. Philosophers such as Comte de Mirabeau and Denis Diderot produced political, philosophical, and obscene writings simultaneously.

The dramatic cultural changes that occurred during the French Revolution—from new attitudes to divorce, the repudiation of the monarchy, and the curtailing of Church control—can be tied in part to the critiques found within French pornography. This type of political pornography reached its apex (or nadir, depending on one's point of view) in the 1790s in France and ebbed after the trial of Marie Antoinette.[23] While many of the political arguments about pornography and many of the themes and tropes it relied on were set by the Revolution, changes in the relationship between society and desire continued to occur with the rise of new forms of representation, new political alignments, and new controls by the state.

Across the Channel, England developed its own pornographic tradition, one that also gained currency in the rejection of older forms of government.[24] While English pornography evolved against the historical controversies around religion, governance, and empire, by the eighteenth century these currents merged with a middle-class culture and began to generate significant works such as *Fanny Hill,* or, more formally, *The Memoirs of a Woman of Pleasure* (1748 or 1749). *Fanny Hill* fit into a broader literary development as it followed the transition from the epistolary novel to that based upon plotting, character development, and description.[25] Pornography did not remain isolated; the pornographic novel rose in form alongside the more "canonical" one.[26] With the French Revolution, English pornography became more overtly politicized as texts, writers, and ideas were influenced by the wave of revolutionary sentiment that spread across Europe.[27] This English tradition of political pornography continued well into the nineteenth century, bolstered by the continued participation of political radicals such as William Dugdale and John and Benjamin Brookes and by their republication of pornographic, political texts. As the Queen Caroline Affair demonstrated, pornography could cross the political divide, serving either radical or conservative masters equally well.

In the German states new immoral books emerged after the Enlightenment tradition during the late eighteenth and early nineteenth centuries and generated new definitions of obscenity based on the emerging definitions of bourgeois citizenship, rather than the overlap of politics and sexuality. As Sarah Leonard demonstrates, Germany lacked the philosophical and anticlerical traditions of obscene writing found in France or England but remained aware of the burgeoning of sexual and revolutionary radicalism through the availability of French texts. The overlap between political and sexual enticements were firmly established when Germany began to develop its own canon. The German texts differed from classical "erotic" works by eschewing titillating details, but the police and guilds saw them as "lewd and immodest" and developed definitions of *obscenity* to counter their circulation.

Leonard shows that German obscenity emerged at a critical period between the Napoleonic Wars and the formation of the German Empire, when older ties and allegiances were broken down and new requisites for citizenship emerged. In this context pornography combined the questioning of sexual and social contracts with critiques of the emerging pattern of bourgeois sexuality. Works such as *Beloved of Eleven Thousand Women, Memoirs of Lola Montez,* and *Memoirs of a Singer* raised questions about citizenship, gender, and the erotics of the modern world. In these three examples the key theme of social wandering becomes set against the emerging bourgeois values of hard work, progress, stability, and gender difference. Althing's novel, *Beloved of Eleven Thousand,* follows a downwardly mobile character as he makes his way through a sexually and politically fragmented world. The dissolution of family, trade, and citizenship leave him vulnerable to vagaries of modernity and its seductive forces. *The Memoirs of Lola Montez* recounts the personal history of the dancer and consort of King Ludwig of Bavaria, who promised her citizenship and elevation to the aristocracy before protests forced Montez into exile and the king into abdication. Montez's memoirs denounced radicalism and extolled the value of loyalty in the fragmenting political world. In contrast, Wilhelmine Schroeder-Devrient, a political and social radical expelled from Dresden for her participation in the uprisings in 1848, purportedly wrote *The Memoirs of a Singer.* Her fictionalized memoirs recount the sexual life of the "modern" woman who documents her history for the benefit of "science." Neither the conservatism of Montez nor the radicalism of Schroeder-Devrient precluded the works' reception as "immoral." Instead, the definitions of *obscenity* worked across the political spectrum even as pornography, by having characters carve new social and sexual contracts, addressed new political realities. Obscenity, as her essay demonstrates, maintained its status as politically corrupting even as the basis of politics changed.

Despite the changing relationship between pornography and society, as a product, pornography showed great continuity. Pornographers continued to print texts using letterpress, to illustrate them using woodcuts and copper plates, and to sell their works in markets, fairs, and bookshops in the first half of the nineteenth century. Even the texts remained fairly standard. *Fanny Hill,* for example, continued to gain prestige in the nineteenth century, and editions in English, French, Italian, and German poured off the presses.[28] Pornographers had an established body of knowledge, a preexisting consumer base, and a repertoire of pirated texts, ideas, tropes, and examples.

By the midcentury, however, three related contextual developments began to transform the trade: the overlap between the sexual and political spheres began to break down, pornographers focused on consumer products, and states across Europe concerned themselves increasingly with moral surveillance of their subjects. As revolutions soured the upper classes on the ideals of radical change, the ties between revolution and pornography began to unravel.[29] By the 1860s most governments, including those in England, France, and Germany, began national campaigns to control their populations through the censorship of sexual ideas. The state intervened with the justification that it needed to help the weak—particularly the young, poor, and female—who remained susceptible to immorality. The essays by Annie Stora-Lamarre, Colette Colligan, and me demonstrate how these topologies emerged in the nineteenth century as oversexed and implicitly corruptible. The focus on hypersexualized women, children, and perverts correspond to the typologies that Foucault delineated as emerging in the modern world. Pornography became another disciplinary regime that overtly said what other forms of discourse both aroused and tried to silence. Pornographic tropes began a new form of political work in the nineteenth century as overt and confrontational politics lost its hold over the expression of sexual ideas.

Symbols that maintained cultural currency were adapted to the broad cultural changes of the period as writers recycled figures and tropes and applied key themes to new circumstances. As Stora-Lamarre demonstrates, the idea and image of the sexually rampant women remained central to French pornography throughout the nineteenth century; despite this dominance, however, the image of women underwent a series of broad transformations. The books of l'Enfer written by men and contained by male censors demonstrate a changing conception of female sexuality. These shifts illustrate the cultural memory of masculine desire as the nineteenth century struggled with the impacts of democracy, industrialization, the expansion of consumer culture, and nationalism.

Stora-Lamarre argues that the changing ideals of female sexuality link the broadest debates about the nation to the minutest form of perversion. Early-nineteenth-century works saw sexually voracious women as adventurers who climbed the social ladder. By the 1830s female heroines, whether nubile adults or precocious children, became more voracious and driven by monstrous desires; they no longer controlled their world and their sexuality, but, as early femme fatales, were now at the mercy of them. Once driven by great passions, by 1900 female characters became industrialized: sex became reduced to manipulation, and love and lust gave way to mechanization. In France the outpouring from the pornographic press and the importation of works that detailed ever more perverse practices created a crisis in democratic ideals. According to critics, the masses' familiarity with such terrible creatures could only corrupt reason as the crowd gave way to the audience. During the fin de siècle it was posited that this debased audience included women who would eschew faithfulness and virtue in favor of lust and excitement. According to this line of reasoning, the absence of morality on the part of men and women would weaken the nation. The control of fictional creatures and their supposedly real-life counterparts became integral to the functioning of the Republic. The early pornographic tradition became caught in the ebb tide of political alignments; having once served the Revolution, by the late nineteenth century it began to limit the efficacy of people's abilities to rule. This mutability gets to the center of debates about pornography's relationship to politics in the modern world: as a consumer product, pornography became unaccountable to political allegiances, even though it had political connotations that remained formidable.

Colligan demonstrates that racialism underwent substantial revisions during the same period. Early in the nineteenth century abolitionist texts raised the issue of sexual violence for humanitarian purposes, but, once raised, racialized, sexual violence continued to circulate as a trope. Pornographers picked up the implicit sexual tension between denunciation and prurience in abolitionist literature and created a new flagellant, racialist pornography out of an older humanitarian tradition. The beaten female slave served many masters: from arousal that wedded titillation to political action, sexual parodies that exploited homoerotic tension through the medium the female body, and chastisements for female aspirations that served as counter-nationalist propaganda. As Colligan demonstrates, sexual exploration divorced itself from the social roots of abolition, allowing the idea of the slave to cross literary forms and remain contextually mutable. The reworking of the slave narrative, in turn, became a strand in the fabric of English flagellation literature. Flagellation, long considered the English vice, emerged at the intersection of a long-standing racialism, an emerging consumerism, and a progressive past; theories of sadomasochism (S-M) that see the practice as playing with power for liberationist purposes need to take this past into their accounts.

In a similar process, in which pornographers made use of preexisting symbols and tropes, incest underwent extensive renovation. Before the nineteenth century the trope of incest was used in negative propagandistic campaigns such as those against Marie Antoinette. In the late nineteenth century pornographers began to develop the theme of incest as a positive pleasure rather than a negative example. My essay charts fantasies of incest in the late nineteenth century and the transference of desire within the family. Incestuous pornography—produced, sold, and read by men—created a fictive access to children's desires. As readers used such texts to look into the fictional minds of children, the fictional children looked out with longing on the men who read. Children in these works were doubly sexual: they became not only sexual objects, worthy of erotic contemplation, but also sexual subjects who actively desired the attention. By engaging in sexual intercourse with children (often in a forced embrace), adults liberated children's desires in this model. The shift in the meaning of incest in pornography shows the ways that consumerism made use of existing tensions and tropes to whet, make, and meet emerging desires.

Taken together, the essays by Stora-Lamarre, Colligan, and me show the conservative turn that pornography took over the course of the nineteenth century. As these essays demonstrate, pornography became another path toward disciplining, examining, and enjoying the politically subordinated in European society, a path that complemented patterns of censorship, even as the state justified such patterns based on the purity of those under question.[30] It is here that one can see the connection between what are often thought of as individual perversions and broader cultural patterns. Deviance, a modern concept, emerged in relation to the exigencies of consumer culture, shaped and organized by the illegal market. At the same time, this market responded to the broader culture and choreographed the emergence of identities in conflict with the modern state. Gender roles, the family, the racial order, and heterosexuality contained paradoxes that pornography elaborated in ways that both supported and undercut official morality. The state would be hard-pressed to argue that it supported incestuous rape or racialized discipline, but it remained incapable of offering an alternative logic to the ones that so fully emerged from other, state-sanctioned realms. By shedding its overtly political messages and, instead, contributing to a covert politics of consumption, by ignoring the rules of aesthetics when desirable, adopting them when useful, and satirizing them at every possible turn, pornography counterbalanced the more bourgeois processes of refinement—artistic, ideological, hygienic—that dominated the polite world. The obscene and aboveboard, however, had the same roots in the expansion of culture as an item for consumption.

Inexpensive paperbacks, pamphlets, and photos were joined by postcards, penny-in-the-slot machines, and films encouraging circulation across the class structure.[31] At the same time, the rapidly expanding European empires provided new opportunities for a popular, symbolic imperialism. Malek Alloula has tied the erotic postcard to the popularity of imperialism.[32] Photographs and illustrations from Asia, Central America, and Africa flooded back to Europe, allowing all levels of European society to see concrete images of imperialism and European dominion. Images of naked and partially naked Algerian, "Moorish," South African, and Caribbean women permeated the metropolises of Europe, corroborating fictional accounts of nonwhite sexuality. Even stamps produced by the imperial governments showed images of naked natives well into the twentieth century. The invention of motion pictures in the 1890s allowed early displays of female nudity, and cinematic pornography emerged with either *Le Voyeur* (1907) or *A l'écu d'or ou la Bonne Auberge* (1908). French filmmakers pioneered the pornographic film, but German and Italian filmmakers quickly followed. These silent films erected few linguistic barriers, becoming staple fare at brothels and traveling between towns in France and, more covertly, airing internationally.[33]

Across Europe, states responded to the emergence of consumer pornography by increasing the tenor of criticism against pornography and by emphasizing the vulnerability of suspect populations; both the state and pornography focused on women, on people of color, on children and the young, with ever greater attention. Most European states let the police, the customhouse, and the courts winnow out the obscene on the ground, while organizations and state agencies joined together into international organizations to confront the problem. They lobbied for the passage of new, but largely ineffective, legislation. National governments began to work together, share information, and organize censorship campaigns; these measures hampered but did not end the trade.

The formation of the social sciences between the 1880s and 1920s allowed emerging disciplines such as anthropology, sociology, criminal justice, and psychology to investigate sexuality as an academic pursuit separate from erotica. As social sciences legitimated the objective study of sexuality, *pornography* became a catch-all term to include those works that did not neatly fit within scholarly inquiry. In essence, as legitimating functions broke away from pornography, pornography lost its claim to a social function apart from arousal. Yet a relationship between the newly compartmentalized schemas for addressing human sexuality continued, however much social scientists tried to divest themselves of the stigma of prurience; sexologists used pornography to define emerging sexual pathologies, while writers and publishers exploited new categories of identity to organize and sell pornography.[34] Thus, the study of sex and the sale of sex continued to be mutually reinforcing, both economically and intellectually. Consumerism and science formed a reciprocating relationship as pornographers marketed their works according to specific sexual appetites and scientists studied, labeled, categorized, and created etiologies for emerging desires. While pornography became a more discrete concept, it did not exist in isolation as either a locus for ideas about sexuality or as a category of constraint.

After World War I the "cult of the body" developed as a reaction to repression, the war, and the problems of modern, urban society. This "cult" withstood political division: artists, intellectuals, and ideologues looked to the body as a central icon of the human condition and used it to symbolize social decay or cultural superiority. The symbol of the body was strengthened by the rise of nudism, the back to nature movement, the expansion of physical culture ideals, and the increase in youth groups, all of which legitimized the prevalence of sexuality and the nude. The rise of the physical culture movement and the Free Body Culture movement in Germany advocated a return to nature as a way to combat the degeneration of industrial capitalism and urbanization. According to these movements, individuals needed to re-attune their bodies to the outdoors and reject the poison of industrial society. These claims were made against commercial culture, but magazines, photographs, pulp fiction, films, and books followed suit and touted the qualities of the nude physique.[35] Erotic enough to function as a wellspring of masturbatory fantasies, these displays were also desexualized enough to pass censorship boards. As Thomas Waugh has demonstrated, homoerotic "beefcake" and hetero-erotic "cheesecake" emerged from this milieu, and the circulation of such ideas and images functioned to form as well as meet emerging desires.[36] During the 1930s the political Right took radical action to end the problem; when the National Socialists seized power in Germany in 1933, one of their first acts was to burn a cache of such decadence: the Institute of Sexual Science's books and papers. Nevertheless, they developed their own cult of the body during the interwar years. Nazi ideals incorporated elements of pornography into public art. Thus, fascist regimes took pornography, and the liberal reaction to it, as emblematic of the excesses of liberalism but could not avoid its persuasive power. By the 1930s the pornographic had become synonymous with social decay.[37]

These forms of banned pornographic film, photography, and literature, as well as the semi-legal images of nudism and bodybuilding, carried into the postwar world.[38] World War II and its aftermath also contributed to an American cultural influence in Western Europe; pornography proved no exception. GIs' "pin-up girls" became a public model of sexuality. The American "porno" film and magazine shortly followed. As the American culture industry began to dominate European markets during the postwar years, so American influence began to be felt in pornography, as magazines such as *Playboy* reached Britain and the Continent.

Censorship again emerged when politically liberal states sought to contrast their regimes with fascist and communist ones. Britain, France, West Germany, and the Netherlands, in particular, saw liberalism as superior to the cultural controls enacted in the Communist bloc, but this position raised the problematic issue of moral censorship. In 1960s and 1970s European governments reversed social policy by legalizing pornography based upon new standards: if any element of the work had artistic, historical, or literary merit, it had a redeeming social value and should not be censored. This standard created new types of pornography and new levels of profitability; pornographers began to defend their works based upon the social value of sexual pleasure.[39]

As long as it stayed illegal, pornography appeared as a reservoir of the hidden desires of humanity, creating a confrontational stance with the state. Pornography revealed hidden, hierarchical relationships once legalization occurred. The mixture of gender expectations, sexual scripting, and consumerism quickly stripped away whatever libratory value pornography billed itself as having.[40] This process occurred twice in the late twentieth century, first during the 1960s and 1970s in Western Europe and then during the 1980s and 1990s in the Eastern bloc. In both instances the political values of pornography lessened as its economics became more pronounced with legalization. The loss of political backing that won it legitimacy encouraged pornography to take a commercial turn. No longer working under the rubric of expressing a higher self, pornographers developed niches for expression of the low self that functioned in dialectic with American importations. As the relaxation over censorship allowed pornography to go mainstream, the 1960s and 1970s seemed to be a "pornographic moment" in Western Europe. The rise of the new Left and the focus on personal liberation resulted in a broad acceptance of sexually explicit materials.

When the Scandinavian countries decriminalized pornography in the late 1960s, Americans entered the market, driving out local producers. In response, France erected trade barriers by taxing imports, which encouraged a resurgence of the French pornographic film.[41] Most nations, however, did not develop a platform for the defense of indigenous pornography and allowed their products to be swamped by American imports. The conflict between American cultural hegemony and the meaning of sexuality in the local context has laid the groundwork for many of the developments in late-twentieth-century pornography. There is, however, one major caveat: although American publications, companies, and ideas have succeeded, American criticisms have failed. The American antipornography movement, spearheaded by feminists and the religious Right, has been generally disregarded across Europe, with the notable exception of Britain, where it joined an older tradition of censorship. This rejection cannot be reduced to a failure of feminism or an absence of religiosity. In Russia a symbolic religiosity peacefully coexists with a pornographic pop culture. Feminism has made as equally important an impact in France as it has in the United States, but feminist criticisms of pornography have not; there female authors such as Pauline Réage resist this analysis of pornography by showing the complexity of desire for women just as Leopold von Sacher-Masoch's work did earlier for men. In short, American pornography sells better than American critiques.

The rejection of feminist antipornography analyses also raises the issue of a confrontational stance in sexual politics. As John Phillips argues here, the relaxation of censorship, though never complete, has allowed for the emergence of a literary pornography for gays, lesbians, and women. A pornographic literature by women for the female market is no small development, given that the tradition of inventing female desires that fit with men's fantasies formed the backbone of the pornographic tradition from Aretino forward. Rewriting tropes has allowed women to create their own sense of sexual subjectivity, but these attempts must be placed in historical context. Works such as *Story of O* might very well explore the female masochist impulse, but the accretion of meanings around sadism and masochism and the patterning of such a work after earlier formulations such as *Venus in Furs* limits the value of assessing the work as representative of a "true female nature." While disentangling true desire from the pressures placed on women to recreate their desires to fit within a male world remains impossible, ignoring the ways that the male world has conditioned female desires seems just as wrongheaded. The value, then, of examining such works might emerge from exploring the reverberations of such conditioning and seeing them as a response to older works—a distaff rewriting of a previously male perspective. Literary pornographers can either confront those patterns or omit their own desires through self-censorship. According to Phillips, such self-censorship has impeded the free play of imagination: the attempt to match desire to political inclinations saps the creativity out of sexuality and gives rise to banality. We either confront the edge of sexuality or cede it to even more problematic constraints.

Clarissa Smith argues in her essay that the impact of partial legalization in Britain has been muted despite its long tradition of illegal pornography. *Banality* seems to be the watchword, but, whereas Phillips sees self-censorship and the authorial inability to confront politically unpleasant desires as causing banality, Smith, in examining popular culture, sees it emerging from the tension between the law and the market. The British government legalized soft-core pornography but controlled its distribution and continued to outlaw hard-core defined by fetishes, penetration, and "the angle of the dangle." Once pornographers developed a legal and profitable niche, they tended to stay there. According to Smith, this resulted in corporate and cultural stagnation. Smith examines the manner in which pornography, despite cultural criticisms against it, remains a business that negotiates the law, the chain store, public opinion, and consumer tastes to find a market. Rather than viewing pornography as a body of content that responds only to a patriarchal belief about women, Smith argues that we must see pornographers as responding to a wide variety of imperatives and constraints on their products even as they are scapegoated for sexual excess and social problems. British pornography focused on soft-core images of the female body because, in many ways, British society allowed them to do so. Producers negotiate between chain stores' attempts to stay on the right side of the law, a rising acceptance of female nudity in the daily press, and community concerns about morality. Pornography made for a curious form of capitalism; it has been constrained not only by the market but also by the conflicting demands for free expression and for social responsibility.

In both the French and the British examples, legalization shifted the relationship between pornography and society from confrontational to commercial. Publishers no longer had to work in an underground economy or fight for the legitimacy of sexual information. The greater the room afforded to sexual publications, the more reason for producers to stay within accepted cultural boundaries. Sexual liberation as a banner for pornographic publications has given way to sexual conformity, particularly since the advent of a more globalized market.

The shift from a confrontational stance to a commercial one that the West saw in the 1960s was repeated in Eastern Europe with the legalization of pornography in the 1990s, even though its legalization emerged more from a general weakening of the state than from a commitment toward sexual liberation. Once the state abandoned cultural control, Eastern European pornographers pulled upon international traditions, local talent, and current conditions to develop new forms of pornography. The ideological and economic bankruptcy of postcommunist society made pornography (along with other forms of sex work) an area of economic growth. Three essays in the volume document this shift. Katalin Szoverfy Milter and Joseph Slade analyze the economics of Hungarian video, Maryna Romanets explores the continuities between socialist realist literature and Ukrainian pornography, and Eliot Borenstein questions the politics of Russian men's magazines and avant-garde literature. All three examine the place of indigenous pornography in a globalizing economy.

Milter and Slade's approach, like Smith's, emphasizes the economics of the industry. Milter and Slade look at the formation of the hard-core video industry, in which the lack of legislation allowed an unfettered global capitalism to influence content, production, and distribution. As Milter and Slade demonstrate, pornography became a big business in the global economy and crossed national boundaries in search of expanded markets, cheaper production sites and labor pools, and novelty. This pornographic economy has been bolstered by technological innovations. In the 1980s the growing availability of home video allowed consumers to avoid seedy, pornographic theaters and lowered the cost of production. In the 1990s distribution was again made easier with the rise of the Internet, which allowed easy access to pornography from home, and falling prices helped dismantle the economic limitations to computer access in Europe. National control of pornography, never as powerful as imagined, seems to be over. Pornography is part of the European and global community, and legislators have to enter the fray in exploring how, when, or whether to intervene.

American distribution companies have consolidated the worldwide market even as Hungary situated itself as an important production center. The need for hard currency encouraged the Hungarian government to rent studios at reduced rates in the early 1990s, and poor economic conditions encouraged an influx of actresses and actors into the industry. State support, cheap talent, and limited morals legislation brought an influx of producers to Budapest, stimulating a Hungarian dominance in European productions. These productions self-consciously situated themselves against the American dominance of the industry by emphasizing anality, local color, and Magyar "naturalness"—a cultural standard no less idealized than the *Playboy* "college girl" look.

The burgeoning global economy in sexuality creates cultural beliefs about women, about regions, and about sexual behaviors at the same time that it reconfigures the state's stance toward economic development. The simultaneous stagnation of British pornography and the boom in Hungarian production demonstrate the manner in which the law affects the economy and the ways that constraint affects form; content emerges in these two essays as much from the economy as from culture.

In contrast, Romanets's and Borenstein's essays explore the political meanings of pornography. In part this difference emerges from these two authors' examinations of the divide between high and low culture. Both Romanets and Borenstein see the eruption of post-Soviet pornography as a significant reworking of cultural ideals; in both Ukraine and Russia national liberation has also come to mean sexual liberation. In both regions high and low cultural forms of pornography confront the cultural legacies left by Communist control. A national style seems particularly relevant during the post–Cold War period of intense political and economic change. At the same time that national controls are crumbling, nationalist sentiments have taken root. Like others across Europe, pornographers in the former Soviet bloc have begun to define themselves against the emergence of a global market.

Maryna Romanets's essay raises a critical issue concerning the explosion of pornography as a release from the authoritarian prudery of Soviet society. While the widespread eruption of sexualized images allows Ukrainian society to break away from the hygienically desexed body that served the state, the rapidity of their absorption has created a cultural shock as both high and low art engage the body. In her survey Romanets finds that high literature and "porno-pulp," while reinscribing the body with meaning, cannot escape a fictionalized past. Writers channel symbols of Ukrainian history into symptoms of the Ukrainian present. On one hand, representations of bodies responding to passion undo the neutered sexless social realism of Soviet culture. On the other, Ukrainian pornography emerges out of a formulaic tradition of socialist realism that deadened the creative impulses. Romanets also argues that low pornography, like its socialist-realist antecedents, relies upon stock characters and plots, and this derivative pornography contributes to the commodification of female sexuality. Given the historical disempowerment of men in relation to the state, the hypersexualized objectification of women speaks to a "crisis in masculinity." If the culture demands that women sacrifice their own sense of sexual subjectivity to bolster the wallets and egos in an impoverished patriarchal culture, it appears as if we return to nineteenth-century models, when Western European societies used their weakest members to sustain a sense of importance and augment the failures of emergent capitalism. In contrast, literary pornographers rewrite gender roles, postcolonial inheritances, and national myths into dramas that point toward the symptoms of contemporary decay. Myths of the past—such as those of Roxolana, the demonic succubus, or the oedipal hero—become symbols of the present conflicts over contemporary culture and life. The most complicated formulations make use of preexisting symbols to explore the place of sexuality in a rapacious society.

The split between pornographic high and low culture remains central to understanding the shock waves produced in both Ukraine and Russia; while low culture re-creates a commodification of female sexuality, high culture addresses the problems that emerge from rapid change. Both speak across new national divisions at the same time that they use the metaphor of sexuality to try to "fix" the serious problems in Eastern Europe's culture, economy, and society. While Ukrainian pornography pays particular attention to the postcolonial realities after Soviet control, Russian pornography responds to the same realities by trying to create a masculinist sexuality to maintain an international sense of superiority. In Ukraine the attempt to supersede Russian control and wipe the memory clear of subordination encourages a pornographic culture that subordinates women in order to hold up masculine heterosexuality. In Russia the desire to hold onto the phallic energies developed during the Cold War contributes to an erotic nostalgia, even though the Soviet state itself spurned pornography.

Pornographers in the former USSR now find themselves swamped by the same glossy *Playboy*-style domination faced earlier in Western Europe. In reaction, as Eliot Borenstein demonstrates, pornographers are creating a sense of "Russian" sexuality—largely defined by linking heterosexuality with hypermasculinity, references to a fictional past, and symbols of former military greatness to develop a niche for themselves. In creating Russian pornography (rather than just pornography for Russians), Russian men's magazines posit men as the losers of international politics and sexuality as a means for addressing the international imbalance; sexuality works as an allegory for working out the relationships between gender, liberalism, and nation in an Eastern Europe that has become embattled and embittered. The satiric novel *Blue Lard* by Vladimir Sorokin intervenes in this emerging tradition in its reworking of the Soviet past by blurring the line between high and low culture. Neither sexuality nor culture, in Sorokin's formulation, remains sacrosanct. By using sexuality to lampoon both Russian cultural superiority and an aggressive masculine sexuality, Sorokin attacks the bases of a developing nationalist rhetoric. Pornography, then, remains political.

With the return to politicized pornography in post-Soviet Russia, we appear to come full circle and once again seem to "prove" the relationship between sex and subversion, pornography and politics. The affirmation of heterosexual male privilege in the context of the insecurities brought by capitalism and liberalism plays itself out in the symbolic subordination of women in Russian society much as it did in eighteenth-century French pornography. The censorship of ideas that contravene in this tradition reverberates as a political act. But the meanings produced in this context are remarkably different. In early modern pornography the political rhetoric of sexuality was set against the controls established by the monarchy, the church, and the aristocracy. In more recent permutations Russian pornography critiques the Western, liberal tradition using the technologies and symbols that the West developed over the last two hundred years. Psychic inequalities, whether imagined or real, current or historical, cascade along the lines of historical interrelationships. In reimagining the sexual present and past, lowbrow Russian pornography attempts to undo individual and national emasculation with a bit of good old-fashioned misogynistic objectification. In turn, the former nations of the Soviet bloc rework a sexual history to counter the disenfranchisement and emasculation left by the Soviet state. The cascading back and forth creates a vortex of sexual and nationalist energy that occasionally erupts into national dramas and political crises but most often testifies to the dreary remnants of unsatisfied desire. Pornography becomes a way to represent the legacy of dearth and to surmount the pain of history through its representation of sexual plenty.

This search for sexual plenty has shattered simple binaries—if those ever even existed. As the final essay by John Phillips attests, East and West, male and female, producers and consumers, have become blurred in the context of a global technology and a cyber-community. The realm of transsexual Internet pornography calls into question not only older sexological models of perversity but also the impact of a contextualized sexuality, as one cannot even clearly identify the location or the meaning of context on the Internet. Transsexual Internet pornography illustrates the impact of technology on all levels of sexual culture. The technologies of medicine cross with the technologies of delivery to create new versions of sexuality, gender, and pornography—ones that nullify any modicum of essentialist desires. The meanings of male and female, of heterosexual and homosexual, of imaginary and real, begin to melt away once one acknowledges that desires cross categories as easily as they cross borders in the contemporary world. It is this nebulousness that continues to stimulate and frighten, that threatens to liberate and pervert. If the pornographic moment across Europe has had any repercussions, they might be stated thus: the age of pornography has undercut any sense of sexual fixity, and, despite this lack of permanence, sexuality saturates society.

Thus, this volume offers no simple conclusions. Censorship and the curtailment of legal pornography created a reservoir of sexual desires deemed perverted and thought to corrupt the citizenry in the nineteenth century; the close analysis of these works demonstrates that pornographers created representations just as socially and culturally problematic as more recent permutations. Their already illegal status and relatively cumbersome technologies might have limited the spread of the ideas, but these works informed important groups of people about sexuality, no matter how fictional those ideas may have been. It seems like small solace to argue that the curtailment of distribution around ideas about children, women, or people of color constrained the distribution of pornography if such banned works could still be attained by those who legislated on behalf of children, women, and people of color. In that moment the hierarchical relations of Western European society were mirrored in pornography and the law. Censorship did not solve the problem, nor did legalization make it disappear. Whether partial or more complete legalization occurred, as in the United Kingdom or Hungary, respectively, the production of problematic images continued. If the concern is the treatment of women, for example, the wide acceptance of soft-core in a partially legalized market actually does little to raise women's status, especially when images in pornography are accompanied by those in the daily press. Full legalization certainly extends the industry of pornography and makes room for new sources of taxation, but it does little to limit the expansion of sexual images and products and merely places sexual culture at the mercy of a global market.

Individuals who want the state to make citizens moral through the censorship of sexual ideas, who want the state to leave sexual images alone, or who want to understand the meaning of modern sexuality must face pornography's multifaceted roles: pornography whets desires, calms dissatisfactions, paves political alignments, bolsters a heterosexual order while simultaneously undermining it, exacerbates nationalist tensions, feeds the global economy, and critiques that economy's dominance. Pornography, then, despite a seemingly simplistic message about sex, bodies, and orgasms, does complicated cultural work that nullifies any sense of certainty.

Despite all of this, as sexual identity, the search for pleasure, and the rise of consumerism become more integral to daily life, pornography's messages have moved from margin to mainstream. If pornography links modernity to the major stages in Western society before the French Revolution, as Lynn Hunt has argued, then pornography has shepherded European society into the postmodern age. It has become a clichéd claim that pornography spearheaded the growth of Internet technologies, but, even before the Internet, pornography ramped up the pace of communications, making its mark on pulp novels, postcards, film, and video. As new technologies of communication appeared, pornography found room for the libidinal, and it did so because people paid, and still pay, to have their desires expounded.

These desires do not appear unbidden but need to be called into existence. In one sense pornography merely articulates what is thought but cannot be said in other realms. In another sense pornography, like any other cultural form, remains a powerful way to affect consumers. Just as one can be changed by reading Alexander Pope's *Essay on Man,* one can be influenced by reading John Wilkes's *Essay on Woman,* the pornographic satire of it, at least to the extent of deflating the original's seriousness. So, too, can other pornographic ventures affect the reader. Pornography can transform not only the way one reads familiar cultural icons but also the sexual terrain itself. For those unfamiliar with transsexual culture, access to Internet she-males can call up new desires and new constellations in the sex/gender relationship. Pinning down an exact relationship between desire and pornography remains impossible, but the range of relationships bears noting: Colligan demonstrates that pornography attested to the preexistence of latent erotic associations in abolitionist writings; John Phillips concludes that literary pornographers expanded the erotics of homosexual desire; and Clarissa Smith shows that publishers curtailed content to walk the fine line of legality. Taken together, these essays argue that pornography alternately elaborates, confronts, and restricts desire; all of them see pornography as potent, but each sees a different casual link between desire and display.

The authors in this volume also find contradictory conclusions about the effects of this potency. Part of the disagreement may well stem from the types of pornography under scrutiny. Incestuous pornography is harder to bear than gay pornographic fiction; racial flagellant pornography continues to be more problematic than soft-core. Beyond the subject matter, however, remains the fundamental issue of the ways that power ramifies through society and whether or how to disrupt it. Pornography and the battles about it pinpoint the sexual tensions in society, whether between citizen and subject, man and women, children and adults, national and global. As the essays in this volume demonstrate, tropes about children as desiring subjects, women as sexual viragos, or whipping as a painful pleasure emerged at the intersection of subject and citizen in the nineteenth century; in the twentieth century, as citizenship in the state has been extended to groups of people previously excluded, globalism has reduced the nation into a series of cultural markers for sale. Citizenship no longer offers safe harbor, if it ever did. The Roxolana myth, the image of Magyar smoky sensuality, and Russian machismo became signs of sexuality sold within the nation and to the broader world of virtual tourists. Niche marketing has made national clichés into hard currency. Most states seem quite willing to hawk their cultural heritage and allow impoverished people to sell themselves for much needed currency, with a few key exceptions.

While liberal sexuality has largely overlapped with the liberal state since the 1970s in Western Europe and since 1989 in Eastern Europe, allowing people to speak of their desires and define their own sexuality, the acknowledged parameters of desire continue to expand. The acceptance of new sexual identities and desires has created a libidinal explosion; there is more pornography and more types of pornography going to more places than two hundred years ago. From the dismantling of heterosexual normativity to the acceptance of deviant acts such as fellatio and cunnilingus as well as more esoteric practices such as S-M, anal sex, multiple partners, the lexicon of popularly acknowledged sexual acts has multiplied. Furthermore, pornography plays a complicated political role overtly as writers try to reckon and wrestle with the meaning of the body politic and as individuals and groups respond to the politics of bodies. The cacophony of pornographic expression creates a subversive potential at the same time that it might very well engender a political backlash. States across Europe have curtailed civil rights in the case of child pornography to maintain their status as legal bodies and to follow American law. For other types of pornography it remains to be seen how far this acceptance will go or how long it will continue. Battles over sexuality have divided the United States for the past few decades; European states seem to be entering into the same divisive formulations, if the Sorokin affair and quasi-fascist political groups have their say. Asking for moderation from pornography, however, would be like asking for moderation of desire itself.

Perhaps that is the only firm conclusion this volume can offer; pornography illustrates the wealth of desires woven into the fabric of European history: desires about empire, about nation, about self and other, about plenty and dearth, about mechanization, democracy, wandering, stability, offspring, pain, pleasure, and politics. Pornography loads these longings onto the fragile frame of the human body to detail the petty and grandiose pleasures wrought from sex. Released from constraint, desire continues to beckon, allowing polymorphous perversity to transmutate into new cultural forms; yet pornography also seems to illustrate the banality, the search for novelty, and the constant search for sensation in a consumer age. The attraction, adoption, and revulsion toward pornography illustrate the allures and crises of sexuality in the contemporary world.

Notes

1. Marilyn Yalom, *A History of the Breast* (New York: Ballantine Books, 1997); Isabel Fonseca, *Bury Me Standing* (New York: Vintage Books), 56.
2. See Joan Hoff, "Why Is There No History of Pornography?" in *For Adult Users Only: The Dilemma of Violent Pornography,* ed. Susan Guber and Joan Hoff (Bloomington: Indiana University Press, 1989), 17–46.
3. Laura Kipnis, *Bound and Gagged: Pornography and the Politics of Fantasy in America* (New York: Grove Press, 1996), 162.
4. Thomas Waugh, *Hard to Imagine: Gay Male Eroticism in Photography and Film from Their Beginnings to Stonewall* (New York: Columbia University Press, 1996), 6.
5. For discussions of pornography in Russia, see Marcus C. Levitt and Andrei L. Topokov, eds., *Eros and Pornography in Russian Culture* (Moscow: Ladomir, 1999); Paul W. Goldschmidt, *Pornography and Democratization: Legislating Obscenity in Post-Communist Russia* (Boulder, Colo.: Westview Press, 1998); Laura Engelstein, *The Keys to Happiness: Sex and the Search for Modernity in Fin-de-Siècle Russia* (Ithaca: Cornell University Press, 1992), 359–420.
6. Linda Williams, *Hard Core: Power, Pleasures, and the "Frenzy of the Visible"* (Berkeley: University of California Press, 1989).
7. Joan Hoff argues that detailed histories of pornography would interfere with the political agenda of social control. See Hoff, "Why Is There No History of Pornography?" For discussions of the problem of doing academic work on sexuality, see Rachel P. Maines, *The Technology of Orgasm: "Hysteria," the Vibrator, and Women's Sexual Satisfaction* (Baltimore: Johns Hopkins University Press, 1999), ix–xvi; Waugh, *Hard to Imagine,* xv.
8. Robert Darnton, *The Literary Underground of the Old Regime* (Cambridge, Mass.: Harvard University Press, 1982); Lynn Hunt, ed., *The Invention of Pornography: Obscenity and the Origins of Modernity, 1500–1800* (New York: Zone Books, 1993); Iain McCalman, *Radical Underworld: Prophets, Revolutionaries and Pornographers in London, 1795–1840* (Cambridge: Cambridge University Press, 1988). See also Lynn Hunt, ed., *Eroticism and the Body Politic* (Baltimore: Johns Hopkins University Press, 1991).
9. Waugh, *Hard to Imagine,* 8.
10. Paula Findlen, "Humanism, Politics, and Pornography in Renaissance Italy," in Hunt, *Invention of Pornography,* 52–54; David O. Frantz, *Festum Voluptatis: A Study of Renaissance Erotica* (Columbus: Ohio State University Press, 1989), 4–6.
11. Walter Kendrick, *The Secret Museum: Pornography in Modern Culture* (New York: Viking, 1987), 12–32.
12. David Gaimster, "Sex and Sensibility at the British Museum," *History Today* 50, no. 5 (September 2000): 10.
13. For the former, see Gérard Lenne, *Sex on the Screen* (New York: St. Martin's Press, 1978); and Edward de Grazia, *Girls Lean Back Everywhere: The Laws of Obscenity and the Assault on Genius* (New York: Random House, 1992); for the latter, see Andrea Dworkin, *Pornography: Men Possessing Women* (New York: Putnam, 1982); Su-

san Griffin, *Pornography and Silence: Culture's Revenge against Nature* (New York: Harper and Row, 1981); Catherine A. MacKinnon, *Feminism Unmodified: Discourses on Life and Law* (Cambridge, Mass.: Harvard University Press, 1987); and Catherine A. MacKinnon, *Only Words* (Cambridge, Mass.: Harvard University Press, 1993).

14. Hunt, *Invention of Pornography,* 10.
15. Frantz, *Festum Voluptatis,* 9–11, 43; Findlen, "Humanism, Politics, and Pornography in Renaissance Italy," 74–75.
16. Findlen, "Humanism, Politics, and Pornography in Renaissance Italy," 55–56.
17. Frantz, *Festum Voluptatis,* 142–143.
18. See David Foxon, *Libertine Literature in England, 1660–1745* (New Hyde Park, N.Y.: University Books, 1965), 38–43, for a discussion of the publication information.
19. See Lynn Hunt, "Obscenity and the Origins of Modernity," in Hunt, *Invention of Pornography,* 21–24; Wijnand W. Mijnhardt, "Politics and Pornography in the Seventeenth- and Eighteenth-Century Dutch Republic," in Hunt, *Invention of Pornography,* 287; Patrick Kearney, *A History of Erotic Literature* (Hong Kong: Dorset Press, 1993), 101.
20. David Stevenson, *The Beggar's Benison: Sex Clubs of Enlightenment Scotland and Their Rituals* (East Linton, UK: Tuckwell Press, 2001), 33–35, 41–45, 183–185.
21. For discussions of sexuality, the Enlightenment, and libertinism, see G. S. Rousseau and Roy Porter, eds., *Sexual Underworlds of the Enlightenment* (Chapel Hill: University of North Carolina Press, 1988); James G. Turner, "The Properties of Libertinism," *Eighteenth Century Life* 9, no. 3 (1985): 75–87; Catherine Cusset, ed., *Yale French Studies* 94 (1998): special issue: "*Libertinage and Modernity.*"
22. Robert Darnton, *The Forbidden Best-Sellers of Pre-Revolutionary France* (New York: W. W. Norton, 1995), 21.
23. Lynn Hunt, "Pornography and the French Revolution," in Hunt, *Invention of Pornography,* 312–314.
24. Rachel Weil, "Sometimes a Scepter Is Only a Scepter," in Hunt, *Invention of Pornography,* 125–153. For a discussion of gender and sexuality in the formation of British politics, see also Anna Clark, *The Struggle for the Breeches: Gender and the Making of the British Working Class* (Berkeley: University of California Press, 1995).
25. For a history of *Fanny Hill* see Foxon, *Libertine Literature in England;* William H. Epstein, *John Cleland: Images of a Life* (New York: Columbia University Press, 1974); Kearney, *History of Erotic Literature.*
26. Doreleis Kraakman, "Pornography in Western European Culture," in *Sexual Cultures in Europe: Themes in Sexuality,* ed. Franz X. Eder, Lesley Hall, and Gert Hekma (Manchester: Manchester University Press, 1999), 112–113.
27. McCalman, *Radical Underworld.*
28. See Henry Spencer Ashbee, *Cantena Librorum Tacendorum* (1885; rpt., New York: Documentary Books, 1962), 60–91.
29. Gary D. Stark, "Pornography, Society, and the Law in Imperial Germany," *Central European History* 14 (1981): 206.
30. Alison Smith, *The Victorian Nude: Sexuality, Morality, and Art* (Manchester: Manchester University Press, 1996), 48; Stark, "Pornography, Society, and the Law in Imperial Germany," 204.
31. Paul Hammond, *French Undressing: Naughty Postcards from 1900–1920* (London: Bloomsbury Books, 1976). See also Lisa Z. Sigel, *Governing Pleasures: Pornography and Social Change in England, 1815–1914* (New Brunswick: Rutgers University Press, 2002), 119–155.

32. Malek Alloula, *The Colonial Harem* (Minneapolis: University of Minnesota Press, 1986).

33. Al Di Lauro and Gerald Rabkin, *Dirty Movies: An Illustrated History of the Stag Film, 1915–1970* (New York: Chelsea House, 1976), 43–46, 52–54.

34. John K. Noyes, *The Mastery of Submission: Inventions of Masochism* (Ithaca: Cornell University Press, 1997), 50; [Charles Carrington], *Forbidden Books: Notes and Gossip on Tabooed Literature* (Paris: For the Author and His Friends [Carrington], 1902), 33.

35. Peter Jelavich, *Berlin Cabaret* (Cambridge, Mass.: Harvard University Press, 1993), 176–183, 154–165; Gideon Reuveni, "Failure Is Success: The Struggle against Pulp Writings and the Construction of Bourgeois Identity in Germany," MS.

36. Waugh, *Hard to Imagine,* 183, 176–205.

37. For a fuller discussion of pornography and the symbolics of social decay during the interwar years, see Carolyn Dean, *The Frail Social Body: Pornography, Homosexuality, and Other Fantasies in Interwar France* (Berkeley: University of California Press, 2000).

38. Lenne, *Sex on the Screen,* 139–140.

39. Kendrick, *Secret Museum,* 188–212.

40. For a discussion of the relationship between consumerism, business practices, and pornography, see Richard Ellis, "Disseminating Desire: Grove Press and 'The End[s] of Obscenity,'" in *Perspectives on Pornography: Sexuality in Film and Literature,* ed. Gary Day and Clive Bloom (London: Macmillan, 1988), 26–43.

41. Joseph W. Slade, "Pornography in the Late Nineties," *Wide Angle* 19, no. 3 (1997): 4–5.

Wanderers, Entertainers, and Seducers

Making Sense of Obscenity Law in the German States, 1830–1851

Sarah Leonard

In October 1850 the police in Berlin confiscated the first full translation of *The Memoirs of Casanova von Seingalt,* published by Gustav Hempel in Berlin and translated by Ludwig Buhl.[1] During the brief period between the liberalization of the press laws following the political uprisings in 1848 and the codification of a new Prussian Legal Code in 1851, Hempel took the opportunity to republish the *Memoirs,* volumes that had been notoriously banned in the 1820s.[2] One result of the revolutionary demonstrations in 1848 was the suspension of a police ordinance from 1819 that authorized the police in Prussian territories to confiscate publications that offended "religion, morals, and civil order." As the existing ordinances had been suspended and new laws had not yet been issued, the police used a previous judgment to condemn the volumes. They explained, "because of the reputation of the book, a closer analysis is not necessary." It was already well known, they wrote, "that in the description of his life removed from all civil order, the author supplies a description of his amorous adventures, dissecting almost every manner of sensual gratification and laying it before the eyes of the reader." They were furthermore not to be detracted from their efforts by a lack of explicit content. According to this report, the author's "elegant, light, veiled language" made *Casanova's Memoirs* more attractive and, as a result, more dangerous.[3]

In lieu of confiscations, which would have only been effective locally, Berlin's police chief recommended a general ban on the work. Notice of this ban would be sent to chiefs of police in major cities in the Prussian territories.[4] Reports from these regional governments came in over the next five years: in 1856 another edition of *Casanova's Memoirs* appeared in the free city of Hamburg; a year later a knockoff, *Casanova, Memoirs of a Libertine,* appeared in installments. The authorities in Trier confiscated a copy of the original *Memoirs* from a bookseller named Peter Braun. In 1857 they wrote again to report that they had found two more copies of *Casanova's Memoirs.* The first was confiscated from a private lending library run by "Sicius of Saarlouis," who was also found in possession of a second illegal work, *The Memoirs of Lola Montez* (also published in 1851). The second copy was found in the library of a bookseller based in Trier by the name of Lintz. In each case the reports were careful to note that the offending works had been confiscated and safely tucked away in the archives of the local police.[5]

The flurry of reports surrounding the reappearance of *Casanova's Memoirs* in the early 1850s introduces the central problem that will concern us here: what counted as "obscene" in the German states during the first half of the nineteenth century? It is one thing to document that the police confiscated particular books in particular places. It is another thing entirely to explain their method—why these titles in particular?

In 1851 a new law adopted in Prussia authorized the police to confiscate so-called *unzüchtige Schriften* (literally, "lewd" or "immodest" writings) and allowed courts to prosecute distributors.[6] The central term *unzüchtige* was left (perhaps deliberately) vague, and the Prussian police also referred in their reports to publications that "injured modesty or morals" (*verletzt die Schamhaftigkeit und Sitte*).[7] Because the legal language was general enough to allow for broad interpretation, we are left to ask how and why the police confiscated certain publications and not others. Finding an answer to this question, I would argue, requires that we temporarily suspend our own assumptions about morality and shame. With few exceptions the publications that were confiscated in early-nineteenth-century Germany bear no relation to our own twenty-first-century definitions of obscenity. We know that unauthorized reprints of sexually explicit literature such as *Thérèse Philosophe* were produced by German booksellers as early as the 1830s, but they seem to have been largely ignored by the police. In 1828, when the first edition of *Casanova's Memoirs* appeared, a liberal journal complained not about the work's veiled sexual content but, instead, about the protagonist's roving lifestyle: "Casanova is not only the most common of libertines, but also a swindler, gambler, bandit, and vagabond. A more potent moral poison does not exist."[8] Like the authors of this article, early-nineteenth-century German police and courts were more concerned with writings that were suggestive rather than graphic—with books that offered knowledge of relations between the sexes but also knowledge of strange, transitory lifestyles, far-flung places, and lives spent in pursuit of pleasure.

This gap between nineteenth-century definitions of "immoral and obscene writings" and our own alerts us to the complexities of providing any historical account of obscenity law—especially one that does not simply focus on censorship. A detailed analysis of our own attitudes toward obscenity, for example, would necessarily be complex. Where would we start? Would we begin with constitutional debates about protected speech and individual rights? With attitudes toward sexuality and gender that have changed dramatically over the course of the last century? Where would we add ideas of privacy and exposure, of politics and public lives? Any historical study of this category needs to be equally alert to the historical contingency of attitudes, anxieties, and material conditions.

What follows is an exercise in trying to understand a particular legal category, *unzüchtige Schriften,* as it was written down and interpreted in the German states during the first half of the nineteenth century. As the language of the law provides few clues, we have to examine the content of the texts themselves as well as the historical context of the world in which they circulated. From there we can proceed backward to a potential understanding of historical actors actually engaged in interpreting laws and making decisions. One of the central tasks of such an exercise (to borrow a phrase from Paula Findlen) is to identify the matrix of issues that inform the historical meaning of obscenity—that is, to identify the questions, tensions, and struggles that informed contemporaries' approach to the problem of the *unsittliche Schrift.*

The first half of the nineteenth century is framed by two major upheavals: the Napoleonic Wars, leading to massive territorial restructuring of the German territories; and the revolutionary uprisings in 1848–1849. The years in between were the era of the German *Biedermeier*—a term that often evokes images of quiet middle-class homes and political reaction on the part of nervous European monarchs. Historians have shown, however, that the relative quiet of this period belies important changes at the level of political expectations, social attitudes, and material realities. During these decades Germans were continuing important dialogues about political inclusion, state building, and civil society that had begun in last decades of the eighteenth century. Liberal governments were established in the German states of Baden and Württemberg, and in Bavaria the power of the monarch was limited by a constitution.[9] This was also a period in which territorial restructuring, the secularization of church lands, and urbanization shifted people's sense of physical identity. The assurances and exclusions of guild systems and professional concessions were slowly giving way to an ethos of free trade. Germans hotly debated the proper roles of women and men and, from this, relations between the sexes.[10] In short, these were decades during which the many constitutive elements of social identity were in flux.

I will argue here that several of the books singled out by the police for confiscation and prohibition treated these questions of political and religious allegiance, place, and social and gender roles at length. They responded to questions generated within a newly emerging bourgeois culture—in particular, concerns about shared identities and isolated individuals, the sources of virtue and vice, and the nature of relationships between the sexes. These were matters of enormous importance within this society. The engagement of these texts with problems of social and political identity seems to have been one of the things that attracted the attention of the police and courts.

During the first half of the nineteenth century the police in the German states were forced to reinvent the basis of their authority. Germans had long tolerated an exceptionally active police presence on the grounds that it helped maintain "order, safety and tranquility." By the early nineteenth century the values that stressed collective states of "order and tranquility" were challenged by a growing preoccupation with individuals—particularly vulnerable individuals in need of protection. The literature of the prerevolutionary period stressed the importance of reading in the creation of an educated citizen, capable of self-government. But where we might expect to find language of rights-bearing individuals, we are more likely to find comments about vulnerable individuals. This was particularly the case with women, whose inner lives were subjected to intense scrutiny on grounds that they were exceptionally pliable and uniquely prone to "passionate enthusiasm" (*Schwaermerei*). Men, too, were imagined to have highly mutable interior lives, open to suggestion, corruption, and enthusiasm. If the police had long justified their authority by reference to the social order, by the 1850s they began to stress their protection of individuals.[11]

This shift in focus can also be seen in the evolution of the laws concerning *unzüchtige Schriften*. In language borrowed from the French Penal Code, a Prussian police ordinance adopted in 1819 condemned all books that "offended against religion, morality, decency, or civil order" (*gegen Religion, Sittlichkeit, Anstand und Bürgerliche Ordnung verstossen*). Similar laws adopted in other German states used slightly different language, prohibiting "injury to modesty" and "public nuisance." It is this language that we see at work in the police documents regarding *Casanova's Memoirs*. Protected here were collective values. By the 1880s the law (now a national law for a newly unified nation) required the explicit depiction of sexual organs with the intent to arouse. This law insisted on a clinical definition of the "immoral publication" and stressed not only the "intent" of producers but also the effect of such works on the *individual,* rather than the community.[12] In other words, over the course of the nineteenth century the legal understanding of the "immodest or immoral publication" became increasingly focused on explicit sexuality and its effect on the individual reader or viewer. It did not, however, start out that way.

In her collection *The Invention of Pornography* Lynn Hunt advances a hypothesis: obscenity, she argues, is linked in important ways to the "origins" of modernity.[13] She defines *modernity* in terms recognizable to most of us: stressing links between obscenity and Humanism, the scientific revolution, the Enlightenment, and democracy. In her account of these originating moments of the early-modern period, Hunt describes important links between modern knowledge and "obscene" knowledge. While her treatment of modern history is complex, she nonetheless stresses a triumphant vision of the modernity in which social, political, and religious hierarchies were successfully challenged and replaced by democracy, secular public opinion, and scientific method. The darker sides of modernity—the isolation, violence, and exploitation that accompanied it—are left out of her account.

Germany, with its fragmented, hesitant, and ultimately catastrophic path to modernity, is conspicuously absent from Hunt's treatment of European development and therefore of the history of obscenity.[14] But Germany, too, experienced modernity—sometimes as a fascinating and dangerous foreign important, other times in its own internal dynamics and uprisings. We take up the question of obscenity, or the *unsittliche Schrift,* at a time of great potential and possibility for Germany—a period that begins with the reorganization of territories and ends in the heady "pre-March" days before the revolutionary uprisings in March 1848 forced supporters of democracy into exile, retreat, and immigration.

The German Pornographic Tradition

The production of illicit literature in the German states during the late eighteenth and early nineteenth century was fundamentally different from that of France. Germany did not, for example, witness the outpouring of anticlerical philosophical works that characterized eighteenth-century French print culture. In part this had to do with the particular nature of religious politics and regional variations within the German states. While Germany's Catholic minority was certainly the target of salacious attacks, religion was not as closely linked to absolutist power as it was in a centralized nation such as France. Furthermore, figures of the German Enlightenment were less occupied with attacks on religious authority and more concerned with providing rational programs for legal, political, and social reform within the existing frameworks of small absolutist states. "Discipline and Order" (*Zucht und Ordnung*) were the watchwords of a new bourgeois culture that emerged in the late eighteenth and early nineteenth centuries. This German *Bürgertum* (a term simultaneously denoting citizenship and social and economic standing as a member of a broad range of middle classes) was linked not by shared institutions but by a growing civil society based in large part on the circulation of print.[15]

If Germany did not produce a body of philosophical and anti-clerical works like those that accompanied the French Enlightenment, German readers did have an enormous appetite for French imports of all kinds.[16] French books traveled into German borders via publishers in the more liberal states of Baden and Württemberg as well as Danish-controlled regions in the north. By the 1830s German readers were able to buy inexpensive reprints and translations of French libels, memoirs, and even classics of philosophical pornography. Of the pornographic works that did circulate in the German states, most took the form of pirated versions of French texts and knockoffs and translations of French originals. German publishers were happy to produce unauthorized reprints of proven French titles, as this method allowed them to avoid paying authors for their work. Johann Scheible, a publisher based in Stuttgart, took advantage of the liberal press laws and proximity to France and ran an extremely successful trade in hastily translated and cheaply printed French books and pamphlets.[17] Scheible published illicit works under a separate imprint and did not include such titles in his catalogs. We know of the existence of this separate imprint from police records of confiscations and from the records of the German booksellers' guild, which took the unusual step of suspending Scheible's professional affiliation on grounds of piracy.[18]

Imported French books were central artifacts of French philosophical and political life, and their importance should not be underestimated. In the imaginations of many readers in the German states, France was not only associated with the promise and violence of its revolution but also with a large body of imported publications, many of them sexually suggestive. The danger posed by these French imports was double: for one thing, they threatened to import experiments in republican government; at the same time, critics charged that the immorality of French books threatened the vulnerable inner life of German readers. Writing in the wake of the Napoleonic Wars, Wilhelm von Humboldt asserted, "it has never been more necessary to shape [*bilden*] and consolidate the inner form of character than now, when external circumstances and habits are threatened by the terrible power of universal upheaval."[19] It is noteworthy that Humboldt's vision of defense was not one of institutions and armies but was based, instead, on the development of a strong inner life.

Early-Nineteenth-Century "Immoral Books": Wanderers and Womanizers

Despite the dominance of French publications, a few original works of so-called immoral literature did emerge out of the German states. In the early decades of the nineteenth century a few books were published in Germany that became synonymous in the German imagination with the threat posed by immoral books. The best known seems to have been *The Memoirs of Casanova*, a sprawling memoir that combined firsthand accounts of political figures and events, descriptions of life at European courts, and veiled references to sexual affairs with always fascinating women. Casanova offered his readers unpretentious accounts of a large and diverse world of political and philosophical dynamism, a clear and elegant defense of Deism, in addition to suggestive (thought not explicit) interludes with women up and down the social scale.

The books discussed in this essay all fall into a particular category of works referred to by contemporaries as "gallant" literature—this focus is not by design but is, rather, the fruit of following the trails left by the authorities who confiscated and condemned books. Because the authorities focused on gallant works while ignoring others that might (to our sensibilities) seem like better candidates for condemnation, it is worth saying a few words by way of introduction about this genre. The German literature of gallantry seems to depend on a strong, central narrative voice that can be real or fictional. The narrator provides a lens through which the reader experiences several things: extensive travel (focused on range rather than depth); romantic encounters (usually short-lived) followed by philosophical remarks on human nature, romantic love, or the roles of the sexes; and close encounters with historical figures or events, also followed by remarks on political power, human nature, and the behavior of crowds. This was a literature that was conceivable only in a world in which such questions as the nature of political authority, of human nature and crowd behavior, and of sexual contracts were subject to debate.

Before initial publication of *Casanova's Memoirs* between 1822 and 1828, the most recognizable name in illicit German literature was "Althing," the pseudonym of Christian August Fischer. According to records kept by the Prussian police, Fischer was a former professor at the University of Würzburg. In the early 1820s he had been sentenced to a jail by Bavarian courts for publishing "libelous works" but avoided prison by fleeing to Bonn, a town that had recently been awarded to Prussia after the Napoleonic Wars.[20]

References to Althing's works often appear in late-eighteenth- and early-nineteenth-century sources. Althing's books were collected, for example, by one of the most famous bibliophiles of the Napoleonic period, Geheimrat von Krenner, whose collection forms the basis for the Bavarian State Library's "Giftschrank," or "poison chest."[21] August Prinz, who was himself constantly in trouble with the authorities for publishing illegal books, provides us with another reference to Althing.[22] Prinz, who delighted in the misfortunes of others (especially his competition), tells his readers of a case in 1827 involving a bookseller by the name of Ernst Klein. Klein, it seems, had brought copies of *The Brief Tales of Althing* to the Leipzig book fair, where booksellers gathered each spring to sell their wares. According to Prinz, the copies of the offending book were confiscated by officials from the booksellers' guild and publicly burned. This not only represented a loss of revenue for Klein (booksellers worked on a small profit margin, and the loss of business no doubt hurt); it also signaled exclusion from professional goodwill. Klein was indignant that Friedrich Brockhaus was allowed to sell illegal copies of *Casanova's Memoirs,* while he was publicly humiliated and stripped of his goods.

Despite the notoriety of *Casanova's Memoirs,* Althing is perhaps more relevant to a study of the early-nineteenth-century German attitudes toward obscenity because his works were originally written and published in German. Fischer [Althing] was the author of many books, including *The Almanac of Curiosities* (1825); *Secret Stories of a Prisoner* (1825); and *On Relations of Women with Men* (1800). Here we will be concerned with a particular title attributed to Althing, *The Beloved of Eleven Thousand Ladies,* published in 1804 with no imprint or publication date.

As very little is known about Fischer or his publications, we must work with the small pieces of evidence that we do have. If the publication date is to be believed, *The Beloved of Eleven Thousand Ladies* appeared during the period of political turmoil, alignment, and realignment in the German states coinciding with the Napoleonic Wars. Between 1800 and 1815, 60 percent of the German population changed rulers, as small duchies were consolidated and ecclesiastical lands were folded into secular states. Many of the traditional local ties and allegiances that had shaped daily life were in flux, and German booksellers were able to take advantage of these political realignments and reorganizations to publish illegal pamphlets and books.

The lack of imprint on *The Beloved of Eleven Thousand Ladies* would have protected the publisher and printer from prosecution. This meant that booksellers would bear the brunt of the substantial financial losses associated with confiscations. Because we know something about the illegal book trade in general, we can make some guesses about where the book might have appeared. Stuttgart, in the Kingdom of Württemberg, is one likely source of such works, as it was one of the main centers of the illegal book trade. The books might also have been published in the Danish-controlled city of Altona, which bordered directly on the Free German city of Hamburg. August Prinz and other publishers established a tradition of publishing illicit literature there that flourished into the 1860s.[23]

The material qualities of the original copy itself provide only a bit of information about the publication. Printed on less expensive paper, most likely sold unbound, the printing quality is good, without serious typographical errors or any apparent haste in publication. This would differentiate it from inexpensive publications printed hastily on low-quality paper with little care for typography or quality. Who might have bought such a book? The content was by no means practical, and its purchase could not be justified in terms of use value. In early-nineteenth-century Germany many people were still suspicious of publications that were strictly entertaining. Middle-class readers continued to be attracted to "useful" books—those offering instruction on some part of life, from household economy to medical remedies and courtship manuals. Those who bought books like Althing's would most likely have been people with some disposable income. It is also possible that such a book was available in small lending libraries, where readers could borrow popular titles for the equivalent of a few pennies.

Turning to content, what is the substance of the story that contributed to Althing's reputation as one of the most notorious authors of immoral fiction? *The Beloved of Eleven Thousand Ladies* tells the story of a male protagonist, Rudolph, who wanders from adventure to adventure, living by singing and acting, his wits, and a willingness to take advantage of opportunities as they present themselves. From the outset his story is one of downward social and economic mobility. Rudolf's life story begins with the choice of his aristocratic mother, who is left destitute by the death of her father and is faced with the choice of becoming a nun or marrying a fur trader—a *Bürger*—who is beneath her social caste. She decides to marry in spite of its effect on her social status, and Rudolf is the offspring of this union.

Rudolf's early experiences provide an education in the harsh reality of the individual's isolation. When the father fails to return from a fur-trading trip one day, the family finds itself immediately abandoned by those around it. Friends and business associates quickly drop all connections with Rudolf's widowed mother, and the family is left to live by its wits. Rudolf is enrolled in a singing school at the local church, where he learns skills that will later support him. Already at the beginning of the story, then, the world is described as one that is harsh and uncertain: fathers die, leaving daughters desperate and uncared for; husbands fail to return from business trips; friends and associates are quick to abandon unprofitable connections when it suits their purposes.

Left to make his way on his own, Rudolf begins a journey that will take him to cities all over the German states and into France. He wanders through a series of misadventures, many involving sexual encounters with women that are hinted at but never described. His first introduction to romance is through Rosalie, the daughter of his singing master. She provides "practical lessons" on the art of love to the boys in the singing school. After a month of initiation into the ways of love, Rudolf has his first insight into the perils of such attachments. For a blissful month, Rudolf explains, he was convinced of his lover's sincerity and fidelity. Yet the romance comes to a screeching halt "when an accident convinced me that it would be folly to depend upon the faithfulness of women. I did not yet know that the love affairs of entertainers don't last long, but my lady singer quickly provided me with evidence."[24]

The story continues as Rudolf moves from town to town, working with troops of actors and singers, putting on a variety of plays. "I was now in the prime of life and imagined in my twentieth year that the energy of youth and the ardor of fantasy would never fade. I fluttered around everywhere and was as changeable as a chameleon."[25] At each stop along the way he is embroiled in another love affair, almost always ending with the realization that the woman in question is dishonest and unfaithful. During one of his stops an adulterous sexual affair with an innkeeper's wife ends when he discovers that the woman in question has yet another lover. From this he begins to formulate ideas about the female sex: "Ladies, I would beg you all for forgiveness, had these adventures not reconciled me more than a little to your sex, and had I all my life maintained the belief that for you, sincerity and fidelity are imagined virtues."[26]

When he finally does meet a virtuous young woman, she is dressed as a man. On his way to Nantes, Rudolf encounters Josephine, the daughter of a count who has disguised herself as a man in order to travel the open roads unaccosted. She does so in order to be reunited with her lover, a young man from a merchant family who is deemed unsuitable for marriage. In light of Josephine's virtue Rudolf begins to revise his view of women: "I myself, who until this point had seen these frivolous and seductive creatures only through the lens of sensuality, who could not look at any woman without immediate infatuation, I felt for this woman a solemn reverence."[27]

He surprises himself by spending the night with Josephine without trying to seduce her, and her presence awakens virtues in him that he was unaware he possessed. After spending a chaste night together, he and Josephine travel to a free city, where they plan to stay. When Josephine's father tries to capture his daughter, Rudolf is nearly shot. Josephine is dragged away, leaving Rudolf shaken by the risks he has taken and the loss of this exceptional woman.

Rudolf's revised views of women are quickly dashed, but he spends little time bemoaning his fate. After a good meal he recovers his composure and revisits the recurring question of women: "When the danger had passed, I began to reflect on the vicissitudes of fate. I ruminated on all the adventures that had found me and came to the inner conviction that, in one's relations with women, caresses are the only thing one has."[28] He concludes that never again will he be the protector of princesses on the run. And that night, after a good meal, Josephine is quickly forgotten as a new woman—the innkeeper's wife—begins to occupy his attention. She, too, brings him only danger: after a night of love he wakes up to find that his money purse is gone. The innkeeper demands payment, and, when he cannot pay, the innkeeper brings him to the local authorities. Sentenced to jail for an unspecified period with only water and bread, Rudolf gives up his ring to pay the debt and goes on to the next town, having lost his money, his ring, and his illusions.

What accounts for the outcry over a work that, after all, was suggestive but never explicit? While it is clear to the reader that Rudolf is sexually involved with the women he encounters, there are no descriptions of physical intimacy. Nor does the work linger on the beauty or attributes of the women involved. Instead, we are presented with a world of mercenary men and women willing to switch loyalties at a moment's notice, who transgress established social order, and to seize every opportunity presented to them to advance their own self-interest.

Making sense of how and why such a text was included in an emerging canon of immoral publications requires attention to context. To begin with, Althing's *Beloved of Eleven Thousand Women* commented at length on the problem of relations between the sexes—a topic that received considerable attention in the novels, advice literature, and pedagogical works of the period. Marriage was a topic of some concern in the early nineteenth century. According to Prussian law, considerable financial hurdles had to be overcome in order to earn the privilege of marriage. Reform-minded figures such as Theodore Gottlieb von Hippel argued that legal obstacles to marriage should be abolished.[29] To his mind, such financial restrictions constituted a barrier to happiness and companionship—as well as to the true intimacy between two people that aided in self-development. These historically specific expectations of marriage were linked to the emerging values of the German middle classes, which, for a moment in the early nineteenth century, stressed marital intimacy and emotional proximity over sexual difference. For an increasingly self-conscious German bourgeoisie, for whom sociability and companionship were the watchwords of a good marriage, Althing's stories were a fundamental challenge to these emerging ideas of personal and collective virtue.

If Althing stressed sexual difference over emotional proximity, his vision of women's "nature" was also at odds with emerging expectations of female virtue. In the world Althing inhabits, women are not to be trusted. The women he encounters are seductresses, thieves, adulterous wives—and sometimes all three. Whatever virtues women possess are learned, not inherent. Furthermore, in Rudolph's world men do not reap moral benefits from their intimacy with women. Trusting women is foolhardy and dangerous, apt to put men in precarious situations as they defend the honor of (indefensible) women. Rudolph concludes that the virtue women possess is the product of education rather than nature, and men's inherent sense of chivalry dissipates quickly by experience with women.

A second important context for understanding the status of Althing's story can be found in the broader portrait of an unstable social world. Rudolph's rapid decline in social status—his mother's initial fall from aristocrat to *Bürger* and his equally swift decline from *Bürger* to itinerant entertainer—could easily be read as offending established notions of social order. In many German states actors had traditionally occupied a special legal status as members of a "disreputable profession." Like executioners and skinners, actors had been denied membership in guilds, the privilege of marrying outside their social caste, and inclusion in collective organizations. By the early nineteenth century the laws that constituted this special legal status had been abolished. Nonetheless, the social stigma associated with "disreputable trades"—and with outsiders in general—still informed the space they occupied in people's imaginations.[30] Rudolph is also a wanderer who travels from place to place. He seems to have no state citizenship—a legal status that conveyed honor and position and signaled official membership in the community. Furthermore, he has no clear class position, having lost both aristocratic lineage through his mother's marriage to a *Bürger* and eventually his status as a *Bürger* upon his stepfather's death. With no citizenship, no professional allegiances, and no family, Rudolf lives outside the structures of life that define identity.

It bears repeating that *The Beloved of Eleven Thousand Ladies* was published at a time in which social and political loyalties were in flux. Political allegiances were fluid as some states allied themselves with Napoléon, others with Austria, and still others were created out of whole cloth. Thus, Althing's depiction of a world of self-interest, competition, and shifting loyalties should be seen not as a reflection of external realities but as one way of depicting the possibilities of such a world.

It is, in a sense, only through attention to context that the status of such works as obscene and immoral makes sense. Focusing on the censorship efforts of absolutist states goes only so far in revealing how and why such a work was considered obscene. It also helps to consider how the emergence of new values and realities associated with the German *Bürgertum* shaped definitions of the *unsittliche Schrift*. Althing describes an alternative world to that of bourgeois self-development, thrift, hard work, and virtue. Relationships between men and women do not ennoble the soul or promote empathy (as contemporaries hoped). Instead, people pursue wealth, power, and pleasure—usually at the expense of others. In the world Rudolf describes, it is true that "caresses are all one has."

If we return to early-nineteenth-century laws concerning "indecent" literature, we will remember that the language of the law in several German states prohibited publications that "offended against religion, morality, or civil order [*bürgerliche Ordnung*]." Later in the century the injury to the individual mind became the basis of secular obscenity law, but in this earlier period *Sittlichkeitsdelikte*—literally, crimes against "customs" or "morals"—still stressed the collective offense to the community.[31] Books such as *The Beloved of Eleven Thousand Ladies* were labeled "immoral" not only, or even primarily, because they portrayed a relaxed sexual morality. Gallant books depicted a world in which self-interest, corruption, downward social mobility, and physical dislocation were the norm. The constitutive elements of social status—place, family, profession—were shown to be precarious. In Althing's world individuals were left to look after themselves in the face of fierce competition and indifference on the part of others. Such ideas about human nature contradicted an emerging middle-class culture of sensibility.

Having briefly considered one of the most notorious works published in early-nineteenth-century Germany, we will look at two more publications before returning to some of the broader questions posed at the beginning. The next case concerns *The Memoirs of Lola Montez, Countess of Landsfeld,* originally published in 1851 following the uprisings of 1848–1849 and falsely attributed to Lola Montez. The timing of the publication is not an accident, as the real Montez played a key role in the politics of the period. Like *Casanova's Memoirs* and *The Beloved of Eleven*

Thousand Ladies, The Memoirs of Lola Montez were widely circulated, reprinted, and imitated. We also know from the multiple references to Montez's *Memoirs* in police documents that the publication was also confiscated from peddlers' boxes, lending libraries, and bookstores throughout Germany.[32]

Much like the two works we have considered up to now, the illicit status of Lola's *Memoirs* is puzzling unless we consider the context in which the two hefty volumes were published. Here, again, we encounter a case in which historically specific questions were treated in illegal texts. Political tensions, conflicts, and developments are apparent in the flood of publications surrounding the Montez affair. These were conflicts between the Bavarian monarch and the Catholic Church, between absolutism and popular representation, and between Munich's citizens and the influence of outsiders.

The basic facts of the story—which must be differentiated from the multiple ways these facts were interpreted—are as follows. In 1846 a twenty-four-year-old Scottish dancer who went by the name of Lola Montez (her real name was Betsey Watson) came to Munich with hopes of being a dancer in the Royal Theater. After being rejected by the director of the theater, Montez appealed directly to the Bavarian king, Ludwig I, in hopes that he would exert his influence and get her a job.[33] Ludwig was immediately taken with the beautiful young dancer, and the story of his infatuation spread quickly to cities throughout the German states and abroad through a body of pamphlets, ballads, and books.[34]

Ludwig had had many affairs up to this point, and it seems that the Bavarian public had come to accept this as normal behavior for the energetic, art-loving King Ludwig. What made this affair different, however, was the political situation in Munich, the broader tenor of political events in the pre-March days leading up to the revolutions of 1848, and the particularities of the woman in question. Prior to Montez's arrival, political and religious tensions already existed in Munich. The Bavarian state had a constitution crafted early in the nineteenth century that established representative bodies based on social caste and granted basic rights including religious freedom. Vying with these formal principles was the still very potent power of the monarch, who was nonetheless answerable to the constitution. Furthermore, there were long-standing conflicts between Munich's Catholic majority and a Protestant minority. To complicate the situation even further, popular protests in the 1830s, prompted by the rising price of beer and the July Revolution in France, had prompted Ludwig to clamp down on Munich's citizens. It was into this scene that Lola Montez entered. And it was through her, and through publications about her, that these preexisting questions about monarchical power, religious toleration, and popular sovereignty would be decided.

Almost immediately after her arrival, Munich's Catholic government took a stand against Montez. In order to secure her own interests, Lola allied herself with liberals and Protestants against the Catholic majority. Uncomfortable and ultimately untenable armed camps formed, with King Ludwig, Lola, Protestants, and Liberals on one side and the powerful Catholic ministers and Jesuits on the other. In 1847 the chain of events began that would eventually lead to popular uprisings and the abdication of King Ludwig. Early in that year Ludwig promised that he would make Lola the countess of Landsfeld, thereby ennobling her. In order to be granted aristocratic status, however, Lola would have to be naturalized as a Bavarian citizen. By law this could not be done without approval by the ministers of state. The king's request was denied.

Faced with the failure of the ministers to grant Lola Bavarian citizenship, Ludwig dissolved the government, overruled the ministers' decision, and made Montez a citizen and a countess. Meanwhile, this expression of absolutist power prompted popular protests, as angry citizens gathered in front of Lola's house and the king's palace. With the help of the government, protesters were able to get a warrant to have Lola expelled from Bavaria. Lola was arrested, escorted across the Bavarian border, and forced into exile in France. Amid uprisings in Munich and cities throughout the German states in March 1848, Ludwig abdicated his throne and joined Lola in France.

Such a story was too good for German publishers to miss. In 1849, shortly after Ludwig's abdication, none other than Johann Scheible in Stuttgart published *The Memoirs of Lola Montez, Accompanied by the Intimate Letters of King Ludwig of Bavaria.* Scheible's publication, which was allegedly based on the real love letters that had disappeared from Lola's house, was promptly banned by the Prussian police. In 1851 the Berlin bookseller Carl Schultz published *The Memoirs of Lola Montez, Countess of Landsfeld,* translated from the original French and attributed to Montez herself. This second set of memoirs was banned from lending libraries in Prussia.

Turning to the *Memoirs of Lola Montez,* we can begin by considering their physical form and the tricky question of authorship. Published in nine separate volumes, on inexpensive paper, and probably sold unbound, the *Memoirs* were small and light enough to be carried by itinerant peddlers or hawkers. The volumes were probably inexpensive enough to attract a range of buyers. Inside, readers were treated to an elegant lithograph of Montez herself, dressed in riding attire with a pastoral scene in the background. In 1851, three years after she was marched to the border of Bavaria and forcibly expelled, German readers were treated to a portrait of her in the French countryside. The attribution of the *Memoirs* to Montez is almost certainly false, and bibliographers list the author as French writer Hughs de Cortal. Nonetheless, I would argue that it is crucial that readers in mid-nineteenth-century Germany thought that they were reading the words, confessions, and stories of Montez herself.

The introduction to Lola's *Memoirs* begins by inserting her life story into the political events of the day. She frames her decision to write in terms of an effort to clear King Ludwig's name. In the process Lola also addresses her political enemies—the "rabble of 1848," or those who participated in the revolutionary uprisings. "Sire! Here we hand over our memoirs to the public. It is your poetic thoughts (the thoughts of a man of art, a philosopher) that I hope to reveal—your sometimes strict but always weighty judgements, the lofty thoughts of a liberal, magnanimous, and elevated king. These I present to Europe—the same Europe that has today sunken into bungling, vacuous, helpless and godless materialism."[35] In an answer to the host of pornographic songs and lampoons that circulated ridiculing the king and, with it, the principle of monarchy, the author of the *Memoirs* took the opportunity to condemn democracy. Lola gives as good as she gets, and, just as she has been painted as a courtesan, a "fallen woman," she uses the same language to condemn political protestors. Although she does not, she states in the preface, "want to linger too long on politics, so as to not weary the reader," the book's first comments are saved for a condemnation of the revolutionaries (the "prostitutes" of 1848): "We do not wish to speak more than is necessary about those prostitutes of the time of 1848, who have more than once earned our contempt, who demeaned themselves in that they descended to the street and formed a partnership with the rabble [*Gesindel*] with those false supporters of republican ideas."[36] The fictional Lola is true to her word and limits her discussion of politics. She turns, instead, to the details of her own personal story.

The bulk of the *Memoirs,* which are peppered with antirevolutionary remarks, present the reader with a hybrid genre: the traditions of the Bildungsroman, or classic novel of education, are fused with a story that is part gallant memoir, part travel narrative. Like Casanova and Rudolph, Lola roams the world encountering exotic places and people and having romantic encounters with strange men. At the same time, Lola's *Memoirs* tell the story of her growth from girl to woman and the knowledge she gleans along the way. The *Memoirs* are centrally concerned with three things: the nature of sexual difference and of relations between the sexes; political events (particularly her relationship to them); and the customs of different "peoples" or nations.

The fictionalized Montez relates stories of her childhood and comments on the education of women and the role of false education. "The moment in which the young girl enters the world, she is pure and true, representing the beautiful ideal created by nature. But education entirely erases this innocence, this inborn purity." Education encouraged women to dissimulate, to act falsely. "This hypocrisy, which has become the rule, and many other ills of our modern society, which I could fully enumerate, were the determining origins of the European upheaval, to which France gave the signal in 1848."[37]

She refers to revolutionary protesters as the "rabble" and condemns the hypocrisy of the French. Like Althing, Lola takes up the question of relations between the sexes, but in her case the conclusion is different. In the *Memoirs* Lola contrasts her views of marriage with those of a woman named Brown, a "cold, organized woman [who] had her head where her heart should be." Brown, it seems, "stood by her ideas about marriage. She saw in this beautiful relationship only a business arrangement. Marriage seemed only to be useful, insofar as it brought women a good position." Lola takes up this question of the sexual contract in several other contexts. She relates the example of her mother, who, she explains, "had no other dowry than her beauty and the name of her family." Lola insists that the marriage between her mother and father "was not business, speculation, or commerce, as it so often is these days in Europe (especially France)."[38]

This question comes up again when Lola relates the story of her own first marriage. The tale of this marriage begins when the young Lola is thirteen and almost done with her education. Her mother proposes that Lola should agree to an arranged marriage with a sixty-year-old Englishman; when Lola protests, her mother assures her that she has no say in the matter. She is "rescued" from this fate by an unscrupulous Irish officer by the name of Thomas James, who urges the young Lola to flee with him, promising her that he will protect her from a disastrous marriage. When James abducts her and marries Lola "for the sake of appearances," we hear that Lola has already lost her virginity. In a chapter entitled "The Abduction" she explains: "The young girl of fourteen was no longer innocent. She awoke tarnished by a shame that she neither asked for nor understood."[39] Trapped with a man who seduced and grudgingly married her, Lola begins to explore the possibilities of passion outside of marriage, pursuing numerous flirtations which may or may not (it is not entirely clear) result in extramarital sexual encounters.

In spite of these veiled references to premarital and extramarital sex, we still have to ask what exactly was at stake in official condemnations of these *Memoirs* on grounds of "indecency," for there was much that was troubling about the *Memoirs of Lola Montez* beyond hints about sexual intercourse. And here it seems fair to ask: was it politics, draped in an alluring tale of exotic places and famous people, that concerned the authorities? Was it sex, veiled in the "serious" rhetoric of politics? Or was it, rather, the values of place and social order, which were so clearly disrupted by the life story of Montez? Like Rudolf, "Lola" the protagonist of the *Memoirs,* was a wanderer, having lived in Ireland, India, and England before landing in Bavaria. Furthermore, she made her living as an entertainer, which necessitated many moves and categorically excluded her from "respectable" society.

Yet by 1851 both the language of German laws and the historical context in which those laws were interpreted had changed. As we saw earlier, Prussian press laws crafted in 1851 specified that publications were considered indecent if they offended feelings of shame or modesty in the reader. In other states similar laws were adopted.[40] The language of religious authority and civil order had dropped out and, with it, the idea that the community, rather than the individual, needed protection. By the 1850s a text such as Montez's *Memoirs* would theoretically have been read for the possible damage to the individual.

At the same time, the political context for interpreting the laws had changed. The growth of the first German women's movement in the 1830s and 1840s culminated in the active involvement of women in the uprisings of 1848 as they called for emancipation and citizenship. This meant that Lola's complaints about the status of women—about their "sale" in marriage—were published in an atmosphere in which such questions were enormously heated. The reestablishment of political order in 1851 also meant that questions of gender equity and citizenship had to be put to the side. This was particularly easy to do if the "failure" of the revolution could be blamed on the irrationality of crowds (as in the introduction to Lola's life story). This was especially the case after the failure of the revolutions to achieve even moderate goals. And the question of politics—as ancillary as it seems in the *Memoirs* themselves—cannot be ignored. As absolutist governments tried to reestablish the legitimacy of their rule in the wake of 1848, the story of the deposed King Ludwig reminded readers of the arbitrary nature of monarchical rule. In short it seems that old concerns about wanderers, strangers, and outsiders coexisted with new ones about political and social revolution.

The Memoirs of a Singer

Turning to our last case, we finally encounter a work that bears some resemblance to our own notions of obscenity. *The Memoirs of a Singer* focused explicitly on the problem of sexual knowledge. It is also the first text we will discuss focused on graphic depictions of sexual acts, and it is clear that the author intended to arouse the reader.

The Memoirs of a Singer (*Aus der Memoiren einer Sängerin*) was published in 1861 by the notorious publisher of illegal books, August Prince, in the Danish-controlled city of Altona.[41] In keeping with the tradition of Casanova and Lola Montez, *The Memoirs of a Singer* was based on the life of a recognizable public figure. In this case the author was identified as the famous Wagnerian opera singer, Wilhelmine Schroeder-Devrient. Like Montez, Schroeder-Devrient was known for her work as an entertainer and artist: before joining Dresden's opera in 1822, where she worked closely with Wagner, she had traveled widely, singing for opera companies throughout Europe. Finally, like Montez, Schroeder-Devrient's real-life biography intersected with the political unrest surrounding 1848. As a supporter of democratic reform, Schroeder-Devrient was an active (and easily recognizable) participant in political uprisings in Dresden. When the revolution failed, she was banished from Dresden; thereafter, she stopped singing and retreated into private life until her death in 1860. A year after her death the first volume of *Memoirs of a Singer* appeared.

The book drew on some of the conventions that had been developed within the small corpus of German pornographic writings. Of the first volume of the memoirs the sexologist and historian of pornography Paul Englisch declared that it was "without doubt the best erotic novel of German origin published in its time, one that brought people immediately and everywhere into contact with the name of the famous German singer, Wilhelmine Schroeder-Devrient."[42] This judgment hinged on the high quality of the writing and story. And, indeed, framed as a classic story of a young woman's introduction to sexual knowledge and knowledge of the world, the writing was careful and well rendered, with a plausible woman's voice.

As nothing is known about its reception or the size of the press run, it is difficult to corroborate Englisch's insistence that the book made Schroeder-Devrient widely known throughout German-speaking Europe. It does seem likely that the singer was readily recognizable, though only in part because of the *Memoirs* and the controversy surrounding their authenticity (certainly, such publicity was not bad for sales, a fact not lost on Prinz). Schroeder-Devrient was also known because she had a distinguished career of her own.[43] Her story was made even more compelling by the fact that her public participation in the revolutionary uprisings Dresden in 1849 essentially ended her career. Her life was also unconventional in other ways: she married three times, divorced twice, traveled widely, and made her own living.[44]

The Memoirs of a Singer is a carefully crafted memoir that conforms closely to the chronology of the real singer's life—and this careful correspondence worked to convince readers of its veracity. The story itself is a narrative of sexual education. It is framed by a letter, supposedly written by the mature Schroeder-Devrient, to a doctor and friend. This friend has offered a hypothesis—that one's moral character is tied directly to one's introduction to sexual life—and the singer agrees to put his hypothesis to the test. In the letter that frames the preface, the singer addresses the doctor directly: "I am sending you what I wrote a few days ago, and you will have to decide for yourself whether I am being candid or not. I have tried to answer your first question, and in so doing I have convinced myself of how right you were when you once told me that sexual and moral character develops according to the particular circumstances under which one becomes aware of the carefully veiled secrets of love. At any rate, I find that this was true for me."[45]

What follows is a description of the narrator's childhood as the daughter of two actors and her adult life as a well-known opera singer, performing in major European capitals and encountering well-known figures, such as the aging Goethe. The life story serves as a vehicle, however, for the discovery and growth of sexual knowledge. The sexual scenes are graphic, but, seen through the eyes of a demure female narrator (almost certainly fictionalized), they maintain a tone of innocence and delight in the pleasures of the body.

Unlike *The Memoirs of Lola Montez,* which directly addressed a public audience, *The Memoirs of a Singer* works on the premise that what is being revealed is something intimate, private, not intended for distribution or public consumption. This is solidified with reference to the singer's otherwise respectable exterior. "In my whole circle of my acquaintances," she writes, "I am considered a completely virtuous and so-called 'cold woman.'" Treating the reader to the details of her sexual education, the *Memoirs* instead reveals a sensitive, intelligent, and widely curious woman. We hear that she is first made aware of the secrets of sexuality when she inadvertently sees her mother and father having sex in their bedroom. Later she is introduced to the pleasures of sexual love by a female cousin.

The Memoirs of a Singer was almost certainly the creation of writers and publishers hoping to make a profit; nonetheless, the book deserves to be situated in the political context of the period. If the sexual content of the story was largely borrowed from classics of erotic education, the life story itself reflected the particular tensions of postrevolutionary Germany. Alongside episodes of sexual awakening, the readers of the book were treated to the life story of a remarkable contemporary woman. If the fictional Lola Montez condemned the revolutionary activists of 1848, the "singer" sacrifices her home and career for political principles. Furthermore, the singer (like her real-life counterpart, Schroeder-Devrient) lived an exceptional life for a woman of the period. She earned her own living, divorced twice, had close ties to prominent feminists, and participated actively in the calls for women's political rights in 1848 and 1849. Prinz, who was himself jailed for his involvement in the 1848 uprisings in Hamburg, probably relished the opportunity to publish such a story. The failure of the revolution meant that hereditary monarchs throughout the German states were increasingly concerned about political unrest. Thus, a story that portrayed a revolutionary and feminist in a positive light would have been frowned upon by the authorities.

Once again, it is not easy to separate sexual obscenity from larger questions of politics and lifestyle. The scenes and language depicted in *Memoirs of a Singer* were graphic enough to rise to the legal level of "offending shame and modesty." Yet the book was potentially "morally offensive" in other ways. And, again, the story portrayed the life of a wanderer—in this case an artist and revolutionary, who moved regularly and was forced into exile by the authorities in her adopted home. The book also made reference to political events—in this case the failed revolution and the fate of those exiled, displaced, and defeated as a result of it

Having looked at these three cases, let's return to the question posed at the outset: is it possible to link the interpretation of obscenity law in mid-nineteenth century Germany to the emerging experience of modernity? Or, to put it in more specific terms, is there historical logic to the choices of the police and courts as they raided bookstores, peddlers' boxes, and private lending libraries in the early and midcentury in search of titles that offended against "religion, morality, decency, and civil order" and later the "sense of shame and modesty of the reader"? If we consider this small body of German memoir literature, it seems to me that connections can be made between the problem of immoral books and the historical preoccupations and attitudes of nineteenth-century Germany.

One of the themes that links these books is a preoccupation with insiders and outsiders. These were not "modern" concerns per se, but they did express a world in which rooted identities, particularly local identities, were in flux. Although this fascination with mobility and wanderers was not new, it meant new things in a world in which political allegiances, professional identities, and social structures were changing rapidly. Seen in this context, it is perhaps not surprising that the central—in fact, decisive—moment in the Lola Montez affair concerned her status not as an aristocrat but as a Bavarian citizen.

Perhaps the link between democracy and obscenity is nowhere more apparent than in the host of perspectives expressed within the context of the Lola Montez affair, in which sexuality was harnessed to a series of conflicts over religion, the limits of monarchical authority, and the nature of the "masses." Lola's *Memoirs* served as one of many vehicles to express a characteristically German ambivalence about the unknown terrors unleashed by democracy and a "world turned upside down." The condemnations of the crowd offered by the Montez memoirs were only one of many such attacks on the people involved in protests. Public opinion, generated to a great extent by the efficiency of print culture in spreading news, could be mobilized in powerful ways.

Finally, it is surprising how much these so-called immoral and obscene publications and the debates surrounding them reveal about the emerging values of the German middle classes. New attitudes toward community, toward marriage and the proper relationship between the sexes, are thrown into sharp relief by the (often quite different) worldview articulated in "obscene books." Emerging orthodoxies of gender difference—which attributed "natural" inborn virtue to women—were loudly dismissed by writers such as Althing. We would be hard-pressed to find anything "liberating" in Rudolph's description of women as savvy, dissimulating, and self-interested. Nonetheless, such visions of women offer an alternative to a growing cult of domesticity.

If, as historians of France have argued, the illicit books of the Enlightenment linked sex to knowledge and knowledge to freedom, people in nineteenth-century Germany were far more ambivalent about both freedom and knowledge. Books were often labeled "immoral" not because of explicit sexual content but, rather, because of the "knowledge" they seemed to convey: knowledge of the private lives of kings and queens, of criminals and vagabonds, of adulteresses and singers—knowledge of what it might mean to live unattached to a guild, caste, or family.

Notes

1. *Aus den Memoiren des venetianers Jacob Casanova de Seingalt, oder, Sein Leben wie er es zu Dur in Böhmen niederschrieb* (Leipzig: F. A. Brockhaus, 1822–1828).
2. Geheimes Staatsarchiv Preussischer Kulturbesitz, Berlin (hereafter GStA), HA I, rep. 77, tit. 380, no. 7, bd. 1, pp. 1–3. *Berlin, 16. October 1850, Report to the Police in Berlin to Interior Minister Manteuffel, Concerning the Translation of The Memoirs of Casanova.*
3. GStA, HA I, rep. 77, tit. 380, no. 7, bd. 1, p. 2.
4. GStA, HA I, rep. 77, tit. 380, no. 7, bd. 1, p. 48. Berlin, 11 September 1856, reports from the provincial governors concerning the circulation of *Casanova's Memoirs.*
5. GStA, HA I, rep. 77, tit. 380, no. 7, bd. 1, pp. 55–67, reports from the regional governments in Hamburg and Trier to the Prussian interior minister concerning the circulation of the two editions of *Casanova's Memoirs, Casanova: Memoirs of a Libertine,* and *The Memoirs of Lola Montez.* According to the authorities in Berlin, another knockoff, *The Casanova of Hamburg,* was confiscated by the police in Hamburg in October 1857.
6. *Strafgesetzbuch für die preussischen Staaten vom 14. April 1851,* para. 151.
7. GStA, HA I, rep. 77, tit. 380, no. 7, bd. 1.
8. "Gelehrte Sachen," *Allgemeiner Anzeiger* 69 (1829): col. 69.
9. On this period, see the classic account by James Sheehan, *German History, 1770–1866* (Oxford: Oxford University Press, 1989).
10. On sexuality and gender relations in prerevolutionary Germany, see esp. Dagmar Herzog, *Intimacy and Exclusion: Religious Politics in Pre-Revolutionary Baden* (Princeton: Princeton University Press, 1996); and Isabel Hull, *Sexuality, State, and Civil Society in Germany, 1700–1815* (Ithaca: Cornell University Press, 1996).
11. For a discussion of *Schwärmerei* and its relationship to political autonomy, see Doris Kaufmann, *Aufklärung, bürgerliche Selbsterfahrung und die "Erfindung" der Psychiatrie in Deutschland, 1170–1880* (Göttingen: Vandenhoeck und Ruprecht, 1995).
12. On German legal language, see Rudolf Schauer, *Zum Begriff der unzüchtigen Schrift* (Leipzig: Rossberg'schen Buchhandlung, 1893).
13. Lynn Hunt, ed., *The Invention of Pornography: Obscenity and the Origins of Modernity* (New York: Zone Books, 1993).
14. Historians of Germany have produced very little scholarship on pornography or obscenity. Some of the best work on the topic remains that of the German sexologist

Paul Englisch. His two works on erotic literature make several references to the German tradition: *Geschichte der erotischen Literatur* (Stuttgart: J. Püttmann, 1927); and *Irrgarten der Erotik: Eine Sittengeschichte über das gesamte Gebiet der Welt-Pornographie* (Leipzig: Lykeion, 1931). Most of the recent work on the topic done by historians has focused on the period between national unification in 1871 and the outbreak of World War I in 1914. See, for example, Gary Stark, "Pornography, Society and the Law in Imperial Germany" *Central European History* 14, no. 3 (1981): 200–229; Georg Jäger, "Der Kampf gegen Schmutz und Schund. Die Reaktion der Gebildeten auf die Unterhaltungsindustrie," *Archiv für Geschichte des Buchwesens* 31 (1988): 163–191; Mathias Gross, "Die Evangelische Sittlichkeitsbewegung im Deutschen Kaiserreich," (master's thesis, University of Hamburg, 1994).

15. There is a growing body of work on civil society in Germany. See, for example, Hull, *Sexuality, State and Civil Society;* and Ian McNeely, *The Emancipation of Writing: German Civil Society in the Making, 1790s–1820s* (Berkeley: University of California Press, 2003).

16. There is a rich body of scholarship on the sexually explicit attacks on the Catholic hierarchy and the monarch in the decades leading up to the French Revolution. See, for example, Robert Darnton, *The Forbidden Best-Sellers of Pre-Revolutionary France* (New York: W. W. Norton, 1996); and Lynn Hunt, *The Family Romance of the French Revolution* (Berkeley: University of California Press, 1992), esp. chap. 4.

17. Scheible's published catalogs, which did not include the illegal works he published under a separate imprint, contained many titles translated into German from French originals. References to Scheible's illegal activities can be found in the records of the German *Börsenverein* (the official organ of the German book trade). Information on the *Börsenverein*'s investigation of Scheible, see records at the Sächsisches Staatsarchiv Leipzig I (465), *Börsenverein der deutschen Buchhändler zu Leipzig.*

18. Sächsisches Staatsarchiv Leipzig I, 467, Akte des Börsen-vereins der deutschen Buchhändler 2u Leipzig, 1842.

19. Wilhelm von Humboldt, *Werke,* qtd. in Sheehan, *German History,* 364.

20. GStA, HA I, rep 101E, Lit F, no. 10, *Die Zensur und der Debit der von dem ehemaligen Universitätsprofessor zu Würzberg Dr. Christian August Fischer herausgegebenen Schriften und Bücher, 1824.*

21. Bayerische Staatsbibliothek München, *Alte Remota Prohibita* (I).

22. August Prinz, *Der Buchhandel vom Jahre 1815 bis zum Jahre 1843: Bausteine zu einer späteren Geschichte des Buchhandels* (Altona: Verlagsbureau, 1855). On Prinz, see Englisch, *Irrgarten der Erotik.*

23. Englisch, *Irrgarten der Erotik.*

24. Christian August Althing, *Der Geliebte von Elftausend Mädchen* (1804): 33–34.

25. Althing, *Der Geliebte von Elftausend Mädchen,* 69.

26. Althing, *Der Geliebte von Elftausend Mädchen,* 82.

27. Althing, *Der Geliebte von Elftausend Mädchen,* 110–113.

28. Althing, *Der Geliebte von Elftausend Mädchen,* 118–119.

29. Theodor Gottlieb von Hippel, *On Marriage,* trans. Timothy F. Sellner (1774; rpt., Detroit: Wayne State University Press, 1994), originally published anonymously.

30. On this topic, see Kathy Stuart, *Defiled Trades and Social Outcasts: Honor and Ritual Pollution in Early Modern Germany* (Cambridge: Cambridge University Press, 1999).

31. For more on the police and notions of "discipline and order," see Hull, *Sexuality, State, and Civil Society;* Marc Raeff, *The Well-Ordered Police State: Social and Institutional Change through Law in the Germanies and Russia* (New Haven: Yale University Press,

1983); and Alf Lüdke, *Police and State in Prussia, 1815–1850,* trans. P. Burgess (Cambridge: Cambridge University Press, 1989).

32. GStA, HA I, rep. 77, tit. 380, no. 7, bd. 1.

33. For an excellent account of the political context of the Lola Montez affair, see Veit Valentin, *Geschichte der deutschen Revolution* (Berlin: Verlag Ullstein, 1930), esp. 1:101–140 and 1:385–397; a more recent account is given in Sheehan, *German History,* 632–633.

34. On Montez's life, see Doris Foley, *The Divine Eccentric: Lola Montez and the Newspapers* (Los Angeles: Westernlore Press, 1969); and Isaac Goldberg, *Queen of Hearts: The Passionate Pilgrimage of Lola Montez* (New York: John Day, 1936). One of the sources of conflict in Munich was the tension between the Catholic Church and the monarchical authority of Ludwig. This tension is expressed by Lola's contemporary, Paul Erdmann, in *Lola Montez und die Jesuiten: eine Darstellung der jungsten Ereignisse in München* (Hamburg: Hoffmann und Campe, 1847).

35. *Memoiren der Lola Montez, Gräfin von Landsfeld* (Berlin: Carl Schultze Buchdruckerei, 1851).

36. *Memoiren der Lola Montez,* 4.

37. *Memoiren der Lola Montez,* 8.

38. *Memoiren der Lola Montez,* 38.

39. *Memoiren der Lola Montez,* 120.

40. Schauer, *Zum Begriff der unzüchtigen Schrift.*

41. On Prinz's illegal publishing activities, see Englisch, *Irrgarten der Erotik;* and Heinz Sarkowski, "Hinweise auf August Prinz," intro. to Prinz, *Stand, Bildung, und Wesen des Buchhandels* (1856; rpt., Heidelberg: Carl Winter, 1978).

42. Englisch, *Irrgarten der Erotik,* 58.

43. "Wagner and His Singers," Victor Fuchs, New York Public Library Performing Arts Division, clippings file: Wilhelmine Schroeder-Devrient.

44. Fuchs, "Wagner and His Singers."

45. *Aus der Memoiren einer Sängerin,* attributed to Wilhelmine Schroeder-Devrient (Amsterdam: n.p., 1909). I was unable to find an extant copy of Prinz's 1861 edition of the book, but I was able to find a later reprint.

Censorship in Republican Times

CENSORSHIP AND PORNOGRAPHIC NOVELS LOCATED IN L'ENFER DE LA BIBLIOTHÈQUE NATIONALE, 1800–1900

ANNIE STORA-LAMARRE

The collection of books called "L'Enfer de la Bibliothèque Nationale" (the Hell Collection of the National Library) summons images brimming with the forbidden, "the cunning refinements of the carnal novel," the fantastic universe whose meaning waits to be uncovered. A multitude of questions arise concerning these works' origins, their organization in catalogs, their history. This collection of roughly nine hundred works have missing or fanciful dates and lack acknowledged authors; they vary in literary genre and narrative texture, and yet they bear surprising testimony to a despised and relegated production. These books produced new historical patterns of desire by drawing out a cartography of pleasures. In turn, these censored books point to the line between acceptable and unacceptable in the Republic of Letters, when democracy made it more difficult to hinder freedom of thought. During the Third Republic (1870–1914), at a time when the written word became a means of mass communication, in whose name was the objectionable eradicated?

Masculine and Feminine in the Books of l'Enfer:
A Location Abhorred

As Henry Miller wrote in "Obscenity and the Law of Reflection," to discuss the nature and meaning of obscenity is almost as difficult as talking of God.[1] Those who have seriously tried to find the meaning of the word have been forced to admit failure. Indeed, at the end of the nineteenth century jurists, moralists, politicians, and physicians indiscriminately used the adjectives *obscene, lewd, pornographic, licentious, dirty,* and *impure.* According to the dictionary produced by Paul-Émile Littré, obscenity is "what openly hurts decency."[2] While allowing wide room for interpretation, this bouquet of adjectives and this definition are interesting in that they call forth the exciting and the forbidden. As the *Bulletin Continental* pointed out, to nail down obscene writing, one cannot rely on style, which can hide "manure," or on a "deceitful" preface, which, in the guise of virtue, gives praise to the cultivation of vice.[3] "Obscene" written works do not belong to a specific literary school, as erotic novels appear in all periods and in many styles. On the other hand, morality leagues designated pornographic books as "carnal novels," novels of the flesh and pleasure that saw life only in its original carnality. All revolves around the flesh, all goes back to the flesh; the plot of such books revolves around mere succession, "a constant quest for cunning refinements, hidden caresses, whose only goal is to rouse the beast resulting in the slow death of the heart and the conscience." There is no possible ambiguity; when pursued, obscenity is invariably linked to sex and desire.

It is in the L'Enfer de la Bibliothèque Nationale that one finds the forbidden books. The poet Guillaume Apollinaire tells us that this abhorred location, L'Enfer, created by order of the First Consul after the Vatican Library's "Hell," is a small library of nine hundred volumes, consisting of erotic novels, pamphlets, and drawings.[4] The name *Hell* comes from the fact that these books were initially to be burned; while waiting for an auto-da-fé, they were amassed on shelves to allow the destruction of a considerable number of them at a time. The threat of fire is one of the mythological elements of the book; throughout the centuries written works condemned by the Ecclesiastic Tribunal or by a Court of Law were burned, joined by an effigy representing the author if he were on the run.[5] Some of the books in L'Enfer came from police seizures, some from customs, and some were obligatory deposits for national collections. To expedite the process, Fernand Drujon explains, burning was replaced by pulping at the beginning of the nineteenth century. The works to be destroyed were placed in sealed bags and carried to the factory under escort by a police officer or a civil servant. They were weighed at the beginning and at the end of the journey, lest a loss or subtraction occur.[6]

The Catalogers

Hell has its puppet masters, the catalogers. They came from the world of libraries and from the police, chiefly editors previously prosecuted for editing or selling prohibited books. They were book fanatics, in love with this curious library, whose biographies bear testimony to a certain antiestablishment spirit. Jules Léopold Gay (1809–1883) was born in Paris on 2 August 1809.[7] He was the son of Dominique Gay, an editor who founded the Russian Court's Library in St. Petersburg. In London Jules met Désirée Véret, a socialist, whom he married in 1834. In March 1848 he published, in a single issue entitled the *Communist,* a piece professing his materialism. He was also a founding member of the International Alliance for a Socialist Society (of Bakunist allegiance). Jules Gay specialized in publishing erotic novels, earning him numerous trials. Having had his publishing license revoked, he first fled to Brussels, like others such as Charles Baudelaire's publisher Poulet-Malassis. His major work, *The Bibliography of the Principal Works regarding Love, Women, and Marriage, and Facetious, Rabelaisian, Scatological, or Satirical Books,* was published in 1861; the three hundred copies sold out in a matter of months. To prepare for the subsequent editions that followed for over ten years, he gathered documents, studied the big sales catalogs of the time, and accumulated notes from bibliophiles, a labor cut short by his death in 1883.

On the opposite side of the political spectrum, Albert Drujon, born at Troyes in 1845, was a lawyer by training and spent his entire career, beginning in 1870, on the police force. He used catalogs, put together thanks to censorship reports written under the Restoration, large collections such as the *Universal Monitor* and *Gazette of the Tribunals* and literary sources such as the *French and Foreign Review of Literature and Fine Arts,* whose last issue is dated 3 December 1829.[8] What remains of these lives is the opus: the catalog. It bears witness to the immense labors of erudition and detective work. The books they cataloged were often anonymous; their original editions revealed neither the place, nor the date of publication, and often contained no indications to identify the author, printer, or publisher. Yet these bibliographers shed light on an "underground" culture, that of erotic publishing.

Dressing Up the Forbidden Book: Preface, Title, Vignette

The prefaces of the catalogs to L'Enfer books clarify the catalogers' arguments and justifications. As Claude Duchet underlines, the preface ignores the confrontation between the judged and the judge, and the codes of acceptability function plainly and clearly in the preface.[9] In the preface to his catalog Jules Gay inverted values and played with paradoxes. Respectability lay with those who enjoyed this literary genre, the "very reserved" and "very discreet" individuals whose behavior was most exemplary, in contrast to the debauched and hypocritical people who shunned it with care. Thus, taking sides with the prohibited book, Gay managed to pose as a militant, resisting the collusion of civil and religious powers. The titles in L'Enfer, the printers' information, the suggestive names of the authors and publishers—for example, *Gifts for Three Sexes; Almanac of Galant and Erotic Follies* for 1889, printed by Erotic Follies Society Press; *Golden Balls*—all contrast, however, with the proper tone of the prefaces to the catalogs. Most of the names of the bookstores are equally unambiguous and refer explicitly to eroticism: *At Cupid's Bookstore, The Library of Eros's Disciples.* The presses are listed in Amsterdam, London, Geneva, and Brussels. Gustave Brunnet points out that in the eighteenth century most forbidden books came from Holland and Belgium, Amsterdam and Brussels.[10] The names of the publishers emerge when there was trouble with the law. These include Gay, father and son; Charles Hirsch; and the Briffaut brothers. The authors generally hid behind pseudonyms; this anonymity is easily explained by the prosecutions that this type of publications could incur. The pseudonyms, such as Henri de Balence, were adorned with noble titles, of which these novelists seem particularly fond. Toward the end of the eighteenth century metaphoric names—such as *A Flagellant Love, Erosmane* (Erotomaniac)—were preferred, undoubtedly for their evocation of erotic practices.

A Culture of the Forbidden

The vast majority of authors of l'Enfer literature were men. The accumulation of obstacles against feminine erotic expression stems from a more general dissymmetry, underlined by the historian Alain Corbin.[11] According to him, in spite of efforts by historians to tease out a feminine voice, women's history is constructed by echo, through a masculine discourse. Thus, it is necessary to delineate the systems of representations, the kernel of anxiety that regulated language and masculine behavior. Indeed, the books of L'Enfer illuminate the figures of pleasure, who were impersonated by women. These representations are singularly dated. In the eighteenth century women were given noble names, for example, "Caroline de Saint-Hillaire," or a first name followed by a social station, such as "Thérèse, Philosophe" (Philosopher). Eighteenth-century novels reveal a certain number of constants. The young woman is sensitive and beautiful, with unruly desires and an irrepressible thirst for love.[12] The heroines Fanny Hill, Thérèse Philosophe, and Margot la Ravaudeuse (Seamstress) are orphans, or at least they have no material resources. By reading gallant literature, eighteenth-century heroines began their initiation toward love.

In contrast, the 1830s became a time of exalted and morbid heroines, such as the famous Countess Gamiani, whose adventures enthralled the nineteenth century. This erotic masterpiece of clandestine literature was reprinted forty times between 1833 and 1930 and ranked first among forbidden literary reprints.[13] At the end of the century, through reediting, Gamiani embodied perversion-turned-woman; sprung from an absinthe-infested dream, offering all the characteristics of decadent literature. Gamiani is "cerebral," a homosexual whose sexual behavior is "monstrous." *The Novel of Violette,* another big erotic best-seller, was the posthumous work of a "Masked Celebrity," attributed to Théophile Gauthier. Violette is a young girl who hungrily tries all the pleasurable perversions that her ingenious lover can teach her. Violette, her "body plump with desire, finds nothing revolting in lesbianism, complicated by vigorous male loves." Shared desires unite these characters—Gamiani, the femme fatale, and Violette, the woman/child.

The industrialization of vice set the stage for the nineteenth-century femme fatale. By 1900 women were represented in art at an intersection of complacency and violence, a staple of the twentieth-century morbid and gory eroticism. Woman sowed pleasure, lust, and death through passion. Literary works of the fin de siècle also attested to a fascination with the young woman and her initiation into pleasure. It was about making young women "half-virgins," for the necessity of virginity permeated both the universe of the erotic novel and moralistic discourse. At the end of the nineteenth century licentious eroticism made room for "crude" debauchery and the world of the sex worker. Titles no longer spoke of love but of "carnal passions," "bizarre pleasures," "lubricity," and "pornographic ejaculations." In this era of the masses the individual woman disappeared in favor of categories: "Les Petites vicieuses" (The Small and Vicious), "Les Enrôleuses" (The Bewitching), "Les Demi-vierges" (The Half-Virgins), "Les Mangeuses d'hommes" (The Man Eaters), and "Les Tueuses d'âmes" (The Soul Killers) illustrate the dregs of the genre.

The titles used repetition to arouse desire: "La Petite vicieuse envoyée chez les proxénètes" (Little Vicious Girl Sent to the Pimps). In these novels sex is crudely displayed; it is detailed. Industrial civilization fragmented the human body, mechanized it. Industrialized sex was evoked at the very moment when an accelerated production of this type of publication was occurring. Of the 210 books that Louis Perceau cataloged between 1800 and 1920, there were 26 books from between 1800 and 1835, 35 published just in 1890, and 34 in 1891. To counterbalance the power of these "pleasure travelers," the titles insisted on the man's virility: "Les Révélations érotiques d'un bandeur" (The Erotic Revelations of a Man with a Hard-on); "La Vengeance d'un fouteur" (A Fucker's Revenge). The absence of any moral connotations in the terms used to define the "man with the hard-on" served the cult of manliness. In general, masculine homosexuality did not appear in the titles. One notes only 2 titles out of 210 cataloged by the journalist, politician, technical secretary of big dailies, songster, storyteller, and bibliophile Louis Perceau. These titles are "Pédérastie active (Active Pederasty), "L'Homosexualité d'un prince" (A Prince's Homosexuality).[14]

The Cartography of Pleasures

The books of L'Enfer map the spaces of pleasure, whose main characteristic is enclosure. The degeneracy happens in convents, in boarding schools, or in houses of pleasure. The titles leave room, however, for vaster geographic areas, emphasizing, for example, the sadomasochistic literature from England, "a country hungry for decency and respectability" but which turns out to be a fertile breeding ground for vice. Russia is also a favorite setting for erotic literature at the end of the nineteenth century; the titles, such as "Souvenirs d'une princesse russe" (The Memories of a Russian Princess) and "Mémoires d'une danseuse russe" (The Memoirs of a Russian Dancer), play on the exotic to ensure success; these are perversions and turpitudes that could only be Slavic. With a degenerate aristocracy in the background, plebeian crowds and savage peasants come to the fore. Eugène de Vogüe sees in the Russian character, "still a bit Tartar, an exceptional alliance of qualities and flaws that could topple the state of manners into unbelievable debauchery."[15] The clichés are explained not only by a rise in French nationalism but also out of a desire to denounce an archaic regime, deemed incompatible with the democratic ideals of the Third Republic.

The colonies—Algeria, Indochina, and the Antilles Islands—also provided an exoticism sought by erotic literature. It was the scorching sun that provoked piquant and orgiastic scenes. "Chaudes saturnales" (Hot Bacchanales) and "Promenades en Alexandrie" (Strolls in Alexandria) staged the refinements of the Orient—its lust, its bizarre and cruel pleasures, its bloody joys, and its ferocious instincts. According to Pierre Cabanis, a precursor to the hygienists, hot countries produced tempers in which sensitivity dominated the forces of motion, which explains the bizarre quality of minds becoming addicted to pleasure, leading men to the perverse.[16] In these exotic novels the corset-wearing woman of the bourgeoisie was contrasted with the half-naked savage woman, who willed herself to any enslavement. The exotic book conformed to the norms of domination of that time.

The cartography of pleasures was organized uniformly around the logic of enclosed spaces, in which roles followed a social hierarchy that favored men. Furthermore, ideas about the world conformed to public opinion, contributing to these caricatures. Such was the fate of England, Russia, and, of course, the Orient. Despite their evident links to the social world, L'Enfer books hurt the cause of Republican puritanism by speaking about sex. Their existence testifies to the ethical and social crisis; by the diversity it revealed, l'Enfer showed a society preoccupied with alternative sexual desires. These desires constituted a real challenge for the Republican moralist.

The Crime of the Pornographic Book

The spread of obscene writing surprised and disoriented French society at the end of the nineteenth century. The image of the "pornographic volcano spilling deadly lava" came to represent the historical issues that arose around the question of pornography. In what would seem to be the sermon of a popish preacher, one can detect criticism about the dynamic role of the cities, the fast development of the written press in a commercial and capitalist economy, and also the effects of generalized schooling and literacy. In this new society formidable problems were appearing that threatened to weaken traditional social institutions. The contemporary sociologist of morality wondered when this folly of desire and pleasure would stop, what would be the consequences of the written initiation to sexual liberty, and where would these deviations, degeneracy, and carnal excess lead society? The unrest created by "pornographic" production led to defense mechanisms that were obviously not new to the period. Yet one gets the feeling that something singular happened at the end of the nineteenth century with the change in social purists' ideas, whose evangelical message concerned the education and regeneration of the masses' morals and the organization and establishment of a large number of morality leagues. How did the league member tabulate the effect of a vastly multiplied print production with increased literacy, which in turn broadened the readership and in particular the female readership?

The City; or, How Crime Crosses Borders
Not having a definition of what constitutes obscene writing allows us to discuss the question of pornography as a function of the historical situation and the needs of the moment. In denouncing the cities, the social observer of the time denounced vice's potential audience—anonymous people, free to read what they chose; troubled people in danger of seeking refuge in the sexual fantasy world. "Impure Paris," "Gallant Paris," symbolized France's lust.[17] The growing audience corresponded to a new organization of the market that tended to constitute itself in a more coherent manner first at the national then at the international level. The revolution in travel brought on by an expansion of railway connections and faster and more regular trains favored the development of commerce; open tracks went from 1,900 km in 1850 to 23,000 km in1880, allowing obscene writings easy access to cities, while new postal routes anonymously carried their "infamous" lots.

From this conquest of national space followed the progressive organization of a European and a world market through steamers, telegraphs, and trains. But new judicial and institutional structures also followed, as colonization allowed European and North American commerce to extend its grasp across the entire planet. Vice crossed borders easily.

The Snowballing Effect of Vice

Indeed, it was on the grounds of the transformation of society that the intellectual and moral elite agonized over the negative effect of reading the wrong material. Cities served as background for the expansion of pornography to the masses. This space was a haven for lust and fostered an industrial market for erotic print matter. Such was the view expressed by the participants of the Congress on "Workers' Gardens" and other large international conferences against pornography that took place at the end of the nineteenth century.[18] A political and social analysis underlay the discussion. At a time when a rural exodus was perceived as a major scourge, the city grew ever more dangerous in that it exerted a great attraction for rural populations. For abbé Lemire, creator of the workers' gardens, the city lured rural youth with its pleasures and fake riches; in contrast, the village appeared gloomy and depressed. The denunciation of the city was done in the name of individual land ownership—a founding principle for future society. Technological progress and the surfeit of industrial production created a crisis in the numbers of unemployed. The crusade against the city was not undertaken, however, around the idea of owning one's own land; progress itself was denounced as divisive. Of course, this was not a new analysis. Most philosophical essays on social problems were concerned with the contradictory effects of progress, and there was considerable doubt and skepticism among the virtuous citizens of the Republic. The repercussions were not automatic. Science would not necessarily work for the greater good; education would not enable man to manage his knowledge; Democracy would not necessarily lead to the power of reason. By not blindly believing in progress nor giving up its benefits, entrepreneurs of morality followed a median line of reasoning.

The analysis of the urban setting was crucial to building a consensus between the promoters of rural land ownership and those who exalted the progress of the city. Both parties agreed to denounce the dangers of urban vice. The city constituted an amplified space of debauchery, filled with theaters, music halls, revues, balls, concert bars, "filthy places, where everything reeks of lust, alcoholism, and death." In this dangerous street the written word had a privileged place. It caught the eye through billboards, and "raunchy" posters for novels—adorned with woodcuts—were shown in enticing displays. Writing was a shape-shifter; poisonous periodicals, naughtily illustrated, pornographic novels, and posters invariably were spotted by the moralist in the vicinity of a school, as if to underline the extreme danger. Newspaper vendors disseminated printed matter on the streets with this or that summary of a sensationalistic, illustrated novel to anyone who wanted it, "even to children." The multiplication of risqué papers demonstrated their ubiquity in social life and was described by the leagues as a "boa bloated with sullied paper." *Gil Blas* was founded on 19 November 1879 by Auguste Dumont, news-paper entrepreneur.[19] The most sought-after publisher was the Baron de Vaux, the author of the famous "inflammatory front page gossip," which he signed as "Le Diable Boîteux" (The Limping Devil) or Asmodée. (The Limping Devil was the model for Maupassant's novel *Bel Ami*.)[20] This sort of press was not in opposition to the books in L'Enfer de la Bibliothèque Nationale; both spoke about sex and desire. These productions were carefully separated, however, by the moralist. The risqué press was disqualified by its popular readership: "The people read and de-vour without ritual," whereas books, geared toward a small elite, could not possi-bly be as dangerous. This comparison could be found at the very foundations of the Republican civil society, mother of the democratic order.

The Relationship between Mass and Elite

The dangers of improper reading generated major anxieties. The vice industry forced open the traditional barriers isolating the places of pleasure. It took over the street, causing "gangrene [in] the populations, these giants, these colossal bod-ies, at once so formidable and so weak." This anxiety was constant. Gustave Lebon provided a theoretical framework for these ideas with the concept of "crowd psy-chology."[21] He showed civilization in a mortal danger from the crowd's blind and destructive power. At a time when universal suffrage was adopted, this conception of the masses was foremost a political one. The philosopher Alfred Fouillée (1838–1912) explained the transition from the idea of the "people" to that of the "masses" as a crisis for democracy.[22] According to his analysis, when the people struggled for their rights against oppression, intelligence developed, but, when the masses became the dominant force, the opposite occurred. Democracy was the stage for those who no longer needed reason. Thus, Fouillée concluded, by a kind of historical irony the very virtues of modern societies, freedom and brotherhood, were the seeds of their own demise. Georges Fonsegrive contended that, to un-derstand the effects of art on the public, one needed to consider the "indistinct" masses versus the elite. Thus, he said, "for those who have not received appropriate initiation, the Greek statue, masterpiece for some, is obscene for others."[23] A work of art would be deemed pornographic according to its audience. In this view what was scandalous was the display of a piece of work at an inappropriate venue.

A vain warning! Publications multiplied. The cheap price of pamphlets and licentious volumes made them accessible to all. The customer base became im-mense. This situation precluded the classification between the masses—subject to influence and corruption—and the elite. The sources of corruption were every-where, and all classes were infected. Crowd theory as described by Gustave Lebon seemed insufficient. Theorists turned to thinking about the diversity of the audi-ence. Building on Gustave Lebon's work, Gabriel Tarde carried out an analysis of a public's psychology, creating a more sophisticated model than crowd formation to explore intellectual and social evolution.[24] Tarde disagreed with Dr. Lebon in the latter's assessment that his was the era of crowds; instead, Tarde argued that it was an era of "public" or "publics"—a very different concept. A new sociability emerged with the development of the daily news, which fostered important associations between readers. The public increased and diversified. The readers chose their newspapers; the newspapers sorted their readers—a mutual selection took place, generating a mutual adaptation. Ultimately, Tarde put forward the problems of the press's influence on society, the molding of the reader, and the suggestive power of literature.

As early as 1802, Pierre Cabanis, the founder of psychophysiology, demonstrated that the world imprints itself on an individual's ideas, opinions, and desires. His disciple Bénedict Morel wrote that the brain is the organ of the soul.[25] Armed with these social and medical theories, moralists projected their own fantasies on the base effects of the obscene writing as "alcohol for the brain." Under the influence of these books that acted as a narcotic, the mind suddenly would lose its balance and become psychologically troubled and physically ill. Healthy individuals would lose their autonomy, their freedom, their self-control. The carnal book cut the worker from his work and inflamed the woman's imagination, turning her into a dangerously sensual psychological being.

The Corrupted Woman Reader

The psychiatrist Scipio Sighele insisted on women's vulnerability to emotion and their susceptibility to a certain vague and soft poetry.[26] The novel plunged the female reader into an excited, confused atmosphere, provoking secret thoughts and desires previously unknown to her. According to him, some women cheat on their husbands in thought before deed: "long are the falls of the soul, the pathological case of Messaline aside, women go through a slow period of depravity and evolution, during which the book exerts a shadowy influence and often acts as devilish temptation. Consequently, the novel deflowers the woman's heart, twists her conscience, and lays the ground for the soiling of her mind and body." As an example, Sighele provided George Sand, who, by ennobling the love affairs between coachmen and ladies, had eased—mind you, only eased—the fall of young women into subordinate arms. If literature's suggestions contributed to real failings in the private sphere, its devastating effects were recast in the social world. The sociologist Paul Bureau contended that the proper organization of the private sphere and the family made people vigorous and strong. Alcoholism led to a mad people. An adulterous affair, while a personal choice, also created a habit in popular opinion and would lead to divorce.[27]

Social observers examined not only the way vice was displayed but also what nourished it and found that the times called for delirium, dreams, and fevers. Divorce in the real world served as a support for romantic fictions; moreover, the problematic book provoked the situations of "vice," however specific: divorce, Malthusianism, decadence, and crime. The discussion of the Naquet Law, voted in on 27 July 1884, allows us to consider the social and moral effects of the deleterious book. Novels, for example, encouraged divorce; this was a political "fact" of utmost importance. Victor Russe, in his doctoral thesis in law published in 1908, wrote that lawmakers were inspired by ideas expressed by the phalanx of novelists and dramatists leading the movement in favor of divorce.[28] According to him, three factors contributed to this result: literary individualism, judicial or even economical individualism, and finally feminism, supported by socialists. Russe's example of literary individualism was Paul and Victor Marguerite, who wrote "that after the long suffocation by the monarchic and religious reaction, one had dared to open the door only barely. Fresh air has not yet reached the innumerable prisons of bad marriages."

In this battle over morality adversaries of divorce feared that through familiarity divorce might acquire moral legitimacy. Paul Bureau referred to Naquet, who wrote in 1869 in *Religion, Ownership, Family:* "In the name of human rights, of the inalienability of individual freedom, of the right to happiness, one proclaims with that an indissoluble marriage is a cause of degeneracy for the species, an institution that generates vice, misery, and death." At a time when the law on divorce gave "vice a legal frame" by legitimizing it, books describing adultery appeared especially threatening. They acclimated the reader to a world free from any physical constraint, in which chaos ruled carnal relationships between the sexes. They made divorce banal in the public mind, legitimized the affair, and seduced the married woman away from conjugal faithfulness by painting the lover with attractive features. They showed women "confused," "exalted," and "unnerved," courting below their station. Woman was tempted by a "dream Casanova." The "crime of the pornographic novel" reached the home, dividing spouses by introducing the idea of a shared and mutual boredom. It sowed the germs of discord, unfaithfulness, and licentiousness in the very heart of the home. It was a crime against the social body. For Dr. Féré the adulterous woman was even worse than the prostitute for her crime struck against the family and through the family against society as a whole. For his part, under the novel's influence, man weakened the home by placing his mistress higher than his legitimate wife.[29] Thus, real and imaginary facts fed on one another and increased the moralist's anxieties. According to the moralist, unnatural vice did not even try to hide. It was on the street. The number of infanticides increased, and, in a noteworthy change, the juries, by their leniency, were complicit with the "moral debasement of their fellow citizen." Were they not, after all, a reflection of the public opinion that they embodied?

Without hesitation, the moralist put Malthusian contraceptive practices at the top of the hierarchy of infractions that destabilized the family. The moralist explained the use of contraception by highlighting the immoderate search for pleasure, the individual's rebellion against the most normal and healthiest of constraints, and the desire to maintain one's independence, even if this meant giving the word *independence* its most irrational or immoral meaning. Here the situation became more political; the disintegration of the family, the public disorders created by immoral behavior, and the increase of the number of divorces led to a cradle strike. The novel shared a large part of the responsibility for this social deterioration. It featured attractive creatures closer to Sappho or Messaline than to a woman soon to be mother. Malthusian booklets, "pornographic" in nature, weakened the institution of marriage and set the stage for the childless family. They constituted a menace to political democracy. They jeopardized the future of the race, destabilized the workplace, and weakened the nation. That was why moralists accused Malthusianism of obscenity.

In this society that felt threatened by degeneracy, the novel was thought to lead to crime, which was nothing other than the symbol and sign of a degenerate lifestyle. The moralist worried about a crime epidemic created by suggestions made on weak minds, women's in particular, with their "weak and broken-down souls." Here belongs Mrs. Lafarge and her infamous poisons, who analyzed herself and her reading habits in her memoirs and who explained the ways the novel accustomed her to the idea of crime, promoted her hatred for her husband, and fostered the idea of killing him to live happily ever after with her lover. The motives for this crime seemed particularly worrisome because crime literature did not simply give a whiff of crime, according to analysts, but reeked of it all over, and what was exceptional became the rule. For Sighele literature was "a vast hospital leading society in a fatal journey to a moral decline." At heart, for the public and particularly those women susceptible to a romantic view on crime and suicide, the pornographic novel contained an incendiary power. Action must be taken everywhere against this "horrible leprosy." Faced with vice's banality, the reader was no longer able to tell good from evil but came to consider evil an ordinary or, worse, necessary component of life. To his horror the moralist felt he was witnessing the birth of a new mentality, one so soaked with immorality that it became imperceptible. This climate of anxiety explains the moralist's obsessions with uniting the country's intellectual and social elite in a cleansing project for society. It was the time of the leagues.

The Time of the Leagues

Social militants noted that immorality persisted despite the multiplication in the number of charities. They decided that the time had come to develop vast organizations in order to make the masses more responsible. The question of organizing the struggle arose at a time that appears dominated by leagues—against alcoholism, tuberculosis, and infant mortality, in favor of instruction and education for the young, for morality, and for retirement. The existence of leagues led to the passage of the French law on the creation of associations, voted in on 1 July 1901. The willingness to engage in innovative thinking about the struggle against immorality can be seen in Protestant-inspired leagues concerned with the individual's moral awakening, responsibility, and participation in collective work. These militants construed the leagues as vast enterprises, established on a scale never seen before, alone able to face a new responsibility: the moral edification of the majority. In France the Central Federation against Public Immorality serves as a good illustration of this concept. The federation comprised over a hundred regional sections that created vigilance committees. Each committee pursued a specific, practical task, such as attacking "filthy" literature.

One of the dominant ideas of the program set forth by the French League consisted of calling on public authorities to promulgate repressive laws. The laws were key: in modern society laws were thought to be one of the most important factors in education because through them each new generation learns about justice. But, above all, for the member of a league, acting on the state for the promulgation of laws meant having a commitment to politics. The state, which had been so active in educating the masses, would have to be made to use the laws and courts against corruption; it must prevent progress from degenerating into licentiousness; it must define society's use of progress, wrote the Redress League. Thus, lawmakers had a crucial role. They would determine, based upon tradition and the principles of modern law, when repression was necessary. The requested repressive measures were justified by the state of the capitalist market, which triggered the dissolution of moral values. The league argued that, in this market age of supply and demand, if suggestive titles, pornographic novels, and loud illustrations were not on display in the bookstores, then the public would not think of them. Applying repressive laws had the great advantage, according to the league, of uniting the individual and the state in action. This constant demand for repressive legislation can also be explained by the fact that many league members moved in political circles and were convinced that the state had a mission in the field of moral reform. In this institutional struggle against obscene writing, a league member was to be judge and jury. He acted in the name of the league in order to protect public opinion and in order to play a political role in the state. He was moved by a willingness to establish a modern mentality, thanks to the weapons provided by the law and the citizens' goodwill.

Education

Repressive legislation was accompanied by another remedy: education. The constant education of the public opinion should be mandatory, said the league. The dual strategy of repression and education appeared to be more effective than either one alone. "When the souls are confused and do not understand themselves, when the flesh is overexcited, order only happens because there exists a demand for it." While the philosopher Edmond Goblot asserted his agreement with the policy of book censorship, he warned against delusions that might be created by suppressing a few unhealthy publications. Pornography was the result of the corruption of morals, rather than its cause. This was why, concluded Goblot, education was essential. Through education the league reconnected with the great improvement project of the nineteenth century—the regeneration of the laboring classes.[30] This educational strategy was inspired by the Anglo-Saxon and American models, often cited as examples because they embodied the spirit of reform. Eugène Budé from Geneva praised the contents of the Boston American Library. The sociologist Paul Bureau insisted on the remarkable leadership of the American elite as "exceptionally modern, exceptionally virtuous," who did not dissociate morality from social and economic life.[31] These new humanists left behind the traditional assistance they deemed archaic and worked toward the founding of schools, libraries, and popular universities that would strengthen the health of their fit brothers. Here emerges their modernity. They dreamed of creating societies of moral support, after the models of New York, Philadelphia, and London.[32]

Joining Forces

The strategy of combining constraint and enlightenment allowed the leagues to unite social and political forces against sex and debauchery. At a time of doctrinal divisions, these leagues offered a common goal to the atheist, the papist, and the social, religious, and political constituents of France through the belief that there could be no progress without higher ideals. By demanding only repressive legislation, they might have alienated believers in a "new spirit" that rejected constraint in a period when freedom of the press had just begun to flourish. In contrast, a strategy based on education alone that emphasized the individual's responsibility to play an active role in his or her own regeneration would antagonize the "children of tradition." The dual approach thus allowed the movement to avoid a right-wing drift toward law and order as well as a left-wing drift toward anarchy. Its advantage was to facilitate consensus. Its relative flexibility allowed each man to clarify his ideology and to choose the most suitable type of action. This dual way also allowed the incorporation of modern democratic values with the most important traditional values.

Censorship Everywhere

Repressing obscene writing was a universal problem. Criminal vice crossed borders easily, and the deterioration of the nation, denounced by all of the leagues, was on everyone's mind. Such was the view of the participants at the International Congress against Pornography, which took place in Paris on 21 and 22 May 1908, when participants pointed out that a narrow reading of territorial rights interfered with the law's functioning.[33] Pornographic catalogs were printed in several languages and sent in bundles to foreign countries. A publishing house would have correspondents, travelers, and warehouses in the cities of multiple nations. The clever organization of the clandestine commerce hindered repression: no longer connected to a storefront on an actual street, all it took was a simple flat in a private person's house, without a sign or marking, a closed door opened only to the initiates. Ads in the paper and prospectuses were distributed openly to someone's address, if requested; catalogs and publications were also sent covertly in sealed envelopes. Action had to be taken everywhere.

Creation of the International Bureau against Immoral Literature

Numerous associations, formed at the end of the century to protect their populations against immoral publications, contributed to the founding of the international bureau. The first international congress took place in Bern in 1896, when Christian, mainly Protestant, purists decided to campaign against the dissemination of obscene books.[34] Protestant circles initiated a vast campaign against "filthy" literature. The members referred to the Gospel as a source of individual and social progress. They wanted to send a message of morality and hope. Geneva expected to play the role of Europe's ethical capital. By the wealth of its associative life, the city represented a model for French moralists. The number of benevolent institutions was impressive.[35] In 1883 the Swiss Association against Immoral Literature was founded in Geneva. Its origin was in a letter sent by a certain Louis Bachelard to the Consistory of the Protestant Church dated 22 August 1883, indicating that the French-speaking region of Switzerland was inundated by a flood of novels and newspapers, with their serialized stories, containing pages and description of an exceptionally obscene character. Bachelard proposed the creation of an association to establish an impassable dike against pornography. Although it was supported by the Consistory, the Swiss Association against Immoral Literature was independent. In a modern conception of secularism it remained disassociated from religious authority in order to sidestep a denominational classification and, instead, call on all available moral forces at a national and international level.

In 1893 the historian Eugène de Budé (1836–1910) founded the International Bureau against Immoral Literature and warned, when talking about pornography, against bovine plague or phylloxera.[36] This international bureau very quickly became an information agency, a precious source of intelligence available to any association whose mission was the repression of pornography. The bureau worked toward pan-national unity: its motto, "no division in our ranks," asserted that men of all denominations and of all nationalities should unite for the destruction of their "vile enemy." The National Vigilance Association, so instrumental in the battle against immoral literature, argued that joining forces at the international level was necessary: "the rogues get richer by selling obscene paintings and books found in every country." Accordingly, like-minded people must unite. A special relationship already existed between Geneva and Paris to fight immorality. The French Federation to Redress Public Morality, led by the minister Louis Count of St. Etienne, depended on the Continental branch of the British Federation, whose general secretary had been located in Geneva since 1885. The links between Geneva and Paris were further strengthened by exchanges between the National Protestant Church of Geneva and the French Lutheran Church.

It is therefore not surprising to see that in 1908 two antipornography societies jointly called for an international meeting to unite all men and women against this evil—one was from Geneva, the Swiss Association against Immoral Literature; and one was from France, the Society for Protesting Public Licentiousness founded in 1894 by the senator René Bérenger. Bérenger (1830–1915) was a moral entrepreneur who campaigned against white slavery, for Sunday rest, and for woman's moral regeneration. He presided over the General Society of Prisons, founded in 1877, as well as the Society for the Patronage of Freed Prisoners to rehabilitate the guilty. Legal and accepted immorality, he contended, led to crime. Bérenger's objectives included working for the reform of the penal code and integrating the development of public education and public morality. He helped to create two particularly important laws, the law of conditional parole of 14 August 1885 and the so-called law of suspended sentence.

The burgeoning of issues contributed to a desire to tackle social problems and fight the social diseases of the time. The participants invited to these conferences remained invariably the same: European moral elites. Émile Cheysson provides an example; he was the president of the Society for Public Hygiene and Public Medicine and a member of the General Society of Prisons, of the National

METHODIST COLLEGE LIBRARY
FAYETTEVILLE, NC

Agricultural Society, of the Popular League for Sunday Rest, of the National League against Alcoholism, and of the Central Union for the Patronage of Freed Prisoners. There were also a few female participants from public aid charities such as Mrs. Paul de Schlumberger, the countess of Caraman, and even the Marquess de Castellane, a member of the International Union for the Protection of Young Women. This mix did not indicate a diverse audience. On the contrary, those vulgar and weak-willed readers who succumbed to such nasty publications were excluded from these meetings. Those who prevailed were a certain type of expert, the technocratic bourgeoisie, best able, according to the leagues, to join forces and stop the contamination.

Europe in Danger

The reports written by French and foreign delegates detailed a European map of dangers provoked by immoral literature. Georges Leconte, president of the Société des Gens de Lettres, took upon himself the responsibility for seeking the best conditions for French intellectual expansion and for studying the demoralizing effects of books and pictures on society. According to him, the traffic in these loathsome "libelles" constituted a shameful situation for all citizens and a danger for professionals, "the shame of being confused with those exploiting vice, the vice of having liberty curtailed through a necessary repression."[37] Similar anxieties could be felt throughout Europe. From all the reports emerged the singular idea that the purchase of obscenity led to sexual desire and activities. The delegation's report insisted on moral decay caused by the enormous dissemination of obscene pictures and books that were published in the name of science, hygiene, and art. In Germany Joseph Pappers, a teacher from Cologne and first secretary of the Federation of Men's Societies for the Fight against Public Immorality, railed against private printings that allowed "publishers and editors without scruples" to work around the law. Worst yet, he added, an ounce of artistic intention for private editions protected the crudest filth against the law. A mound of catalogs and modern books thus flowed freely, with alluring titles such as *L'Amour est mon péché* (Love Is My Sin), *Le Troisième sexe* (The Third Sex), *La Faisense d'anges* (A Woman Making Angels), *Fiancée secrète* (A Secret Fiancée), *Femmes infidèles* (Unfaithful Women), *La Liberatrice* (The Liberator), and *Un Favoris de femme* (A Woman's Favorite).

A Cartography of Fears

The delegates of the Goethe Committee in Dresden, in 1890, found that illustrated postcards, photography, and pseudoscientific literature were the most pernicious. German lawyers lamented, as did their French colleagues, about the vagueness of the term *obscene,* which left too much room for interpretation to the court. The Society against Public Immorality asked the German Reichstag to pass a law to protect the morality of the public. "If an artist, by trade, is not shocked by illustrations, what about the people?" For these activists the crime was the dissemination of works that offended public morals. As in France, the debate concerned not only morality but also society because the diffusion of pornographic material was seen as a threat to the country's vital interests.

The English report by Alexander Coote, a member of the National Vigilance Association, used medical explanations to argue that the bacteria of bad literature introduced infection into an individual's morality. In an important difference from French law, English law did not recognize the author's intent when determining the criminality of publishing obscene books or obscene paintings. This became the model for those working against pornography because it allowed a more effective repression against this sort of literature. Moreover, in England, if a magistrate proved that a book or a picture was indecent, a search warrant would be delivered, allowing the police to enter a shop or home and confiscate the work. Other laws, such as England's vagrancy laws, allowed any person selling indecent pictures or photographs on the streets to be arrested by the police and charged by a magistrate for up to three months of hard labor. This legislation showed that merry old England, at the turn of the century, made room for discipline and morality, key Victorian values. Above all, at a time when English eroticism was everywhere in Europe, its legislative forces attempted to provide an effective answer and set itself as an example to other European countries.

Reports from Belgium and Switzerland, two French-speaking countries, both accused France of flooding them with an avalanche of filthy publications. Yet they also congratulated France for providing an example on how to fight against pornography. The law of 7 April 1907 proposed to strike at clandestine commerce by attacking the means of production and distribution and penalizing the circulation itself. Henceforth, France looked abroad to attack evil at its root: the production of obscene literature. Crime must be fought everywhere. The conference on 21 May 1908 attempted to facilitate the communication of documents to allow each nation to prosecute culprits living on their territory. The international conference, held on 18 April 1910 at the Musée Social, hosted by the French government, granted this wish. Senator René Bérenger represented France, and each participating state envisaged the creation of an office for the repression of obscene publications. These offices would be in constant communication with one another to coordinate their efforts.[38] Their unifying principle was adopted unanimously by all participating countries at the closing ceremony held on 4 May 1910. The removal of jurisdictional boundaries would be approved either by direct communication between the judicial authorities or through a diplomatic or consulate agent.

The conference ended with the proposal for the future study of neo-Malthusianism. At that point all delegates unanimously denounced the danger of that "vile propaganda incurred by the nations for drying up the very sources of life." The congress set the stage for the great battle over contraception that led to the anti-abortion law of 20 July 1920. At the time when nationalism played on the theme of racial purity, a close collaboration was set between the Home Office at Whitehall, the Central Authority for Belgium, the German Police Authority in Berlin, and the Interior Ministry in Paris to break up the networks responsible for the circulation of obscene literature. The 1910 understanding bore fruit; the "criminals" came under worldwide, infallible scrutiny.

Conclusion

L'Enfer gives surprising testimony to the representation of male desire in pornographic books of the nineteenth century. During the Third Republic, Thérèse no longer philosophized. Industrial civilization fragmented and mechanized bodies, and the skilled woman gave way to a lifeless automaton servicing an endless cycle of lovers. The industrialization of vice corresponded to the new situation of the written word; it had become a means of mass communication at the end of the century, thanks to the industrialization of publishing and an increased demand from a largely successful literacy campaign. For the first time the entire society was open to the printed word; vice was no longer confined to small pockets of readers, as it had been in the Old Regime. Horrified, the moralist felt that he was witnessing the birth of a new mentality so saturated with immorality as to be imperceptible. The censorship of pornographic books, at a time of freedom of the press promulgated by the Third Republic, stems from these anxieties. From the 1880s to the 1900s legislative powers gained more strength with the laws of 2 August 1882, of 16 March 1898, and 7 April 1907,[39] which provided the executive with an increasingly sophisticated repressive arsenal. By 1910 calls for order became more strident, the great purification of the souls accelerated, and the liquidation of L'Enfer went hand in hand with the march to war, the ultimate purifier of moral disorders.

Notes

This essay was translated by Olivier Lessmann.

1. H. Miller, *L'Obscénité et la loi de réflexion* (Paris: Losfeld, 1971), 7–9.
2. P. E. Littré, *Dictionnaire de la langue française* (Paris: Librairie Hachette, 1882).
3. J. Cart, "De l'influence de la littérature sur la moralité publique," *Bulletin Continental, Le Bien Public,* no. 12 (1880): 92–95.
4. G. Apollinaire, G. Fleuret, and F. Perceau, *L'Enfer de la Bibliothèque Nationale: Iconographie descriptive et raisonnée complète à ce jour des ouvrages composant autre célèbre collection avec un index alphabétique* (Paris: Mercure de France, 1913), 10.
5. P. Pia, *Les Livres de l'Enfer: Bibliographie critique des ouvrages érotiques dans leurs différentes éditions du XVIIème siècle à nos jours* (Paris: C. Coulet, 1978).
6. F. Drujon, *Catalogue des ouvrages écrits et dessins de toute nature poursuivis, supprimés ou condamnés depuis le 21 octobre 1814 jusqu'au 31 juillet 1877* (Paris: E. Roeyre, 1879), preface.
7. Archives of Brussels, Foreign Policy, J. Gay file, no. 5.579.
8. Drujon, *Catalogue des ouvrages écrits et dessins de toute nature poursuivis.*
9. C. Duchet, "L'Illusion historique: L'Enseignement des préfaces (1815–1832)," Le Roman historique, special issue, *Revue d'Histoire Littéraire de la France* (Paris: Armand Colin, 1975), 245–267.

10. G. Brunet, *Imprimeurs imaginaires et librarires supposés. Études bibliographiques suivie de recherches sur quelques ouvrages imprimés avec des indications fictives de lieux ou avec des dates singulières* (Paris: Librarie Tross, 1866).
11. A. Corbin, "Le Sexe en deuil," in *Une Histoire des femmes est-elle possible?* ed. Michelle Perrot (Paris: Rivage, 1984), 142.
12. P. Fauchery, *La Destinée féminine dans le roman européen au XVIIIe siècle: Le Destin féminin et les morales* (Paris: Armand Colin, 1972), 46–52.
13. *Gamiani ou deux nuits d'excès par Alcide Baron de M. A. Venise, chez tous les marchands de nouveautés* (Brussels: n.p., 1871).
14. Apollinaire, Fleuret, and Perceau, *L'Enfer de la Bibliothèque Nationale.*
15. Vicomte Eugène Melkior de Vogüe, "De la littérature réaliste à propos du roman russe," *Revue des Deux Mondes,* 15 May 1888.
16. P. Cabanis, *Rapport du physique et du moral: De l'influence des climats sur les habitudes morales* (N.p.: Caille et Ravier, Pas de lieu d'édition indiqué dans les catalogues de la Bibliothèque Nationale, 1802): 134.
17. M. Ducamp, *Paris, ses organes, ses fonctions et sa vie dans la seconde moitié du XIXe siècle,* vol. 1 (Paris: Hachette,1878). See also the works of C. Virmaitre, *Paris galant, Paris Génonceaux* (Paris: Genonceaux, 1890); and C. Dalou, *Paris impur* (N.p.p., 1889).
18. *Congrès sur les Jardins Ouvriers,* 1908, Congress on Workers' Gardens, opening speech by M. Méline, 51–52.
19. *Gil Blas, illustré hebdomadaire,* Bibliothèque Nationale (BN) fol. Lc2 3968, May 1891–April 1903.
20. National Police Archives, *"Le Diable boiteux," BA 1037.*
21. S. Barrows, *Distorting Mirrors: Visions of the Crowd in Late Century France* (New Haven: Yale University Press, 1981).
22. A. Fouillée, "Le Suffrage universel," *Revue des Deux Mondes* 15 (1888): 104–120.
23. G. Fonsegrive, *Art et pornographie* (Paris: Bloud, 1912).
24. G. Tarde, *L'Opinion et la foule* (Paris: F. Alcan, 1901), 5–6.
25. B. Morel, *Traité des dégénérescences physiques, intellectuelles et morales de l'espèce humaine et des causes qui produisent des variétés de maladie* (Paris: Bénédict Auguste, 1857).
26. S. Sighèle, *Littérature et criminalité,* preface by Jules Claretie (Paris: Giard et Brière, 1908).
27. P. Bureau, *Études de morale et de sociologie: La Crise morale des temps nouveaux,* preface by Alfred Croiset (Paris: Bloud et Gay,1907).
28. V. Russe, *Réforme du divorce: Étude historique et critique* (Paris: Thèse de Droit, 1908).
29. C. Féré, *Dégénérescence et criminalité: Essai physiologique* (Paris: Alcan, 1881).
30. E. Goblot, *Qu'est-ce que la pornographie?* Third National Congress against Pornography, Lyon, 24–26 March 1922.
31. Bureau, *La Crise morale des temps nouveaux,* 357.
32. P. Desjardins, *Le Devoir présent* (Paris: Armand Colin, 1892), 76.
33. National Archives, Paris, F. 17.652, International Conference againt Pornography, Musée Social, 21–22 May 1908.
34. Geneva University Library, item relating to a campaign against immoral literature, Bern Congress, 1897.
35. E. Mittendorff, *Les Institutions philanthropiques genevoises, leur origine, leur développement et leur état actuel* (Geneva: BPU, E 680/8, AEG: 1580).

36. The letter of Louis Bachelard, 22 August 1882, is found in the Church Archives of Geneva, Compagnie des Pasteurs, Ba 4612/1880 BPU, Geneva.

37. E. Haraucourt, *Congrès National du Livre* (Paris: Cercle de la Librarie, 1917).

38. Royal Archives, Brussels, Foreign Police, 732–733. Intelligence transmitted by foreign authorities according to the Paris, 1910, arrangement.

39. A. Stora-Lamarre, *L'Enfer de la Troisième République: Censeurs et pornographes* (Paris: Imago, 1990).

Anti-Abolition Writes Obscenity

THE ENGLISH VICE, TRANSATLANTIC SLAVERY, AND ENGLAND'S OBSCENE PRINT CULTURE

COLETTE COLLIGAN

From the late eighteenth century to the mid-nineteenth century the flogged slave woman was a ubiquitous rhetorical and visual image in England largely introduced by transatlantic abolitionism. The image appeared in parliamentary debates, abolitionist pamphlets and newspapers, visual arts, and slave narratives. The flogged slave man did not have the same abolitionist appeal,[1] but the image of the flogged slave woman was repeatedly reproduced for public consumption, provoking Christian compassion, abolitionist zeal, and, disturbingly, prurience. Through the long nineteenth century this image underwent a series of literary and visual repetitions and transformations influenced by the English libidinal investment in the whip—what Ian Gibson has called the "English Vice."[2] Showing how this preoccupation influenced the reception and reproduction of the image of the whipped slave woman, I focus on four moments in both abolitionist and obscene print communities: its early emergence and reception among English abolitionists; its appropriation by a publisher of obscenity in the 1880s; its later appropriation by another illicit publishing ring in the 1890s; and, finally, its apparent disappearance by the early twentieth century. The transformations this image undergoes are, to say the least, unexpected. The traffic of this image between mainstream and clandestine print communities demonstrates that the preoccupation with racialized sexual violence around slavery was not simply a Romantic secret or a Victorian peccadillo. The appropriation of slavery imagery was not only part of an emerging commodification of sexuality but also part of a growing underground obscene print culture that fed off cultural fantasies and thrived on their repetition and expansion.[3] The image of the flogged slave woman remains with us today, albeit transformed. In fact, the history of this image requires another prurient viewing in order to expose its current manifestations and to question its repetition.

The Prurient Gaze: The Flogged Slave Woman among English Abolitionists

In the early nineteenth century English politics and culture were preoccupied with transatlantic slavery and its ethos of violence. Statutory law abolished the slave trade in 1807 and colonial slavery by 1833. In the 1830s and 1840s transatlantic abolitionist movements flourished, especially under the initiative of Quakers, nonconformists, and evangelicals. In the early 1850s Harriet Beecher Stowe's American antislavery novel, *Uncle Tom's Cabin,* enjoyed enormous commercial and popular success in England, both benefiting from and nourishing the English appetite for real-life American slave narratives.[4] As Audrey Fisch observes, the public spectacle of fugitive slaves, such as Frederick Douglass, who would describe their personal experiences under slavery and provide proof of its atrocities by displaying their scars, was also popular among mid-Victorian audiences.[5] The English were politically neutral but were rapt observers of the American Civil War, which finally ended in 1865. At the end of the century the British were still concerned about the persistence of slavery around the world: in parts of South America, the Ottoman Empire, and, as David Livingstone discovered, Africa. Between 1880 and 1920 roughly 124 texts were published in Britain on the subject of slavery.

Over the century competing interests mottled the English perspective on slavery in the Americas. Christian humanitarianism underlay abolition campaigns. Rivaling economic investments in the East and West Indies also determined many people's stance on abolition in English colonies. Later, during the American Civil War, the English reliance on cheap cotton led many British citizens to denounce abolition as economically disruptive. For many others, however, the persistence of slavery in America consolidated an English sense of national superiority for having abolished it first.[6] While humanitarian and economic investments underlay public interest in transatlantic slavery, so too, in some instances, did English prurience. Karen Halttunen has shown that the humanitarian impulse made fashionable by the eighteenth-century cult of sensibility was often aroused by a "pornography of pain." As she argues, sentimental portraits of suffering and tortured animals, women, and slaves satisfied a sadistic spectatorship that helped shape the new erotics of cruelty in the late eighteenth century.[7] Information about the graphic violence and corrupt sexuality of the slave system produced sympathy and disgust among many British citizens, but for some it also elicited sexual arousal and fantasy. This history developed around the circulation of images of the flogged slave woman, first introduced in abolitionist print communities.

To understand this history, one must recognize that the English sexual preoccupation with the whip indelibly underwrites it. In the nineteenth century flagellation was widespread in the English home, school, army, and prison. By midcentury, with the passing of the Whipping Act of 1862 and escalating debate about corporal punishment, flagellation was increasingly rejected as a form of punishment.[8] Nonetheless, corporal punishment informed Victorian men's early experiences. For many it was regarded as the privilege of public school education, where beatings tested and formed the gentleman. In *The English Vice* Gibson famously describes this widespread cultural investment in flagellation. Flagellation obscenity was one of the earliest genres to dominate English obscenity when it became an active trade in the early nineteenth century.[9] Much of this literature survives, and even more is recorded in Henry Spencer Ashbee's late-nineteenth-century bibliography of erotica, which includes a treatise on flagellation that cites obscene works on the subject. Ashbee also comments on the relationship between whipping and sexual excitement. "It cannot be denied," he writes, "that to some constitutions flagellation is a powerful aphrodisiac, an active inciter of sexual enjoyment."[10]

Theories about nineteenth-century English flagellation obscenity have inaccurately tended to homogenize it. Following Freud, Steven Marcus suggests that, despite the variety of flagellation fantasies, all of them present "the same unvarying idea"—that of the boy being beaten by the phallic mother, who is a surrogate for the father. He argues that the fantasy blurs sexual identities as a "last-ditch compromise with and defence against homosexuality." For Marcus flagellation obscenity represents one of the earliest, albeit unconscious, forms of homosexual literature.[11] Gibson concurs, arguing that the fantasy represses and displaces homosexual desire. While these psychoanalytic readings are important for disclosing the layers of the flagellation fantasy—in which manifest content sometimes disguises latent meaning—they ignore its historical specificities and mutations by always reading the fantasy as a homosexual one.

Historically, the association between whipping and sexual pleasure probably emerged through the combined stimulation to the genital area and public exposure of genitals and buttocks. This form of sexual pleasure undeniably emerged within all-male communities and was profoundly homoerotic, but it also explored other sexual desires and was subject to outside influence. Flagellation literature was already in vogue in the eighteenth century, as Edmund Curll was charged with obscene libel in 1727 for publishing Johann Heinrich Meibomius's *Treatise of the Use of Flogging in Venereal Affairs*. Flagellation also appeared in obscene writing as a perversion to provide *piquance* to the sexual act. Flagellation is briefly featured in John Cleland's *Fanny Hill* (1749), for instance, to demonstrate an aberrant desire.[12] By the early nineteenth century flagellation obscenity developed into a separate genre that catered to the English sexual proclivity exclusively and accumulated its own set of conventions. An early, and often reprinted, example includes *Venus School-Mistress* (c. 1810). By the 1830s, as Iain McCalman shows, George Cannon specialized in elite, high-end flagellation obscenity such as *The Birchen Bouquet* (c. 1830), *The Exhibition of Female Flagellants* (c. 1830), and *Elements of Tuition and Modes of Punishment* (c. 1830). Besides a concentration on the shape of the buttocks, flagellation obscenity focuses on the binding of the victim, his cries for mercy and writhings, the reddening and bleeding of his buttocks, the quality of the birch, and, finally, the reaction of the spectators. While the most frequent flagellation scenario involved a strict schoolmistress (a Mrs. Birch or Miss Switchem) beating a boy, there were numerous varieties: a schoolmistress beating a girl, a man beating a boy or a girl, a wife beating her husband to titillate his flagging sexuality, a girl seeking revenge on her schoolmistress, and so forth.[13] Toward the end of the century, once flagellation was an established genre of obscenity, its sexual deviance seems to have diminished with its ubiquity. It therefore incorporated more contemporary forms of sexual deviance into the flagellation narrative such as sodomy, tribadism, transvestism, and interracial sex.[14]

Recent and controversial scholarship has shown that the English sexualized images of the flogged female slave in early abolitionist discourse and imagery because of their predisposition to flagellation and sexual violence. Mary Favret, in her essay entitled "Flogging: The Anti-Slavery Movement Writes Pornography," argues that Romantic abolitionist rhetoric in parliamentary debates and pamphlets demonstrates a prurient fascination with the flogging of black female slaves that "imported the difference of race into" the already existent flagellation fantasy. She suggests that descriptions of slave flogging nourished the English "sexual investment in the whip": "What abolitionist tactics contributed to the literature of flagellant erotica was an explicitly racialised sexuality, where black women, substituting for the usual blushing white boy, were displayed as erotic objects for the punitive desires of (usually) white men." Although she overgeneralizes about the sexual relationships found in flagellation obscenity, Favret argues provocatively that the abolitionist focus on the flogged, naked body of the slave woman was the safest and most politically effective fantasy for a group of gentlemen to entertain: it "prompt[ed] the men of England to recognize their power—and desire—to act" but did not unman them by encouraging an overidentification with the image of the flogged black woman.[15]

Marcus Wood's *Blind Memory* extends Favret's thesis to the visual arts. Discussing English visual representations of flogging from early abolitionist movements against the slave trade to later movements to end slavery, he argues that such depictions were regularly "contaminated by pornography." He also acknowledges an important point: flagellation obscenity did not flourish *until* the height of abolition. The image of slave flogging "contaminated" flagellation obscenity as much as it contaminated the abolitionist image. In his discussion of sexualized representations of the flogged slave woman, Wood focuses on a copper engraving entitled "The Flagellation of a Female Samboe Girl" by William Blake that accompanied John Stedman's *Narrative of a Five Year's Expedition against the Revolted Negroes of Surinam* (1796). He discusses how this engraving, which displays a slave woman who has been stripped and flogged, invites prurient viewing: "Staring front on at an almost naked and physically magnificent young woman, who is pushed right up against the viewer, it is hard not to become compromised. Blake seems to be inviting us to enjoy the sexual frisson elicited by such suffering beauty. [. . .] [His] image teeters on the verge of pornography in order to confront us with our own corruptibility." Wood, like Favret, suggests that Blake demonstrates sympathy for the slave but inflames the passions in order to elicit political action— what one might identify as an abolitionist strategy of political arousal.[16]

Wood tends to oversimplify the sexual fantasies that emerged around the image of the flogged female slave as an aggressively heterosexual one that centers around a white man's sexual domination over a black slave woman. He discusses an engraving from an 1805 version of Stedman's *Narrative* that visualizes the same whipping scene as depicted in Blake's engraving, but Wood ignores the complexities of the fantasy it suggests. As he notices, this image curiously whitewashes the flogged slave woman, but it also depicts the white men gazing at the half-naked black overseers. It demonstrates how race is manipulated to construct fantasies about abased white women but also reveals the homoerotic desire that so often underwrites English flagellation.

From the beginning, then, the image of the flogged slave woman in abolitionist print culture roused sadistic flagellation fantasies about whipping white women, fantasies that were superimposed on the homoerotics of flagellation. The fantasies that emerged around this image were layered, complex, and often incoherent, revealing the competing and confluent influences of English flagellation and transatlantic slavery in the early history of England's obscene print culture. The discussion of the relationship between the consumption of violent flagellation and the antislavery campaign can also be extended to the slave narrative. Slave narratives, a later abolitionist enterprise and regular transatlantic feature in the English literary market especially after the 1830s, repeatedly displayed the image of the flogged slave woman while focusing on the atrocities and sexual violence of slavery with varying degrees of explicitness. There was a tendency among some nineteenth-century English readers to view slave narratives as racy transatlantic products. Slave narratives were a regular transatlantic feature in the Victorian literary marketplace, consumed by male and female viewers alike. Twenty American slave narratives appeared in English editions by midcentury, many of which appeared in the most respectable of middle-class institutions, Mudie's Circulating Library.[17]

Slave narratives focused on the sexual violence underlying the slave system. *The History of Mary Prince: A West Indian Slave,* for instance, published in London in 1831, alludes to the sexual violence of her white master: "He had an ugly fashion of stripping himself quite naked, and ordering me to wash him in a tub of water. This was worse to me than all the licks. Sometimes when he called to me to wash him I would not come, my eyes were so full of shame. He would then come to beat me." *The Narrative of the Life of Frederick Douglass, an American Slave, Written by Himself,* which appeared both in the United States and Britain in 1845, also points to sexual violence within the slave system. In graphic terms Douglass describes how his master flogs his Aunt Hester in order to display his sexual power:

> He was a cruel man, hardened by a long life of slaveholding. He would at times seem to take great pleasure in whipping a slave. I have often been awakened at the dawn of day by the most heart-rending shrieks of an own aunt of mine, whom he used to tie up to a joist, and whip upon her naked back till she was literally covered with blood. No words, no tears, no

prayers, from his gory victim, seemed to move his iron heart from its bloody purpose. The louder she screamed, the harder he whipped; and where the blood ran fastest, there he whipped longest. He would whip her to make her scream, and whip her to make her hush; and not until overcome by fatigue, would he cease to swing the blood-clotted cowskin. [. . .]

This occurrence took place soon after I went to live with my old master, and under the following circumstances. Aunt Hester went out one night,—where or for what I do not know,—and happened to be absent when my master desired her presence. [. . .] Why master was so careful of her, may be safely left to conjecture. She was a woman of noble form, and of graceful proportions, having very few equals, and fewer superiors, in personal appearance, among the colored or white women of our neighbourhood.

While Douglass vividly details the violence—the method, the weapon, the screaming, and the blood—he is more circumspect about describing its sexual horrors. Instead, he sexualizes his aunt's body to imply her master's lust. Yet the nineteenth-century reader, who was accustomed to coded sexuality, would not have been left guessing about Douglass's meaning.

The Narrative of William W. Brown, a Fugitive Slave, Written by Himself (1847), first published in England in 1849, is another slave narrative that focuses on sexual violence. Like many narratives, it painstakingly describes the instruments of torture: "the handle was about three feet long, with the butt-end filled with lead, and the lash six or seven feet in length, made of cowhide with platted wire on the end of it." In more explicit terms than either Prince or Douglass, Brown also hints at the master's sexual abuse of slave women. In a scene reminiscent of the flogging of Aunt Hester in Douglass's narrative, Brown describes how his master beats the servant girl, Patsey, because she disobeys his sexual command: "Mr. Colburn tied her up one evening, and whipped her until several of the boarders came out and begged him to desist. The reason of whipping her was this. She was engaged to be married to a man belonging to Major William Christy [. . .]. Mr. Colburn had forbid her to see John Christy. The reason of this was said to be the regard which he himself had for Patsey." Slave narratives featured gross acts of violence and allusions to sexuality that far surpassed other nineteenth-century genres. They were more shocking than the most daring sensation novel but circulated freely.[18]

Contemporary English reviews of slave narratives emphasized their violence. As Audrey Fisch notes, emphasis on violence was typical in the reviews of slave narratives. A review of Douglass's narrative from 1846 in *Chambers's Edinburgh Journal* exemplifies this interest in violence with its lengthy quotations of descriptions of flogging in the narrative. Fisch argues that some journals, such as the *Anti-Slavery Advocate,* found the violence educative insofar as it revealed the cruelty of the slave system and the United States itself. She also concentrates, however, on the *Athenaeum* reviews, the middle-class journal that felt that slave narratives degraded the literary marketplace with their gratuitous depictions of violence. A review from 31 March 1855 denounced John Brown's *Slave Life in Georgia* for its "stereotyped accounts of horrors" and "sickening amplifications on the effect of the bull-whip and the cobbling-ladle": "The severities of masters, incarcerations, escapes, captures, floggings, and excessive task-work, occur in one as in another, and we scarcely see how the public is to be instructed by repetitions of accounts so piteous and so harrowing." Similarly, a later review from 4 April 1857 accused the white author of the fictionalized biography *Autobiography of a Female Slave* of "high-flown sentimentality, mixed up with ghastly and minute details of the floggings and brutalities to which slaves are represented as exposed."[19]

Nineteenth-century reviewers and critics also commented on the corrupt sexuality depicted in slave narratives. Slave narratives provided salacious reading that resulted from the widespread verbal and visual spectacle of the flogged slave woman already introduced by abolitionists and fueled by the erotics of flagellation. Even before the popularization of the slave narrative in England in the 1840s, this image was sexually encoded for readers, listeners, and viewers. The *Anti-Slavery Advocate* repeatedly mentioned incidents of sexual abuse within slavery. In March 1857, for instance, it included an interview with a slave woman entitled "A Talk with a Slave Woman" that describes the "criminal intercourse" between a white master and a slave woman: "Some is weak and willin', poor things; but the most on 'em is forced to it. There was Elizy. I know how Massa Tom came in, and I heard him a beatin' her; she screamed and cried, but nobody couldn't help it; And afterwards, when the pretty little thing was born, and the missus saw it, she was ready to kill it."[20] This article would have provoked sexual readings of the jealous mistress and loitering master, characters with which any reader of slave narratives would have been very familiar. In so doing, it tutored readers on how to infer sexuality from suggestive scenes.

If Favret and Wood have concentrated on the early-nineteenth-century fascination with the image of the flogged slave woman, I am interested in its cultural repetitions and transformations through the remainder of the nineteenth century. As this image was circulated, repeated, and transformed, it accumulated the "half-life" of former fantasies. The image of the flogged slave woman titillated English curiosity about racialized sexual violence and incited prurient viewing. Nineteenth-century obscenity, I will show, *confirms* an underlying and understated English sexual response to flogging and the emergence of racialized flagellation fantasies.[21] What was understated in abolitionist print culture found full expression in the nation's underground literature—albeit not until the 1880s.

Slavery Obscenity in the 1880s: William Lazenby's *The Pearl* and *The Cremorne*

The sexualized representations of the flogged slave woman in abolitionist print culture allowed later publishers of obscenity to appropriate the image. In the 1880s obscene stories created and reflected fantasies about the sexual excesses within slavery. Lazenby introduced this genre of obscene writing. He was widely known in London as a prolific publisher of flagellant obscenity. He published old favorites such as *The Birchen Bouquet* (c. 1830, 1881) and original works including

The Quintessence of Birch Discipline (1883) and *The Romance of Chastisement* (1883). In the 1880s, however, he began to add race and slavery to embellish what had become an exhausted genre. Between 1879 and 1881 he was the publisher, editor, and sometime author of *The Pearl*. It remains one of the best-known productions of Victorian obscenity after *My Secret Life* (c. 1888–1894) and *The Lustful Turk* (1828).[22] The magazine features serialized stories, anecdotes, poems, and chromolithographs that are sexually explicit and liberally embellished with flagellation. One of its serialized stories includes a narrative on the flogging and libidinous excesses of a slave plantation in Santa Cruz told by a West Indian schoolgirl to her English school friend.[23] Ashbee, who felt the work featured stories as "cruel and crapulous" as those in Marquis de Sade's *Justine,* indicates that it had a private issue of 150 copies. Marketed exclusively to a wealthy English male clientele, the set appears to have been sold for anywhere between eighteen and twenty-five pounds.[24] In 1882 Lazenby produced a sequel to *The Pearl,* entitled *The Cremorne; A Magazine of Wit, Facetiae, Parody, Graphic Tales of Love, etc.* The title alludes to the Cremorne Gardens on the embankment in Chelsea, which became notorious after dusk, when prostitutes replaced picnickers.[25] Like *The Pearl,* it was also published privately with a small issue of three hundred. Each number initially sold for a guinea. It was also falsely dated back to 1851 in order to confound legislators and vigilante moralists. Similar to *The Pearl* in style and content, it also contains a story about slavery, one that accentuates and parodies the most gruesome aspects of sexual violence and flogging described in slave narratives.

It is within the new historical context of the 1880s that Lazenby's tales appear: at this time abolition in the Americas had been achieved, flagellation obscenity was creatively exhausted, new sexual preoccupations were emerging, and increased imperial encounters were altering cultural fantasies about racialized sexuality. These new contexts led to unexpected results. Lazenby's stories about slavery in the Americas suggest new and developing English sexual fantasies that relate to changing desires, literary tastes, and imperial encounters.

The Pearl serializes the first obscene tale about slavery in the Americas between 1880 and 1881 and demonstrates the industry's emergent interest in its history as an imaginative resource. This story, entitled *My Grandmother's Tale; or, May's Account of Her Introduction of the Art of Love,* describes a variety of sexual activities in explicit detail: lesbian gambols among schoolgirls, sex between members of the upper and serving classes, threesomes, sodomy, voyeurism, and paternal incest. The story adds to this sexual panoply with its attention to the sexual license and violence within slavery. Yet, even before "Kate's Narrative," the embedded story that recounts a schoolgirl's life on a West Indian slave plantation, there is an earlier reference to racialized sexuality. The tutor Mr. T seduces the two schoolgirls with a series of obscene illustrations involving a white girl and a black man: "In the first he [the Negro] is sitting on a chair, playing the banjo, his trousers open, and his great black tool sticking out. She has her eyes fixed on it, while she holds up her dress, and points to a most voluptuous cunt between a pair of widely extended fat thighs, as much as to say 'Look here, Sambo, here is a place that will soon take the stiffness out of your prick.'"[26] Other vignettes follow that similarly draw on widespread Victorian stereotypes about black men as monstrously virile and yet laughable at the same time. The African-American minstrel figure with his banjo seems to have offset the threat of his putative sexual endowments. These pictures, which are described but not shown, introduce the theme of racialized sexuality and suggest the Victorian preoccupation with miscegenation. These pictures, however, supplement rather than complement the story's primary interest in the white man's sexual power over the black slave woman. They suggest an alternative kind of racialized sexual union that both enhances and destabilizes the fantasy that follows in "Kate's Narrative." In fact, the pictures focus on a theme that will emerge in later slavery obscenity.

"Kate's Narrative," which is allotted separate and significant space within *My Grandmother's Tale,* develops the fantasy of white male sexual dominion over black slave women by rewriting scenes from abolitionist reports and slave narratives. In one of its first incidents it appropriates the image of the flogged slave woman, explicitly sexualizing the brutal flogging of a black slave girl by an overseer of ambiguous color acting under the authority of the white plantation owner. As Jim (the white overseer's son who is later haphazardly renamed Joe by the slipshod writer) recounts to Kate: "You know Jim who has the cat, and flogs the slaves when they misbehave. Well, when the women are sent he flogs their backs, but when the girls are sent he flogs their bottoms." Young Jim further describes the sexual nature of the violence as he illustrates how rape follows the beating: "He opened his pantaloons, and out started Oh! Such a big one, it would have frightened you, as he pushed it against her bottom." "She liked it beyond anything," the boy insists as he negates her sexual victimization, "I knew it by the way she stuck out her bottom." After Jim's description of the beating, he and Kate attempt intercourse, having been aroused by the flogging.[27]

Following this flogging incident, the narrative continues to depict white male sexual access to black slave women, demonstrating cultural knowledge about the open secret of slavery. Jim recounts to Kate how he surreptitiously watched his father cavorting with several slave women, regular nighttime visitors who "like to come to him for they get plenty of rum, and are sure of a half-holiday next day." They discover Jim "peeping" on them and subsequently invite him into the room, where he is sexually initiated. As before, Jim's act of telling arouses the youngsters, who now succeed at having intercourse. Jim proceeds to stress the sexual difference of the black women by negatively comparing their genitalia to Kate's "soft round white lips." Kate further explores the crossing of the color line with her descriptions of her father's sexual access to the "almost white" slaves he retains in the house, especially one woman named Nina. Kate eventually has Nina freed and travels to England with her in order to attend school. "Kate's Narrative" thus travels to England, where its tales of white male sexual power over slave women titillate the English schoolgirls, whose response undoubtedly enhanced the erotic effect of the description of West Indian slave life for the story's white male English readers. This story even invokes the slave narrative with its first-person account of slavery, escape, and travel, pilfering from it for a prurient English audience.[28]

A curious illustration accompanies the scene in which Jim finds himself among his father's slave women. The illustration depicts the ithyphallic father and boy surrounded by four naked slaves. There are two versions of this illustration that accompany different editions of *The Pearl* that correspond to the textual erotics in different ways. The first illustration comes from the first edition of the magazine, which is now in Gerard Nordmann's collection in Geneva; the second illustration accompanies a later reprint of *The Pearl* from around 1890. Peter Mendes suggests that the reprint added hand-coloured lithographs based on the originals.[29] While the theme and composition of the illustrations are virtually the same, the difference lies in the visual imagery: specifically, the coloration and characterization of the female slaves. Although more sexually graphic in its explicit portrayal of genitalia and pubic hair, the second illustration portrays a far less bacchanalian scene. The women are composed, with their tidy hair, neat smiles, and decorous jewelry. The illustration also does not emphasize their race, surprising in light of the narrative focus on their sexual difference and availability. If the illustration were not attached to the narrative, one would have difficulty identifying these women as black, let alone West Indian slaves. Whereas the second illustration suppresses the slave women's blackness and sexuality, the first illustration emphasizes both. The women are dark brown in color, their skin starkly contrasting with the pale skin of the men. Their untidy hair and wide grins as well as their protuberant breasts and bottoms at once suggest their degeneracy and sexual libidinousness: these are the women who would prostitute themselves for rum. The bold, hurried lines of the drawing convey a sense of activity not found in the wooden *tableaux vivants* of the second illustration, while the warmer tones suggest the hot, exotic setting of the tropics. Both drawings depict white male sexual license over black female slaves, but the second illustration supplements the text with alternative sexual possibilities. It may be depicting the desirability and sexual vulnerability of mulattoes that the narrative suggests with its introduction of Nina, or it may be invoking the idea of white women's slavery that later slave obscenity would explore. Because little is known about the illustrations that accompanied the magazine, I can only speculate about the significance of the two versions of this illustration. What was the relationship between illustrator(s) and text? Did the illustrator(s) have direct access, or did the publisher simply provide a description or a drawing? Without being able to answer these questions, one must focus on effect rather than intent. Put simply, the visual message is not parallel to the textual one. The second illustration, which possibly dates to ten years after the first, suggests another fantasy related to slavery and racialized sexuality, allowing undeveloped preoccupations to supplement the primary textual fantasy about white male sexual power over black female slaves. Wood, in his analysis of the Stedman engravings, discovers a tendency to whitewash the slave woman in early-nineteenth-century visual depictions of flogging. The second illustration from "Kate's Narrative" may invoke this early visual trend; significantly, it also foreshadows the slave fantasy's turn-of-the-century transformations. As with the pictures described at the beginning of *My Grandmother's Tale,* these illustrations reveal the rich archaeology and layered fantasies of slavery obscenity that revolved around color and race.

The Pearl instigated further sexualized readings of American slavery with its libidinal investment in racialized sexuality and the flogged female slave. Just a few years later Lazenby returned to the same fantasy in *The Cremorne,* emphasizing its sexual violence by obsessively returning to the image of the flogged slave woman. *The Cremorne* includes a story entitled *The Secret Life of Linda Brent, a Curious History of Slave Life* that is a parody of Harriet Jacobs's American slave narrative, *Incidents in the Life of a Slave Girl* (1861). In brief Jacobs's story, told by the pseudonymous Linda Brent, dramatizes her sexual harassment by her master, Dr. Flint, as well as her attempt to frustrate his efforts by having an extramarital affair with a white man, Mr. Sands, with whom she has two illegitimate children. Jacobs's narrative was not as well recognized in England as those of Frederick Douglass or John Brown. It did not appear, for instance, in Mudie's Circulating Library catalogs. Yet, even though her book did not have the exposure of some of the earlier slave narratives, two English editions of the narrative appeared in 1862 as *The Deeper Wrong,* published by the abolitionist London publisher W. Tweedie.[30]

There is little doubt that Jacobs's narrative was appealing to publishers of obscenity because of its sexual content: it is the most explicit of the slave narratives on the subject of sexual abuse. The American slave narrative had already been branded as unnecessarily violent and degraded. Jacobs's narrative was largely praised, and most reviewers only obliquely alluded to its focus on women's sexual exploitation. The *Athenaeum,* however, roundly denounced it in a review from 19 April 1862 because of its sexual content:

> Every fault which an abolitionist novel can have is present in this repulsive tale, which is equally deficient in truth, decency and dramatic interest. "I am well aware," says L. Maria Child, in her Preface, "that many will accuse me of indecorum for presenting these pages to the public; for the experiences of this intelligent and much-injured woman belong to a class which some call delicate subjects, and others indelicate. This peculiar phase of slavery has generally been kept veiled; but the public ought to be made acquainted with its monstrous features, and I willingly take the responsibility of presenting them with the veil withdrawn. I do this for the sake of my sisters in bondage, who are suffering wrongs so foul, that our ears are too delicate to listen to them." Having given this frank intimation of the coming disclosures, L. Maria Child "withdraws the veil." Those only who have an appetite for what is cruel, and a taste for what is unclean, will part on good terms with the strong-minded woman who edits a slave-girl's disgusting revelations.[31]

The review, which questions the narrative's veracity, disparages Child's indecency, and denounces the unspecified slave girl's depravity, demonstrates beyond a doubt that English readers were aware of women's sexual vulnerability within slavery and reveals the interpretive capacities of nineteenth-century English readers to infer sexuality. It also displays self-conscious concern about the indecency of such prurient readings of slave narratives.

Jean Fagan Yellin, the critic who in 1981 established the authenticity of

Jacobs's narrative and subsequently revived interest in it, observes that her slave narrative is the only one "that takes as its subject the sexual exploitation of female slaves—thus centring on sexual oppression as well as oppression of race and condition." In addition to telling Jacobs's story, her narrative relentlessly exposes the great open secret of slavery—namely, black women's sexual victimization by white slave owners: "No pen can give an adequate description of the all-pervading corruption produced by slavery. The slave girl is reared in an atmosphere of licentiousness and fear. The lash and the foul talk of her master and her sons are her teachers." Although Jacobs is generally more explicit about the sexual violence carried out in slavery than her contemporaries, she is often oblique about her own sexuality. Recent critics have observed how her narrative obfuscates, omits, and conceals her sexuality, displacing the plain facts of the abuse and "sexual nonconformity" with elaborate discursivity. Karen Sánchez-Eppler examines how the narrator writes her sexuality to titillate her white women readers but also to conceal her sexual transgression by shifting focus from her sexual vulnerability to her motherhood. Deborah Garfield discusses how Jacobs switches between the roles of speaker and listener in order to underplay her agency in the telling of her indecorous story. Finally, P. Gabrielle Foreman comments on the narrator's strategic use of "undertell" when disclosing information. She observes that Jacobs's undertellings moderate a subject matter that may have been deemed obscene: "Jacobs's confession [of her sexual liaison with Mr. Sands], in contrast, with its emphasis on a rapacious master, could easily collapse for her readers into the arousal of imagined sadistic pornography. Yet Jacobs carefully contains her writing, refusing to describe Linda's more private moments with Mr. Sands, and so distinguishes the more acceptable titillation and resolution of confession and absolution from the pornographic excitement that would be labeled unacceptably illicit in Victorian America." Perhaps it was this combination of unusual explicitness and restraint in Jacobs's narrative that titillated the English publisher, familiar with sexualized readings of slavery and, like other Victorian readers, adept at decoding sexual implications.[32]

Lazenby's *The Secret Life of Linda Brent* is a fragmentary parody of Jacobs's slave narrative that covers only the first years of her life but manages to rewrite the sexual violence described in Jacobs's narrative as sadistic obscenity. It distorts slave women's sexual victimization as grossly carnal and rejects Jacobs's anxious professions of virtue by overtly sexualizing her: she watches a slave and a white overseer copulating, masturbates, and engages in sexual "games" with another mulatto woman.[33] *The Secret Life* dwells particularly on the sexual violence that accompanies white men's sexual access to black women in slave society. The parody lifts the flogging scene from "Kate's Narrative," repeats it four times, and in so doing reveals sadistic fascination with the sexual torture of female slaves. In its descriptions of flogging the parody overwrites the English flagellation fantasy with a racialized flogging fantasy. *The Secret Life* does not follow the fantasy structure that it sets up, however, but is, instead, diverted by another sexual impulse. What begins as a fantasy about white male brutal sexual power over slave women becomes a homoerotic fantasy that includes graphic descriptions of sodomy and male same-sex desire. The parody appropriates the image of the flogged slave woman, by now thoroughly contaminated by sexualized readings and repetitions, as a disguise for its true preoccupation with homoerotic desire.

The first flogging scene in *The Secret Life* features Jacobs's grandmother. It functions primarily to undermine the importance of the grandmother in Jacobs's slave narrative who is the matriarch of the slave community. A freed slave who owns a house near Dr. Flint's, she is at once community leader, moral keystone, and symbol of freedom. Jacobs's narrative only briefly alludes to her grandmother's history as a young slave and never intimates sexual abuse or impropriety; as Foreman observes, her private life is not subject to scrutiny. What she discloses is that "she was a little girl when she was captured and sold to the keeper of a large hotel" and fared "hard [. . .] during childhood." The parody, however, denies the influence that the grandmother holds in the slave narrative as a seasoned older woman who has survived slavery. It imagines her as a young slave girl—Martha, rather than Aunt Martha—still vulnerable to sexual abuse by her "rascally master, the hotel keeper." Ridiculing Jacobs's language of sensibility as well as women's role in the abolitionist movement, the parody imagines Linda's grandmother confessing to "a sympathising anti-slavery lady" about how "her modesty was overcome." The fantasy thus unfolds. In the parody Martha describes how her master, Jackley, detains her for a wealthy and lecherous Colonel who is a guest at his hotel. As she is confined in one of the rooms, the Colonel spanks and birches her while her master watches with "quiet but intense enjoyment." The beating is frankly sexualized: in the manner of English flagellation obscenity, its instrument is the birch, and its focus is the nude buttocks rather than the back, where the slave was usually whipped. Yet the fantasy also relies on the frisson of difference for its erotic effect. The Colonel eroticizes and racializes the woman, revealing the erotics of color, by describing her "beautifully-polished skin—the slight olive tint of which looked far more voluptuous than the white skin of an Englishwoman's." With this slippage the parody reminds us of its English audience and reveals how its erotics depends on racial difference and transatlantic displacement for its effects.[34]

Up until this point *The Secret Life* is a heterosexual fantasy that viciously repudiates the feminist and abolitionist appeal of Jacobs's slave narrative for the victimized slave girl. Yet, as soon as the parody constructs this heterosexual fantasy, it transforms it. What begins as the beating and rape of a black slave girl shifts into a sexual exchange between the two white men where the black girl is never even penetrated. Jackley, pleading the excuse that he must preserve Martha's maidenhead in order to sell it later at a good price, sodomizes the Colonel. Meanwhile, the Colonel performs cunnilingus on Martha, who has her first orgasm. This Sedgwickian triangle demonstrates white male homoerotic desire expressed through the spectacle of the brutalized black woman. Martha is both the pretext and the victim of this homoerotic exchange, her blackness and femininity at once arousing the white men and providing the excuse for their homoeroticism.

A second flogging scene immediately follows the first and also reveals underlying homoerotic desire. Immediately after the assault on Martha, the Colonel cautions her with a story about how he had another intractable female slave, a mulatto named Cherry, disciplined. Giving her up to an overseer, a "great black big fellow," he describes how he watched while she was flogged and sexually tortured:

> Well, he put his great big prick into her; he hugged her close to his black hairy breast, and kissed her pretty little lips with his great thick black ones. More than that, he put his great stiff prick into her pretty little bottom hole, and pushed it in until she was all torn and bleeding, and because she objected to this, and screamed, he flogged her until the skin and flesh of her bottom was all hanging in strips, and her blood ran down into her shoes; and when she screamed he thrust the handle of his whip into her cunt. So that little Cherry was quite subdued, and was laid up for months.

On the one hand, this passage is a heterosexual fantasy about male sexual power over the black woman. On the other hand, it is also a homoerotic fantasy from which the Colonel derives sexual pleasure from watching the black man and knowing that he enacts his sexual will. The Colonel directs his gaze primarily at the imposing physicality and blackness of the overseer. He lingers over the overseer's "great big prick," "black hairy breast," and "great thick black" lips."[35] The black woman, his sexual victim, seems less significant than this racialized spectacle of the virile and brutish black man. The kinds of sexual acts described also reveal the parody's deviation from the typically heterosexual flagellation and flogging fantasies. In addition to heightening the black woman's pain and humiliation, these acts parody heterosexual coitus and make it redundant. This passage, then, allows for homoerotic desire to cross the color line but, in so doing, also exploits the color line in such a way that the Colonel is able to discuss deviant sexuality from a racial remove. In other words, although the Colonel relishes the homoerotics of this flogging scene, he displaces the act of sodomy from white male sexuality onto black male sexuality and depicts sodomy in terms of a brutal male black sexuality that is willing to penetrate any orifice, however unusually. Indeed, this entire passage could be read as an anxious and corrective fantasy in response to the first flogging fantasy, when the two white men commit sodomy. The Colonel's story of the black overseer indulges in the spectacle of manliness and the performance of sexual deviance but removes white male sexuality from an act perpetrated by a black man on a black woman.

The third flogging scene also constructs a heterosexual fantasy only to distort it. It draws from an incident in Jacobs's slave narrative when Dr. Flint punishes the cook by confining her for a day away from her nursing baby and conflates it with another incident on the same page when Dr. Flint ties one of his male slaves up to the joist and flogs him for accusing him of fathering his wife's child. In the parody Dr. Flint binds and flogs the cook, who is the mother of his child. He switches from the English birch, used in the previous flogging scenes, to the American cowhide, a detail that demonstrates knowledge about American technologies of slave torture. Revealing the sexual impulse behind the flogging, the cook for "shame" asks to be flogged on the back rather than the bottom. As with the other flogging fantasies, this one features a display of white male racial and heterosexual power only to interrupt it with the introduction of anal penetration. After flogging the cook, Dr. Flint penetrates her anally with a broom. As before, anal penetration takes the place of penile-vaginal coitus, diverting the course of the heterosexual rape fantasy. Also, as before, the parody distances the white man from sodomy by making sure that Dr. Flint's penis does not perform the act, but, instead, he uses another object.[36]

In these last three flogging scenes, then, *The Secret Life* repeats the image of the flogged slave woman to transform it, becoming otherwise preoccupied with white male sexual deviance, homoerotic desire, and sodomy. The reasons underlying the appropriation of this image also explain its transformation. By the 1880s, first of all, flagellation obscenity had become creatively exhausted and seems to have depended on the inclusion of racial difference or sodomy for its resuscitation. During this period Lazenby's works on flagellation were increasingly turning to depictions of deviant sexual activities. His serialized stories from *The Pearl*, including *Miss Coote's Confession, Lady Pokingham,* and *Sub-Umbra,* each contains reference to flagellation as well as male or female homosexuality. The image of the flogged slave woman functioned as a diversion to introduce male same-sex desire. At the beginning of the 1880s legislators, theorists, and publishers of obscenity began more systematically to discuss homosexuality. There was an emerging awareness of homosexuality in England that preceded the notoriety of Oscar Wilde in the 1890s. If the Foucauldian thesis is true, that the sodomite evolved from an aberration to a species in the 1870s, then the 1880s, at least in England, set about constructing and debating this species. In England's obscene print culture, for instance, narratives about male sodomy and male relationships were being featured more prominently. Lazenby's publication of *Sins of the Cities of the Plains; or, The Recollections of a Mary-Ann* (1881), arguably the first explicit English work of fiction on homosexual identities and communities, suggests the industry's awakening interest in sodomy. The discussion of a criminalized sexual act such as sodomy would have been less anxious at a geographical and historical remove. The addition of racial and cultural difference to the English flagellation fantasy via the image of the flogged slave woman disassociated the fantasy from the English. It thus enabled the inclusion of English homoerotic fantasies about sodomy—already a powerful, but latent, component of the flagellation fantasy— while blaming such acts on the degeneracy of the American plantation owner and the American system of slavery.[37]

The Secret Life also includes a fourth flogging scene, but it is unlike the others. It explores other forms of sexual violence within slavery. More specifically, it examines the idea that Jacobs emphasizes in her narrative: "Cruelty is contagious in uncivilized communities." The parody describes how the regular crossing of the color line corrupts other members of the plantation household. It borrows a scene from Jacobs's narrative when Mrs. Flint forces her to remove her new shoes ("whose creaking grated harshly on her refined nerves") and orders her to run errands barefoot in the snow. The parody recasts this punishment as flogging and describes how Mrs. Flint beats Linda with her new shoes: "she drew my petticoats over my head, exposing my naked bottom to her own gaze, and—worse— the gaze of the precocious little rascal Nicholas." Linda becomes the object of not only Nicholas's erotic gaze but also Mrs. Flint's. This scene reveals a shrewd reading of Jacobs's description of Mrs. Flint's predatory sexual jealously: "Sometimes I woke up, and found her bending over me. At other times she whispered in my ear, as though it was her husband speaking to me, and listened to hear what I would answer." Recent critics, such as Sánchez-Eppler, have suggested that this scene is one of the most graphically sexual in the narrative: once Mrs. Flint enters the bedroom, she "occupies precisely the position of erotic dominance repeatedly denied the doctor."[38] By having Mrs. Flint flog Linda, a punishment that has been repeatedly sexualized, the parody possibly draws on the intimations of other forms of sexual abuse in Jacobs's narrative. Up until this fourth flogging scene, then, *The Secret Life* is a profoundly homoerotic piece that uses the image of the flogged slave woman simultaneously to arouse, displace, and deny this English male homoeroticism. In the final scene, however, it notices another power relationship within slavery—namely, that between the slave woman and the jealous mistress. This final scene demonstrates the astute, albeit vicious, reading of the various forms of sexual abuse described in Jacobs's narrative. It also reveals the historical imbrications of its sexual fantasy: the parody resurrects sexualized reading of the flogged slave woman, recontextualizes the image as homoerotic fantasy, and introduces other fantasies circulating around the sexualized and racialized violence within slavery.[39]

An illustration that accompanies *The Secret Life* adds to its historical complexity. This illustration, like the one from the second edition of *My Grandmother's Tale,* suggests alternative fantasies surrounding the image of the flogged slave woman. It depicts the first flogging scene when Jackley and the Colonel beat Linda's grandmother but whitewashes the grandmother. Nothing in the illustration suggests that the flagellation is racialized and perpetrated in the antebellum South. Moreover, there is no suggestion of homoerotic desire. Sodomy and homoerotic desire were frequently described in nineteenth-century obscenity but were apparently deemed too transgressive for visual depiction. In effect, then, the illustration shows a typical English flagellation scene, indistinguishable from the illustrations in Lazenby's ordinary flagellation obscenity. The illustration seems to revert to the English flagellation fantasy upon which the flogging fantasy is built, omitting reference to racial difference and sodomy and recalling visual iconography that would have been familiar and innocuous to readers of obscenity. The illustration offsets the racial and sexual brutality that it describes and, in so doing, neutralizes the most transgressive and objectionable elements of the parody. More important, with the whitewashing of the grandmother, it both recalls early visual iconography around slave flogging and foreshadows future appropriations of flogging and slave narratives that fantasize about white women as slave victims.

Slavery Obscenity at the Turn of the Century: Charles Carrington and Select Bibliothèque

The underground fascination with slavery in the Americas diminished after Lazenby's imprisonment in 1886. After a decade, however, slavery once again became the subject of obscene publication. The reengagement with this particular phase in history extended from the 1890s to 1910s, driven by a loose consortium of British, French, and American publishers, agents, and interests. The image of the flogged victim retained its fascination but underwent further transformation. Fantasies around this image, preserving elements from flagellation literature and slave narratives, now shifted their focus from the flogged black woman to the white woman.

Accompanying this new development in slavery obscenity was a heightened awareness about its historical and national origins. Lazenby's productions addressed English gentlemen exclusively and dehistoricized slavery to explore homoerotics through racial and sexual domination. Later slavery obscenity, however, addressed men of various national backgrounds and detailed the historical circumstances of slavery in the Americas. Fantasies about the white woman slave that emerged in later slavery obscenity were co-opted by nationalist rivalry. The publishers of later slavery obscenity, such as Charles Carrington and Select Bibliothèque, marketed the titillating image of the flogged white female slave variously for different national audiences. These publishers based decisions about censorship, open or clandestine publication, and cultural ownership upon national sensibilities, proclivities, and legalities.

It was the indomitable Carrington who first returned to the subject of slavery in the Americas. Immersed in the bohemian literary culture of Paris, he also became the most prominent publisher of English and French obscenity in the late nineteenth century. By the end of the nineteenth century, as Mendes observes, Carrington "produced a vast amount of 'scientific,' 'oriental' and flagellatory semi-erotic texts openly, and in addition controlled most of the clandestine trade in pornography for the English-speaking market." He was the bane of Scotland Yard until 1907, when he was deported from France, though he returned in 1912. During his career he demonstrated keen global entrepreneurialism, creating and responding to a market for racialized erotics. He focused on oriental harems, Eastern sex manuals, American slavery, and later even colonial exhibits of Africa. His increased focus on the Americas corresponded to the global expansion of both the English and American traffic in obscenity. After a private interview with St. George Best, Gershon Legman describes how this man acted as Carrington's American agent after the turn of the century. Legman writes that "it was Best's job to smuggle Carrington's pornographica into America, through Cuba and Mexico, and deliver them safely to paying customers and fashionable booksellers in the United States."[40] He did not immediately turn to fantasies about flogging and the white female slave but revealed an early interest in race relations and slavery in the Americas.

As direct evidence of Carrington's familiarity with Lazenby's interest in slavery, he reprinted two of his publications that touch on slavery and race relations in the Americas: *My Grandmother's Tale* (as *May's Account* [1904]) and *The Adventures of Lady Harpur* (c. 1906). The first is a reprint from *The Pearl*, the latter a reprint of *Queenie* (1885). Again directed at wealthy mail-order clients, *The Adventures of Lady Harpur* sold for three guineas.[41] Like Lazenby's stories from *The Pearl* and *The Cremorne*, this novel is fascinated with the libidinal possibilities of the slave plantation and the mythic immensity of the black man's penis; unlike Lazenby's other works, however, it does not focus on the floggings and cruelties concomitant with slavery. This story of father-daughter incest, intergenerational sex, and rape uses West Indian slavery as its backdrop primarily to explore the sexual intermingling of black and white bodies. Although there are occasional references to the history and geography of West Indian and American slavery, the story is mostly concerned with colored corporeality. Queenie, the heroine of the story, expresses the preoccupation that runs through the story: "Although the colour did not much matter, provided that they were equally strong and active, she preferred being fucked by a white man; but that some of the blacks, and especially Sambo, had most enormous tools."[42]

Before his Lazenby reprints, Carrington demonstrated his interest in race relations in the Americas in other ways. In the 1890s and early 1900s, from his base in Paris, Carrington published a series of original, English-language works with American settings: *The Memoirs of Madge Budford; or, A Modern Fanny Hill* (1892), *A Town-Bull; or, The Elysian Fields* (1893), *Sue Suckitt; Maid and Wife* (1893),[43] *Maidenhead Stories* (1894), and *Dolly Morton* (1899). Mendes posits that Best, Carrington's later American agent, may have authored some of these works. He bases his theory about Best's authorship on his discovery that he was publishing stories in an Anglo-American magazine in Paris in the 1890s.[44] Yet it is difficult to determine whether English or Americans authored these works. By comparing typographical features, Mendes convincingly traces all these texts back to Carrington, but they feature different original places of publication: *Madge Budford, A Town-Bull,* and *Sue Suckitt,* New Orleans; *Maidenhead Stories,* New York; and *Dolly Morton,* Paris. Clandestine catalogs, however, indicate that these works were mainly directed to an English market.[45] For the most part the content is no more revealing about their national origins. *Dolly Morton,* with its male English narrator, was most likely authored by an Englishman; however, the other texts blend American and English references.[46] Authorship aside, what is important about the publication history of these texts is that they demonstrate European interest in American sexualities. Moreover, while American sexuality seems to have been a source of interest for a certain class of French and English reader, a certain class of American reader also seems to have been equally interested in European depictions of their sexuality—though not until a few decades later, when these publications eventually reached the United States through recirculation and reprint.

Except for *Maidenhead Stories,* all of these novels focus on racialized sexualities in the United States. The last in the series, *Dolly Morton,* is by far the most noteworthy and deserves closer attention. The earlier texts, however, establish and develop Carrington's interest in the topic. *A Town-Bull* focuses on the sexual escapades of a virile American man who eventually finds himself as the forefather of a Southern commune (his Elysium), whose offspring display a "fine scale of color, from purest white to a rich chocolate brown."[47] The implicit and likely unconscious logic of this story is that indiscriminate sexuality brings the harmonious mixing of races. *Sue Suckitt* explores male same-sex desire by introducing the black man as a well-endowed sodomist. The frenetic sexual combat between a black and white man leaves little doubt about where desire is located in this novel: "Like gladiators they faced each other, standing each lance in rest [. . .] and with a lustful yell they closed, writhed in each other's arms like athletes in a wrestling match, then jutting out their bellies, each seized out his own prick and handling it like a foil in fencing, rubbed them together, titled at each other, stabbed each other, until the cream like gore began to shoot, when, rolling on the floor heads and heals, their salacious mouths sucked frantically each other's sperming spigots."[48] Unlike Jacobs's parody, this novel does not separate the white man from sodomy but explores his participation with interest. Finally, *Madge Buford,* putatively authored by D'Arcy St. John, also focuses on racialized sexuality in the United States. In this novel the black male slave is sexually deviant and degraded—he commits bestiality with a female dog and fellates a male dog.[49] These novels reveal a range of attitudes toward black American sexuality, from playful to debasing, but, as a series, they are significant because they demonstrate Carrington's early publishing interests and suggest the commercial viability of black American sexuality to underground European and, later, American book markets.

It is with *Dolly Morton,* however, that Carrington turned to Lazenby's trade in slavery obscenity. Of Carrington's publications with an American setting, it is the most significant in terms of reproduction, influence, and literary quality. Wilde was reputedly familiar with the novel. Dawes, moreover, places it "as being amongst the very few good erotic works of its period," lauding its historical realism: "even *Uncle Tom's Cabin* leaves a lot out that is to be found in *Dolly Morton*" (287). There is little doubt about what details the novel adds. *Dolly Morton,* like the stories from *The Pearl* and especially *The Cremorne,* reproduces fantasies about the flogged slave woman by overwriting flagellation and slave narratives. The white woman, however, now assumes the role of the flogged female slave. The publication history of this novel makes the transformation of the fantasy all the more interesting, demonstrating how this new fantasy became a matter of nationalist contest and historical revisionism.

Like earlier slavery obscenity, *Dolly Morton* turns to the physical and sexual violence inflicted upon women for its erotic effects. It represents itself as a first-hand account of the American slave system before the Civil War that focuses particularly on the physical and sexual violence inflicted upon slave women. The novel opens in New York in 1866, describing an Englishman's sexual encounter with a prostitute, Dolly. Following their encounter, the Englishman records verbatim Dolly's narrative about her life in the South. Before the Civil War and after hearing about the execution of the white abolitionist rebel John Brown, she moves to Virginia with an abolitionist Quaker woman, Miss Dean, in order to run an underground railway for escaped slaves. The Southerners, however, discover their duplicity and viciously punish them with a whipping. Randolph, one of the Virginian plantation owners, offers to help Dolly if she becomes his mistress. She yields in order to avoid further punishment. The rest of her story documents her sexual victimization as well as that of the female slaves on his plantation. With the onset of the Civil War and the Battle of Fair Oaks in Richmond, Randolph finally loses his hold on and interest in Dolly, eventually allowing her to leave for the North, where she establishes a house of prostitution in New York and meets the original narrator, an Englishman.

Dolly Morton reveals the same generic imbrications that are the trademark of Lazenby's slavery obscenity. The novel's subtitle, which appears in Carrington's original 1899 edition, immediately announces the combined influence of flogging and flagellation: "An account of the Whippings, Rapes, and Violences that Preceded the Civil War in America With Curious Anthropological Observations on the Radical Diversities in the Conformation of the Female Bottom and the Way Different Women endure Chastisement." A novel preoccupied with the whip, it continually reproduces the image of the whipped woman by drawing on flagellation and flogging conventions. Here, in a typical scene, Dolly is stripped and whipped by a lynch mob for her involvement in the running of an underground railway:

> "Now, as to the punishment of the gal. I propose to give her a dozen strokes, but not to draw blood." [. . .]
>
> "You bet I'll lay them on smart, and you'll see how she'll move. I know how to handle a hick'ry switch, and I'll rule a dozen lines across her bottom that'll make it look like the American flag, striped red and white. And when I've done with her I guess she'll be sore behind, but you'll see that I won't draw a drop of blood. Yes, gentlemen, I tell you again that I know how to whip. I was an overseer in Georgia for five years." [. . .]
>
> All the time the man was holding forth, I lay shame stricken at my nakedness and shivering in awful suspense, the flesh of my bottom creeping and the scalding tears trickling down my red cheeks. The man raised the switch and flourished it over me [. . .] .
>
> I winced and squirmed every time the horrid switch fell sharply on my quivering flesh. I shrieked, and screamed and I swung my hips from side to side, arching my loins at one moment and then flattening myself down on the ladder, while between my shrieks, I begged and prayed the man to stop whipping me. [. . .]
>
> "There boys, look at her bottom. You see how regularly the white skin is striped with long red weals; but there is not a drop of blood. That's what I call a prettily whipped bottom. But the gal ain't got a bit of grit in her. Any nigger wench would have taken double the number of strokes without making half the noise."[50]

This passage borrows conventions from flagellation and flogging, blending them in what is now a familiar fashion: the American overseer, for example, wields the English switch and hickory. What is different, of course, about this fantasy is that it imagines the white woman as slave. Dolly, after all, is unquestionably white: "Her skin was as white as milk and without a blemish." While this passage eroticizes her whiteness, dwelling on the red welts that contrast with the white skin of her bottom, it implicitly compares her to a black slave woman. Like a black slave woman, she is tied and beaten by an overseer. This overseer further suggests the parallel between Dolly and the female slave by comparing their responses to a beating.

If this passage only draws an implicit comparison between Dolly and slave woman, another makes the comparison more explicit. Randolph decides to whip Dolly one last time before he leaves her, and he promises, "I am going to whip you as if you were a naughty slave girl." In a few words he sums up the erotics of this novel. The repeated scenes of whipping, inflicted on women of all colors, demonstrate that gender rather than race finally becomes the preoccupying concern in the whipping fantasy—recalling the whitewashing of the slave woman at the beginning of its history. As Randolph bluntly states to Dolly, "you will soon find that many other men besides me are fond of spanking a woman till she squeals."[51]

American slavery, however, still remains the pretext of the fantasy. In many ways *Dolly Morton* is influenced by the structure and themes of a woman's slave narrative as it recounts Dolly's story of prostitution in the South and her "escape" to the North. In effect the novel is a white woman's slave narrative, one that draws on the history of slavery to document a white woman's sexual victimization. The novel literalizes the sexual abuse implied in American slave narratives such as Jacobs's by making *it* the circumstance of bondage, rather than race. While it is not an outright parody of the slave narrative, such as Lazenby's parody of Jacobs, it exploits the slave narrative in order to titillate its predominately male readers with scenes of sexual violence. A later imitation of Carrington's publications confirms this notion that he is borrowing from the slave narrative in *Dolly Morton. Woman and her Slave: A Realistic Narrative of a Slave who experienced His Mistress' Love and Lash,* a novel of unknown date, origin, and pagination, appropriates the slave narrative. This novel is not explicitly obscene and does not preoccupy itself with whipping: its suggestive title functions to establish the book's connection with Carrington but does not fulfill its promise. Instead, the book describes a male slave of mixed race who has a sexual relationship with his white mistress. It appropriates the slave narrative in order to explore another possible sexual dynamic within the slave system. It callously overturns the political protest that is so crucial to the genre by transforming it into an interracial love story: the lovers read *Othello* to each other to disclose their feelings, but he learns to despise his blackness as "unfitted for freedom." While the fantasy is altogether different from that which emerges in *Dolly Morton,* it comments on Carrington's prurient interest in slavery and the slave narrative. It reflects back on *Dolly Morton,* revealing how this text depends on historical contexts and genres in order to fantasize about a white woman being beaten.[52]

This image of the "white female slave" may respond to what Cecily Devereux has discussed as the rhetorical association between prostitution and white slavery by the end of the nineteenth century. As early as 17 January 1880, *Town Talk* developed the connection between the slave trade and female prostitution in an article on the "British and Foreign Traffic in Girls."[53] By 1912 London hosted an International Conference on Obscene Publications and the White Slave Trade. The French and English editions of *Dolly Morton,* however, did not elaborate on this relationship between slavery and the sexual trafficking of white women. Instead, they focused on the whiteness of the flogged woman *only* to displace the fantasy elsewhere. Demonstrating a heightened awareness about the novel's historical and national origins, these editions engaged in nationalist struggles to disown the fantasy. Whereas Carrington's English versions of the novel marketed it as American history, his French versions described it as an expression of the English vice.

Dolly Morton was first published in English openly, rather than clandestinely. Sold to affluent clientele for three guineas, it appeared amid a recrudescence of flagellation literature for which Carrington was known. An early 1896 advertisement for the novel marketed the book to the "Historian, and Students of Medical Jurisprudence," the "Anthropologist," and the "Student of Flagellation."[54] Carrington's later preface, however, focuses on the novel as history. Amassing historical detail around the novel, it reveals detailed knowledge about abolitionist history, referring to Wilbur H. Siebert's study *The Underground Railroad from Slavery to Freedom* (1898) and the "romantic narratives" of Frederick Douglass and John Brown. While, on the one hand, the preface suggests that the novel is a sympathetic historical account of abolitionist history, on the other hand, he uses this history to exploit the image of the flogged woman: "Women who were caught in this business were ruthlessly stripped and whipped—their persons exposed to the lustful eyes of lascivious men and, on many of them, other violences of a far more intimate nature were perpetrated. These ardent Southern men were, after all men in a sexual sense also, and few men can witness the chastisement and skin-warming of pious lovely, white women, without feeling promptings of a passionate nature." He manipulates history, imagining a scenario for which, to my knowledge, there is no recorded fact to suggest the legitimacy of a dubious text. In so doing, he displaces the prurient preoccupation with the image of the flogged woman—now transformed into a white woman—to the annals of American history. As he sets up this history, however, he shamelessly endorses the novel's prurient gaze: "Again we see beautiful women and delicately nurtured, stripped bare under a Southern sun; we hear their cries and pleadings for mercy as, one by one, their robes and petticoats are torn off or tucked up, their drawers unfastened and rolled down; our eyes are shocked and, by an inevitable natural impulse, delighted at the sight of the white, well-developed hemispheres laid bare and blushing to our gaze, only to receive the cruel lash." Using personal and possessive pronouns such as *we* and *our,* he also implicates the reader in this erotic viewing. All subsequent English reprints of his novel were printed clandestinely, a fact that suggests that his historicizing preface was not altogether convincing.[55]

While English editions reimagined history to disown the fantasy, French editions did the same by marketing it as English. Carrington openly published a French translation of the novel in 1901 as *En Virginie*. As Donald Thomas notes, Carrington's publishing activities were relatively unregulated in France because he expurgated French editions of English works. Except for the expurgation of explicit sexual acts, however, this edition remains intact and retains the descriptions of violent flagellation, including the description of Dolly's flogging. His French edition, moreover, includes a preface by Jean de Villiot, a composite pseudonym frequently used by Carrington,[56] that denounces English hypocrisy by juxtaposing strange English proclivities against its legendary prudery. Aggravated by the National Vigilance Association's denunciation of French literature as immoral,[57] Villiot responds to the hoary English tirade by disparaging English sexuality as an extreme of vice and virtue and reproducing the idea of the sexually hypocritical Victorians: "Là, règne cette dangereuse maxime qu'une austérité rigoureuse est la seule sauvegarde de la vertu. Le mot le plus innocent effraye; le geste le plus naturel devient un attentat. Les sentiments, ainsi réprimés, ou s'étouffent ou éclatent d'une manière terrible. Tout pour le vice ou tout pour la vertu, point de milieu; les caractères se complaisant dans l'extrême, et l'on voit naître des pruderies outrées et des monstres de licence."[58] Later, in his "Bibliographie des Principaux Ouvrages Parus sur la Flagellation," which appears at the end of the book, Villiot specifically links flagellation to the English: "C'est incontestablement l'Angleterre qui tient la tête en cette matière."[59] In addition to perpetuating the national and sexual rivalry in this French edition of *Dolly Morton,* Carrington continued to do so in a French series on flagellation entitled "La Flagellation à travers le monde." This series focused largely on English flagellation and identified the act as English. Producing such titles as *Le Fouet à Londres* (1904) and *Étude sur la flagellation [. . .] avec un exposé documentaire de la flagellation dans les écoles anglaises et des prisons militaries* (1899),[60] Carrington sold the series as a spectacle of English vice to a French market steeped in Sade.

By the early twentieth century the image of the flogged slave woman was still circulating in obscene print cultures, not only in England and France but also in the United States. The American trade in obscenity did not emerge until the Irish immigrant, William Haynes, began to publish "improper" books in the mid-nineteenth century. Anthony Comstock, a founder of the New York Society for the Suppression of Vice, helped secure federal obscenity legislation in the United States. After the law's passage in 1873, he claimed to have seized "200,000 pictures and photographs; 100,000 books; 5,000 packs of playing cards; and numerous contraceptive devices and allegedly aphrodisiac medicines."[61] Yet by the end of the century the trade had greatly expanded both in terms of import and export. For instance, obscene cabinet photographs featuring American slaves were sold by mail order to English and American audiences. A clandestine catalog entitled "Strictly Confidential," probably printed in Paris in the early nineteenth century, listed twenty cabinet photographs of "slave negresses" for 25 shillings, or $6.25. These photographs visualize the sexual dominion of the slave owner over his female slaves: "A young planter orders one of them to take off all her clothes. He then seats himself on horseback upon her, clastifying [*sic*] her violently with a whip, and when the climax of his sensual evolutions has been reached, she has to pump his penus [*sic*] with her big lips whereby she finally receives as reward a full avalanche of her master's sperm in her mouth."[62]

As the obscene image of the flogged black slave woman recirculated, fantasies about the white female slave also continued to appear. Other publishers besides Carrington, for instance, imagined the white woman slave. In the first decade of the twentieth century Select Bibliothèque privately printed, first in French and then in English, a series of underground obscene books on American slavery putatively authored by Don Brennus Aléra, a composite pseudonym much like Jean de Villiot.[63] The English editions appeared in 1910: *White Women Slaves, Barbaric*

Fêtes, Under the Yoke, and *In Louisiana.*[64] As the only books in the series trans-lated into English, they demonstrate the peculiar appeal of the subject matter to the English. An advertisement at the back of *White Women Slaves* reveals that these books also had an American audience: they were priced at sixteen shillings, or four dollars. Titles such as *White Women Slaves* finally encapsulate my argument. One of the implicit fantasies surrounding the image of the flogged slave woman at the beginning of its history in England finds literal expression by the end of the nineteenth century but now circulated among British, French, and American publishers and readers, provoking nationalist debates and questions about history, imaginative property, and censorship.

Whipping in the Twentieth Century: The Fugitive Image

By the 1920s the image of the flogged slave woman seems to have disap-peared. I speculate, however, that the image has not disappeared in the twentieth century but has been dehistoricized with its global dissemination. I am not sug-gesting that the historical image of the flogged slave woman does not reappear, yet it generally reappears *outside* the context of the historical slave system. I want to suggest that whipping fantasies are ineradicably linked to the history of sla-very. Regardless of the sexual relationships they imagine, whipping fantasies are predicated on a transatlantic image that emerged in the late eighteenth century.

At the beginning of the twentieth century, while fantasies about the white slave woman were still circulating in English underground literature, the image of the flogged female slave was transformed into the figurative trope of master and slave. This trope had long been circulating in England—appropriated by various reform movements—but, as far as I know, it was not introduced into obscenity until the turn of the century. Carrington himself introduced the trope through his publications. In 1901 he published an underground flagellation novel entitled *Sub-urban Souls: The Erotic Psychology of a Man and a Maid,* which describes sexual domination in terms of the master/slave relationship. Later, in 1905, he also pub-lished *The Mistress and the Slave: A Masochist Realistic Love Story,* which re-verses gender roles but still relies on the figures of master/slave to explore the erotics of domination.[65] This transformation of the image of the flogged female slave at the beginning of the twentieth century marks its figuration at the same time as its most intense globalization. The efflorescence of sales catalogs, obscene publications, and regulatory actions by the early twentieth century demonstrates that the international trade in obscenity experienced unprecedented growth in the West at this time. Although widely recirculated, the image became fugitive.

Every twentieth-century whipping fantasy or practice in the West not only relies on this image but also repeats it. In other words, the image of the flogged slave woman has never disappeared. *Histoire d'O,* written by Dominique Aury for Olympia Press in 1958 under the pseudonym Pauline Réage, demonstrates the in-sidious influence of the image. If the following passage from the novel were placed out of context, one might almost attribute it to a slave narrative; it not only invokes the hierarchies of slavery but also borrows its instruments and language of torture:

> You are here to serve your masters. [. . .] The whip will be used only be-
> tween dusk and dawn. But besides the whipping you receive from who-
> ever may want to whip you, you will also be flogged in the evening, as
> punishment for any infractions of the rules committed during the day
> [. . .] . Actually both this flogging and the chain—which when attached
> to the ring of your collar keeps you more or less closely confined to your
> bed several hours a day—are intended less to make you suffer, scream, or
> shed tears than to make you feel, *through* this suffering, that you are not
> free but fettered.[66]

Similarly, the illustrated advertisements found in any British Telecom phone booth in London today play on a wry English self-consciousness about the rich histori-cal tradition of the English vice. Prostitute cards such as "Strict Victorian Punish-ment Taken," "Genuine Victorian Punishment," and "Victorian Punishment" reverse the gender roles of the typical Victorian flagellation fantasy but also invoke por-nographic nostalgia for the public boys' school. While the advertisements situate beating within an English erotic tradition and do not offer any explicit references to slavery, I suggest that they are also imbricated with the archaeological remain-ders of slavery. Had it not been for transatlantic abolitionism, this image may not have been so enduring.

Twentieth-century theorists of whipping fantasies have overlooked their his-torical origins within the context of slavery. In "A Child Is Being Beaten" (1919), Freud notices how Harriet Beecher Stowe's *Uncle Tom's Cabin* stimulated erotic beating fantasies among his patients. As he recognizes one of the most influential texts on the Western cultural imagination in the nineteenth century, however, he dismisses it and explains how the beating fantasy originates in early childhood.[67] Similarly, in *Erotism: Death and Sensuality* Georges Bataille uses the Hegelian master/slave dialectic to describe the erotics of domination in terms of the taut tension between life and death but overlooks how the history of slavery directly informed G. W. F. Hegel's psychological paradigm of self-consciousness. More re-cently, Lynda Hart has turned to Butlerian theories of performativity and subver-sion in order to defend lesbian sadomasochism as liberating. Acknowledging the use of symbols associated with historical atrocities in S-M role-playing, especially fascist ones, Hart defends such role-playing by suggesting it destabilizes static rep-resentations of power. Yet whipping fantasies are profoundly influenced by a trans-atlantic cultural exchange that began at the end of the eighteenth century, when nineteenth-century abolitionist print communities disseminated the image of the flogged female slave in England and across Europe.[68] Sade's *Justine* (1791) and Leopold von Sacher-Masoch's *Venus in Furs* (1870)—both influential on English flagellation literature, fantasies, and theoretical vocabularies—were also influenced by slavery.[69] Research into abolitionist and obscene print cultures in England recontextualizes the history of the so-called English vice and its global spread.

Such research produces a new, historically grounded theory of flagellation fantasies: one that recognizes that such fantasies are predicated on an image imbricated with the remainders of slavery. Anyone who recirculates this fugitive image, in fantasy or practice, needs to confront its association with the history of slavery and empire.

Notes

1. While the image of the brutalized slave man circulated in abolitionist pamphlets and slave narratives, it was rarely eroticized. Such images typically emphasize his suffering or resistance. For a discussion of nineteenth-century representations of slave torture, see Marcus Wood, *Blind Memory: Visual Representations of Slavery in England and America, 1780–1865* (Manchester: Manchester University Press, 2000), 215–291.

2. Ian Gibson, *The English Vice: Beating, Sex and Shame in Victorian England and After* (London: Duckworth, 1978).

3. Decades of careful scholarship have attempted to reconstruct the elusive history of England's obscene print culture in the nineteenth century, beginning with Steven Marcus's Freudian study of the underground literature in *The Other Victorians: A Study of Sexuality and Pornography in Mid-Nineteenth-Century England* (New York: Basic, 1964). For the most significant scholarship on the subject, see Walter Kendrick's history of obscenity in *The Secret Museum: Pornography in Modern Culture* (New York: Viking, 1987); Iain McCalman's study of the trade's efflorescence from radical postwar politics in *Radical Underworld: Prophets, Revolutionaries, and Pornographers in London, 1795–1840* (Cambridge: Cambridge University Press, 1988); Peter Mendes's annotated bibliography that uncovers information about publishing rings and retail markets in *Clandestine Erotic Fiction in English, 1800–1930: A Bibliographical Study* (Hants, UK: Scolar, 1993); Lynda Nead's account of middle-class anxiety over street consumerism in *Victorian Babylon: People, Streets and Images in Nineteenth-Century London* (New Haven: Yale University Press, 2000); and, finally, Lisa Z. Sigel's discussion of the development of the trade within the social hegemonies of class, gender, and race in *Governing Pleasures: Pornography and Social Change in England, 1815–1914* (New Brunswick: Rutgers University Press, 2002). There are numerous, more focused, studies on specific aspects of nineteenth-century obscenity. These include Gibson's study of English flagellation obscenity; Coral Lansbury's exploration of the connections between medical science, vivisection, and obscenity in *The Old Brown Dog: Women, Workers, and Vivisection in Edwardian England* (Madison: University of Wisconsin Press, 1985); Tracy Davis's discussion of the representation of the actress in Victorian obscenity in "The Actress in Victorian Pornography," *Theatre Journal* 41 (1989): 294–315; William Scheick's suggestion that H. Rider Haggard's *King Solomon's Mines* (1885) functioned as "adolescent pornography" in "Adolescent Pornography and Imperialism in Haggard's "King Solomon's Mines," *English Literature in Transition* 34, no. 1 (1991): 19–30; John Woodrow Presley's tenuous discussion of James Joyce's allusions to *The Pearl* in *Finnegans Wake* (1939) in *"Finnegans Wake, Lady Pokingham,* and Victorian Erotic Fantasy," *Journal of Popular Culture* 30, no. 3 (1996): 67–80; Tamar Heller's study of flagellation in "Flagellating Feminine Desire: Lesbians, Old Maids, and New Women in 'Miss Coote's Confession,' a Victorian Pornographic Narrative," *Victorian Newsletter* 92 (1997): 9–15; James Nelson's examination of Leonard Smithers's involvement in London's obscene print culture in

Publisher to the Decadents: Leonard Smithers in the Careers of Beardsley, Wilde, Dowson (University Park: Pennsylvania State University Press, 2000); and Alison Pease's study of the shifting boundaries between art and obscenity from the 1700s onward in *Modernism, Mass Culture, and the Aesthetics of Obscenity* (Cambridge: Cambridge University Press, 2000).

4. Harriet Beecher Stowe, *Uncle Tom's Cabin, or Life among the Lowly* (London: H. G. Bohn, 1852). Also see Audrey A. Fisch, *American Slaves in Victorian England: Abolitionist Politics and Culture* (Cambridge: Cambridge University Press, 2000). As Fisch observes, *Uncle Tom's Cabin* was so popular in England that it was imitated. In 1852 the English novel *Uncle Tom in England* appeared, appropriating the novel's abolitionist message for Chartist reform and initiating a discourse of "white slavery" that rhetorically linked English workers to American slaves.

5. Fisch, *American Slaves,* 70.

6. Fisch, *American Slaves,* 63; also see Richard D. Fulton, "'Now Only the *Times* Is on Our Side': The London *Times* and America before the Civil War," *Victorian Review* 16, no. 1 (1990): 48–58.

7. Karen Halttunen, "Humanitarianism and the Pornography of Pain in Anglo-American Culture," *American Historical Review* 100, no. 2 (1995): 303–334, esp. 307–308.

8. For the Whipping Act, see 25 Vict., c.18. In *The Representation of Bodily Pain in Late Nineteenth-Century English Culture* (Oxford: Clarendon, 2000) Lucy Bending cites some of the pamphlets that debated flagellation, including Rev. C. Allix Wilkinson's *Reminiscences of Eton* (1888). In the periodical press one of the most curious debates appeared in *Town Talk.* The magazine published correspondence on flagellation that chiefly debated the "indecent whipping of girls." One woman wrote to the editor about how her daughter was birched: she "was compelled to stand before all the other girls in a most indecent way, with half her clothes off and the other half tucked up over her shoulders while the mistress whipped her with a birch rod till the blood trickled down her legs"; see *Town Talk,* 26 July 1879, 3. On 4 April 1885 the magazine published a separate one-shilling pamphlet that collected all the flagellation correspondence; it also promised to sell (by private subscription) another pamphlet that included letters that the magazine had deemed unsuitable for publication. While the magazine claimed to expunge immorality by exposing it, it clearly intended to titillate. Because of its explicit content, the magazine was continually under the threat of obscene libel charges, and it periodically interrupted publication whenever the editor was convicted.

9. Numerous critics, including McCalman, Pease, and Sigel, use the term *pornography* to discuss nineteenth-century obscenity. I follow Kendrick's and Nead's use of the term *obscenity. Pornography* did not enter English vocabulary until 1850 in order to denote sexually explicit literature and art (OED). Such works were more generally referred to as "erotic," "curious," or "forbidden"; see Kendrick, *Secret Museum,* 71. *Pornography* only entered popular usage in the late nineteenth century, most famously with attacks by the *Pall Mall Gazette* against the "esoteric pornography" of Sir Richard Burton's translation of the *Arabian Nights* (1885–1888); see Sigma [John Morley], "Pantagruelism or Pornography?" *Pall Mall Gazette,* 14 September 1885, 2–3.

10. Pisanus Fraxi [Henry Spencer Ashbee], *Centuria Librorum Absconditorum* (London: privately printed, 1879), 445. Ashbee also provides information about brothel houses that specialized in flagellation, naming the "queen of [the] profession" as Mrs. Theresa Berkley. After cataloging her various instruments of torture, he writes that "at her shop, whosoever went with plenty of money, could be birched, whipped, fustigated, scourged,

needle-pricked, half-hung, holly-brushed, furse-brushed, butcher-brushed, stinging-nettled, curry-combed, phlebotomized"; see Ashbee, *Index Librorum Prohibitorum* (London, 1877), xliv.

11. Marcus, *Other Victorians,* 260; and Gibson, *English Vice,* 282.

12. Johann Heinrich Meibomius, *A Treatise on the Use of Flogging in Venereal Affairs* (London: E. Curll, 1718); and John Cleland, *Memoirs of a Woman of Pleasure* (London: G. Fenton, 1749).

13. Mendes, *Clandestine Erotic Fiction,* 215. Also see surviving nineteenth-century editions of Cannon's publications: *The Birchen Bouquet; or, Curious and Original Anecdotes of Ladies Fond of Administering the Birch Discipline* (N.p.: Birchington-on-Sea [Avery?], 1881); *The Elements of Tuition in Modes of Punishment* (London, [c. 1880]); *The Exhibition of Female Flagellants* (London: printed for the bookseller, [c. 1840]). For a description of flagellation fantasies, see Gibson, *English Vice,* 265–268.

14. For more recent commentary on flagellation obscenity, see Tamar Heller, "Flagellating Feminine Desire: Lesbians, Old Maids, and New Women in 'Miss Coote's Confession,' a Victorian Pornographic Narrative," *Victorian Newsletter* 92 (1997): 9–15; and Coral Lansbury, *The Old Brown Dog: Women, Workers, and Vivisection in Edwardian England* (Madison: University of Wisconsin Press, 1985). Both Lansbury and Heller discuss its new trends after the 1870s, showing that flagellation obscenity was not homogeneous in the nineteenth century but, rather, diverse and responsive to changing views about sexuality and deviance. Although they recognize the historicity of the genre, they miss that it is irretrievably linked with the history of slavery in the Americas.

15. Mary Favret, "Flogging: The Anti-Slavery Movement Writes Pornography," *Essays and Studies* 51 (1998): 19–43, quotations on 32, 26, and 39. One wonders, of course, what appeal such a fantasy would have had to the many Englishwomen involved in British abolition movements. Favret argues that women viewers filtered the pornographic gaze. But is it not possible that women, despite their probable gender identification with the victimized woman, were also aroused by the image's suggestion of sexual dissipation? There is evidence that lower- and middle-class women were both vendors and consumers of obscenity from the beginning of the century. "Police" articles and "Law Reports" from the *Times* consistently recorded prosecutions against obscenity throughout the nineteenth century, disclosing that women and families participated in the trade, particularly in the earlier decades; see, for instance, *Times,* 27 February 1850, 7; and 13 March 1851, 8. Also see Sigel, *Governing Pleasures,* esp. 21, which offers a detailed synopsis of the familial character of the trade in the early nineteenth century. That women gazed pruriently upon the image of the flogged slave woman is also a real possibility.

16. Wood, *Blind Memory,* 260, 236–237. Also see John Stedman, *Narrative of a Five Years' Expedition against the Revolted Negroes of Surinam, in Guiana, on the Wild Coast of South America: From the Year 1772 to 1777* (London: n.p., 1796). Wood's most recent work expands on these ideas about the prurience that underlay representations of slavery. More specifically, he discusses the emergence of plantation pornography. His only historical example, however, is Stedman's *Narrative,* which was not an underground publication. His definition of *pornography* is inadequate, generally referring to sexual content rather than a new publishing phenomenon. He also states that "pornography focused on slave imagery flourished in the eighteenth and nineteenth century," but he does not provide any evidence; see *Slavery, Empathy, and Pornography* (Manchester: Manchester University Press, 2003), 89.

17. Fisch, *American Slaves,* 52.

18. Mary Prince, *The History of Mary Prince* (London: n.p., 1831), 13; Frederick Douglass, *Narrative of the Life of Frederick Douglass, an American Slave, Written by Himself* (Dublin: Webb and Chapman, 1845), 5–7; and William Wells Brown, *Narrative of William W. Brown, an American Slave. Written by Himself* (London: Charles Gilpin, 1850), 14–15, 24.

19. *Atheneaum,* 31 March 1855, 378; 4 April 1857, 434.

20. *Anti-Slavery Advocate* (March 1857): 103. Americans read the slave narratives for many of the same reasons as the English. See Charles Nichols, "Who Read the Slave Narratives?" *Phylon* 20, no. 2 (1959): 149–162, quotation on 152. He discusses the commercial success of slave narratives in America and suggests that their "sensationalism" and "thrilling adventures" were partly responsible for their popularity. Although Nichols does not address this point, American reviewers were also aware of the sexual abuse within slavery. A reviewer for the *National Anti-Slavery Standard* describes the "legalize[d] concubinage" and "licentiousness" of slavery as described in Jacobs's narrative; quoted in Jean Fagan Yellin, "Texts and Contexts of Harriet Jacobs' *Incidents in the Life of a Slave Girl: Written by Herself,*" in *The Slave's Narrative,* ed. Charles T. Davis and Henry L. Gates Jr. (Oxford: Oxford University Press, 1985), 262–271, quotations on 270. Karen Sánchez-Eppler, moreover, argues that slave narratives actively enlisted sexual responses from their white female readers to provoke a political response by reminding them of their own sexual vulnerability; see *Touching Liberty: Abolition, Feminism, and the Politics of the Body* (Berkeley: University of California Press, 1993), 104. While there are no examples of obscene appropriations of slave narratives in American obscenity (most likely because the industry was still fledgling), George Thompson's open publications (which he published under the pseudonym Greenhorn) suggest prurience surrounding slavery and sexual violence. He was one of the most popular and prolific authors of the antebellum era who wrote lurid novels about race, urbanization, and poverty in such works as *Venus in Boston: A Romance of City Life* (New York: n.p. [Haynes], [1849]). William Haynes published his works and eventually became the father of the America's obscene book trade; see H. Montgomery Hyde, *A History of Pornography* (London: Heinemann, 1964), 107.

21. Ronald Hyam, arguing that "sexual dynamics crucially underpinned the whole operation of British empire and Victorian expansion," notes that "it can hardly be an accident that all the classics of British erotic literature were written by men who were widely travelled inside and especially outside Europe"; see his book *Empire and Sexuality: The British Experience* (Manchester: Manchester University Press, 1990), 1, 90. For discussions of race in English obscenity, see Pease, *Modernism;* Ruth Bernard Yeazell, *Harems of the Mind: Passages of Western Art and Literature* (New Haven: Yale University Press, 2000); and Sigel, *Governing Pleasures.* For discussions of race in French colonial postcards, see Malek Alloula, *The Colonial Harem,* intro. Barbara Harlow, trans. Myrna and Wlad Godzich (Minneapolis: University of Minnesota Press, 1986).

22. Lazenby dominated the English underground trade in obscenity from around 1873 until 1886, when he was prosecuted and imprisoned in November. He operated his business under various aliases, including Duncan Cameron, Henry Ashford, and Thomas Judd. After 1884 he seems to have collaborated with Avery, who took over control of the trade after Lazenby's imprisonment; see Mendes, *Clandestine,* 4–7. See the *Times* for reports on his prosecutions: 17 July 1871, 13; 16 September 1876, 11; 12 November 1886, 13. See the following underground publications: *The Birchen Bouquet; The Lustful Turk; or, Lascivious Scenes in a Harem* ([New York]: Canyon, [1967]); *My*

Secret Life (Amsterdam: n.p., [c. 1888–1894]); *The Pearl, A Journal of Facetia Voluptuous Reading* (London: printed for the Society of Vice [Augustin Brancart], 1879–1880 [c. 1890]); *The Quintessence of Birch Discipline* (London: privately printed [Lazenby], 1870 [1883]); and *The Romance of Chastisement; or, Revelations of the School and Bedroom* (N.p. [London?]: n.p. [Lazenby?], 1870 [1883]).

23. Santa Cruz, the West Indian island to which the story refers, is presumably St. Croix, now part of the U.S. Virgin Islands. While the island's colonial rulers shifted through history, there was significant English settlement from as early as 1625.

24. Henry Spencer Ashbee indicates that the volume sold for twenty-five pounds; see *Catena Librorum Tacendorum* (London: privately printed, 1885), 345. *The Catalogue of Curiosa and Erotica* (1892) priced it at eighteen pounds, and *Catalogue of Rare Curious and Voluptuous Reading* sold one of its numbers for two guineas; see *Album 7: Catalogues and Prospectuses* (1889–c. 1908), an unpublished collection of catalogs and advertisements at the British Library.

25. *The Cremorne; A Magazine of Wit, Facetiae, Parody, Graphic Tales of Love, etc.* (London: privately printed [Lazenby?], 1851 [1882]). See Ashbee, *Catena,* 357, for publication information on the magazine. For discussion of the Cremorne pleasure gardens, see Donald Thomas, *The Victorian Underworld* (London: John Murray, 1998), 89–90; and Nead, *Victorian Babylon,* 109–146.

26. *Pearl,* 2.153–154.

27. *Pearl,* 3.12, 3.13.

28. *Pearl,* 3.13–15.

29. Mendes, *Clandestine,* 201.

30. [Harriet Jacobs], *The Deeper Wrong; or, Incidents in the Life of a Slave Girl. Written by Herself* (London: W. Tweedie, 1862).

31. See *Athenaeum,* 19 April 1862, 529. For other reviews of Jacobs's narrative, see *Anti-Slavery Advocate,* 1 May 1861, 421; *London Daily News,* 10 March 1862, 2; *Londonderry Standard,* 27 March 1862, 4; *Caledonian Mercury,* 31 March 1862, 3; *Anti-Slavery Reporter,* 1 April 1862, 96; and *Western Morning News,* 5 April 1862, 4. Of these reviews only the *Caledonian Mercury* referred explicitly to the sexual content of the narrative: "These pages give many vivid pictures of the terrible licentiousness which characterise the majority of slaveholders. Thousands of young slaves have Anglo-Saxon blood coursing through their veins" (3).

32. Jacobs, *Deeper Wrong,* 51; Yellin, "Texts," 263. See also Sánchez-Eppler, *Touching Liberty;* Deborah M. Garfield, "Speech, Listening, and Female Sexuality in *Incidents in the Life of a Slave Girl,*" *Arizona Quarterly* 50, no. 2 (1994): 19–49, quotation on 109; and Gabrielle P. Foreman, "Manifest in Signs: The Politics of Sex and Representation in *Incidents in the Life of a Slave Girl,*" in *Harriet Jacobs and Incidents in the Life of a Slave Girl: New Critical Essays,* ed. Deborah M. Garfield and Rafia Zafar (Cambridge: Cambridge University Press, 1996), 76–99, quotations on 77, 80.

33. *Cremorne,* 35, 43, 44.

34. Foreman, "Manifest," 88; *Cremorne,* 12, 4, 8, 10.

35. *Cremorne,* 16.

36. *Cremorne,* 23, 43

37. Michel Foucault, *The History of Sexuality: An Introduction* (New York: Vintage, 1990), 43; see also *The Sins of the Cities of the Plain; or, The Recollections of a Mary-Anne with Short Essays on Sodomy and Tribadism* (London: privately printed [Lazenby?], 1881).

38. Jacobs, *Deeper Wrong,* 43, 19; *Cremorne,* 67, 34; Sánchez-Eppler, *Touching Liberty,* 96.

39. Had Lazenby's *The Secret Life* continued beyond its three numbers, I wonder if it would have focused on other passages that recent critics have found sexually redolent. Later in her narrative Jacobs not only alludes to white men crossing the color line but also to white women who conceive black men's children. She also describes the ill treatment of a slave named Luke by his dissipated master in such terms that lead Foreman to infer homosexual abuse. When speaking of Luke, Jacobs suggests terrible depravity but remains silent about its exact nature, a telling omission considering the link between secrecy and sexual abuse in her world: "Luke was appointed to wait on his bed-ridden master, whose despotic habits were greatly increased by exasperation at his own helplessness. [. . .] A day seldom passed without his receiving more or less blows. [. . .] As he lay on his bed, a mere degraded wreck of manhood, he took into his head the strangest freaks of despotism [. . .]. Some of these freaks were of a nature too filthy to be repeated"; see Jacobs, *Deeper Wrong,* 52, 78, 192.

40. Mendes, *Clandestine Erotic Fiction,* 39–40; *Report from the Joint Select Committee on Lotteries and Indecent Advertisements* (London: Vacher and Sons 1908), 30; G. Legman, *The Horn Book: Studies in Erotic Folklore and Bibliography* (New York: University Books, 1964), 34.

41. *May's Account of Her Introduction to the Art of Love* (London and Paris: n.p., 1904). (The full title of this work is *My Grandmother's Tale or May's Account of Her Introduction to the Art of Love,* which forms a serial in *The Pearl.* The serial was sold as a stand-alone work under the name of *May's Account of Her Introduction to the Art of Love,* the second subtitle. This version is used here. Sigel's essay in this volume uses the serialized version from *The Pearl,* shortened to "My Grandmother's Tale.") *The Adventures of Lady Harpur; Her Life of Free Enjoyment and Ecstatic Love Adventures Related by Herself* (Glasgow [Paris?]: William Murray Buchanan St. [Carrington?], 1894 [c. 1906]). Lazenby's original publication of *Queenie* does not survive. For the publication history of *The Adventures of Lady Harpur,* see Mendes, *Clandestine Erotic Fiction,* 137.

42. *Adventures of Lady Harpur,* 42.

43. I have seen a later 1913 edition of *Sue Suckitt.* It appears with a false wrapper with *La Guerre des Balkans* as its title. This reprint was likely circulated among English-speaking World War I soldiers.

44. St. John D'Arcy, *The Memoirs of Madge Buford; or, A Modern Fanny Hill* (New York: n.p., [Carrington?],1902); *A Town-Bull; or, The Elysian Fields* (New Orleans: n.p. [Carrington?], 1893); *Sue Suckitt; Maid and Wife* (New Orleans [Paris]: n.p.[Carrington], 1913); *Maidenhead Stories, Told by a Set of Joyous Students* (New York: printed for the Erotica Biblion Society [Carrington], 1897); and *The Memoirs of Dolly Morton: The Story of a Woman's Part in the Struggle to Free the Slaves* (Paris: Charles Carrington, 1899). Also see Mendes, *Clandestine Erotic Fiction,* 39.

45. Catalogs gathered in *Album 7* priced these works in British currency: *Catalogue of Rare and Curious English Books* lists *Maidenhead Stories* at one guinea; *List of Rare and Curious Books* prices *A Town-Bull* at one guinea; and *Privately Printed English Books* lists *Miss Dorothy Morton* at three guineas. All of these books eventually found their way to the United States: there are copies, for instance, at the Kinsey Institute. *Dolly Morton,* as I will show, was the most successful book of this kind. It alone found a French audience.

46. *A Town-Bull* was likely authored by an American: it uses an American setting, reveals familiarity with American institutions (the "Savings Bank"), and adopts American spelling ("colored"). *Sue Suckitt,* by contrast, is more difficult to place because it blends references to American dollars with allusions to English flagellation ("birchen rods").

47. *Town-Bull,* 115.

48. *Sue Suckitt,* 41–42.

49. *Memoirs of Madge Buford,* 76–77.

50. *Memoirs of Dolly Morton,* 71–73.

51. *Memoirs of Dolly Morton,* 9, 26, 267.

52. *Woman and Her Slave: A Realistic Narrative of a Slave Who Experienced His Mistress' Love and Lash* (Paris, n.d.).

53. Cecily Devereux, "'The Maiden Tribute' and the Rise of the White Slave in the Nineteenth Century: The Making of an Imperial Construct," *Victorian Review* 26, no. 2 (2000): 1–23; "British and Foreign Traffic in Girls," *Town Talk: A Journal for Society at Large,* 17 January 1880, 1–2. Lansbury's argument that late flagellation obscenity was preoccupied with taming rebellious women may correspond to the increased concern about the white woman slave. Lansbury even equates obscene fantasies with the social regulation of rebellious women: "When suffragettes were seized and beaten by police to the approval of a jeering crowd, when they were bound top a stretcher and force-fed through a tube pushed down their throats by a wardess and attending doctor, the fantasies of pornography became fact"; see Lansbury, *Old Brown Dog,* 122.

54. See Mendes, *Clandestine Erotic Fiction,* 263.

55. John Brown, *Slave Life in Georgia: A Narrative of the Life, Sufferings, and Escape of John Brown* (London: The Editor, 1855); Wilbur H. Siebert, *The Underground Railroad from Slavery to Freedom* (New York: Macmillan, 1898); *Memoirs of Dolly Morton,* ix–x.

56. *En Virginie: Épisode de la Guerre de Sécession* (Paris: Charles Carrington, 1901); and Thomas, intro., *The Memoirs of Dolly Morton* (London: Collectors Edition, 1970), 14. Jean de Villiot was a composite name used by Carrington, especially for his openly published works on flagellation. Hugues Rebell and Hector France may have written for Carrington under this pseudonym. For a fuller account, see Mendes, *Clandestine Erotic Fiction,* 364.

57. The National Vigilance Association (NVA) existed from 1886 to 1953. It advertised its activities and campaigns in the *Vigilance Record* (1887–1932). For discussions of the origins and activities of the NVA, see Edward J. Bristow, *Vice and Vigilance: Purity Movements in Britain since 1700* (Dublin: Gill and Macmillan, 1977), 154–174; and Sigel, *Governing,* 199–255.

58. *En Virginie,* ix. "There reigns the dangerous maxim that a rigid austerity is the only safeguard of virtue. The most innocent word offends; the most natural gesture becomes an indecent assault. Emotions, repressed in this way, extinguish or erupt in a terrible manner. All for vice or all for virtue, but nothing in between; some characters take pleasure in extremes, and we thus see born immoderate prudery and monstrous license" (my trans.).

59. *En Virginie,* 63. "It is undeniably England that takes the cake in this matter" (my trans.).

60. "*Flagellation in London* and *The Study of Flagellation . . . with a documentary on flagellation in English schools and military prisons*" (my trans.).

61. See Ashbee, *Index Librorum Prohibitorum* (London: privately printed, 1877), xxxi–xxxii; Frederick F. Schauer, *The Law of Obscenity* (Washington, D.C.: Bureau of National Affairs, 1976), 13.

62. See *Album 7*. Another set of photographs described in *Album 7* is entitled "The Negro's Revenge." This set reproduces other fantasies and anxieties surrounding slavery, depicting "the young wife of a tyrant violated by a young negro, in revenge of cruelties suffered at the hand of his master."

63. Select Bibliothèque was run by the Parisian publisher Massy, who specialized in flagellation; see *Dictionnaire des oeuvres érotiques* ([Paris]: Mercure de France, 1971), 484–485.

64. See Don Brennus Aléra, *White Women Slaves* ([Paris: Select Bibliothèque], 1910); *Barbaric Fêtes* ([Paris: Select Bibliothèque], 1910); *Under the Yoke* ([Paris: Select Bibliothèque], 1910); *In Louisiana* ([Paris: Select Bibliothèque], 1910).

65. *Suburban Souls: The Erotic Psychology of a Man and a Maid* (Paris: printed for distribution amongst private subscribers only [Carrington], 1901); *The Mistress and the Slave: A Masochist Realistic Love Story* (Athens [Paris?]: imprinted for its members by the Erotika Biblion Society [Carrington], 1905).

66. Pauline Réage, [Dominique Aury], *Story of O* (New York: Grove, 1965), 15–17.

67. Sigmund Freud, "A Child Is Being Beaten," *The Standard Edition of the Complete Psychological Works of Sigmund Freud,* vol. 17 (London: Hogarth, 1955), 180.

68. Georges Bataille, *Erotism: Death and Sensuality,* trans. Mary Dalwood (San Francisco: City Lights, 1986); Lynda Hart, "To Each Other: Performing Lesbian S/M," in *Between the Body and the Flesh: Performing Sadomasochism* (New York: Columbia University Press, 1998), 36–83, quotations on 58, 60.

69. Leopold von Sacher-Masoch, *Venus in Furs* (Paris: Charles Carrington, 1902); Marquis de Sade, *Justine; ou les malheurs de la vertu* (N.p.p., 1791). While Sade's *Justine* was not translated into English as *Opus Sadicum* until 1889, it circulated in French and is referenced frequently in other underground works. Sacher-Masoch's *Venus in Furs,* first published in German as *Venus Im Pelz* in 1870, was a later and lesser influence on English flagellation fantasies. The terms *sadism* and *masochism* were, of course, coined after these authors, revealing how psychological and medical vocabulary were also influenced by the overlapping histories of flagellation and slavery.

The Rise of the Overly Affectionate Family

INCESTUOUS PORNOGRAPHY AND DISPLACED DESIRE AMONG THE EDWARDIAN MIDDLE CLASS

LISA Z. SIGEL

In 1908 Parliament passed a piece of legislation that would seem largely unproblematic. If anything, the passage of the Punishment of Incest Act for England and Wales was grossly overdue. Ecclesiastical courts abandoned the death penalty for incest with the Restoration and then only feebly enforced canon law for cases of incestuous marriage by demanding the guilty do public penance at Lent.[1] When church courts ceased to regulate such behaviors in the nineteenth century, no legal jurisdiction existed for the prosecution of the offense. The lack of legislation did not go unnoticed; the issue of marrying "the deceased wife's sister" produced an over seventy-year debate on the definition of incest. The rather odd twist on the definition was joined by an emerging discussion over the more problematic issue over blood kin in the 1880s.[2] Despite the long discussion over the meanings of incest, the British government did not reach a legal definition of incest or an adequate means to prosecute the offense until the twentieth century. What seems curious about the new law is not its passage but the inability to pass earlier acts and the ambivalence that the consideration of this bill produced. One would think, given the emphasis on morality, the restrictions of sexuality, and the idealization of the home in Victorian and Edwardian England, that the illegality of incest would be ensured. Yet earlier failures in 1899–1900, 1903, and 1907 to pass similar legislation and continued arguments in Parliament against the 1908 bill demonstrate a deep cultural ambivalence toward state regulation of familial sexuality. Even after the state finally acknowledged incest as a social problem, it chose not to pursue it. The early twentieth century became the moment to recognize incest, but that recognition was grudging, late, and fleeting.

Previous scholars such as Victor Bailey and Sheila Blackburn approached the passage of the 1908 bill by looking at the debates in Parliament. Their work remains seminal to an understanding of shifting legal norms; however, they discuss the debates without addressing incest as practice. Others, such as Anthony Wohl and Louise Jackson note the prevalence of incest in the working-class family.[3] Wohl, following the arguments of nineteenth-century social commentators, attributes incest to the crowded conditions of the working-class room. Louise Jackson finds evidence of incest in her examination of court cases of sexual abuse in Victorian Britain. All of these scholars suggest that incest also occurred in middle-class households, but the paucity of sources stymie their attempts to examine the issue. Furthermore, even the available cases of incest do little to explain why individuals committed such acts.

Incestuous pornography allows us to work around both of these gaps and address the mentality of abusers in middle-class culture, or at least those whose fantasies were recorded for a reading public. Victorian men who produced and consumed this subgenre of pornographic literature developed a rhetoric that believed incest to be both enjoyable and consensual, negating the criminal and immoral aspects of the act itself. Examining this rhetoric might begin to explain why, in so many other realms of discourse, ambivalence confounded people's ability to see incest as abuse.

Working-Class Cases and Middle-Class Ambivalence

Nineteenth-century court cases reveal certain patterns in incestuous attacks that make these encounters seem eerily familiar to those conversant with recent incest cases. Most incestuous unions occurred in the house; by and large the father perpetrated the crime and resorted to threats and blackmail to silence the victim, usually the daughter. The "planned-accident" of the incestuous encounter; the mingling of violence, blackmail, and threats; and the assumption of sexual precocity for children tie these cases together. The 1880 case of Richard Cheeseman, father to fifteen-year-old Clara Ann Cheeseman, demonstrates his planning of incestuous rape, even though he later argued that the incident occurred because of a momentary lapse of control; on one occasion he waited until her mother left before he raped Clara Ann in the washhouse, while on another he told the other children to go out to the barn so she could serve him breakfast. On both occasions he threatened to kill her if she told anyone.[4] Harry Ernest Magrath waited until his wife left before having sex with seven-year-old Rose Mary.[5] The planning and violence of such attacks seems incontrovertible. Nevertheless, medical officers did question them. Issues of the daughter's character and previous sexual experience remained crucial to the court's decision. In the Tanner case, in which the father was convicted of an incestuous attack, his sentence was reduced because "the girl was not only dishonest, but of dissolute character."[6] Linda Gordon, in her examination of incestuous attacks in Boston, demonstrates that they had similar characteristics. According to Gordon, "incestuous relationships were carefully calculated and planned in advance to avoid detection"; the maternal figure was absent either through death or disease; men used threats and violence that they themselves denied; the men often rewarded the girls with gifts and affection; and the authorities labeled the victim as "precious" or "sophisticated."[7] While sexual attacks clearly constituted abuse, girls garnered sympathy only if they were very young; the older the victim, the less sympathy and more suspicion the courts displayed. Even if young, the medical and legal communities tended to discount evidence of sexual abuse, including the transmission of venereal disease, if a family member committed the offense.[8]

These cases came to the courts because of the intervention of social welfare workers into the lives of the poor. The awareness of incest as an act grew alongside the rise of child welfare organizations; the language of class became central to understanding the orientation of British concerns around incest. In 1882 the chaplain of Clerkenwell prison reported to a royal commission and a select committee that one-room lodgings caused incest. William Booth stated that "incest is so familiar as hardly calls for remark" in the lives of the poor.[9] Even sexologists believed this: Richard von Krafft-Ebing stated that "external conditions which facilitate their occurrence are due to defective separation of the sexes among the lower classes."[10] The concern by reform groups led to social purity policing but not to radical transformations in the understanding of the family.

Because of the lack of laws against incest, reform groups such as the National Society for the Prevention of Cruelty to Children (NSPCC), which acted as extra-legal child guardians, often found themselves in the situation of trying to find a legal reason for taking children from the sexually abusive home. The National Vigilance Association (NVA) and the NSPCC turned to prosecuting incestuous attacks under the Criminal Law Amendment Act of 1885 because there were no other statutes available. As a result of their firsthand experience with sexual abuse in the home, they began to advocate for new laws regarding incest. To back up their claims about the urgent need for legislation, particularly after the inability to pass the first bill, they began to compile statistics. During 1899 the NSPCC submitted details of eleven cases of incest to the Home Office. One case submitted to the home secretary in 1899 discussed a father, age seventy-four, and daughter, age twenty-three, who lived in an incestuous union. Three children from that relationship had died, but the couple was living with another daughter, age fourteen.[11] Eight of the eleven cases featured father/daughter unions; the others were brother/sister and grandfather/granddaughter. The NSPCC also submitted a memorandum in 1901 to support yet another bill in which they documented 183 cases of incest, most often father/daughter unions, carefully annotated with the number of children produced. Additionally, the Home Office had a list of convictions in Scotland that had its own laws regarding incest. (There incest was punishable by death, although the government sent Scots to serve a prison term in England to avoid the full ramifications of the law.) Scotland averaged six convictions per year from 1896 to 1905, and the Home Office looked to Scotland for a comparison of laws and incidence. New Scotland Yard reported that from 1905 to 1907 forty-six cases were brought to the police, thirty-six cases with girls under sixteen and ten with girls over that age.[12]

Despite the accumulation of data, Parliament refused to pass three incest bills in 1899–1900, 1903, and 1907.[13] Members of Parliament justified this negligence in a number of ways. The earl of Halsbury thought that acknowledging the problem would be worse than the incidents themselves, and Mr. Rawlinson (MP for Cambridge University) thought that passage of the act would increase the opportunity for blackmail. Even in the 1908 discussion, concerns with blackmail remained paramount with Mr. Rawlinson and Mr. Stavely-Hill. The latter added the additional point that young girls would bring charges without foundation, "in regard to an offence of a similar character, charges were brought by two girls which had no foundation whatever in fact."[14] While children's advocates and family members sought to separate the incestuous parent from their children, lawmakers and justices saw girls as somehow already at fault; they worried that the overt sexuality of girls could bring the father's downfall, that girls faked their sexual states, that they rubbed themselves into physical states mimicking sexual abuse, or that girls would falsely accuse their fathers.[15]

Parliament finally passed the Punishment of Incest Act of 1908 because of widespread canvassing by reform groups who emphasized child saving. When the state passed the Incest Act of 1908, however, it did so as much to prevent the debilitation of offspring as to protect children.[16] Mr. Maclean, MP, to justify the act's passage on "sociological grounds," pointed out that "children of weak intellect, idiots, and imbeciles" came from incestuous unions.[17] Mr. Herbert Samuel, MP from Yorkshire, explained that "it was not merely the case of a moral offence affecting grown-up people, but it might entail consequences of a disastrous kind on the offspring which sometimes followed from such intercourse, and from that point of view society had a special interest that should lead to steps being taken to put a stop to it."[18] Their reasoning, while helpful for getting the law passed, shifted the problem from trauma to offspring. The brutality of prosecuted incest cases make it clear that incest functioned as an extreme form of paternal authority enforced through sexual violence; however, only rising progressive demands tinged with eugenicist concerns allowed the state to intercede into that authority.

Furthermore, the passage of the act in 1908 did not produce an increase in the rate of convictions. Only a few convictions, including one of brother and sister living in a long-term marital relation and one previously mentioned conviction that was overturned because of the daughter's dissolution, occurred between the passage of the act and 1914. By then, the NSPCC turned its focus from the family, and "any recognition of child sexual abuse virtually disappeared . . . despite the 50,000 cases of neglect and cruelty reported to the society annually."[19] Social purity workers in both Britain and the United States increasingly looked away from the family and toward the anonymous pervert, thereby making the home once again a "safe" retreat from urban chaos.[20] The turn from familial violence to extrafamilial threats allowed the focus on incest to recede before any systematic attempt to assess or treat the problem could occur. Thus, the family as an ideological force could remain unquestioned.

While this discussion underlines the brutality of incest cases and raises the question of why Parliament refused to pass laws against incest, the cases speak to working-class households; Members of Parliament, officers for the NSPCC, and

concerned sexologists all argued that incest occurred only among the most mate-
rially debased classes. In effect, they created an environmental argument for the
problem of incest. Incestuous desires, however, clearly crossed class boundaries
and existed in the far more comfortable circumstances of the middle and upper
classes.[21] An environmental argument did little to explain the proliferation of incestuous desires in circumstances defined by plenty rather than dearth. To reconstruct these desires we need to make a leap to the fiction of the time. Pornography,
in many ways, is a unique body of literature that gives free reign to sexual desire
around this most hidden of inclinations. Once we begin to look at the pornography of incest, we can see the underlying tensions around the roles of men, children, and the family that might explain the larger ambivalence to legislation.

Incest in Pornographic Novels

The incestuous novel emerged after a major shift in the history of British
pornographic publishing, during which distribution and content underwent a radical change. As Lynn Hunt and Robert Darnton have demonstrated, pornography
emerged in confrontation with the premodern state, and incestuous pornography
works as a case in point. Before the late nineteenth century incestuous pornography largely worked as a form of scandalmongering. To accuse someone of incest
was to impugn his or her Christianity, basic morality, authority, and place in society, and the accusation carried harsh penalties, including a loss of fortune, career,
and, in Marie Antoinette's case, life. As Mary Lindemann puts it, "The political
implications of incest were always negative."[22] Political radicals leveled the accusation of incest against prominent individuals, particularly monarchs and members of the church.[23] Radical republicans in effect were trying to unravel authority
where the state contract and the "family" contract overlapped.[24] That is not to say
that scandalmongering pornography eschewed titillation. Pornographic scandal
sheets accused, condemned, and titillated at the same time.[25] Although Sade gave
France a model for incestuous pleasures, English pornography did not follow his
example. By the 1840s radical English pornography began to die down without
incestuous accusations ever gaining the degree of popularity that they saw on the
Continent.[26] The incestuous trope saw a surge, however, in the 1880s.

Rather than denouncing or documenting incest, as had earlier forms of incestuous scandal sheets, this new type of pornography adapted the theme of incestuous unions to the pleasures of middle-class life. In essence these new
incestuous works replaced the aristocratic or monarchical order with the middle-
class family as the site of forbidden desire. With the shift in the purpose came a
shift in form; the eighteenth-century exposé, epistolary, and other early forms of
the novel gave way to the pornographic novel. The rise of the pornographic novel
comes as no surprise, given the preeminence of the novel overall in the nineteenth
century. Yet the novel, as Nancy Armstrong has pointed out, remained largely the
preserve of the middle class, and the pornographic novel proves no exception. The
rise of the middle-class incestuous novel, in effect, acknowledges three overlapping changes in society: the middle class as central to the new political order; the

novel as the preeminent form of storytelling; and pleasure, rather than disdain, as the point of pornography.

The Romance of Lust (1873–1876) begins the fascination with incest in English pornography. Rumor attributes the book to William Simpson Potter, who edited it while on a trip to Japan.[27] Supposedly, Monckton Milnes (Lord Houghton), Sir James Plaisted Wilde (Lord Penzance), James Campbell Reddie, Frederick Popham Pike, Edward Bellamy, and George Augustus Sala wrote this novel in a round-robin fashion. This group of men formed the backbone of the Cannibal Club, an offshoot of the London Anthropological Society. The joint production of *The Romance of Lust* argues that incestuous desires surpassed the individual and, instead, were shared by these middle-class men, some of whom were quite influential to Victorian society. Monckton Milnes (Lord Houghton) was a member of Parliament and a minor poet; Sir James Plaisted Wilde (Lord Penzance), a judge, contributed to the reform of divorce law; and Frederick Popham Pike was a "barrister of standing." Certainly, Lord Penzance's role as a divorce court judge would allow him privileged access to cases involving accusations of incest; if anyone could rip fiction from the court cases, Penzance would be that person.

In pornographic novels such as the one these men produced, the staging of an incestuous encounter took ingenuity, and authors set up the encounters with great relish. To enjoy incest as fantasy, a great deal of imaginative and cultural work needed to be done in order to set aside the strong social proscriptions and sheer daily details that mitigated against it in real life; in fiction authors recognized and surmounted the social relations that limited incest in life. A "desert island" scenario might be one way to achieve an incestuous union with a minimum of fuss, but authors eschewed this option. Finding a way to achieve incest in context was central to such portrayals: incest did not just happen in these novels; it had to be contrived so that the affectionate family could fully express itself.

In the stories of young people, and most of these stories focus on the incestuous longings of the young, a missing parent often becomes a route to lax discipline. *The Romance of Lust,* for example, kills off the father on the first page to explain the main character's place in the nursery long after he reaches pubescence. His place there allows him to begin his sexual education with his sisters (before his circle of sexually available relatives ramifies). Likewise, a mother's infirmities leaves Eveline open to her brother's and the father's advances in *The Modern Eveline.* Numerous deaths, of mothers, aunts, and female relations of all kinds, give the girls of "My Grandmother's Tale" free rein to explore their desires. The frequent deaths of family members expand the degree of privacy in domestic life in these accounts. As numerous scholars have shown, daily life was still embroiled in overlapping relationships, and privacy was a goal rather than a reality in middle-class homes. The bustle of the nursery, the ubiquity of servants, the predominance of the mother in the daily life of her children, curtailed male access to his offspring. To kill off members of the family in fiction offered a way to circumvent the controls over childhood sexuality.

By eliminating or disabling a parent, authors achieved a type of lax surveillance, but they still needed to create a time free from the strictures of normal life for such encounters. In *The Powers of Mesmerism* (1891), as the title implies, the author uses the devise of hypnosis to allow familial passions to overcome moral scruples. The returning son, Frank, first seduces his sister while she is hypnotized. The sister and brother then corrupt other members of the household and community, including the maid, mother, father, family friends, and extended family. Once Frank chips away at each family member's inhibitions by seducing them during mesmeric trances, each person realizes his or her deepest desires and willingly accedes to debauchery. The device of mesmerism creates a time separate from normal morality in which family members can act out their sexual tensions. Hypnosis, then, absolves responsibility and choice in much the same way that a desert island scenario might have but in a way that allows all the comforts and erotics of home.

In *Sweet Seventeen* (1910) both the writer and the fictional participants minutely plan such encounters. In that novel the mother remains alive to the end, when she finds the father and daughter in an incestuous embrace and drops dead at the sight. Her death leaves the two to assume a marital relationship in public; thus, death does function to liberate the lovers from the strains of maternal control. The novel is set in Paris, the supposed capital of corruption; the setting signals a deviation from normal life and the normal interrelationships of British society. Upon his arrival in Paris, Mr. Oliver Sandcross, the father, throws off his stuffy Anglo-Saxon inhibitions and tries every option for debauchery. Decadence leads to incestuous desires, and Sandcross realizes his lust for his daughter, Fanny. He tries to corrupt her with expensive jewels, trips to the vulgar theater, and blue novels. After a trip to the theater, in which he fantasizes about her seduction, he passionately kisses her, and, when she objects, he spanks her, threatening to wake his wife and to accuse Fanny of immorality. The beating arouses her passions, and they have sex. The passage plays up the wife's sleeping a few doors away at the same time that it emphasizes the lateness of the hour, the quietness of the house, and the wife's insensibility to such tensions.

> "Let me alone!" she murmured, struggling violently. "I'll rouse the house and call for ma!"
>
> "I defy you to, hussy! You know your mother believes in me! I'll lie to her and say you called me to your bed. You dare not do what you say—you will kill her! I'm going to punish you for your assault on me!"
>
> He exposed the swelling cambric drawers of her rotund posteriors.[28]

The invocation of a maternal presence heightens the debauchery of the scene by playing off the possibility of discovery. At the same time, by layering the setting with cues about Parisian corruption, the writer prepares his audience for extravagant sexual expectations. In essence, by carefully setting up the incestuous encounter, the writer plots sexual abandon against the pragmatic controls of familial sexuality.

In *The Pearl*'s serialized story called "My Grandmother's Tale" (1879–1880), the writer sets up numerous incestuous encounters with equal care. The writer frames the vignettes as a series of overlapping encounters that interlock around the theme of incest. The title introduces the incestuous idea; the serialized novel is billed as a rediscovered memoir based on the sex life of the owner's grandmother.

The fictional manuscript owner reads about his own grandmother's randy past, which includes stories of her relations with her father or the owner's great-grandfather. Thus, the voyeurism of reading about a family member's sexual relations is marked as doubly incestuous, and each vignette supports this conclusion. Rather than focusing on the grandmother as the title implies, the story devolves into a series of confessions by schoolgirls and their female sexual associates. In all, May has sex with her father; Kate with her father; Hilda with her uncle; Alice Moreton with her father, Thomas; Susey with her uncle; and, in a brief aside, a grandfather with his granddaughters (at Dick Turpin's gunpoint.)

The writer achieves a second layer of framing in these stories by continuously shifting the narration. Not only do the girls take turns telling their stories and not only are their tales' interrupted by letters of theirs school chums' exploits, but they are also having sex at the same time that they recollect their sexual histories. The frequent interruptions make sex ever present and highlight the girls' sexual sophistication. As Kate recounts her sexual history to May (apparently), the two engage in sexual play. May, on sensing someone behind them, calls out: "'Let me up, Kate, I'm sure there is someone behind us.' 'Nonsense' said Kate, 'it is only your overheated imagination.' 'Oh! It is pushing in—let me up—there is someone fucking me. Oh, Kate, I feel his prick, my cunt is filled with it, do let me up.'" After orgasm the mysterious phantasm melts away without being identified, and the two return to sex play and Kate's sexual history. The continual asides, interjected orgasms, and shifting narration blur temporality, creating the implication that all the girls are equally randy at all points in their sexual histories. The convolution in the framing also dislocates volition. Did May desire the stranger? "Oh, never mind, let me get on with my story," as Kate puts it before continuing to tell her history.[29]

When the tales recount incestuous unions, the framing likewise disperses responsibility and volition among participants. In one story Tom, the gardener's son serves as a sexual and informational conduit between May and her father. "He told me many curious things; among others, that papa was in the habit of fucking our milk-maid Sarah in the hayloft."[30] Tom and May hide themselves in the hayloft so that they can watch her father with the milkmaid. The sight of her father's sexual adventures affects May's passions as she discovers her desire for him. "The sight of my father's prick had a curious effect on me. At first I did not like to look at it, but at length the amorous feeling overpowered every other."[31] As May watches her father have sex with Sarah, Tom fills the gap between her desires and circumstances, while the writer plays up the incestuous tension. "I was leaning forward on the hay, and Tom over me, his prick and balls resting on my naked bottom; but as soon as papa commenced fucking Sarah, he lodged his prick in my cunt. He then timed his strokes, so that each time papa pushed I felt Tom's prick driving into my cunt."[32] May forms her intention to copulate with her father (after she has sex with the groom), but, before taking May's newly formed incestuous desires to any conclusion, the writer turns to the story of the father's new mistress, Kate, whose narrative continues the theme that May's began.

Kate also grew up in the country without female controls over her life or sexual urges, and she also began her sexual adventures early with the servants of the household. In both stories the rural setting allows the girls freedom and gives the fathers more authority of the lives of their offspring. The writer removes the strictures and interruptions, the compressed relations of urban life, and, instead, creates an idyll where knowledge of sex occurs in nature. In Kate's example, set in the West Indies, children of slaves, overseers, and owners romp naked and free to examine one another's genitals. Upon seeing her father have sex with a servant/ slave, Kate becomes aroused. She arranges to substitute herself for her slave so she can have sex with her father. Her plans succeed, and after sex he initiates a conversation about seducing his daughter. She colludes with him and has sex the next night in the guise of her slave's friend. On the third night they both acknowledge their desires and their transparent deceits.

> "Tell me, my darling, was it you in Nina's bed last night?"
>
> "It was I, dearest papa; was I very wicked?"
>
> "No, my darling, you gave me the sweetest pleasures I ever had in my life. Did you enjoy what I did to you then?"
>
> "I did indeed, it was most delightful."
>
> "May I do it to you again?"
>
> "You may, dear papa, if you like."[33]

The framing of the story allows the readers to see the multiple scripts as they play out. The access to the daughter's desires allows readers to see the multiple ways in which she fakes her innocence; she arranges indiscretions, fakes her virginity, and speaks only of her desires as a response to his. At the same time, we can see the father as desirous but also the unwitting tool for satisfying female lusts. He responds to scripts set in motion by his daughter. The girl's faked innocence heightens her desirability and the father's pleasures at corruption. It also provides the grand justification for the father's actions: he does not compel his daughter; instead, he is compelled by her.

The Modern Eveline (1904) takes the logic of the seductive daughter delineated in earlier stories even farther. Eveline makes a careful study of her father's habits and idiosyncrasies. "My quick woman's wit, my habit of close observation, a restless spirit of inductive reasoning all combined to arrive at a thorough knowledge of his inner character."[34] She dresses, acts, and molds herself to his tastes and seduces him into giving trinkets and quick caresses, remaining in control to the point that he pre-ejaculates at their first attempt at intercourse. After their failed interlude, he avoids her, making her "certain he had been forming resolutions to restrain his passion."[35] Eveline makes no such resolutions. Caressing him during a performance of *Faust,* she incites him to attempt intercourse again. (The Faustian reference hints, of course, that incest is the ultimate sexual knowledge.) This time he performs more successfully, and she fakes her virginity by crying out: "Papa! Papa! You are killing me! Oh, it is too much! I cannot bear it—indeed you hurt me dreadfully! Good Heavens! I shall die! Take it away—oh!" After their mutual orgasm, Eveline grabs a hairpin and pricks her genitals to produce blood for him to find, while she "swoons." She denies her orchestration of the event and, instead, explains her acceptance of the incestuous union because of Voltaire's work on Charlemagne. "Great men are excused faults which in ordinary people are crimes. In my eyes you are a great man."[36] Her careful preparations limit his accountability and convolute desire as her father responds to her transparent manipulations. In each of these stories we can see that girls connive to seduce their fathers; their innocence is false, and their resistance is a cultural script. The girls' narration of the story makes their shammed innocence particularly clear, so that the reader can follow the girl seducing her father even as the reader knows all the tricks that she will play.

The Romance of Lust demonstrates that the play at innocence crosses gender. If anything, boys are even more corrupt than girls and even better suited to a pretense of innocence. The narrator, Charlie, tells of his erotic history that began as a fifteen-year-old boy whose father's death left him to become man of the house. Although he is treated as a child, he lusts for his governess and engages in sexual play with his two sisters. He quickly receives a sexual education—oral, genital, and anal—from an older woman, who eventually shares him with another female friend. He, in turn, enlightens his sisters. From there Charlie's sexual exploits expand as family friends, family members, servants, teachers, school chums, and chance acquaintances become sexual partners. Charlie's relationship with both aunt and uncle (as well as other older women, including his governess and his mother's friends) is predicated upon his fictive innocence. All conspire to seduce the schoolboy, and the schoolboy, Charlie, conspires to let them. Charlie explains his pretense at innocence when he realizes that his aunt will seduce him: "I saw at once that I should be called upon to show myself a man the next day; but I had already felt the advice both my admirable mistresses had given me, as to make all my conquests believe that they were my first fruits. I determined to adhere to the game I was playing, and I foresaw that the pleasure of supporting such a thing would greatly enhance the delight aunt would take in being fucked by my monstrous cock."[37] Charlie maintains his innocence after having sex with his aunt (they all pretend that sex is medicinal to relieve excessive hardness of the penis) even as his uncle butt-fucks him: "He knelt behind me, and spitting on his cock, presented it to my bum-hole, and pressing gently forward, soon sheathed it to the upmost depth. He did not hurt me at all, as I was too much used to be dildoed there to have felt any difficulty of approach, but I deemed it politic to beg him to be gentle from time to time, as if it were a virgin vale he was entering."[38]

Inequality and inexperience disappear behind Charlie's play-acting of virginity. As Charlie's real innocence disappears beneath his ever-expanding experiences, descriptions of sexual acts highlight these unions as incestuous and underscore the deviance of the characters' desires. Early in volume 1, when Charlie seduces his sister Mary, very little mention of their relationship is made during the description of two bouts of cunnilingus and three of intercourse. Only after luncheon, and another round of oral sex and intercourse, does Charlie conclude, "Thus delightfully ended the first lesson in love taught to my sister, and such was my first triumph over a maidenhead, doubly enhanced by the close ties of parentage between us."[39] Even that brief mention of their blood relationship is not repeated when Charlie seduces his other sister, Eliza. Only toward the end of volume 2 and well into volume 3 does the novel start to exploit the erotic tension around incest. When Charlie has sex with his aunt and uncle, the writer begins to emphasize their relationship, even to the point of giving her organs a distinct family resonance. As Charlie exclaims, "Oh, my most gloriously cunted aunt, do I fuck you?"[40] Charlie then refers to both aunt and uncle only by their familial titles, rather than by their given names; their familial relationships define the character of their pleasures, and perversity begins to dominate their dialogue.

Nonetheless, the novel continues to rely upon a pretense of innocence when it incorporates the stigma against incest as plot device. The aunt conspires with Charlie to blackmail Charlie's lover, Ellen, into a ménage à trois. They plan for the aunt to find Charlie and Ellen in bed together. When the aunt bursts in, Charlie pretends to rape the aunt in a mixture of lust and revenge. "She gave a subdued scream, and called to Ellen to come and prevent me from violating her. Ellen came, but wisely would only look on while I worked away manfully. 'Ellen, why don't you pull him away—he is ravishing me—and oh, horror!—commiting incest.'"[41] Ellen refuses to help the aunt escape because, if she does, the aunt can tattle on Ellen's indiscretions. The three enter into a mutually assured destruction pact at the same time they enjoy one another's favors. The scene delineates the tit-for-tat relationship between indiscretions; incest equals premarital sexuality as illicit acts. The scene also creates a sham of force—where force and pretense meet remains indistinguishable to the character, Ellen, but clear to the reader.

The framing techniques used in these stories remove the encounters from real-life traumas; at the same time, however, the narratives keep track of how real-life incest might occur. Real delight at a trifle becomes a coquettish acceptance of a father's desires in *Sweet Seventeen,* "My Grandmother's Tale," and *The Modern Eveline;* a girl's disgust becomes a ploy to maintain her fictive innocence; a hymen becomes a lump of alum; and confusion becomes a way to force others to declare their desires. Even faints, pain, and blood are all translated in these stories into shams. Across the works authors maintain the contrast between the imaginable horror if the story happened in real life and the fictitious play at horror as part of the erotic framing. As part of this convolution of reality, these stories interrupt the fantasy of orgasmic pleasure to deal with the mundane problem of reproduction. Kate's father ejaculates in Nina, her slave in "My Grandmother's Tale." The other girls in that series rely upon syringes and withdrawal. Eveline has a slight deformity that will not allow impregnation. After undergoing surgery to have it repaired, she only masturbates her father until impregnated by another man. The *Romance of Lust* advocates the careful avoidance of the menses. This focus on reproductive practicalities defines "harm" as pregnancy, rather than incest itself. In doing so, these stories present a *looking-glass* version of incestuous rape—one that distorts the very practicalities that it illuminates.

Despite the attention to play-acting and the jocular tone in the descriptions, most of these works sharpen the edge of violence and emphasize disparities in power. In doing so, the distortions of incestuous rape that they take part in become clear. In *Sweet Seventeen,* when Oliver Sandcross has sex with his daughter, the author not only emphasizes their blood relations but also exaggerates their disparities in age. When the father has sex with the daughter, the author combines the language of incest with that of pain and violence. "One fierce lunge and [her hymen] gave way, as Sandcross felt every inch of his huge fatherly organ nipped by the sore, excoriated lips of his daughter's virgin cleft."[42] By enhancing the "fatherly" state of his huge organ and the "daughterly" state of her virgin cleft, the text reinforces their familial relationships as a central part of the sexual act and exaggerates their physiological disparities. After intercourse he tucks her into bed as if she were "his tiny little baby girlie," and she becomes younger still: "As her nervous system gradually reverted to its normal state of quietude, so the babyish look returned to her violet eyes, and her face was as full of innocence as heretofore."[43] The author infantilizes her in the passage, even though in previous descriptions she is clearly postpubescent. Incest does not equalize their status as lovers; instead, the sex act exacerbates their differences and underscores the incestuous act as violent and pedophilic.

The Autobiography of a Flea (1885) also explores asymmetrical power relations. Like *Sweet Seventeen,* it advocates blackmail as a way to overcome girlish scruples and weds the language of violence to the act of incest. When the local priest finds fourteen-year-old Bella locked in a passionate embrace with her lover, he blackmails her into sexual relations. Rather than uphold his bargain, however, the priest also tells her uncle, Mr. Verbouc. Both the priest and uncle remonstrate her for the affair before raping her. Father Ambrose and Mr. Verbouc hold her down and take turns with her. That midnight the uncle steals into her room, surprising her, and a "struggle ensues." Mr. Verbouc wins the "battle" by shooting "a hot stream of trickling fluid into the furthest recesses of her womb."[44] While Bella is half-fainting, he turns her over and sodomizes her. The narration emphasizes the violence and corruption of the scene: Bella trembles with "surprise and terror at the nature of the crime"; she yells that it is "horrible," "monstrous," and cruel"; Mr. Verbouc's penis is a "weapon"; the incestuous embrace is described as "the lamb in the clutches of the wolf, the dove in the talons of the eagle—merciless."[45] What begins as rape becomes some sort of painful pleasure, however, as Bella submits and learns to enjoy not only the incestuous embrace but all others that the priests and her uncle arrange. Sex with her uncle transforms her: "Bella, young, child-like, and so lately innocent, had suddenly become a woman of violent passions and unrestrained lust."[46] The violence of the scene and the descriptions highlight the asymmetrical power relations and call into question the play on violence that other works detail. The author weaves violence and submission to authority together as an explanation of incestuous pleasures.

Even in mother/son incest, the sublimated violence around the dynamics of gender remain the same; *Realistic Pleasures Gathered from the Diary of a Sybarite* (1900–1901), a pirated excerpt from *Amatory Episodes,* advocates maternal rape to overcome female scruples. In that story the widowed mother of Charles, a fifteen-year-old schoolboy, has an affair with the Colonel. Charles watches them through a spy hole, and, when the Colonel leaves, he launches himself onto his mother. "All her movements to escape only made it more easy for the standing prick already pressing hard against her frightened cunt to engulf itself up to the hilt, and the youth mad with lust and determination to fuck his mother began working away within her with all his might."[47] After raping her a few times, she consents to his embrace. In *The Romance of Lust* Charlie's friend Harry wants to join in the affair between his own mother and Charlie. The two boys decide to arrange a surprise attack on Harry's mother to weaken her defenses against incest. Harry barges in on his mother after seeing her have sex with Charlie. To encourage her to submit to his own embrace, he drops hints of all her indiscretions. When she tries to reject him, he responds by saying, "Oh, no, mama, I can't [leave you], indeed, my own mama. I mean to possess you, what harm can there be in returning to whence I came."[48] Blackmail and violence are woven into the accounts through plot devices, descriptions, and imagery.

The mother's position as desirable, authoritative, and vulnerable opens room for a sublimated violence to her position. She is both desired and loved, but that love limits her son's place in the world. The plot requires some type of violence against the mother to liberate the son. In *Amorous Adventures* mother and son begin a counter-affair after the maternal rape, characterized by its relationship to the Colonel's passions. Charles continues to watch his mother and lover and remains energized by their embraces; their sexual encounters become his foreplay. The Colonel also seduces Charles. Eventually, the Colonel discovers the mother and son, and the three complete the triangle. After an interlude of orgasmic pleasures, the mother dies, leaving son and lover to continue in their homosexual and libertine embraces. Mother is but a step toward wider pleasures, and her death liberates Charles. Mother, then, is not the only site of desire, and mother love leaves little room for the happily ever after fantasies that father/daughter tales seem to generate.

If we look at incestuous pornography as a whole (*Sweet Seventeen, The Romance of Lust, The Modern Eveline, Realistic Pleasures, Autobiography of a Flea,* "My Grandmother's Tale," and *The Powers of Mesmerism*), there are two central tales—one about boys and one about girls. In both stories youths are precocious, corrupt, and sexual. In both stories the young desire their parents and those who function in the position of parental authority. And in both stories the framing shifts volition from adults to children, absolving adults from responsibility. The difference between these stories occurs at the level of violence and sublimated violence. Violence and plays on violence are used against girls and women. While all characters have lusts and enjoy sex, only boys and men employ violence to achieve it. And this violence, in both descriptions and plots, brings the female characters back into the family. Rape, seduction, and blackmail all force girls and women to explore their most perverse delights, but ultimately this process also returns them into personifying exactly what men want; they become the embodiment of men's desires and then willingly become the accessory to men's further sexual adventures. Furthermore, once seduced, the girls cannot leave; they remain sexual subsidiaries to the men in their families. Even the growing sentimentality over "mother" in Edwardian society did not preclude a bit of maternal rape in incestuous fiction; the love of mother barely elevates her from her position as female and inherently available. The position of girls, lacking the authoritative context, leaves them even more vulnerable. Sex with daughters, nieces, and granddaughters intensifies their position within the family, while familial sex for boys becomes a proving ground for their adult masculinity.

Incestuous fantasies clearly develop within the power dynamics of Victorian society, even though they transgress the limitations placed on sexuality in that society. They implicitly conceive of the maternal presence as tamping down sexuality in the family; while mothers have their own desirability, their overdeveloped sense of morality makes them dangerous to erotic games. The books reinforce the place of girls in the family while serving as a launching ground for boys toward the wider world. Children are at once both tempters and victims, and, even when they act as tempters they still kowtow to paternal authority. Adult men in these novels remain authoritative and distant, only momentarily touched by an erotic accessibility. The writers paint these men at their prime—physically strong, lusty, financially secure, well dressed, well fed, well versed. Despite their erotic transgressions, the men bear all the marks of respectability. The distant father (or uncle or grandfather) unbends long enough to take part in erotic encounters without ever losing his place as final arbiter in the family. Male characters are not supplicants but beneficiaries. They accept incestuous encounters as their rightful due. In essence these novels set the stock characters of the Victorian family in motion; the naughty schoolboy, the stern father, the desirable daughter, even the weeping mother all perform the tensions over Victorian sexuality in a charade about the family. This charade successfully absolves men of responsibility and mitigates the onus of violence. Whereas most forms of literature or amusement deflect attention from the tensions around familial sexuality, pornographic literature elaborates, exposes, and exaggerates them in a way that disperses responsibility and makes abuse into apologia.

Readership and Psychological Disjunctions in the Family

The relationship between narration, content, and readership intensifies the mitigation of responsibility. Across these works the young person becomes the voice of incestuous desires. This displacement of the narrative voice followed earlier pornographic works that fictionalized the female voice such as *The Memoirs of a Woman of Pleasure* (1748–1749), *The Lustful Turk* (1829), and *The Seducing Cardinal's Amours* (1830) in which male writers created a female narrator and a fictive female subjectivity.[49] Likewise, late-nineteenth-century incestuous pornography either assumed the narrative voice of the child (*The Romance of Lust* and "My Grandmother's Tale") or used an omniscient voice, heavily reliant on dialogue (*The Modern Eveline*) to allow young people to tell their own stories of desire. Through the narration writers access the voice of youths, who in turn desire the adults. Noteworthy here is the lack of narration by adult male characters; in none of the stories do adult men relate their desire for members of their family. Through this pattern of narration the writers dislocate volition by making the young look upon adults with desire, rather than acknowledging that adults long for sexual relations with their children.

The narration seems particularly revealing when set against the patterns of readership. At the end of the nineteenth century distribution, price, and accessibility curtailed the readership. Pornographers used the social register and the society pages to pick likely clients and sent catalogs "to officers in the Army and Volunteer force" and to students at elite schools such as Eton and Winchester.[50] In effect they sought to expand distribution by sending notices to the wealthiest and most suited clients for the works. The price of pornographic publications guaranteed a certain social class of users. *Romance of Lust* cost between four and twelve pounds.[51] *The Pearl* (priced in francs, dollars, and pounds) cost eighteen pounds for the complete set.[52] As W. Hamish Frasier has shown, middle-class households budgeted between five and eight pounds a year for books, magazines, and lending libraries. Even the relatively inexpensive *Autobiography of a Flea* (five pounds, ten shillings) would be hard to sneak into a household budget so tightly constrained. Few women or children had that pleasure in Victorian and Edwardian England. Only middle-class men, and comparatively well-to-do ones at that, could afford such an expenditure.

The production, distribution, and consumption of such incestuous works demonstrate the context in which incestuous fantasies circulated. The meanings of incestuous pornography would look quite different if children read and fantasized about such unions, but they did not. These works circulated within the realm of middle-class men, even though the narration argued that children reciprocated that sentiment and arranged such encounters. In reading these works, middle-class men could think about sexuality in the family in a way that was cut off from other family members. These fantasies clearly took place in families like theirs. The girls and boys are carefully educated; the furniture is all fine (and sturdy); there are grottoes, lawns, and even tree houses for hidden encounters. The opera, the theater, books, and music conspire to bring out passions. Mothers nap, rather than serve, and fathers barely concern themselves with work. Governesses, boarding schools, and maids all figure prominently in the tales; the markers of class mark the fiction. Thus, middle-class men could explore fictionalized family relations in ways that the rest of the family could not, creating a psychological disjunction within the family; men could see the world and their children in a certain way that children could not foresee.

This psychological disjunction between members of the family appeared in a variety of forms; the end of the nineteenth century witnessed a series of crises over gender roles, the family, and the meanings of sexuality. The "Maiden Tribute" scandal, the pitched battles over suffrage, the rise of the New Woman, and the Oscar Wilde scandal magnified the fissures of Victorian gender and sexuality to the public gaze. In each of these crises the breakdown of unity in public demonstrated the illusory nature of familial accord in private. The "Maiden Tribute" scandal showed Victorians that rich men purchased the innocence of the young, implicitly breaking the contracts of familial fidelity, of class separation, and of age-appropriate sexual interchanges. The Oscar Wilde scandal not only raised the issue of the "love that dare not speak its name" (i.e., homosexuality), but also publicized the cross-class alliances that Wilde made with the young male prostitutes who testified against him. Furthermore, Wilde was both married and a father. Sexual intercourse broke ranks with the familial sexuality that supposedly contained it. The New Woman and suffrage movements demonstrated the breakdown of separate spheres and the intrusion of women into public life as women and girls began to carve out new roles and identities for themselves. In response, middle-class men began to develop new styles of aggressive masculinity that celebrated chivalry, character, and action. Alongside these high ideals, however, came the well-known brutality that cemented severity to masculinity.[53] Beatings, bullying, and a distrust of intellect and introspection created a style of aggressive masculinity that, when fused with the expression of sexual desires, became particularly problematic. Jonathon Rutherford has shown that "the homophobia of the schools precipitated sexual ambivalence, frustration and a predisposition to sexual brutality."[54] Men turned this violence against women, as Angus McClaren explains: "Such anger was evidence to the feeling that many men harbored at the turn of the century, the sense that if there was a crisis of masculinity it was primarily due to the fact that women were unilaterally redefining themselves and thereby the relations of both sexes."[55] When such pitched battles over sexuality occurred in public, little wonder that violence over gender and sexuality played out in fantasy.

The boundaries between fantasy and reality remained nebulous, particularly when they involved children. Children remained vulnerable to adult manipulation because of their diminished legal rights coupled with their inflated cultural status. The erotics around childhood can be seen in the relationships between adult men and young girls. For most of the nineteenth century the age of consent remained twelve for girls; it was raised to thirteen in 1875 and then to sixteen in 1885, after the "Maiden Tribute" scandal.[56] Even after that date child prostitution remained a problem, although men continued to frequent child prostitutes and remained relatively untouched by the stigma of perversity or criminality. In a period when Lewis Carroll could not only have special friendships with little girls but also take them on holidays with their parents' consent and photograph them naked, the sexual tension between older men and girls could be both acknowledged and ignored. Furthermore, the desire for children edged into a desire for incest. As Louise Jackson points out in reference to an 1885 case of a barrister charged with indecent assault and exposure, the erotics of childhood overlapped with ideals of fatherhood. In that case the barrister offered to give the eleven-year-old girl "lovely presents" in exchange for love. Twenty-five years later an admirer of fourteen-year-old Florence Tate wrote her: "My dear little one—I have not forgotten you, and am longing to see you again. Now keep a good little darling, and love me as your dear old dad."[57] In these cases the network of family and friends precluded incestuous associations, so the men created fictive incest where none existed. The longing for children and the desire for an uncomplicated sexual love spilled over from prostitution into a broader "cult of the child." Nineteenth-century fiction, whether pornographic or domestic, imbued the child with innocence, beauty, and an emotional transparency that *Peter Pan* and *Alice in Wonderland* immortalize. Childhood became a special time, characterized by a charm and physicality that clearly had latent sexual implications.

Childhood as a ripe symbolic category in society emerged alongside changing family models. The rise of a domestic ideology and separate spheres differentiated the roles and meanings of family members leaving a number of related legacies for Victorians. First, the family emerged as the center of the emotional world.[58] Nancy Anderson argues that "the emotional attachment within the Victorian family was all the more intense, in contrast to earlier and also twentieth-century family, because the rigid Victorian code of morality, restricting extra-familial heterosexual relationships, damned up libidinous feelings within the home."[59] Second, gender expectations intensified, particularly for girls. Leonore Davidoff and Catherine Hall found earlier in the century that father/daughter relationships developed erotic overtones as daughters stepped into the physical and psychological roles of their mothers upon their mothers' deaths.[60] The channeling of sexual energies within the family, the emotional replacement of mothers by daughters, and even the increase in cases of incest at the courts do not mean a rise in rates of incest. Instead, it demonstrates a shift in the emotional resonance of family.

It is this home as the center of erotic energy that Freud attempted to address with his theories of psychoanalysis. The simultaneous emergence of incestuous pornography and Freudian theory seems too suggestive to be ignored. Both mediums took up the problem of incest at roughly the same time, and both centered their stories on children's desire. Turn-of the-century Viennese medicine and late-nineteenth-century British pornography might seem worlds apart, yet both medicine and pornography must also be understood as seeping across porous borders; the types of discourse were not completely separate. Pornography and sexology influenced each other at the margins of their disciplines.

Sexuality in International Communities

By the end of the nineteenth century the production, distribution, and consumption of British pornography became an international affair. British pornographers moved to the Continent in an attempt to outwit legal authorities. In Britain proper the Home Office, the National Vigilance Association, and the police increased pressure against pornographers during the 1880s. The passage of the Post Office (Protection) Act of 1884 made it illegal to send obscene or indecent materials through the mail, and the police used it and the earlier Lord Campbell's Act (1857) to arrest pornographers. The main publishers, William Lazenby, Edward Avery, Harry Sidney Nichols, and Charles Carrington, fled to Paris, where they set up mail-order businesses. By 1900 Paris became the distribution center of pornography intended for England (as well as the Continent).[61] The international trade connected Amsterdam and Rotterdam, Antwerp, Budapest, Barcelona, Berlin, and Genoa.[62]

To give a few examples, William Lazenby published *The Pearl,* which contained "My Grandmother's Tale," in 1879–1880, before he fled to Paris; Avery reprinted the work from the abandoned sheets.[63] Charles Carrington produced *The Modern Eveline* in 1904 from Paris. Lazenby published *The Romance of Lust* in 1873–1876 in London; in 1900 Versteeg, "then operating in Paris to meet the continuing demand from Parisian booksellers during the Paris Exhibition of 1900," reprinted it.[64] *The Autobiography of a Flea,* first published in London in 1885, quickly became part of the French-speaking world; it was advertised in French and sold in Paris by 1887. Three years later printers working in Brussels or Amsterdam shipped it to shops in Paris.[65] Brancart in Amsterdam and Avery in London reprinted *The Power of Mesmerism,* originally a Lazenby production.[66] Photographs and watercolors also available through mail-order augmented literary production and allowed a further expansion of the international market. Printing and publishing crossed national boundaries, and pornographers produced and sold their work to an international audience.

The extent of the trade remains unknown, but the volume of mail entering Britain suggests its magnitude. To stem the flow of incoming pornography, the Home Office and the Postal Office began to seize packages from pornographers as they entered the country; they confiscated over 12,000 packets from Carrington alone.[67] The policy gained momentum when the Home Office began to issue orders for multiple seizures at a time.[68] When the Postal Office began tracking letters addressed to pornographers, they scrutinized 3,724 outgoing letters, even though this policy remained in place for a short time.[69] Furthermore, these pornographers spoke not only to an English audience, although that was their primary outlet, but to a European-wide community of users. The national tradition here intersected with the international dispersal of information and ideas.

Pornographers began to organize their catalogs by the works' ability to meet consumer tastes and began to spell out the main focus of the work and emphasize its particular perversions. Carrington described *Sweet Seventeen: The True Story of a Daughter's Awful Whipping and Its Delightful if Direful Consequences,* an incestuous work, as "the thrilling narrative of a Father's sin and a Daughter's yielding ignominy": "It would seem to us that there have always been such men, daring, passionate, and wilful, like the unprincipled father here sketched; always such daughters, big, buxom, handsome and sensual as the utterly marvelous creature pourtrayed in these fiery pages."[70] Pornographers used such descriptions to sell works to their clientele. For those interested in visual images pornographers offered photographs of "Family Orgies. Mother and father seduce 10 year old daughter"; "Two sisters"; "Prohibited love" between brother and sister; "aunt and nephew"; "brother and sister, age 14 and 12"; and watercolors of "between brother and sister."[71] The shift in content seems tied together as part of a growing segmentation of the international market.

At the same time that pornographers published incestuous fantasies and marketed them across Europe, theorists such as Krafft-Ebing and Freud began to develop models of sexuality. To do so, they relied upon case studies, oral histories, historical examples, and works of pornography. Krafft-Ebing, for example, coined the term *masochism* after Leopold von Sacher-Masoch,[72] and Freud made use of Krafft-Ebing's work to develop his own theories. Pornographers then incorporated the taxonomical models developed by sexologists back into their works and into their catalogs. In one catalog that reads like Krafft-Ebing's index, Carrington promised illumination on the topics of "nympho-maniacs, onanists, exhibitionists, necrophilists, practicers of bestiality, Sadists, Masochists and erotic maniacs in general; both male and female."[73] What we have in effect is a psychology of sexuality tangentially built on pornography, which in turn was oriented toward new psychological theories. Theory and pornography developed in tandem, only loosely linked but pointing in the same direction. Against the international spread of such ideas it seems unsurprising that sexologists picked up on the erotic motifs in pornography and addressed the erotic energies circulating in the family that pornography elaborated. The development of Freud's theories regarding incest can usefully be put in this context.

Jeffrey Masson places the development of Freud's theories about incest in the European, rather than Viennese, context. In Masson's account Freud's early ideas were influenced by his time spent in Paris in the 1880s. There he was exposed to the work of Ambroise Auguste Tardieu, who wrote on parental physical abuse, including sexual abuse of children. Freud also seems to have been exposed to the works of subsequent scholars who continued to investigate sexual attacks on young girls. Freud attended lectures and autopsies of physical and sexual abuse cases by Professor Brouardel, Tardieu's assistant and replacement. (Freud's library contained works by Tardieu and Brouardel on sexual violence against children.) After linking his patients' hysterical manifestations to early sexual trauma, he developed what he called "a new motto: What have they done to you, poor child?"[74] This work culminated in Freud's 1896 paper "The Aetiology of Hysteria," in which he explained his original seduction theory; according to Freud, the premature sexual "seduction" of offspring resulted in later hysterical symptoms.[75] Masson makes the case that Freud believed that his patients suffered from often brutal incestuous encounters that later resulted in the manifestations of hysteria. By 1897 he believed that the father most often committed abuse, but then, later in the same year, he began to theorize that sexual abuse was really sexual fantasy on the part of the child.[76] This shift in Freud's thinking took place against the backdrop of two highly publicized cases of child abuse that raged in the Viennese press: the Hummel case, which involved the abuse of a seven-year-old girl; and the Kutschera case, in which a stepmother murdered the child Anna and defended herself with accusations of Anna's depravity and sluttishness. Larry Wolff makes clear that Freud's renunciation of childhood sexual abuse occurred in tandem with the widespread discussion of parental brutality and depravity in Vienna.[77] In France concerns over incest culminated in the 1890s in new legislation and judicial interest, including the dissolution of parent's rights.[78] The growing awareness of incest as abuse across Europe makes the shift in Freud's thinking particularly significant and remains central to ongoing controversies about the direction of Freudian theory.

Scholars have denounced Masson's work on a number of counts.[79] Some argue that Freud never renounced the reality of incestuous attacks. Others demonstrate that, because of a lack of evidence, Freud acted as a responsible scholar in appropriately modifying his position. Still others point out that his patients experienced trauma but not necessarily sexual trauma.[80] Even with these modifications (that Freud continued to be concerned about abuse, that he acted appropriately given a lack of evidence, and that his patients' traumas were not necessarily sexual in nature), Freud's theories still place incestuous desire in childhood and make it a root of psychological development.

In the 1890s Freud began to argue that the fantasy of parental seduction occurred in the children's minds, not the parents. As Freud explains: "If the hysterical subjects trace back their symptoms to traumas that are fictitious, then the new fact which emerges is precisely that they require such scenes in fantasy, and this psychical reality requires to be taken into account alongside practical reality. This reflection was soon followed by the discovery that these fantasies were intended to cover up the autoerotic activity of the first years of childhood, to embellish it and raise it to a higher plane."[81] From this position he developed the oedipal complex, the bedrock of his theories on sexual development and thus social development. Freud argues that "it represents the peak of infantile sexuality, which, through its after-effects, exercises a decisive influence on the sexuality of adults." In *Three Essays on the Theory of Sexuality,* published first in 1905 and then revised and further annotated in the 1910s and 1920s, Freud outlines the development of infantile sexuality as rooted in familial love. Infants desire their parents' love, Freud explains, and "it is in the world of ideas that the choice of object is accomplished at first."[82] In the realm of ideas children's sexual impulses are organized toward the parent of the opposite sex. Children's fantasies are incestuous but necessary to sexual and psychological development. Overcoming these incestuous desires forms the basis of puberty, a stage necessary for the "progress of civilization." Freudian theory thus organizes sexuality around the issue of incestuous fantasy and places these fantasies in the minds of the young. Childhood fantasies about incest (rather than adults' fantasies about children) became central to psychological theory for over a century.

At first glance it appears as if Freudian theory would be easily applicable to pornographic novels written during the same period. *Sweet Seventeen,* for example, seems to illustrate Freud's theories about incestuous desires almost perfectly. In a Freudian reading of that novel the daughter unconsciously seduces her father. Their relationship leads to her mother's death, which in turn elevates the daughter to the maternal position. The daughter's desire for the father, her jealousy and violence toward the mother, and her achievement of adulthood through her replacement of the mother seem like an example of the Electra complex par excellence. Likewise, in *Realistic Pleasures* the son's viewing of his mother's and pseudo-father's sexual activities arouse his jealousy, desire, and competition. Ultimately, the son absorbs the phallic energy of adult masculinity and consummates his relationship with his mother (and with the Colonel). These straightforward applications of Freud's theories to pornography might appear to illuminate the dynamics of desire in the family; however, they obfuscate the direction of desire by seeing it flowing from children toward adults, rather than the reverse. Since men, rather than children, wrote and read this pornography, we need to consider these fantasies as a product of men's desire. Men wrote children in particular ways, and men read about their offspring as reciprocating their own desires. Pornography and Freudian theory then fit together, but they do so because they emerged together, shared a basic narrative structure, and together displaced desire onto children.

Furthermore, both Freudian theory and incestuous pornography themselves emerged against the backdrop of new prosecutions against incest. Middle-class pornography clearly aped and then elevated the processes of incestuous rape detailed in working-class court cases. If we take a moment to consider the implications of these pornographic stories in the context of real-life incestuous desires, we can see the way these stories play off of them. Pornographic narratives recycled the violence, the blackmail, the problems with maternal authority over childhood sexuality, into a middle-class milieu. The timing of these three developments around incest—incestuous prosecutions and agitation for new laws, the emergence of incestuous pornography, and the evolution of Freudian theory—remains merely suggestive. The synchronicity can be interpreted in a number of ways from the simplest, that social welfare made the consideration of incest unavoidable in other realms, to the crudest, that the spread of fantasies of incest in pornography began to affect thinking and practice at some broad cultural level. Despite the inability to pin down an exact relationship, it seems well worth noting that the emerging consensus argued that the young supposedly desired adults, rather than the reverse.

All told, between the 1880s and 1914 the incestuous novel transferred the location of desire from adults onto children so that fictional children longed for their parents and engineered their own seductions or attacks. The novels detailed a type of middle-class incest that made adult men both erotic and authoritative. Middle-class men reading these accounts could fantasize about precocious children who looked back on them with an equal measure of desire. At roughly the same time Freud developed his position on human sexuality that made the Oedipus and Electra complexes central to psychological and social development. In doing so, he put aside earlier concerns about sexual trauma and focused on the fantasies of incestuous desire in the young. Against these developments Parliament's inability to legislate against incest begins to make sense. When members of Parliament showed concern over fathers' and families' reputations rather than children's welfare, they iterated a similar dislocation of desire and confusion over volition displayed in other realms. The simultaneous displacement of desire appears as more than mere coincidence.

In essence we have three different versions of the same problem. The similarity of responses to it—despite the vast differences in their tones—suggests that incestuous desires threaded across European society in ways that remain unrecognized. I would further suggest that the similarities of incestuous desire in each permutation emerge from a deep distrust of children and an equally deep acceptance of male erotic powers. Fantasies of incest placed the father as center of the family—distant, desirable, and authoritative—and it was this position on which each of the sources agreed. In each version of this image men as writers, consumers, members of Parliament, and sexologists saw something sexual at the heart of the family, but the absolution of male responsibility remained so compelling that they chose not to examine it further. If the pornography of incest allows access to the mentality of middle-class abusers, then it is hard to see where mentality ended and a broader cultural view began.

Notes

I would like to thank Anna Clark, Colleen Doody, Lesley Hall, Peter Stearns, Valentina Tikoff, and Jennifer Trost for reading earlier versions of this essay.

1. Anthony Wohl, "Sex and the Single Room," in *The Victorian Family: Structure and Stresses,* ed. Anthony Wohl (New York: St. Martin's Press, 1978), 208–209.
2. For a fascinating case study of the "dead wife's sister" problem, see Karen Chase and Michael Levenson, *The Spectacle of Intimacy: A Public Life for the Victorian Family* (Princeton: Princeton University Press, 2000), chap. 5.
3. Victor Bailey and Sheila Blackburn, "The Punishment of Incest Act 1908: A Case Study of Law Creation," *Criminal Law Review* (1979): 708–718; Wohl, "Sex and the Single Room," 197–216; Louise Jackson, *Child Sexual Abuse in Victorian England* (London: Routledge, 2000).
4. Public Records Office, Criminal Court Papers 1/8/8; hereafter abbreviated as PRO, Crim.
5. PRO, Crim 1/8/2.
6. Public Records Office, Home Office Papers 144/1093/195754; hereafter abbreviated as PRO, HO.
7. Linda Gordon, *Heroes of Their Own Lives* (New York: Penguin Books, 1989), 210, 212, 213, 232, 217.
8. Roger Davidson, "'This Pernicious Delusion': Law, Medicine, and Child Sexual Abuse in Early-Twentieth-Century Scotland," *Journal of the History of Sexuality* 10, no. 1 (2001): 67–68, 75.
9. Bailey and Blackburn, "Punishment of Incest Act 1908," 710.
10. Richard von Krafft-Ebing, *Psychopathia Sexualis,* trans. from the 12th ed. (New York: G. P. Putnam's Sons, 1965), 501.
11. PRO, HO 45/9747.
12. PRO, HO 45/10357/152169.
13. From these Home Office reports it is clear that the British government knew about the high rates of incest. HO 45/9747. The Home Office also knew that over a quarter of the cases for rape of girls under sixteen were incestuous. Bailey and Blackburn, "Punishment of Incest Act 1908," 713.
14. *Hansard's Parliamentary Debates,* vol. 191, 26 June 1908, 282.
15. The division surgeon of the police offered compelling testimony about the sexual abuse of Elizabeth Emmanuel that included the absence of a hymen, chronic irritation of the labia and vagina, and dilation. He found the physical evidence consistent with her statement of incestuous rape. His cross-examination consisted of asking whether the "marks might have been produced by the finger," to which he assented. PRO, Crim 1/15/6.
16. Bailey and Blackburn, "Punishment of Incest Act 1908," 717. Sybil Wolfram makes the argument that, while the literature existed on inbreeding, it was not cited in the passage of the act because inbreeding seemed less problematic than it has become since the passage of the act. Wolfram seems to be overlooking the differences between eugenics and genetics in this argument. See Wolfram, "Eugenics and the Punishment of Incest Act 1908," *Criminal Law Review* (May 1983): 308–316.
17. *Hansard's Parliamentary Debates,* vol. 191, 26 June 1908, 283.
18. *Hansard's Parliamentary Debates,* vol. 191, 26 June 1908, 284.
19. Leonore Davidoff et al., *The Family Story: Blood, Contract and Intimacy, 1830–1960* (London: Longman, 1999), 214.
20. Davidson, "'This Pernicious Delusion,'" 75.

21. Nancy F. Anderson demonstrates that incestuous tensions marked the relationship of Thomas Macaulay and his sisters; the relationship of Dorothy and William Wordsworth; that of Robert Browning and his sister Sarianna; Benjamin and Sarah Disraeli; Lord Byron and his half-sister; and Virginia Woolf and her half-brother, George. Anderson, "The 'Marriage with the Deceased Wife's Sister Bill' Controversy: Incest Anxiety and the Defense of Family Purity in Victorian England," *Journal of British Studies* 21, no. 2 (Spring 1982): 70–74.

22. Mary Lindemann, "The Many Lives of Beautiful Charlotte: The Guyard Incest Case in Eighteenth-Century Hamburg," presented at the American Historical Association meeting, Boston, 2001, 6.

23. Lynn Hunt, "The Many Bodies of Marie Antoinette: Political Pornography and the Problem of the Feminine in the French Revolution," in *Eroticism and the Body Politic,* ed. Lynn Hunt (Baltimore: Johns Hopkins University Press, 1991), 108–130.

24. Sara Maza, "The Diamond Necklace Affair Revisited," in Hunt, *Eroticism and the Body Politic,* 84.

25. Lynn Hunt, intro., in *The Invention of Pornography: Obscenity and the Origins of Modernity,* ed. Hunt (New York: Zone Books, 1996), 34–35, 43.

26. Lisa Z. Sigel, *Governing Pleasures: Pornography and Social Change in England, 1815–1914* (New Brunswick: Rutgers University Press, 2002); Iain McCalman, *Radical Underworld: Prophets, Revolutionaries and Pornographers in London, 1795–1840* (Cambridge: Cambridge University Press, 1988), 204–231.

27. Henry Spenser Ashbee, *Catena Librorum Tacendorum* (1885; rpt., New York: Documentary Books, 1962), 188–189; Peter Mendes, *Clandestine Erotic Fiction in English, 1800–1930* (Aldershot: Scolar Press, 1993), 236–237.

28. *Sweet Seventeen: The True Story of a Daughter's Awful Whipping and Its Delightful if Direful Consequence* (Paris: [Charles Carrington], 1910), 28.

29. *The Pearl* (1879; rpt., New York: Grove Press, 1968), 514. The full title of this work is *My Grandmother's Tale or May's Account of Her Introduction to the Art of Love,* which forms a serial in *The Pearl.* This essay uses the serialized version shortened to "My Grandmother's Tale." The serial was also sold as a stand-alone work under the name of *May's Account of Her Introduction to the Art of Love.* That version is used in Colligan's essay in this volume.

30. *Pearl,* 408.

31. *Pearl,* 409.

32. *Pearl,* 410.

33. *Pearl,* 449.

34. *The Modern Eveline; or, The Adventures of a Young Lady of Quality Who Was Never Found Out* (1904; rpt., New York: Grove Press, 1970), 57.

35. *Modern Eveline,* 83.

36. *Modern Eveline,* 88.

37. *The Romance of Lust* (1873; rpt., New York: Grove Press, 1968), 237.

38. *Romance of Lust,* 252.

39. *Romance of Lust,* 57.

40. *Romance of Lust,* 261.

41. *Romance of Lust,* 373.

42. *Sweet Seventeen,* 35.

43. *Sweet Seventeen,* 37.

44. *The Autobiography of a Flea, told in a Hop, Skip, and Jump, and Recounting all his Experiences of Human and Superhuman Kind, both Male and Female; with his curi-*

ous Connections, Backbitings and Tickling Touches; the whole scratched together for the delectation of the delicate, and for the Information of the Inquisitive, etc. (1887; rpt., New York: Carroll and Graf, 1983), 79–80.

45. *Autobiography of a Flea,* 70, 71, 73, 77.

46. *Autobiography of a Flea,* 81.

47. *Realistic Pleasures Gathered from the Diary of a Sybarite* (Alexandria [Paris: Duringe and Smithers?], 1900–1901), 73.

48. *Romance of Lust,* 382.

49. For discussions of the female narrator, see Lucienne Frappier-Mazur, "Truth and the Obscene Word," in Hunt, *Invention of Pornography,* 209, 211; Julia Epstein, "Fanny's Fanny: Epistolarity, Eroticism, and the Transsexual Text," in *Writing the Female Voice: Essays on Epistolary Literature,* ed. Elizabeth C. Goldsmith (Boston: Northeastern University Press, 1989), 135–153, 149.

50. PRO, HO 144/192/A6657D; Society for the Suppression of Vice, *Abstract of the Seventy-sixth Annual Report for 1879,* 1.

51. British Library, album 7, item 25, "Catalogue of Rare and Curious English Books" (London: n.p., 1903).

52. Mendes, *Clandestine Erotic Fiction in English,* 200–204.

53. J. A. Mangan, "Social Darwinism and Upper-Class Education in Victorian and Edwardian England," in *Manliness and Morality: Middle-Class Masculinity in Britain and America, 1800–1940,* ed. J. A. Mangan and James Walvin (New York: St. Martin's Press, 1987), 135–159; Jonathon Rutherford, *Forever England: Reflections on Masculinity and Empire* (London: Lawrence and Wishart, 1997).

54. Rutherford, *Forever England,* 15. See also Ian Gibson, *The English Vice: Beating, Sex and Shame in Victorian England and After* (London: Duckworth, 1978), 99–143.

55. Angus McClaren, *The Trials of Masculinity: Policing Sexual Boundaries, 1870–1930* (Chicago: University of Chicago Press, 1997), 31.

56. Jackson, *Child Sexual Abuse,* 2–3; W. T. Stead, "The Maiden Tribute of Modern Babylon," *Pall Mall Gazette* 42, no. 6336, 6 July 1885, 1–6; no. 6337, 7 July 1885, 1–6; no. 6338, 8 July 1885, 1–5; no. 6340, 10 July 1885, 1–6. See Judith R. Walkowitz, *City of Dreadful Delight: Narratives of Sexual Danger in Late-Victorian London* (Chicago: University of Chicago Press, 1992), 81–134.

57. Qtd. in Jackson, *Child Sexual Abuse,* 123.

58. Loftur Guttormsson, "Parent-Child Relations," in *Family Life in the Long Nineteenth Century, 1789–1913,* ed. David I. Kertzer and Mario Barbagi (New Haven: Yale University Press, 2002), 265.

59. Anderson, "'Marriage with the Deceased Wife's Sister Bill,'" 70.

60. Leonore Davidoff and Catherine Hall, *Family Fortunes: Men and Women of the English Middle Class* (Chicago: University of Chicago Press, 1987), 346–348.

61. "Report from the Joint Select Committee on Lotteries and Indecent Advertisements" (London: HMSO, 1908), 18–19.

62. Pornographers shipping to London included G. Arthur of Switzerland, alias A. de Sailles of Paris, J. Berge of Rotterdam, C. Carrington of Paris and Brussels, alias H. Robert of Paris, Charles Chaillon of Paris, alias Charles Offenstadt, L. Chaubard of Paris, H. Daragon of Paris, Jean Fort of Paris, A. Mazoyer of Lyons, alias L'Economie of Lyons, H. Pouwells of Paris, the Novelty Warehouse of Barcelona, Charles Schraeter of Barcelona, and Senor Zarubaly of Barcelona. PRO, HO 151/9, 414–415.

63. Mendes, *Clandestine Erotic Fiction in English,* 200–203.

64. Mendes, *Clandestine Erotic Fiction in English,* 238.

65. Mendes, *Clandestine Erotic Fiction in English,* 127–130.

66. Mendes, *Clandestine Erotic Fiction in English,* 214.

67. See PRO, Home Office Papers, 1898, HO 45/9752/A59329.

68. PRO, HO 45/9752/A59329, HO 144/9752/A59329, HO 151/6, HO 151/7, HO 151/8, HO 151/9.

69. PRO, HO 45/9752/A59329.

70. Mendes, *Clandestine Erotic Fiction in English,* 396–397.

71. British Library, album 7, catalog 12, "Strictly Confidential" (Paris, c. 1903); album 7, item 9, "Erotic Photos" (1902); cup 803.f.20, item 5, "A Catalogue of Rare Curious and Voluptuous Reading," n.p., 1897.

72. John K. Noyes, *The Mastery of Submission: Inventions of Masochism* (Ithaca: Cornell University Press, 1997), 50.

73. Carrington, *Forbidden Books,* 33.

74. Qtd. in Jeffrey Moussaieff Masson, *The Assault on Truth: Freud's Suppression of the Seduction Theory* (New York: Farrar, Straus, and Giroux) 117.

75. Masson, *Assault on Truth,* 135–136.

76. Wolff, *Child Abuse in Freud's Vienna* (New York: New York University Press, 1988), 205.

77. Wolff, *Child Abuse in Freud's Vienna,* 208–209.

78. Jeffrey Weeks, *Sex, Politics and Society: The Regulation of Sexuality since 1800,* 2d ed. (London: Longman, 1989), 31.

79. For a fascinating discussion of historicity and interiority in reference to Freud and the seduction theory, see Carolyn Steedman, *Strange Dislocations: Childhood and the Idea of Human Interiority* (Cambridge, Mass.: Harvard University Press 1994), 77–95.

80. See, for example, M. F. Bristow, "Review of *Assault on Truth,*" *British Journal of Psychiatry* 160 (May 1992): 722–724; Joel Kupersmid, "The 'Defense' of Sigmund Freud," *Psychotherapy* 29, no. 2 (Summer 1992): 297–309; Jay Greenberg, "The Ambiguity of Seduction in the Development of Freud's Thinking," *Contemporary Psychoanalysis* 37, no. 3 (2001): 417–426; David H. Gleaves and Elsa Hernandez, "Recent Reformulations of Freud's Development and Abandonment of His Seduction Theory," *History of Psychology* 2, no. 4 (November 1999): 324–335.

81. Qtd. in Masson, *Assault on Truth,* 131.

82. Sigmund Freud, *Three Essays on the Theory of Sexuality,* 6th ed., intro. Steven Marcus, trans. James Strachey (1962; rpt., New York: Basic Books, 1975), 91. Freud also discusses oedipal desires in *Totem and Taboo* and *The Interpretation of Dreams.*

Old Wine in New Bottles?

LITERARY PORNOGRAPHY IN TWENTIETH-CENTURY FRANCE

JOHN PHILLIPS

French culture has long been perceived by the English-speaking reader as somehow more "erotic" than Anglo-Saxon culture.[1] This impression is partly due to the large numbers of pornographic publications that have been imported from Paris since the sixteenth century, first into England and later into the United States, but also to the peculiarly French association of pornography and subversion—hence, the fascination that the genre has held for well-known and highly regarded writers from Rabelais to Robbe-Grillet. This historical tradition of literary erotica was invigorated in the eighteenth century by the enormous popularity of libertine writing[2] and, in the modern period, by the Surrealists and later by Roland Barthes and the Tel Quel group, all of whom vigorously opposed censorship and were responsible for an intellectual fascination with the Marquis de Sade, which had considerable influence on the twentieth century's artistic and cultural output.

The subject of this essay, therefore, is precisely this "literary" erotica that appears to be more deeply rooted in the French than in other Western literary traditions. My use of this elitist-sounding term partly serves to distinguish it from the popular erotic novel, as a separate genre, although the boundaries between the two are by no means clear, especially in the contemporary period. Pornography in general might be said to contain many elements characteristic of so-called popular fiction (e.g., erotic themes, violence, travel to exotic places, the extended use of colloquial, even vulgar, language). Indeed, the tendency of the pornographic text to cross generic and cultural boundaries is part of its subversive character, unsettling the conventions and expectations associated with social and cultural stereotypes. If the novels I shall refer to have a claim to be part of the literary canon, however, it is chiefly because they have a sophistication of form that makes them interesting on a textual as well as on a sexual level. On the other hand, the exclusion of pornography that lacks such formal properties can in no way be taken to imply that such writing is less socially or morally acceptable.

In this brief survey, then, I shall aim to provide an overview of so-called literary pornography in twentieth-century France, describing the main trends of its evolution and focusing on some landmark examples.[3] Over the course of the twentieth century the erotic has found expression in the work of many well-known French novelists and poets writing in every major literary movement or period from Surrealism at the beginning of the century through the avant-garde or modernist literature of the 1930s, 1940s, and 1950s, the more liberal climate of the so-called *Emmanuelle* era in the 1960s and 1970s, the new AIDS-driven puritanism of the 1980s and 1990s, to the greater pluralism of the third millennium. I shall consider the extent to which the genre is innovative in the twentieth century or whether it merely exhibits a repetition of themes and forms familiar from a reading of seventeenth- and eighteenth-century libertine literature. In particular, I shall consider the role and status of women as writing subjects and "written about" objects. At the same time, any discussion of pornography in a particular national or cultural context must be underpinned by a precise understanding of relevant terminology as well as by close familiarity with the workings of censorship in that context, and, before charting the evolution of the representation of sex in modern French literature, I shall therefore address these related aspects.

Definitions

In antiquity the word *pornographos* bore little relation to our contemporary notion of pornography as writing or images that aim to arouse sexually, since it merely denoted a type of biography, "the lives of the courtesans," which was not necessarily obscene in content. In fact, it was not until the nineteenth century that the dictionary definition of the word was widened to include "the expression or suggestion of obscene or unchaste subjects in literature or art" and began, therefore, to assume a pejorative meaning.

The etymology of the word *obscenity,* by contrast, is dubious. Its modern definition of "indecent" or "lewd" is preceded by the archaic meaning of "repulsive" or "filthy" (OED). Some recent commentators have suggested that the word originally meant "off the scene," referring, in other words, to actions in the classical theater that were too shocking to take place "onstage" in full view of the audience.[4] What all of these definitions have in common is their subjective basis, for what is "repulsive" or "shocking" to some will not be so to others. When used in a sexual context, moreover, the word reveals a profoundly negative attitude to the sexual functions and to sexual pleasure. For Susan Sontag: "It's just these assumptions that are challenged by the French tradition represented by Sade, Lautréamont, Bataille, and the authors of *Story of O* and *The Image*. Their assumption seems to be that 'the obscene' is a primal notion of human consciousness, something much more profound than the backwash of a sick society's aversion to the body."[5] Like *pornography,* then, *obscenity* has acquired a negative charge in a Western culture conditioned by the puritanism of Christianity, a negativity that legal definitions have reinforced.

Concepts of obscenity are central to antipornography legislation in Britain and the United States as well as in France. In Britain the law currently defines *obscenity* as "anything that may deprave or corrupt persons who are likely to read, see or hear the matter contained or embodied in it."[6] In the United States the so-called Miller Test is still the predominant legal definition of obscenity. According to this test, which originated in a 1973 case tried before the U.S. Supreme Court, *Miller v. California,* there are three criteria: (1) does a work as a whole appeal to "prurient interest"? (2) does it depict or describe sexual conduct in a "patently of-fensive way"? (3) does it lack serious literary, artistic, political, or scientific value?[7] A recent ruling by the Canadian Supreme Court, masterminded by antipornogra-phy campaigners Catherine MacKinnon and Andrea Dworkin, defines obscenity according to the harm it does to women's pursuit of equality.[8]

These definitions of obscenity are dangerously vague, since they all depend upon the inescapable subjectivity and cultural relativity of other terms, such as *indecent, deprave, corrupt, prurient, offensive, value, harm,* and *equality,* embed-ded in them. In the French law of the last two centuries the concept of "bonnes moeurs" (which roughly translates as "public decency") is equally vague and cul-turally relative, as the history of censorship clearly shows—how many of us would consider Flaubert's *Madame Bovary* or the racier pieces in Baudelaire's best-known collection of poems, *Les Fleurs du mal* (*The Flowers of Evil*), a threat to public morals now?

Censorship in France: A Brief History

The Paris of the twentieth century, if not of earlier centuries, is associated in the popular imagination with liberal attitudes to pornography, an association that does have a basis in fact. British, Irish, and American writers of the modern period, whose work contained erotic elements, found a haven in Paris, the "city of culture and tolerance."[9] Indeed, Maurice Girodias's Paris-based Olympia Press (and its earlier avatars, Obelisk Press and Éditions du Chêne) made a great deal of money in the 1930s, 1940s, and 1950s, publishing in English what are now regarded as classics of the modern erotic canon.[10]

It is certainly true, generally speaking, that for most of the century there has been a great deal less censorship in France than in Britain or the United States. Until the late 1950s Britain's draconian obscenity laws were the most restrictive in the world, while in 1950s America, during the McCarthy era, the publication of erotic works could be construed as communist subversion.[11] When one begins to examine the detailed history of French censorship, however, an essential prereq-uisite to the proper understanding of the workings of censorship in twentieth-century France, things appear a little more complicated.

Books have been considered dangerous in France, as in other European coun-tries, since the early days of printing in the fifteenth century, when the Catholic Church realized the power of the medium and the need to watch out for danger-ous material. Robert Netz sees the burning of Martin Luther's "heretical" writ-ings in 1523 as the beginning of a long history of book censorship in France.[12] Until the eighteenth century this censorship was both religious and political in motivation, with the king controlling the publication of all works by the end of the sixteenth century, though by far the largest number of prosecutions were for books attacking the Church.[13] By the eighteenth century such controls had become severe, with a form of pre-censorship exercised by numerous royal censors and the galleys and even the death penalty threatening authors and printers who flouted the laws. In 1759, 40 percent of prisoners held in the Bastille were there for book-related crimes.[14]

This situation, nevertheless, gave rise to a flourishing "under-the-counter" trade in banned books, most of which came into the country from abroad. These included anti-Catholic and antimonarchy pamphlets (or "libelles") and porno-graphic tales of lascivious monks and nuns that began to make their appearance at the beginning of the eighteenth century. Much of this "pornography" was sa-tirical in nature, aimed at both the church and the monarchy.[15] As Robert Darnton points out, however, eighteenth-century Frenchmen did not distinguish a genre of pure pornography from other types of fiction, the notion of pornography itself not appearing until the nineteenth century.[16] Hence, the term *philosophical books* was used by booksellers to denote material of any kind that fell into the forbidden cat-egory. Because of the increasing uses of obscenity to subvert the ancien régime in the third quarter of the eighteenth century, then, it is arguable that the pornographic, indistinguishable from other forbidden discourses, played a significant role in cre-ating a climate favorable for revolution.[17]

In 1789, following the Revolution, the National Assembly abolished all cen-sorship, but it was not long before the return of even more repressive controls: in 1793 it was decreed by the Terror's ruling Committee of Public Safety that any author or printer of works inciting opposition to the status quo would be sentenced to death.[18] This set the tone for the whole of the next century, from Napoléon to the Third Republic. In the early nineteenth century censorship increased dramati-cally. In particular, the law of 17 May 1819 introduced a very important article (art. 8), extended in scope and severity in 1822, which was to form the basis of print censorship until 1881, and, indeed, would be reactivated in 1958, upon Charles de Gaulle's return to power. This article allowed for the imposition of heavy fines and up to five years' imprisonment for "any offence against religious and public morals, or against public decency," including mockery of the state religion.[19] It is this law that was used to prosecute Baudelaire's *Les Fleurs du mal* and Flaubert's *Madame Bovary* in 1857. Baudelaire was fined three hundred francs and ordered to remove six poems from the collection. Flaubert was acquitted, though the judge insisted that the novel was blameworthy, in that it did not fulfill literature's mis-sion of "elevating the mind and purifying our morals."[20]

Altogether, twenty-four writers were tried in nineteenth-century France on the grounds that their work offended "public decency."[21] Two main fears underlay this vague and changeable concept of public morality: that "immoral" works were a threat to public order and social stability; and that "innocence" must be pro-tected.[22] Although article 8 was replaced in 1881 by a law that declared the press to be free and all references to religious morality and absolutes such as public mo-rality, God, and the state had disappeared, "offence against public decency" remained the basic principle of censorship of the written word, and the thinking be-hind it lingered on, influencing the direction of and providing justification for censoring legislation in the twentieth century. Moreover, Catholicism continued to exercise a repressive influence outside French law, by means of Rome's *Index of Prohibited Works*.[23] At the end of the nineteenth century there was some public concern, encouraged by the church and other guardians of morality, that a "wave of pornography" threatened to undermine social values. Consequently, regional "leagues," or committees, were set up to keep an eye on bookshops and take ac-tion against the authors and publishers of obscene literature.[24] The actions of these antiobscenity leagues drove erotic literature underground, by reinforcing a repres-sive legislation that affected not just pornography but all writings about sex, in-cluding technical works about contraception.[25]

Throughout the twentieth century, as indicated earlier, the defense of *bonnes moeurs* has remained the basis of all censorship laws in France, although both world wars and the Algerian War of 1955–1962 also saw extensive political censorship. In the first half of the century erotic works by even well-known writers such as Guillaume Apollinaire, Pierre Louÿs, and Georges Bataille suffered the fate of all obscene erotica of the period of being restricted to private circulation among friends and acquaintances or to under-the-counter sales and did not appear in legal edi-tions until 1970. In laws of the postwar era the protection of youth, above all, has been the overriding aim. For instance, in 1949 it became illegal to expose minors under eighteen to publications of a "licentious or pornographic nature." In 1958, upon General de Gaulle's election to the presidency, the scope of this provision was widened considerably, to the point of forbidding display of such material "in any place whatever" and advertising for it "in any form whatever." Many comic books were suppressed under this law and, at the very least, authors and editors were obliged to exercise self-censorship.[26]

The period since the end of the war until the end of the 1960s could be con-sidered a period of extreme censorship. The principle of the protection of youth, together with the defense of public morality, were the basis of all prosecutions of adult fiction during this period, Maurice Girodias's Olympia Press becoming a par-ticular focus of attention for the authorities under this legislation. Henry Miller's *Tropic of Capricorn* and *Tropic of Cancer* were banned for "offence against pub-lic decency in the medium of print." After "L'Affaire Miller" came "L'Affaire *Lolita*," with the prevention of the publication of Vladimir Nabokov's novel, and Olympia's English-language editions of Sade's *La Philosophie dans le boudoir* (*Philosophy in the Boudoir*). Apollinaire's *Les Onze mille verges* (published as *The Debauched Hospodar*) and Bataille's *Histoire de l'oeil* (*Story of the Eye,* published as *A Tale of Satisfied Desire* by Pierre Angélique) all came under scrutiny by the government authorities. In the 1950s the Brigade Mondaine (or "Vice Squad") made frequent visits to the Olympia Press's offices, taking books away and issu-ing banning orders and lawsuits, which Girodias swiftly contested.[27] Meanwhile, Jean-Jacques Pauvert was famously prosecuted from 1954 until 1958 for publica-tion of the Marquis de Sade's complete works. During this period he was heavily fined and the works ordered to be confiscated and destroyed. *Les Onze mille verges,*

which had reappeared in 1948 under a false Dutch provenance, was repeatedly prosecuted until the 1960s, and, when it was finally published openly by Régine
Deforges in 1970, it had to include a warning that it should be "kept out of the
hands of minors." *Histoire de l'oeil* and other works by Bataille were also the object of numerous prosecutions at this time.[28]

What, then, of literary censorship in France since the 1960s? A 1970 edition of *Magazine Littéraire* announced on its front cover that there was no censorship in France—"Il n'y a pas de censure en France."[29] Yet in the very same year
Pierre Guyotat's *Éden, Éden, Éden,* an obscene novel apparently set in the Algerian War, was the subject of an order banning all advertising of the book and its
sale to minors. Jérôme Lindon, head of the Éditions de Minuit, launched a peti-
tion against the ban, which was signed by many well-known writers, including Jean-
Paul Sartre and Louis Aragon.[30] Since that date, despite a drop in the number of
book prosecutions following the defeat of de Gaulle, books continue to be seized
and their editors threatened with fines and prison sentences. Throughout the 1970s,
for example, Bernard Noël's surreal exotic fantasy, *Le Château de Cène* (1969),
among others, was still banned or prosecuted in France.[31] In 1975 *Histoire d'O*
was seized in Brussels bookstores, having been banned in Belgium since 1965,
and in 1977 the publisher François Maspero declared that twenty-one of his books
had been banned since 1969.[32]

The book and press censorship provisions of the new Penal Code, which came
into force on 1 March 1994, have been welcomed by some as the most liberal that
France has ever known, and yet Jean-Jacques Pauvert regards one article of the
code (article L 227–24) as a "masterpiece of censorship," because of the vagueness of its terms. The article makes it illegal "to manufacture, transport or broadcast by whatever means . . . any message of violent or pornographic character or
the nature of which seriously injures human dignity."[33] As Pauvert observes with
regard to this "catch-all" piece of repressive legislation, "the effectiveness of any
censorship law increases . . . with the vagueness of its terms."[34]

Whereas Pauvert still sees the pernicious effects of direct manifestations of
censorship in law, Maurice Girodias places the emphasis on indirect and more
subtle forms of control. In his autobiography, *Une Journée sur la terre,* Girodias
draws depressing conclusions concerning the evolution of censorship in recent
years, seeing the state's control of individual sexuality becoming increasingly sophisticated: "Whereas under the IVth Republic, de Gaulle and Pompidou, control
was exercised through application of the obscenity laws which remained on the
statute books until their abolition by Giscard d'Estaing, the Socialist record since
1981 has been scarcely less uninspiring, even if the State now employs the innovation of soft-porn on the TV as a means of conditioning sexuality into approved
channels."[35] For Girodias, as for Philippe Sollers, censorship in contemporary
France is no longer the political and moral censorship of the nineteenth century
but, rather, a manipulation of thinking. In the contemporary French media the erotic
is controlled, sanitized, reduced to banality, so that it has ceased to be effective as
a weapon of subversion.[36]

Literary Eroticism in Twentieth-Century France

At the end of the eighteenth century, the century of Sade and of *libertinage,* of the collapse of both monarchy and church in the French Revolution, eroticism in France appeared to go underground. The repressive measures introduced by Robespierre during the Terror marked the beginning of a long period of sexual repression. The adoption of the Napoleonic code and, later, the return of the monarchy encouraged a general decline in the production of pornographic literature.[37] Sex took refuge in the mushrooming medico-legal discourses of the period,[38] peeping out only occasionally from the pages of a literature policed more than that of any other century, and was largely avoided and displaced throughout the nineteenth century as a subject of mainstream literature by the convention of romantic love. By the end of the century, however, more and more educated French readers were consuming Laclos and Sade in secret, and there was a renewed interest in Sade as a literary and philosophical ancestor, particularly among the writers and poets of what was known as the Decadent period (c. 1870–1900). For Jean-Jacques Pauvert the real turning point came around 1905, when the generation of young writers, led by the symbolist poet Guillaume Apollinaire, began to express themselves.[39] Pauvert argues that the early 1900s saw profound changes in attitudes, influenced by important new work in the sciences and in philosophy: Freud published his *Interpretation of Dreams* in 1899 and *Three Essays on Sexuality* in 1905, destroying forever the notion of childhood innocence, while Henri Bergson, Max Planck, Niels Bohr, and Albert Einstein all shook the foundations of a logical positivism that had dominated scientific thinking for most of the previous century. A new, modern spirit was abroad; it was a spirit of uncertainty and disillusion with the old values of religion and the old ruling dynasties.

Born in 1880 and dying in 1918, victim of the Paris influenza epidemic, Apollinaire symbolized in both his life and his work this passage from the absolute certainties of the nineteenth century to the new doubts and relativities of the twentieth. During his short life he did perhaps more to hasten the advent of an *esprit nouveau,* and especially to promote the reading of erotic works, than any other writer of the period.[40] *Les Onze mille verges ou les amours d'un hospodar,* which appeared secretly in 1907, was of its time. Not only did it reflect topical events (the victory of the Japanese over the Russians at Port Arthur in 1904–1905), it was, for some, Apollinaire's masterpiece, bursting with a plurality of meanings and full of a playfulness that make it very much an erotic novel for the modern era.

In spite of its many qualities, *Les Onze mille verges* is, of course, typical of most erotic output up until the mid-twentieth century in being authored by a man and thoroughly male centered. In this respect Apollinaire's erotic imagination merely reflects the structures and prejudices of the patriarchal society in which he lived. It is also noticeably Sadean in influence and characteristic of the genre as a whole in representing homosexual acts (e.g., sodomy, male-to-male fellatio) as interesting diversions rather than as substitutes for heterosexual activities. In this sense Apollinaire's pornographic writings (the equally obscene *Les Exploits d'un jeune Don Juan* appeared the following year in 1908) can be seen as an homage to Sade. Indeed, the young poet did more than any one else in his time to redis-cover the divine marquis for twentieth-century readers. In addition to the novels, he also edited a collection of erotic writings by others, notably Aretino, Baffo, Nerciat, Cleland (the author of *Fanny Hill*), and, above all, Sade.[41] In the intro-duction to his Sade anthology he rightly predicted that, though neglected by the nineteenth century, Sade would come to dominate the twentieth.[42] Indeed, it was this edition of extracts from a number of Sade's writings that kindled the enthusi-asm for Sade of many of his surrealist friends. In addition to his own erotic out-put and his work of editing the erotic writings of others, Apollinaire compiled a catalog of all the pornographic works in La Bibliothèque Nationale.[43]

Despite this clear fascination with the genre, Apollinaire's work in this area has generally been despised by critics, judged to contain no literary value, and reduced to the level of a mercenary pursuit.[44] For Jean-Jacques Pauvert, however, it was in his "enfers" that Apollinaire's love of life and freedom found its stron-gest expression, though evidence of this interest in the obscene can be found in many of his less explicitly erotic texts, including the poetry.[45] Rather than being the creations of a dishonest, puerile, and therefore less-well-developed poetic sen-sibility, as most commentators have maintained, the pornographic writings form an integral part of Apollinaire's oeuvre. The poet's surrealist friends, notably André Breton, Louis Aragon, and Robert Desnos, recognized this at once. For Desnos, for example, Apollinaire was not so much a great erotic writer as a great modern poet, a midwife at the birth of cubism and champion of the new, there being no fundamental distinction to make between his poetic and his pornographic writ-ings: "*Les Onze Mille Verges* is a modern book, and together with *Calligrammes,* Apollinaire's masterpiece."[46] His eroticism was a positive manifestation of the spirit of playful innovation that characterized the intellectual life of Paris in the early years of this century. The most innovative painter of his generation, Pablo Picasso, thought that *Les Onze mille verges* was the finest book he had ever read. It was Aragon, however, who saw more clearly than any other that Apollinaire's sexual-ization of poetry was not only radically modern but intensely creative: "A clear awareness of the links between poetry and sexuality, the awareness of a profaner and of a poet, is what places Apollinaire at a conspicuous point in history."[47] Of all Apollinaire's writings *Les Onze mille verges* is the best example of this mar-riage of poetic creativity and modernist subversion.

Apollinaire's encyclopedic knowledge of the history of pornography, his fas-cination with obscenity, and his ludic tendencies all help to explain why *Les Onze mille verges* reads as an affectionate parody of the Sadean text,[48] rather than as a classic of the pornographic genre, as some have described it. If Apollinaire looks back for his inspiration to Sade and the eighteenth-century libertine tradition, he does so with a surreal inventiveness and an impish sense of humor that are thor-oughly and unmistakably modern.

The strangest case of erotic literature in the twentieth century, according to the writer and critic Sarane Alexandrian, was Pierre Louÿs (1870–1925). Consid-ered by contemporaries such as Mallarmé, Valéry, and Gide as one of the foremost poets of his time, Louÿs has since fallen out of fashion somewhat, a neglect that may in part be a negative response to the astonishing scale of his erotomania.[49] After his mid-thirties Louÿs stopped publishing work of any kind, remaining cloistered in his study. He died twenty years later, half-blind, semi-paralyzed, afflicted by a nervous condition, and tortured by insomnia.

Louÿs's erotic writing, above all, celebrates his adoration of young women, displaying a particular penchant for Sapphic love. Lesbianism obsessed Louÿs. Indeed, many of his works focus on this activity: apart from *Trois filles de leur mère* (1926), *Aphrodite* (1896) and *Les Chansons de Bilitis* (1898) are the best novelistic examples, though there are also short stories about girls in convent schools, indulging in Sapphic pleasures. For J.-P. Goujon this preoccupation with Sapphism goes beyond the obvious voyeurism of a male writer to express a real fascination with female sexuality, as something autonomous and independent of men.[50] Like Apollinaire, Louÿs follows a tradition stretching back to the eighteenth century, when an entirely male-authored erotic genre favored the inclusion, for voyeuristic purposes, of scenes of lesbian lovemaking.[51] Thus, in Louÿs's *Trois filles de leur mère* female homosexuality is presented from a heterosexual male perspective, offering voyeuristic objects for the male reader. Louÿs takes Freud's view of the polymorphous perversity of the child literally: of three debauched sisters who repeatedly pleasure one another and the young man who lives next door in every way imaginable, it is the youngest of the three who is seen to be the least restrained.

Trois filles de leur mère was just one among the numerous obscene works written by Louÿs and published secretly after his death. All of Louÿs's work in the genre, none of which is ever mentioned in literary histories, reflects the characteristic obsessions of its author. For Jean-Paul Goujon four main themes inform Louÿs's erotic interest in the female body—in addition to Sapphism, these are incest, scatology (or coprophilia), and sodomy.[52] To this list we can also add a particular interest in little girls, although the Louÿs case in no way conforms to the stereotype described by Stephen Heath: "The point of the little girl is her existence before womanhood, supposedly before sexual life, before the critical moment 'when the stream and river meet' as C. L. Dodgson (Lewis Carroll) could put it: investment in an untroubling image of female beauty, avoiding any reality of women and men."[53] The *fillette* of Louÿs's fiction is not the creature of prepubescent innocence that we might expect, the Lolita who fascinates Humbert Humbert *because* of her girlishness, so much as the self-assured and street-wise Zazie,[54] the child who always gets the better of the adults around her and who is far more depraved than they are. As Goujon observes: "In Louÿs's work, children are fully conscious of sex, which seems to be the only game available to them, and even their domain: the only activity in which they really excel. A strange inversion, according to which children usurp the place of adults and even end up making them dance to their tune."[55] The *gamines* of *Trois filles de leur mère,* so typically Louÿsian, far from being the sweet, innocent things beloved of the pedophile, are simply younger and smaller versions of their prostitute mother—"three daughters who take after their mother," as the French title has it.

At the level of form *Trois filles de leur mère* is strongly informed with an ironic and parodic humor, and the construction of the text is founded on plurality and excess at all levels: the parodic exploitation of existing forms (autobiographical narrative, personal diary, "books that are read with one hand"),[56] a bold use of vulgar expressions, and a complete lack of sexual inhibitions are combined with a textual polyphony generated by the multiplication of narrative voices and the active role that the reader is encouraged to play. These innovative elements certainly make this novel far more than simple pornography. Thus, while it is true that Louÿs is by no means the first writer of the genre to innovate at the level of form,[57] he made an important contribution to the inventiveness of the French pornographic tradition and, in certain respects, went much farther than his literary and generic antecedents.[58]

The transgressive fictions of Georges Bataille, together with his profoundly intellectual theories of the erotic, dominate the midcentury in France and, in a sense, look both backward and forward: both the extreme obscenity and the sadomasochistic contents of his fiction owe much to Sade, while the theoretical basis of his eroticism, in particular, his presentation of the human subject as disintegrated, his belief in the essential autonomy of the text, and the generally unsystematic nature of his philosophical method seem to prefigure the plural discourses of postmodernism and its textualization of the subject and the world. As Bataille's first and probably best-known erotic fiction, the artistically innovative *Histoire de l'oeil* (1928) has, of all his works, attracted the most critical attention. This novel, indeed all of his fiction, can be said to enact in extreme fashion and graphic detail the links between sex and death and the irresistible need for humans to transgress, theorized later in his study of the nature of the erotic in human culture, *L'Érotisme.*

Presenting the Gallimard edition of Georges Bataille's complete works, published in 1967, Michel Foucault declared him to be one of the most important writers of the century.[59] In the same decade the French avant-garde elevated Bataille's work to near cult status, mainly thanks to *Histoire de l'oeil*, regarding the author, who had died in 1962, as an antiestablishment hero. As Susan Suleiman points out,[60] many of the other leading French cultural heroes of the 1960s and 1970s (including Barthes, Kristeva, Sollers, Foucault, and Blanchot) wrote about him at length. To this list of French intellectuals, Suleiman rightly adds the name of the American writer Susan Sontag, whose seminal essay on literary pornography, "The Pornographic Imagination," drew the attention of Anglo-American readers to Bataille, praising his work as "the chamber-music of pornographic literature," with *Histoire de l'oeil* "the most accomplished artistically of all the pornographic prose fictions I've read."[61] Sontag's work excepted, this interest in Bataille among Parisian intellectuals did not spread outside France until the 1980s, when a sudden fashion for his work is perhaps attributable, as Michael Richardson suggests,[62] to the rise of postmodernist criticism. There are a number of reasons for this neglect, not least a repulsion among Anglo-Saxon scholars for the pornographic and sacrilegious elements of the fictional writing. The author's personal reputation as, at best, a maverick intellectual with eccentric and eclectic interests (e.g., cave paintings, numismatics, mysticism, shamanism)[63] and, at worst, an unbalanced erotomaniac, with suicidal tendencies and a taste for human sacrifice,[64] doubtless contributed to this unwillingness among the academic community in the United Kingdom and the United States to make Bataille part of the twentieth-century canon.

Superficially, at least, the texts appear no less idiosyncratic than their author, portraying a twilight world of fin de siècle decadence, peopled by self-indulgent, upper-middle-class manic depressives who throw frequent convulsions for no apparent reason other than alcoholic or narcotic inebriation or sexual frenzy. As Bataille argues in *L'Érotisme,* work and violence are incompatible,[65] so it is hardly surprising that the sexually violent world of his fiction is inhabited predominantly by the leisured classes. In the pages of Bataille's novels *la Belle Époque* lingers on.

The themes to which Bataille incessantly and obsessively returns might also be considered rebarbative by many readers. All of his fiction can be said to enact in extreme fashion and graphic detail the links between sex and death, and the irresistible need for humans to transgress, theorized later in *L'Érotisme* (alongside the more predictable Sadean scenario of sadistic murder, a fetishistic attachment to urination, e.g., is a dominant erotic theme in *Histoire de l'oeil*).

Bataille continued to write pornographic fiction until his death in 1962, but his obsessive and masochistic concentration on the role played by pain and death in eroticism exercised a lasting influence on French literary pornography.[66] In the 1950s, for example, *Histoire d'O* and *L'Image* contained strong echoes of this link between Eros and Thanatos.

The first French pornographic novel of the century known to have been written by a woman, *Histoire d'O* was published in 1954 by Pauline Réage, a pseudonym for Dominique Aury. Lucienne Frappier-Mazur rightly considers this text to represent the penultimate stage in the evolution of erotic writings by women, in that it depicts male domination and female subjection from the victim's point of view for the first time.[67]

For many feminists, however, *Histoire d'O,* in which the eponymous heroine is subjected to all conceivable brands of male violence, was a voyeuristically pornographic account of female objectification that could not possibly have been the work of a woman. Some believed that the novel was the result of a group effort, like the erotica produced on demand by Anaïs Nin, Henry Miller, and others in the 1930s and 1940s. Others were persuaded that Alain Robbe-Grillet's wife, Catherine, had written the book, a theory bolstered by the appearance in 1956 of the novel *L'Image* by the pseudonymous Jean de Berg, which had similar sado-masochistic themes, was dedicated to Pauline Réage, and contained a foreword signed with the initials "P.R." (It had also been suggested that these initials were, in fact, those of Alain [Paul] Robbe-Grillet.) Most, however, felt that *Histoire d'O* was the work of a man—probably Jean Paulhan himself—and that the use of a female pseudonym by a male writer was nothing more than a convention of the erotic genre, designed to titillate the male reader even more, by suggesting that the novel was the confession by a real woman of events that had actually taken place, another convention of the genre. Andrea Dworkin, for example, speaking of the genre as a whole, argued that "the female name on the cover of the book is part of the package, an element of the fiction. It confirms men in their fantasy that the eroticism of the female exists within the bounds of male sexual imperatives."[68]

Forty years later, with both Paulhan and his wife long dead, the personal issues framing the writing of this novel seem trivial. Dominique Aury's disclosure in the 1990s that she was indeed the author of the book should serve to remind us all, however, of the dangers of drawing either artistic or moral conclusions from a writer's presumed identity: are we not, each of us, a complicated mix of personae, social, psychological, and sexual?

While Réage's book was thoroughly traditional, even classical in form, Emmanuelle Arsan's *Emmanuelle,* written only four years later, though not officially published until 1967, could not have been written before the end of the 1950s. Arsan's novel is certainly very "literary" in form (a fact that might surprise those readers familiar only with the film and its sequels), but its optimistic, life-affirming conception of eroticism and its portrayal of female sexual autonomy are completely alien to the morbid and guilt-ridden eroticism of Bataille. For Pierre Mandiargues *Emmanuelle,* like *Les Onze mille verges,* represents nothing less than a new spirit of eroticism,[69] and for Jean-Jacques Pauvert the novel marks the beginning of a new, permissive era, the "Emmanuelle era," which lasted until 1985, the year when AIDS came to full public attention in France.[70] Among many important contributions to the erotic genre in the 1960s, Pierre Klossowski's three-volume *Les Lois de l'hospitalité* (1965) is notable for its exploration of sexual independence and of the boundaries between reality and the imagination.

It was during this permissive era that Tony Duvert and other homosexual French writers (e.g., Jean Demélier, Renaud Camus, and Dominique Fernandez) also published their explicitly homoerotic works, openly projecting homosexuality in a positive light for the first time.[71] *Récidive,* which was originally published by Duvert in 1967, is one of the first examples in France of the pornographic novel written specifically for the homosexual reader. Other works in this category include novels with an explicitly lesbian perspective, such as Violette Leduc's *Thérèse et Isabelle* (1966) and Monique Wittig's *Le Corps lesbien* (1973). All of these writers have produced a substantial number of critically acclaimed works that represent a considerable step forward from the point of view of sexual politics, though some, like Duvert's, are highly controversial. Duvert's positive portrayal of homosexual themes was in part a reaction to the largely negative portrayal of the homosexual in previous literature, for example, as "an agent for the dissolution of society in Proust, an agent of death in Cocteau, a symbol of all that is conventionally evil in Genet,"[72] and also a reaction to antigay legislation of the day: while it is certainly true that the 1960s saw a gradual relaxation of sexual mores in France, this was also a period in which legal sanctions were introduced against homosexuality for the first time.[73] Moreover, there was still a good deal of intolerance among the populace at large, especially outside sophisticated intellectual Parisian society, in the provinces, which provide the setting for much of Duvert's fiction.[74] Homosexuality had remained a clandestine activity throughout the 1950s and 1960s.

Even among the Parisian intelligentsia, attitudes were slow to change: neither Roland Barthes nor Michel Foucault ever "came out."[75]

Duvert stands at a crossroads in the literary representation of homosexuality, for, in spite of his aggressively positive approach to homosexual issues, the effect of Duvert's portrayal of homosexuality as furtive and sordid behavior is unavoidably negative. There are, furthermore, pederastic/pedophilic elements in Duvert that demand attention from the point of view of a sexual politics, as does the sexual violence that runs throughout his work. His writing is artistically interesting, then, precisely because its representation of homosexual desire is conflictual, and on a political level its pederastic themes seem especially relevant to current concerns about pedophilia.

In past literature homosexuality had largely been depicted in stereotypical terms, with homosexuals portrayed as drag queens or at the very least as effete or effeminate.[76] Undoubtedly, the most positive aspect of Duvert's writing, from a political viewpoint is his dismantling of such stereotypes, representing homosexuality as a fluid rather than a fixed position. In *Récidive,* Duvert's first novel, it is the *process of construction* of homosexual identity that is foregrounded, undermining attempts to view homosexuality as a fixed essence, which is why *Récidive* might be termed a "homotextuality," since this is the term that has been used to stress the mobile nature of a homosexual identity that is constantly being constructed and deconstructed in changing social contexts.[77]

The representation of homosexuality in Duvert as fluid and resisting fixed categorization is in itself sufficient reason to reread him now, given the recent emphasis of Queer Theory on the destabilization of identity and sexual and gender hierarchies.[78] Although much of Duvert's writing is now over twenty, and *Récidive* over thirty, years old, its privileging of circularity, repetition, and fragmentation, as well as its representation of gender and sexual identities as unstable, put it very much in tune with both modern gay theory in particular and what François Lyotard called the "postmodern condition" in general.[79]

The Emmanuelle era, then, was a unique period, during which sexual discourses were relatively free of legal or moral constraints, reflecting the sexual freedoms enjoyed in Western society as a whole, a time when Duvert could actively champion the sexual rights of the child in his essays and fictions, without becoming the target of a hysterical witch-hunt, and when Alain Robbe-Grillet, the leader of the New Novel movement in France, could make films and write novels in which very young females are depicted as objects of male sexual violence, without any overt sense of moral condemnation on the author's part. Robbe-Grillet's *Projet pour une révolution à New York* (1970) is both typical of the author's preoccupation with young girls as erotic objects and its most direct and most daring expression.

With AIDS in the mid–1980s, however, came a new puritanism, which called for abstention from uncontrolled pleasure and advocated a return to the chastity of the pre-pill era. In the United States pro-censorship forces, organized by Andrea Dworkin and Catherine MacKinnon, began to push for legislation to ban all pornography. (In 1983 they achieved their first legal victory with an antipornography law that was passed by the Minneapolis City Council.) The 1980s was also the decade when political correctness emerged from U.S. university campuses, threatening artistic freedoms. Admittedly, the pro-censorship and political correctness lobbies appear to have had little direct impact on French political and cultural life—there is, significantly, no equivalent of Dworkin or MacKinnon in France—but, as we saw earlier, censorship found other ways of justifying its continued presence in French society.

Among feminism's many positive achievements has been the emergence, from the 1970s onwards, of a female eroticism, written, like *Histoire d'O* and *Emmanuelle,* from a female viewpoint, but, unlike Réage's novel, addressing the growing economic and sexual independence of women and shunning the phallocentric sexual imagery that characterizes the style of Emmanuelle Arsan. The political and social revolution of 1968 was also a clear turning point for women's erotica: "In France, the link with the 1968 'events' seems unmistakable. 1968 launched the women's movement which, despite many feminists' hostility to erotica, has inspired more women to 'write themselves' in their own words, hence an unprecedented upsurge of erotic novels whose tone is altogether new."[80]

It is true that some female writers of the erotic, even in very recent times, have continued to ape their male counterparts, producing a pornographic literature for the male reader. *Fantasmes* by Aurélie Van Hoeymissen (1998), for instance, has strong Sadean echoes in its depiction of a fifteen-year-old girl who discovers the sexual power she is able to exert over her male teachers. Although inverting the genre's usual stereotype of male instructor–female student when it comes to sex, the novel nevertheless rehearses many themes familiar to readers of a predominantly male-centered genre: autoeroticism, lesbian initiation, instruction in heterosexual love techniques, and orgiastic initiation.[81] In the same year the male author Michel Houellebecq's *Particules élémentaires* (1998) reinforced the Sadean fantasy of a utopian world in which women are readily available and male satisfaction guaranteed. On the other hand, the last three decades have also seen the emergence of a large number of French women authors, writing about women's sexuality with women readers in mind. Some mainstream female novelists have increasingly emphasized eroticism in their work, making more explicit what were previously undercurrents: Marguerite Duras, for example, in *L'Homme assis dans le couloir* (1980) and *L'Amant* (1984) and Annie Ernaux in *Passions simples* (1991). Indeed, it is no exaggeration to say that the 1990s especially have seen an explosion of erotic creativity on the part of French women writers and filmmakers, many of whom wish to represent women's sexuality as active, autonomous, and self-determining. This trend is typified in the novel by Françoise Rey (*La Femme de papier* [1993]), Virginie Despentes (*Baise-moi* [1994]), Catherine Cusset (*Jouir* [1997]), and Catherine Millet (*La Vie sexuelle de Catherine M.* [2001]) and in the cinema by Catherine Breillat (*Romance* [1999]). The work of Alina Reyes is a particularly good example of this character of French women's erotic fiction in the contemporary period. Her first, highly successful novel, *Le Boucher* (1988), foregrounds the intense physicality and the ephemerality of erotic experience, occurring outside emotionally based relationships, and celebrates the erotic body, whether male or female, as fragmented and objectified like pieces of butcher's meat: "And the butcher who spoke to me of sex all day long was made of the same flesh, but warm, and soft and hard in turn; the butcher had his good and his lower parts, hard to please, eager to burn their life out, to transform themselves into meat. And my flesh was the same, as I felt the place between my legs grow hot at the butcher's words."[82]

Conclusion

In general, then, much twentieth-century erotic French literature appears superficially to repeat topoi and structures perfected by libertine writers. Modern erotic authors are heavily inspired by eighteenth-century texts rediscovered after more than a century of censorship (the championing of Sade by Apollinaire and the Surrealists at the beginning of the century is a good example of this trend, which many others will follow, including Aragon, Bataille, Réage, Klossowski, and Noël). As in the eighteenth century, this *ars erotica* tradition[83] is characterized by a concern especially with pedagogical as well as erotic aims (i.e., the spreading of sexual knowledge and the banishment of sexual ignorance and repression).[84] Many modern erotic novels also rehearse the familiar and long-established convention whereby young females are initiated into sexual experience by older men and women (e.g., *Emmanuelle*). Above and beyond these general similarities between modern and older traditions of an *ars erotic* in France, however, can be distinguished a number of important differences and innovations. If we are to summarize the main trends affecting the erotic and pornographic genre in France during the course of this century, four distinct changes stand out above all else.

First, and most important, *ars erotica* is redefined in the light of Freud's discovery of the unconscious, of infantile sexuality, and of the role of parents in the formation of our desires. The Surrealists were the first to explore the mine of the unconscious and see "l'amour fou" as a disruptive power that could unleash the repressed. Women thus began to lose their idealized status as objects of male veneration as mothers or virgins with no sexual desires of their own. Freud's investigations of human sexuality showed that women are just as sexual as men and are just as interested in writing about sex. Consequently, the male-centeredness of the genre gradually lessened, as more female authors began to write and publish erotic works dealing with female sexuality, pseudonymously to begin with (Dominique Aury writing as Pauline Réage, e.g., and the real identity of Emmanuelle Arsan is still unknown to all except her publisher) and eventually as openly as their male counterparts. More and more explicitly erotic works by women have appeared, especially during the 1990s (e.g., Reyes, Despentes, Rey, and Cusset).

Second, by the 1960s gay and lesbian works, written by and for gay men and women, began to appear more openly in France. The best-known and most talented of this wave of homosexual writers are Violette Leduc, Monique Wittig, Renaud Camus, and Tony Duvert.

Third, from the 1970s onward, French erotic fiction increasingly became a part (and some would say a very lucrative part) of mainstream literary production, and we can witness a gradual erosion of generic boundaries: between the literary genres of autobiography and fiction as much as between what is regarded as conventional and pornographic writing. For instance, there has been a burgeoning of self-confessional novels relating sexual experiences by established women writers (e.g., Duras, Ernaux, and Millet) in ways that have shocked some critics (passages in Duras's *L'Homme assis dans le couloir,* e.g., uncritically depicting female masochism outraged some of her feminist readers). Erotic writing has become informed by a plurality of discourses, addressing, for instance, the representation of love and sexuality in a manner that firmly establishes a broad appeal to the general (especially female) reader or reflecting aspects of social and political realities. This blurring of borderlines between genres is partly due to the increased influence of women writers in this area and partly to a desire on the part of writers to place representations of sexuality in a wider social context.

Fourth, and last, in part due to changing social mores and the decline of religious belief, direct forms of book censorship have virtually disappeared in France, although they have to some significant degree been replaced by indirect forms of censorship, less overt, more insidious. In spite of a certain idealized vision of Paris as the mecca of sexual freedom, even a cursory reading of the history of censorship in France suggests that, though perhaps comparing favorably in this area with the even more puritanical Anglo-Saxon world, the country of Robespierre and Napoléon, of Madame de Gaulle and the Brigade Mondaine, has a long tradition of rigid controls in publishing, and, though they may have lessened in the postwar period, we can still find striking instances of their damaging effects. Maurice Girodias, the head of the Olympia Press in Paris, was a spectacular casualty of the illiberal forces of Gaullist France: "By the mid–1960s, he had collected four to six years in suspended prison sentences, $80,000 in fines and an eighty-year ban on all publishing activity."[85] While a persuasive case can be made that, in this century in particular, censor and censored have at times enjoyed a parasitical and "mutually perpetuating" relationship, with prosecuted books attracting considerably more public interest,[86] censorship has also caused undeniable harm, both directly, in terms of the penalties imposed, and indirectly, in leading to the pre-censorship or self-censorship of authors and publishers anxious to avoid scandal or prosecution (an effect of censorship, which is obviously difficult if not impossible to measure).

Even at the beginning of the twenty-first century, censoring discourses are not entirely absent from the francophone world. A recent issue of the Swiss daily *Le Temps,* for example, devoted a double-page exposé to the increasing ubiquity of pornography in the media, drawing attention to the need to protect our children "dans cette ambiance de harcèlement libidinal" (in this atmosphere of libidinous harassment).[87] This exposé claims (1) that sexual imagery is omnipresent in the media and especially in advertising and magazines aimed at the young; (2) that such imagery focuses on fellatio and sodomy, practices not long ago considered taboo and perverse; and (3) that pornography inhabits a "harsh and violent universe" in which women are the victims. The article is replete with false assumptions (e.g., regarding the predominantly violent content of pornography or the "perverted" nature of certain consensual practices), but, above all, the dangers of such journalism lie in its underlying premise that the young inhabit a universe of sexual innocence that must be preserved from contamination by the "real world" (a premise curiously contradicted in another section of the feature by the admission that, "between 4 and 6 years of age, children are bursting with sexual excitement").

Such exposés in the popular European press are by no means rare in the current climate of concern about pornography, especially in relation to pedophilia, and literary pornography may serve a useful function here in helping to redress the balance of perspectives, providing opportunities for the safe exploration of the erotic in all its complexity, sometimes within the framework of loving relationships but also outside the norms of sexual behavior established by contemporary social and political discourse. It is in this sense that all pornography continues to play a transgressive role, both at a political and a personal level, and we have seen that French literary pornography, in particular, has preeminently played this role for centuries. Pornography is still a "limit" genre in more than one sense: on the one hand, in the potential it offers as an antiestablishment discourse for the evolution of new forms and new ideas and, on the other, as a uniquely powerful medium for the emancipation of thinking about sexuality and the creative representation of sexual desire.

Notes

1. Much of the material in this essay appeared in a different form in my book *Forbidden Fictions: Pornography and Censorship in Twentieth-Century French Literature* (London: Pluto Press, 1999). I am grateful to the publishers for permission to reproduce this material here.
2. By the mid-eighteenth century French publications predominated in the genre; see Lynn Hunt, "Obscenity and the Origins of Modernity: 1500–1800," in *Feminism and Pornography,* ed. Drucilla Cornell (Oxford: Oxford University Press, 2000), 370.
3. The word *pornography* and its derivatives are used descriptively, but not pejoratively, in this essay to denote any writing that transgresses sexual taboos with the sole aim of exciting the reader sexually.
4. See Linda Williams, "Second Thoughts on Hard Core: American Obscenity Law and the Scapegoating of Deviance," in *Dirty Looks: Women, Pornography, Power,* ed. Pamela Church Gibson and Roma Gibson (London: BFI Publishing, 1993), 47 n. 1.
5. Susan Sontag, "The Pornographic Imagination," in *Perspectives on Pornography,* ed. Douglas A. Hughes (New York: St. Martin's Press, 1970), 153–154.
6. The Obscene Publications Act, 1959.
7. See Williams, "Second Thoughts," 48–49.
8. See Williams, "Second Thoughts," 54.
9. John de St. Jorre, *The Good Ship Venus: The Erotic Voyage of the Olympia Press and Its Writers* (London: Pimlico, 1994), preface.
10. The best known of these were Henry Miller's *Tropic of Cancer* and *Tropic of Capricorn;* Samuel Beckett's trilogy, *Molloy, Malone Dies,* and *The Unnamable;* J. P. Donleavy's *The Ginger Man;* Vladimir Nabokov's *Lolita;* Pauline Réage's *Story of O* (published in English and French); and William Burrough's *Naked Lunch.* For a full and fascinating account of the history of the Olympia Press, see de St. Jorre, *Good Ship Venus.*

11. Even publication in Paris by an American author was risky: Vladimir Nabokov, for instance, initially wanted the Olympia publication of *Lolita* to appear under a pseudonym for fear of losing his teaching job at Cornell University; see de St. Jorre, *Good Ship Venus,* 125.

12. See Robert Netz, *Histoire de la censure dans l'édition* (Paris: PUF, 1997), 13.

13. Between 1678 and 1701, for example, roughly half the books seized had religious contents, with very few concerning the internal politics of Louis XIV; see Netz, *Histoire de la censure dans l'édition,* 37.

14. Netz, *Histoire de la censure dans l'édition,* 45.

15. The best account in English of the trade in forbidden books in eighteenth-century France is Robert Darnton, *The Forbidden Best-Sellers of Pre-Revolutionary France* (London: HarperCollins, 1996).

16. Darnton, *Forbidden Best-Sellers of Pre-Revolutionary France,* 87.

17. See Darnton, *Forbidden Best-Sellers of Pre-Revolutionary France,* 169–246, for a detailed analysis of the political power of the printed word. Although, as Darnton himself concedes, the hypothesis of a causal link between the printed word and political radicalism is difficult to prove, there is some evidence that the French authorities believed in it: in 1823 *Les Liaisons dangereuses,* which had appeared in 1782, was condemned to be destroyed by a Paris court for having helped cause the Revolution of 1789; see Nicholas Harrison, *Circles of Censorship: Censorship and Its Metaphors in French History, Literature, and Theory* (Oxford: Oxford University Press, 1996), 28.

18. Netz, *Histoire de la censure,* 75.

19. Netz, *Histoire de la censure,* 85.

20. Cited by Netz, *Histoire de la censure,* 91.

21. See Harrison, *Circles of Censorship,* 53.

22. See Netz, *Histoire de la censure,* 90–91. From the seventeenth century onward the advance of pornography was closely linked to the development of the novel in France, so that, by the end of the 1740s, pornography had espoused novelistic forms and both traditions were well established. Indeed, both pornography and the novel were attacked for inciting desire, and both were often associated with libertinism; see Hunt, "Obscenity and the Origins of Modernity," 367–371.

23. The Index Librorum Prohibitorum was not officially ended until 1965; see Harrison, *Circles of Censorship,* 11.

24. Netz points out that, far from constituting a "wave of pornography," only twenty-one books per annum on average ended up in the Bibliothèque Nationale's "Enfer" between 1890 and 1912 (*Histoire de la censure,* 99).

25. See Netz, *Histoire de la censure,* 98.

26. See Netz, *Histoire de la censure,* 111–113, for the detail of this legislation and its effects.

27. See de St. Jorre, *Good Ship Venus,* 67.

28. See Netz, *Histoire de la censure,* 116.

29. *Magazine Littéraire,* no. 37 (February 1970).

30. For a detailed discussion of the "Guyotat Affair," see Harrison, *Circles of Censorship,* 174–180.

31. See Netz, *Histoire de la censure,* 117.

32. See Netz, *Histoire de la censure,* 117–118.

33. Jean-Jacques Pauvert, *Nouveaux visages de la censure* (Paris: Les Belles Lettres, 1994), 188.

34. Pauvert, *Nouveaux visages de la censure,* 189.

35. Hugh Dauncey, summarizing Girodias's views in "Publishing, Pornography, and Personal Freedom: L'Affaire Dreyfus, l'Affaire Miller, l'Affaire Lolita, and l'Affaire Kissinger," *French Cultural Studies* 3 (1992): 208.

36. See Dauncey, *French Cultural Studies,* 2.

37. See Lucienne Frappier-Mazur, "Marginal Canons: Rewriting the Erotic," *Yale French Studies* 75 (1988): 119.

38. For a detailed account of this process, see Vernon A. Rosario, *The Erotic Imagination: French Histories of Perversity* (New York: Oxford University Press, 1997).

39. See Jean-Jacques Pauvert, *Anthologie historique des lectures érotiques. De Guillaume Apollinaire à Philippe Pétain, 1905–1944* (Paris: Stock/Spengler, 1995), 8.

40. See Pauvert, *Anthologie,* 15.

41. "Les Maîtres de l'amour," Bibliothèque des Curieux.

42. *L'Oeuvre du Marquis de Sade* (Paris: Bibliothèque des Curieux, 1909).

43. Guillaume Apollinaire, Fernand Fleuret, and Louis Perceau, *L'Enfer de la Bibliothèque Nationale* (Paris: Mercure de France, 1913).

44. Pascal Pia, in *Apollinaire,* "Écrivains de toujours" (Paris: Seuil, 1965), practically ignores the poet's pornographic output, merely observing that the two erotic novels were written to make much needed money, while Julia Hartwig (*Apollinaire* [Paris: Mercure de France, 1972]) suggests that these pseudonymously published works have little artistic merit and respect for their author will prevent them from ever seeing the light of day.

45. In Apollinaire's best-known collection of poetry, *Alcools,* for instance, there are many instances of erotic imagery, such as this potentially blasphemous yet visually amusing and delightfully original image from *L'Ermite:* "O Seigneur, flagellez les nuées du coucher / Qui vous tendent au ciel de si jolis culs roses" (O Lord, flagellate the clouds of sunset / That thrust such pretty pink arses at you in heaven).

46. Robert Desnos, qtd. by Pauvert, *Anthologie,* 76; my trans.

47. Preface to a clandestine edition of *Les Onze mille verges,* ed. René Bonnel in 1930, and qtd. in Jean-Jacques Pauvert, "Un Pornographe ou les deux Guillaume," *Magazine Littéraire* (November 1996): 50; my trans.

48. Apollinaire was accused of stealing the *Mona Lisa* and imprisoned for six days in 1911. He was briefly famous for this and almost thrown out of the country.

49. The erotic was certainly not a peripheral activity for Louÿs: his heirs discovered four hundred kilos of erotic writings on his death, a recently published anthology of his work in the genre covering more than a thousand pages; see Jean-Paul Goujon, ed., *Pierre Louÿs: L'Oeuvre érotique* (Paris: Sortilèges, 1994), xvii. Louÿs's interest in the history of eroticism as evidenced by the many unpublished works he wrote on the subject, led Goujon to describe him as a "real encyclopedist of sex" (xxix); see also Sarane Alexandrian, *Histoire de la littérature érotique* (Paris: Payot, 1995), 291.

50. See Goujon, *Pierre Louÿs,* xxx.

51. See Frappier-Mazur, "Marginal Canons," 116 n. 13.

52. Goujon, *Pierre Louÿs,* xxviii.

53. Stephen Heath, *The Sexual Fix* (London: Macmillan, 1982), 107.

54. Raymond Queneau's tomboyish young heroine in his classic novel, *Zazie dans le métro.*

55. Goujon, *Pierre Louÿs,* xxx; my trans.

56. It was Jean-Jacques Rousseau who coined this expression in the eighteenth century to denote pornographic novels, read as masturbatory aids; see Jean-Marie Goulemot,

Forbidden Texts: Erotic Literature and Its Readers in Eighteenth-Century France (London: Polity Press, 1994), x; originally published as *Ces livres qu'on ne lit que d'une main* (Paris: Éditions Alinea, 1991).

57. Since the eighteenth century, in particular, the erotic genre in France has shown strong ludic tendencies; witness, for example, the parodic mises en scène of Nerciat's *Le Doctorat impromptu,* Diderot's *Les Bijoux indiscrets,* or Crébillon fils's *Le Sopha,* not to mention the many linguistic and formal innovations to be found in Sade's fictions.

58. Alongside these works by Apollinaire and Louÿs, Louis Aragon's *Le Con d'Irène* (1928) is worthy of mention: an explicit yet sensitive portrayal of an invalid's sexual frustrations, Aragon's complex novel is probably one of the best examples of French literary pornography of the period.

59. Georges Bataille, *Oeuvres complètes,* vol. 1 (Paris: Gallimard, 1970).

60. Susan Rubin Suleiman, "Pornography and the Avant-Garde," in *The Poetics of Gender,* ed. Nancy K. Miller (New York: Columbia University Press, 1986), 118.

61. Susan Sontag, "The Pornographic Imagination," *Story of the Eye* (London: Penguin, 1982), 106 and 111; also in Douglas A. Hughes, ed., *Perspectives on Pornography* (New York: Macmillan and St. Martin's Press, 1970), 131–169.

62. Michael Richardson, *Georges Bataille* (London: Routledge, 1994), 3.

63. Bataille never held a university post.

64. Richardson refers to the "violent swings of his personality"; for this critic the author's surreal and perplexing compositions, "L'Anus solaire" and "L'Oeil pinéal," "bear witness to his disturbed state, which caused him to seek treatment with the psychoanalyst, Adrian Borel" (Richardson, *Bataille,* 20). He certainly liked to live life on the edge, experimenting with Russian roulette and blood sacrifice. In the 1930s he founded the magazine *Acéphale,* which gave rise to a secret society of the same name. It was rumored that the members planned human sacrifices, though there is no evidence that any were actually performed (see Alain Arnaud and Gisèle Excoffon-Lafarge, *Bataille,* "Écrivains de toujours" [Paris: Seuil, 1978], 18).

65. Georges Bataille, *L'Érotisme* (Paris: Minuit, 1957), 48.

66. Other pornographic works by Bataille include *Ma mère, Le Bleu du ciel, Le Mort, Madame Edwarda,* and *Les Larmes d'Eros.*

67. See Frappier-Mazur, "Marginal Canons," 123. The final stage of this evolution is presumably the representation of female sexuality from the female standpoint and for the female reader.

68. Andrea Dworkin, *Pornography: Men Possessing Women* (London: Women's Press Ltd., 1981), 34.

69. See Pauvert, *Anthologie,* 10.

70. See Pauvert, *Anthologie,* 27.

71. It is true that previous French writers had written and published novels with homoerotic themes. Indeed, there is a long tradition of homosexual writing in France, the twentieth century being particularly rich in this kind of literature. From Marcel Proust to André Gide, from Jean Cocteau to Jean Genet, homosexual themes run through the work of some of the century's major French authors. But few of these works were as explicit as those of this permissive era.

72. Christopher Robinson, *Scandal in the Ink: Male and Female Homosexuality in Twentieth-Century French Literature* (London: Cassell, 1995), 70.

73. See Robinson, *Scandal in the Ink,* 78.

74. It appears that public opinion was more hostile in 1975 than in 1968; see Robinson, *Scandal in the Ink,* 30.

75. The homosexual text is perhaps the best example of writing censored by critical authority in France during the latter half of the twentieth century. Robinson argues that critics have either played down or ignored homosexual elements in the life and work of writers such as Proust and Gide or, if they have acknowledged them, have linked them to perversion and criminality; see Robinson, *Scandal in the Ink,* vii. Indeed, Robinson suggests that gay Catholic writers such as Julien Green and Marcel Jouhandeau have been critically marginalized in favor of straight Catholic writers such as Bernanos and Mauriac, whom Robinson considers much less interesting from an aesthetic point of view (Robinson, *Scandal in the Ink,* 92 n. 7). This is less surprising when placed in the wider context of societal attitudes to the homosexual in general; as late as the 1960s, for instance, homosexuality was considered an illness that medicine could cure (see Porot, *Manuel alphabétique de psychiatrie* [1960], cited by Robinson, *Scandal in the Ink,* 20).

76. For Robinson "Proust, Cocteau and Genet all work to the same stereotype of maleness, one which by definition consigns the homosexual to an inferior 'feminine' role" (Robinson, *Scandal in the Ink,* 71).

77. See E. Apter, *André Gide and the Codes of Homotextuality* (Stanford: Anma Libri, 1987); and Owen Heathcote, "Masochism, Sadism and Homotextuality: The Examples of Yukio Mishima and Eric Jourdan," *Paragraph* 17, no. 2 (July 1994): 174–189.

78. I am referring, in particular, to the work of Butler and Sedgwick; see, for example, Judith Butler, *Bodies That Matter: On the Discursive Limits of Sex* (London: Routledge, 1993); and Eve Kosofsky Sedgwick, *Tendencies* (London: Routledge, 1994).

79. François Lyotard, *The Postmodern Condition* (Manchester: Manchester University Press, 1984); originally published in French as *La Condition postmoderne* (Paris: Les Éditions de Minuit, 1979).

80. Frappier-Mazur, "Marginal Canons," 120.

81. Sade's Juliette and the guileless Eugénie, from his *La Philosophie dans le boudoir,* are unmistakable models.

82. Alina Reyes, *Le Boucher* (Paris: Seuil, Points, 1988), 11; my trans.

83. My argument challenges Foucault's hypothesis that there is no modern *ars erotica* in the West but only a *scientia sexualis.*

84. From the sixteenth century this literature develops pedagogical functions, analogous to those found in works of the Orient, a pedagogy that helps erotic writing to get through the screen of censorship. This pedagogical character is obvious in the titles of works: *L'École des filles, L'Académie des dames, Le Doctorat impromptu, L'Éducation de Laure, La Philosophie dans le boudoir, L'École des biches, L'Éducateur.* . . . Throughout the eighteenth century love is not represented as a primitive instinct but as an art that can be learned—hence, the great number of libertine "romans d'apprentissage." This trend continues in the twentieth century. For example, in *Roberte, ce soir,* the central volume of Pierre Klossowski's trilogy, *Les Lois de l'hospitalité* (1965), the text explores the triangularity of desire (subject, object, mediator) in scenarios in which the partner is given or lent. The novel also exemplifies a pedagogical structure that dates back to the sixteenth century.

85. De St. Jorre, *Good Ship Venus,* 273.

86. This is the main thesis of Harrison's *Circles of Censorship.*

87. *Le Temps,* 17 December 2002, 2–3.

A Perfectly British Business

STAGNATION, CONTINUITIES, AND CHANGE ON THE TOP SHELF

CLARISSA SMITH

It used to be complaints about scantily clad ladies in provocative poses, but now opponents of girlie magazines are applauding the accumulation of dust on British newsagents' top shelves as sales of soft-core plummet. In defiance of the claims of antiporn campaigners that pornography can only proliferate if allowed high street outlets, this branch of sexually explicit production seems to have had its day. All the major UK publishers have felt the effects of waning sales and diminishing profits as "top-shelf lovelies" have been replaced by more profitable sandwiches in high street newsagents. The decline of the girlie magazine could simply be ascribed to competition from new media formats, but the picture is more complex than a linear movement of consumer preference from page to screen. Research and debate about "pornography" have tended to favor exploration of content and effects, ignoring investigation of the market and the political and institutional frameworks that determine the professional production of top-shelf magazines: the economics of the trade are generally judged to be exploitative and therefore to be condemned, not investigated. Thus, very little reliable empirical and statistical evidence exists.

In the twilight zone, regulated and curtailed by a legal system that grudgingly acknowledges profitability but not probity, soft-core pornography has rarely been considered as a business. The details of who owns what; the production contexts of girlie magazine publishing; and the costs of staffing a magazine, commissioning articles and photography, and preparing layout, print, and distribution are discussed only in the context of scandalized exposés of the possible harms of smut for profit. Traditionally, discussions of pornography have failed to engage directly with either the producers of pornography, except as the vilified and shadowy figure of the "pornographer," or readers of such material except where those readers "confess" to the ways in which pornography has contributed to their corruption.[1] Where women's voices have featured in accounts of the pornography industry, it has generally been as victims either of its production processes or of its use in social or personal situations.[2] These accounts, with their attendant focus on the "harms" of pornography, have also tended to sediment the gender divisions of "male perpetrator" and "female victim" so that pornography has achieved dubious status as *the* subordinating representational regime underpinning patriarchy. The central characters in the pornography drama have not, of course, gone unchallenged, but, where authors have raised important questions about porn's monolithic status within academic, legal, and social discussion, their interventions are not problem free. They tend to valorize certain "transgressive" practices of producing and using pornography, thereby contributing to a further hierarchizing of desire with "radical" or politicized porn at the top and the more mundane and widespread use of mass-market porn at the bottom. The recuperation of some producers as "sex radicals" does not illuminate the more mundane activities of the "pornocrats"—those publishers whose intentions are not taboo busting for political ends but, rather, for economic rewards.

Beyond being an object of concern, pornography is a continuously expanding phenomenon, constantly able to "reinvent" itself (although the extent to which its favorite representational tropes are reinvented is the subject of some dispute), utilizing new technologies such as CD-ROM, video, and the Internet in order to reach ever more consumers. The exploitation of new technology is matched by an ability to cater to increasingly specialized markets: for example, the rise of materials addressed to gay and lesbian consumers and the growth of sadomasochism (S-M) materials. These expansions have seen pornography move from a very narrow availability to what at times seems like very mainstream acceptability.[3] Although its expansion is a fascinating area for exploration and investigation, I focus here on stories of stagnation and contraction: one high-profile publisher has recently proclaimed the death of the UK's traditional soft-core business.[4]

This essay focuses on one sexually explicit media form: British soft-core publications available at high street newsagents.[5] The UK pornographic publishing market can be divided into two spheres: material that does not violate current laws in force (i.e., legal material) and everything else. My concern here is the legally available material easily accessible through the network of newsagents throughout the United Kingdom. In the past two years the soft-core scene in Britain has changed substantially with the decision by the British Board of Film Certification (BBFC) to pass seven explicit videos for R18 certification on appeal.[6] This has meant that sex shops are finally able to sell explicit and close-up shots of actual penetration; in line with this relaxation of the BBFC guidelines has been a major increase in the number of hard-core magazine titles on sex shop shelves. These magazines are excluded from my discussion here as they are primarily confined to licensed premises rather than the high street newsagents.[7] Material available on the top shelf in Britain is still the softest soft-core in Europe, and my focus here is limited to the traditional adult magazines featuring glamour pictures of women (usually alone but sometimes with a female partner) in various states of undress.

In delineating my area of study, I take an industry classification rather than a definition derived from moral or aesthetic discourses. By focusing on one narrow (and peculiarly British) section of the adult trade, I am attempting an analysis that recognizes the specificities of individual pornographic forms and their commercial determinants.[8] This position can be defended by noting Linda Williams's comments on the scarcity of writing about "actual texts" that has led to the polarization of the debates such that pornography is either totally divisible from or entirely conterminous with other forms of cultural production.[9] Williams observes that "pornography may not be special, but it does have a specificity distinct from other genres."[10] That specificity lies in its representational intention to arouse its viewers/readers sexually, and it is this quality that sets porn as a genre apart even as it might share some of the representational tropes of more "mainstream" or "respectable" forms. Studies of sexually explicit material often flatten out the medium-specific qualities of, for example, video or photography in order to make the generalizable case about pornography. This categorization has produced an essentialist tendency that finds continuities and uniformity of content in material ranging, for example, from photographic images of children to depictions of sexual activities between consenting adults in videos marketed to gay men. The concentration or distillation of the "essence of pornography" distorts the ways in which we could understand the production and uses of individual forms of sexually explicit materials,[11] leading to claims such as Simon Hardy's that "the appearance of colourful diversity belies uniformity of content and quality and the fact that, like brands of washing powder, 'top-shelf' magazines are almost all owned by the same two or three parties."[12] Like washing powder and many other mass-produced commodities, pornography suffers from a surfeit of contempt that manifests itself in characterizations of the category's homogeneity and, following from that, the uniformity of possible responses to, or expectations of, its subsets. However much the products may appear alike on the shelves, this cannot be an indication of the ways they are used once removed from there. Although issues relating to content and consumption are not for discussion here, the accusations of banality are precisely symptoms of the tendency, found in theory as well as "commonsense" discourse, to produce pornography as genre and form without boundaries, thereby avoiding the material elements of its production and reception in favor of its social role as the repository for all things abhorrent. Accusations of misogyny and the corrosive influence of big business are often deemed sufficient analysis of material production.

The magazines on the top shelf in the United Kingdom are, and have been, predominately aimed at a heterosexual, male market, but there have been brief forays into publishing for heterosexual women and, more successfully, gay men. British porn is produced by big businesses responsible for most of the titles on the shelves: the top producers rank amongst the United Kingdom's top 150 publishers and between them account for more than 85 percent of magazine production.[13] Apparently, for many commentators this is all we need to know. Little is understood about the organizational and institutional priorities of these companies, nor is there much understanding of the role of smaller, independent publishing operations that contributed to a buck-the-trend growth of the market during the 1990s, but who needs to know about the activities of pornographers?

Yet the dimensions of production are vitally important to comprehending the cultural significance of sexually explicit media. Like any other media business, top-shelf magazines are organized around what Joel Best has called the "standard industrial processes of production, distribution and consumption," and in each of these areas a range of regulating agencies supervises the business.[14] Porn publishers, their products, and their customers must negotiate with the discourses that circulate, both to limit and to produce pornography as texts, because pornography has no existence outside of the cultural sphere in which it is produced, circulated, and consumed. It is this focus that I attempt to bring to the fore in this essay by examining the circumstances of top-shelf publishing, its legal and social pressures, and its profits. That pornography makes a profit is indisputable (although the levels of profit are hotly disputed) and is "frequently used as condemnation of it."[15] As a manufactured item exchanged for cash, pornography's profitability is often seen as a measure of its offensiveness.[16] Thus, the current crisis in publishing will seem a matter for celebration by many commentators and academics, but, as they cheer, we are still no closer to understanding the particular structures, imperatives, and regulation of the industry.

The UK Porn Markets

Currently, the United Kingdom's pornography industry is primarily regulated under the provisions of five laws: the 1876 Customs Consolidation Act prohibits the importation of "indecent" materials; the 1953 Post Office Act forbids the distribution of indecent or obscene materials via the post; the 1959 Obscene Publications Act (OPA) prohibits the depiction of actual sexual activity and any other images deemed obscene; the 1978 Child Protection Act makes it an offense to produce or possess any material featuring any sexual depiction of a child; and the 1984 Video Recordings Act ensures all video films are subject to the classification procedures of the British Board of Film Certification—an 18R certificate can be given for depictions of sex to be sold only in sex shops. The definitions underpinning these laws are notoriously slippery: what constitutes the obscene and indecent are largely left to the discretion of the officials who oversee the enforcement of the statutes' provisions.[17] This legislation in large part designates and/or creates the category "pornography," however, and helps to formulate the boundaries that restrain producers' activities and their products.

It is difficult to obtain information, exact or otherwise, on circulation figures, costs, and trends, but commentators on UK porn agree that the production of soft-core publications expanded during the late 1960s and early 1970s.[18] This expansion was encouraged by the success of the American magazines *Playboy* and *Penthouse,* increasingly liberal attitudes to sexual representation, and an economic climate that favored free market entrepreneurs. In 1976 top-selling titles could expect circulation figures in excess of 400,000. In the past decade the market has been estimated at perhaps 10 to 15 percent of all magazine revenue, with a value of £100–150 million. Despite the high revenue, it is also estimated that regular readers account for no more than 6 to 8 percent of the UK male population.[19]

Although soft-core/adult magazines for men performed well during the 1980s, unit sales for individual titles have plummeted since their 1970s' heyday: in 1971 *Playboy* sold 90,000 copies per month in the United Kingdom; it now barely manages a quarter of that, and, if some insiders are to be believed, its sales are as low as 5,000 copies per month. The fall in circulation could be a result of *Playboy*'s increasingly outmoded personality and its American style, but homegrown publications have also had to contend with falling circulation figures. Sales of *Fiesta,* for example, dropped from 238,000 in 1991 to 162,000 in 1996.[20] While the total number of magazines may have increased—an estimated one hundred titles are now produced—individual titles are no longer the cash cows they once were.[21]

Everybody's at It!

In his excavation of the 1990s nostalgic return to the 1970s, Leon Hunt examines the "permissive populism" of British "low culture" of the period, arguing that "permissive populism" offered a "parody" of 1960s liberationist discourses on sex.[22] There are significant problems, as Hunt points out, in delineating particular periods as culturally, politically, and economically self-contained—the 1970s are often described as a time of crisis, while popular culture of the period displayed "an optimism at odds with this impending chaos."[23] Linking the two, according to Hunt, are the expectations of the baby boomers, "the belief that the 'permissive' legacy of the 1960s would manifest itself in a more democratically distributed form. This vulgar hedonism could be found in tabloid populism, not least in its appropriation of pornography and 'sex education' guides, television light entertainment, widely distributed sexploitation films, all testifying to a mythology of lowbrow (male) sexual 'liberation.'"[24] The latter half of the 1970s saw the expansion of Britain's porn industries within Soho and into the provinces: Soho had "54 sex shops; 39 sex cinemas and cinema clubs; 16 strip and peep shows; 11 sex-orientated clubs; and 12 licensed massage parlours."[25] David Sullivan opened the first of his Private Shops in 1978 with plans to expand throughout the British Isles. Sexually explicit materials also became more commonplace and mainstream.[26] The expansion of such materials during this time seems at odds with the facts of British censorship laws, which are generally held to be the most restrictive in Europe.[27] Hunt suggests that the industry's success was due to "the Pornocrats work[ing] *with* capitalism" and that the law was on the side of the publishers in that its inconsistencies and loopholes meant prosecution was difficult and its results uncertain.[28] Yet prosecutions, at least the most high-profile ones, were not aimed at porn publishers per se; in fact, many of the cause célèbres of the 1960s and 1970s featured works of literary merit, or at least that was the defense offered in court. The novels *Lady Chatterley's Lover* and *Last Exit to Brooklyn* were both prosecuted, for example, as were *Oz* and *Suck* magazines. None of these belonged to the low culture brand of top-shelf publications; rather, these were high art or revolutionary publications prosecuted precisely because their emphasis was not on sexual arousal but on "unsettling" themes.[29] There is no space to catalog the period's landmark cases here; it is important to recognize, however, that these cases symbolized for many people the inconsistencies of convictions (juries' decisions were often overturned by the Court of Appeal), but they also galvanized a sense of grievance and opposition to the nanny state that porn publishers then used to justify their own publications. Moreover, these cases introduced the idea that artistic intention removed indecency and/or obscenity, further inscribing the cultural high/low split with a legal definition of merit and confirming for some that there was one law for the arty liberati and another for Joe Bloggs, who just liked looking at girls.[30]

Thus, the permissive legislative moment confirmed the social experience of many that liberation, especially sexual liberation, was something experienced by those wealthy and educated enough to enjoy its highbrow manifestations. The joke that if you remember the 1960s you weren't there is part of a cultural history that celebrates experiences only ever shared by a small urban elite. The 1970s saw popular culture's "negotiation" of the 1960s (particularly sexual) revolution. As Hunt argues, "permissiveness left a lot of people behind, but 'trickled down' in the 1970s, albeit in a rather different form. . . . the real legacy of permissiveness was to be found in Soho, not the Royal Court Theatre."[31] Nowhere was this trend more evident than in soft-core publishing; the 1960s had belonged to *Playboy,* the American import featuring beautiful women, "entertainment served up with humor, sophistication, and spice," and which encouraged the aspirations of its readers. This had been followed by *Penthouse,* an imitator of the successful *Playboy* format, launched in the United Kingdom without the philosophizing of the original and with a determined intent to better *Playboy* by exposing the parts its precursor dared not show. The following decade saw an explosion of sexual material in the United Kingdom; encouraged by the law's concentration on the radical press, sex entrepreneurs expanded their interests: "With the police busy battling against the radical press, with the liberalizing effect of the Obscene Publications Act, a less strict attitude to morals and the emergence of the permissive society, and with the law in a confused and uncertain state, the pornography trade was able to continue expanding at a steady rate relatively unhindered."[32]

The activities of the Dirty Squad (the Metropolitan Police's Obscene Publications Squad) were instrumental in this development: bribery and protection rackets allowed sex shops, cinemas, and publishing to flourish in Soho and its immediate environs.[33] The expansion of the red-light area in Soho was also aided by the relaxation of laws in Denmark and Sweden, enabling a relatively easy supply of material from the Continent. Customs and excise figures are indications of the increasing importation of sexually explicit materials from Scandinavia: in 1960 they had impounded fifty-six hundred books and magazines; the figure was well over two million in 1969.[34] Imported goods have their market, but it was not long before the number of homegrown publications grew to meet demand. Copying formats tried and tested in the United States, Paul Raymond and David Sullivan became household names, and the magazines *Men Only, Club International,* and *Playbirds* had arrived. Each title offered its readers its own special brand of girls and sexual hedonism; critics may be keen to see homogeneity among the titles, but, in fact, purchasers and readers of top-shelf magazines do exercise discrimination in their choice of individual titles. As with any other publication, distinctiveness is a marketing tool, thus content, type of models used, poses adopted, form and tenor of stories, brand of humor, and style of cartoons differentiate the various magazines on the top shelf. In Britain that distinctiveness is most determined by taste and by representational vocabularies of feminine sexuality ranging from ordinary women (readers' wives) to fantasy women (celebrity or glamour girls).

None of the homegrown titles featured what could be considered hard-core pornography, but, as the 1960s and 1970s progressed, there was a race to expose more and more flesh, then pubic hair, and finally gynecological detail. The most enthusiastic of the exposers was David Sullivan, whose two-fingered salute to moral campaigners in the naming of one of his titles *Whitehouse* signaled a determination to exceed the explicitness and daring of his rivals.[35] His titles have continued to operate at what many consider to be the lowest taste level of the top shelf featuring "ordinary" British girls in "strong" poses, thus, as Hunt suggests, the class connotations were very different: "Sullivan's magazines hinted at the upward mobility of the aspiring pornocrat, but solicited an impatient working class 'punter' who wanted the goods delivered at an aggressively lower price. The 'Readers' Wives'—Sullivan's invention—grew out of this ethos."[36] Sullivan has also been likened to Larry Flynt as a tireless champion of the right to publish soft-core and certainly has fought more than his fair share of battles against customs and the police. If *Playboy* and *Penthouse* represent the highbrow of porn publishing, Sullivan's titles have certainly been considered their low Other.

Developments in pornographic publishing have not only gone hand in hand with the attempts to censor or prevent them but have *produced* the very voices that would call for their closure. As Hunt notes, both Bill Thompson and Mary Whitehouse place 1976 as the turning point in porn's fortunes with the failure to prosecute *Inside Linda Lovelace*.[37] At the same time that the porn industry seemed to receive a green light, the "silent majority" received a wake-up call. As the floodgates appeared to be open for a sex shop on every street corner, the Festival of Light and other groups were rallied to oppose porn's march into the suburbs. Feminist arguments against porn were increasingly useful to the moral campaigners, as were the fears of "ordinary" members of the public who were upset at the proliferation of evidence throughout the United Kingdom of the industrialization of sex. As Laurence O'Toole comments, "With neon-lit porn shops setting up near to schools in the heart of middle England, it was only a matter of time before the law bit back."[38] Significantly, moralists had begun to change course on pornography: they had begun to understand that public standards had moved away from the condemnation of heterosexual activities between consenting adults. As Thompson notes:

> they abandon[ed] their public morals rationale against commercial sex in favour of the highly emotive protection of children approach, and to abandon the attempt to utilize the 1959 Act in favour of gaining alternative legislation which outlawed material without the need to go to court. . . . Within a decade they had obtained the Indecent Displays (Control) Act

1981, which curtailed sexual advertisement; the Cinematographic Acts 1982 and 1985, which eliminated sex cinemas; the Video Recordings Act 1984, which reintroduced the concept of pre-censorship into Britain. . . . The most important measure, however, was Clause 3 of the Local Government (Miscellaneous Provisions) Act 1982, which closed hundreds of sex shops and ensured that newsagents became the major suppliers.[39]

The focus on the child as the innocent victim of pornographic publishing was a masterstroke for the campaigners and effectively put publishers on the defensive. In 1980s Britain popular fears about the proliferation of new broadcast media forms through satellite, digital, and online technologies were mobilized toward a new "morality." Fears about new media forms were not, of course, new, and since the 1960s various moral campaign groups had been actively highlighting supposed links between increased levels of "sex and violence" on TV and actual levels of crime.[40] They had also been instrumental in drawing attention to the ways in which "permissiveness" generally was contributing to a decline in morals and the "British way of life." Although the media forms that felt the full effects of moral censure were produced for adult consumption, at the heart of the calls for regulation and censorship were fears about effects on children and the breakdown of the "family"—fears underpinned by homophobia, racism, and the scapegoating of single mothers. A larger history of these fears and debates is not possible here, but successive Conservative governments of the 1980s and 1990s made attempts to revive the nation's sexual morality. These attempts were not without their setbacks, most famously perhaps in the damage done to the "Back to Basics" crusade by evidence of successive Tory government ministers' marital infidelities. More significant than the indiscretions of Tory MPs was the pragmatism of the Thatcherite administration, which often "sacrificed" moral concerns to the broader aims of deregulation and economic liberalism. The populist family values employed in Tory rhetoric were harnessed to that party's general desire to reduce state intervention in both public and private spheres.[41] These two imperatives were sometimes at odds: for example, the government, while welcoming the increased consumer choice and free market possibilities of digital and satellite broadcasting technologies, was unable to countenance the beaming in of the sexually explicit Red Hot Dutch from the Continent to British televisions. Censorship was achieved by banning the advertising and sale of the decoders necessary to receive the station's programming in the United Kingdom.

Concerns over sexually explicit media were not limited to the Right. High-profile campaigns against "pornography and male violence" were also led by Labour MPs and Left-leaning women's groups—for example, Claire Short's 1980s campaign against Page 3,[42] and the Location of Pornographic Materials Bill introduced to Parliament by Dawn Primarolo in 1990 as well as the feminist campaigns "Take Back the Night" and "Off the Shelf." These campaigns used feminist analyses of heterosexuality to mount their critiques and did not limit their demands to banning or reducing availability of sexually explicit materials; they also questioned the moral sanctity of heterosexuality and men's sexual access to women. As

Thompson and others have pointed out, in both the United States and the United Kingdom an uneasy alliance has been forged between the forces of the Right and feminist groups, although the latter would deny that there are formal links, and the former make every effort to distance themselves from the radical critique of heterosexuality. Where the two overlap is in their assertions of pornography's degradation and harm to women and children.[43]

Although the successes of moral and feminist campaigners have been uneven, a number of legislative actions were taken against the production and distribution of sexual materials in Britain throughout the late 1970s and early 1980s. Action against sex shops may well have deflected attention away from the content of the magazines being sold in newsagents across the country. As O'Toole remarks, "British soft-core magazines have become an accepted, if neglected, part of the magazine landscape."[44] Central to this acceptance/neglect has been publishers' willingness to practice self-restraint—a custom O'Toole criticizes as a kind of pragmatic hypocrisy, drawing attention to the industry's claims to be part of a liberated sexual sphere at the same time as it accedes to the requirements of the law as protection from better porn produced in Europe and beyond:[45]

> What is commercial censorship has been masquerading for many years now as moral and legal censorship. The "angle of the dangle"—the notion that a free-standing penis in a photograph may not rise above a certain angle—is not written in law; it is agreed by four parties—the police, the distributors, the magazine publishers and various lawyers—all of whom seem happy for the arrangement to continue. When an editor at *For Women* says that she'd love to show erections but the law won't let her, this is not telling the whole story. It's ironic that mainstream soft-core porners in Britain have in effect taken to hiding behind the law. For so long, porn searched for alibis to excuse and justify itself before the courts. Nowadays, soft-core finds that its alibi for not evolving, for not delivering, actually resides within the law.[46]

I have some sympathy with that analysis, at least in its pointing to the ways in which moral, legal, and commercial imperatives become conflated. But it is interesting that O'Toole should use *For Women* as his example because it is hard to see how *not* including erections actually benefited that publication in the manner he suggests.[47] Furthermore, O'Toole's critique involves a notion of "better" and less sexist porn—clearly, erections are not a guarantee of quality or of less sexism.

It also seems unfair to demand that porn producers should be fighting battles against censorship when they rarely command widespread support from the British public, academics, or politicians. Whereas producers in the States and Europe have been able to mobilize important and popular political sentiment behind their causes of "free speech" and "sexual liberation," British pornographers have fought their battles with the judiciary on their own.[48] The famous obscenity trials of the 1960s and 1970s were mainly concerned with works of literary origin, not those emerging from the offices of self-identified porn publishers, but they were important precisely because they delineated the territory of defense on the basis of artistic merit or some form of social or therapeutic benefit. Magazines were rarely prosecuted under section 2 of the OPA, which entitles the accused to trial by jury. Instead, magazine publication has usually been dealt with under section 3, which allows for a process of "forfeiture" on the judgment of a magistrate: magazines are simply seized from a newsagents or distribution warehouse and placed before the magistrate, who determines whether or not they are obscene and what their fate should be. Under section 3 there are no criminal penalties for the publisher, distributor, or point of sale: the goods are merely destroyed or returned (if deemed not obscene). The fear of this form of prosecution, however, has successfully produced a decidedly cowardly spirit on the part of publishers, distributors, and stockists. The inconveniences of a seizure, the uncertainty of the outcome, and the loss of stock and profits are considerable. As the Williams Committee noted:

> there is a lack of justice in a procedure which allows the large scale seizure of goods and their detention for some time pending the outcome of proceedings. Even if the defendant wins the case he may suffer an effective and substantial penalty. Mr. David Sullivan, a publisher, told us that it was grossly unfair that he should have been deprived of an entire magazine issue for four months only to have the copies returned to him after the magistrates had found they were not in fact obscene; they were then out of date and useless to him and he had suffered a loss of £19,000 despite a court finding in his favour. . . . On the other hand it was put to us that this summary procedure of dealing with bulk pornography provided a far more effective weapon against an illegal trade than any other and that its increasing use in recent times had been crucial in deterring publishers from flouting the law. The publication of potentially obscene magazines was now on such a massive scale that seizure and forfeiture was the only practical remedy, and was both justified and successful in protecting the public interest.[49]

This practical remedy was and is applied unevenly: depending upon which constabulary covers a particular region of the United Kingdom, materials freely available in one city have been subject to seizure and forfeiture in another. Under the leadership of Chief Constable James Anderton, "God's Policeman," Manchester police operated a widespread and very successful seize and forfeiture campaign, which saw top-shelf magazines effectively eliminated from newsagents in the Greater Manchester area in the late 1970s. This strategy worked precisely because there is no real test of the evidence under section 3. Rather, magistrates decide whether on balance the item(s) constitute an infringement of the OPA. When an item has been seized, it is possible for the publisher to challenge the seizure by indicating that he intends to continue to publish the offending item; he can then be prosecuted in a jury trial. Experience has shown that the whole system of deciding on obscenity is flawed and that juries are much less likely to convict than magistrates, so it could be in the interests of publishers to push for a jury trial. Yet most publishers wish to avoid confrontation or an expensive court case and therefore simply accept the decision of the magistrate. Thus, juries have never tested the nature of the offense in a girlie magazine; instead, publishers and distributors have tended to err on the side of caution, giving rise to a peculiarly British kind of product.[50]

The development of a legitimate UK pornography industry has been significantly curtailed by legislation. Both the United States and Europe have seen massive expansions into new technologies from film and video production to Internet sites; in contrast, the UK market has remained largely reliant on top-shelf magazines, a few video spin-offs, and telephone chat lines. Precisely because the laws are so slippery and none of the agencies policing their provisions are willing or able to give precise guidelines to would-be producers of sexually explicit materials, a culture of self-censorship has emerged in the United Kingdom.

Effects on Content

Regulation is not simply a repressive tool: it does not just prevent certain activities; it also forms a set of production imperatives with significant effects on the *content* of magazines. Mainstream availability has been crucial to the success of titles such as *Escort, Fiesta, Men Only,* and *UK Penthouse:* nationwide distribution allows for high-volume sales. As companies operating on the right side of the law, porn publishers have had to be circumspect; breaking the law (or even being suspected of it) is an expensive business. According to David Sullivan:

> The biggest constraint was the law. The biggest problem with the OPA [was] nobody knew what the law was. And nobody knowingly tried to break the law. The police wouldn't tell you what the law . . . what you could and couldn't put in a magazine. My biggest break in publishing, in the seventies, was the day I met the head of the OP Squad. He said, "Listen David, the D[irector of] P[ublic] P[rosecutions] is not too worried about strong shots of single girls, but don't put anything with bondage or that stuff." I said, "I don't do that, but are you saying to me that I can do American style single girl shots and they don't regard that as illegal anymore?" And he said, "That's what I'm saying." So then I published a whole pile of magazines with strong held open pussy shots, and everyone waited for me to get nicked. It gave me a tremendous edge; they didn't know it, but they'd given me a tremendous edge.

Even if they had had the insider information from the DPP, Sullivan's course of action was not open to every other publisher. Sullivan had his own distribution network through direct sales to newsagents and the Private sex shops. For publishers reliant on other companies for distribution and desirous of advertising revenues, a path of respectability had to be treaded. Acceptability and respectability have been two essential ingredients of soft-core publishing in the United Kingdom, although not equally necessary to all publishers. When opposition to soft-core imagery was at its height, publishers formed the British Adult Publications Association (BAPA) to attend government committee meetings and to respond to the various inquiries and lobbies that sought to institute further controls on the industry. According to Sullivan, the BAPA "could never agree on anything"; the failure to agree indicates the ways in which soft-core publishing was never an undifferentiated field of production. A primary objective for the publishers in setting up the association was to convince critics that the industry was capable of self-regulation and able to recognize the boundaries of the respectable and the acceptable without the need for further outside interference. Yet the pressure to be acceptable was not felt equally by all publishers. For Paul Raymond, whose stock in trade was relatively sophisticated sexual imagery, respectability was an essential requirement for advertisers and readers alike. For Sullivan's publications the controlling force of advertisers was much less evident, and readers seemed to enjoy the targeting of "respectability" and "sophistication" in the pages of *Whitehouse* and *Playbirds*. Across the spectrum of soft-core publishing, a system of self-regulation could not bring uniform benefits and indeed would operate to the detriment of publishers whose products thrived on the appearance (at least) of an intention to offend their critics.

Soft-core in Britain has yet to be "tested" by consumers: before it ever reaches the newsagents shelves, it has been through a number of filtering practices designed to mute "offensiveness." Arguably, the role of John Menzies and W. H. Smith has been much more important than the 1959 act in limiting the widespread availability and content of explicit materials. These two companies account for more than 70 percent of wholesale trade in the United Kingdom. The reward to publishers for self-restraint has been a place on the top shelf of the nation's newsagents, through wholesale and distribution deals with those market leaders. All publishers wishing to use the distribution networks of John Menzies or W. H. Smith must submit proofs for vetting by their respective head offices in advance of printing. The publications are therefore subject to those companies' understanding and implementation of "community standards." This does not simply mean the removal of erect penises or photos of couples (for many years the mainstay of "obscenity"): this vetting has very real consequences for the narrative and photographic motifs of British soft-core.

In a fascinating account of working and researching at three men's soft-core magazines, Eleni Skordaki describes how letters sent to the magazines by readers are amended in order to ensure that they will not offend the wholesalers. Skordaki shows the effects on content of the informal and formal regulations that organize the production of porn magazines. Readers are encouraged to write to the magazines with their own sexual experiences: many of them "copycat," replicating the narratives of previously published letters.[51] Despite the copycatting, these letters often require substantial revision or refining in order not to break the rules set by distributors: "distributors' policies can dictate what can or cannot appear in a men's magazine in a way that the *Obscene Publications Act* could never do. Unlike the 1959 Act, distributors adopt concrete criteria of the unacceptable rather than the acceptable. They define what should not appear rather than what should, and can check every issue with that negative checklist in mind—if something is ticked as present, the magazine is penalised."[52]

Besides ensuring that the style of letter was interesting and well written, members of the staff had to pay attention to the theme of the letter to excise any mention of blacklisted activities (e.g., incest, sodomy, and underage sex). Likewise, significant changes were made to letters containing references to alcohol or forms of persuasion in the pursuit of a woman's sexual favors.[53] The removal of any "questionable" justification for a woman's participation in sex was necessary in order to get past the distributors, but, as Skordaki indicates, this significantly changes the nature and motivation of the stories: "The nymphomaniac stereotype legitimates all sorts of sexual exploits which would otherwise be seen as assault and rape. Proclaiming that a woman enjoyed or asked for such experiences is enough to appease censors. From that point of view, censorship not only does not stop the distortion of female sexuality in pornographic imagery, but propagates *further* distortion."[54] Furthermore, distributors' "yardstick" censorship actually contributes to the depersonalized narratives featured in men's magazines. Skordaki gives an example of a letter in which the sexual action in the original is largely driven by the fact that the two protagonists are cousins attracted to each other but unaware of the other's feelings. Because the magazine's lawyer was afraid that this story might constitute an "incest" story for the distributors, that "feeling-generating" fact was removed. Thus, "censorship . . . is not only unable to curb the pornographic reduction of sex into mere body movements, noises and secretions, but instead, encourages it *further* by removing any references to feelings that there might be."[55] Most important, for Skordaki, "These letters, especially in their edited form, also illustrate that censorship which is based on technical criteria of what is an unacceptable act, must necessary [*sic*] ignore intentions and feelings. Mental and emotional conditions cannot be ticked as present or missing with the same ease that a censor can tick whether a feature contains, for example, 'bondage,' 'sodomy,' 'bestiality.'"[56]

This highly suggestive account indicates the ways in which the content of pornography is subject not simply to authorial intentions but to a range of filtering practices.[57] These filtering practices, which are supposed to counteract "its distorted view of female sexuality, and its de-humanized account of sex as an act of mere physiological significance," actually intensify those "problem" elements.[58] In this sense it would seem that the fears of anticensorship campaigners are fully realized in the power of a group of unelected and unaccountable individuals whose interpretation of the law has significant impact upon the content and possibilities of published sexual fantasies. This dimension of production is missing from those accounts that ascribe certain kinds of "typical" behavior to "pornographers" and their readers. Moreover, it suggests that the claims about the inherent "meaning" of pornography that lay stress on the "form" of the material as powerful enough to override readers' moral, ethical, and human senses are at best flawed.

Nevertheless, the attempts to stay on the right side of the law have looked increasingly futile in recent years, not least because developments in other publishing and distribution sectors have changed the magazine landscape. Industry analysts have identified supermarkets as *the* retail sector crucial to the growth of the consumer magazine market: indeed, much of the success of the "new" men's magazines (e.g., *Loaded, FHM,* and *GQ)* is directly attributable to their accessibility via supermarket shelves. According to industry analysts Seymour Monthly Monitor, supermarkets and high-street names such as Woolworth and W. H. Smith account for 59.7 percent of retail sales of magazines.[59] These retailers have no intention of carrying risqué titles; thus, the most dynamic sector of the trade is closed to the publishers of pornographic periodicals.[60] During 2000 sales of adult titles fell again by 7.6 percent. O'Toole suggests that the soft-core market is a "cartel," "a perfectly tight and cozy set-up for those inside the loop, suiting the police, distributors and publishers."[61] This cartel apparently ensures that profits are maximized by keeping within the limits of the law. Over the past decade, however, it has become clear that all has not been as cozy as observers such as O'Toole would claim.

The changes and problems experienced by soft-core publishers are very similar to those that have beset the mainstream magazine market since the 1980s. For example, despite some spectacular successes, the magazine market has experienced damaging drops in overall circulation and advertising spending.[62] Publishers have responded with "narrowcasting": the segmentation of the market into niche areas, with specialized titles targeting narrower groups of "lifestyle" consumers. Industry analysts have identified three factors responsible for the acceleration of this trend from the 1970s: "advertisers wish for more tightly targeted media; the reader's desire for more specialized information; and the publishers' instincts to expand."[63] In an analysis of the structural changes in women's magazine publishing, Stephen Driver and Andrew Gillespie note that "intense competition in women's consumer publishing . . . contribute[d] to an increase in the absolute size of the market."[64] This expansion was largely driven by a small number of publishing houses that expanded both vertically and horizontally in order to maximize audience share and profits and to minimize the effects of shrinking advertising revenue. Similar patterns can be observed in soft-core publishing and are probably best illustrated by focusing on the activities of an individual publisher.

The Northern and Shell Portfolio

Although the company's notoriety as the owners of Express Newspapers is of recent origin, Northern and Shell (N&S) is an established name in pornographic publishing. Founded by Richard Desmond, the company's publishing activities had included a number of music-oriented titles—*International Musician* and *Home Organist*—before winning the franchise for the UK version of *Penthouse* in 1982.[65] The nature of the publishing enterprises and their down-market, homey appeal— one of the most successful formats in the company's portfolio is *Real Wives*—has gained Desmond the nickname the "People's Pornographer," although he is famous for going after any journalist using the epithet "Porn Baron" to describe him. Despite the successes of the company's soft-core titles, Desmond has not been happy to remain on the fringes of publishing: in the early 1990s the company made efforts to widen its customer base with *OK!* (a rival to *Hello!* magazine), *Attitude* (a lifestyle magazine for gay men), *Sindy,* and *Action Man* comics. N&S has aggressively pursued more mainstream ventures and has been able to recognize and respond to gaps in the existing markets that could be exploited without huge investment.[66] The success of *OK!* has been significant for the company, indicating that with the right format it is possible to break into the mainstream, no doubt making the acquisition of a daily newspaper more attractive. The move into more reputable publishing has been driven by Desmond's personal aspirations, which are believed to include a knighthood.

Until very recently, and like other publishers of "pornographic" materials, N&S was relatively invisible in the trade press: the company received little or no attention from industry publications such as *Campaign* or *Marketing*. This invisibility suggests that within the culture of professional advertising, marketing, and publishing the company was considered to have very little relevance. Certainly, most articles profiling the company focused on it as a "producer of pornography" despite its interests in music publishing. Its upstart pretensions were also emphasized in snide remarks about the Duke of Edinburgh opening the offices in Canary Wharf. This commentary has reached dizzying heights since December 2000, when the company successfully acquired the Express and Star Newspapers. In a culture of old publishers N&S has the wrong pedigree, and much scandalized copy details the links between Desmond's "legitimate" businesses and the outrageous activities of his other "filthy trade." Desmond seems rather unmoved by the commentary, remarking to one interviewer: "It's a private business. Wonderful, isn't it?"[67] With the expected doubling of his profits between 1999 and 2001, it would seem, as O'Connor observes, that Desmond has been "underestimated" as a businessman.

What is significant about Northern and Shell is that it has moved into other branches of activity in ways that mirror the practices of other larger and more mainstream media concerns in order to ensure growth and stability. As Driver and Gillespie have argued with respect to mainstream magazine publishing:

> scale appears to confer, potentially at least, a number of advantages. These advantages include: the revenue benefits associated with maximizing audiences across titles; the cost advantages associated with bulk print buying; the power conferred by control over distribution channels; the command over resources necessary to launch, market and sustain new titles, or to acquire them; the spreading of risks through diversification and cross-media ownership; and the ability to reap the rewards of spreading successful publishing formulas across national markets. For those publishers able to exploit these advantages effectively, whilst at the same time managing to foster creativity and innovation at the level of individual magazine titles through organizational decentralization, the rewards have been, and are likely to continue to be, substantial.[68]

Northern and Shell has always sought to operate within a broad field of publishing: although adult content might have been a significant proportion of the company's stock in trade, it has never been its sole raison d'être. As Jonathan Richards, one-time managing editor, put it in a letter to the *Guardian* newspaper, "the group ha[s] the intellectual elasticity to identify opportunities in new commercial environments."[69] In 1991, for example, the company was on the lookout for new areas to develop, and the women's magazine market was one they were keen to enter. Other publishers were investigating the possibility of a sexually explicit magazine for women, and N&S was not about to let the opportunity go to its rivals. Originally conceived as a one-off *Penthouse for Women,* further discussions convinced the editorial team that the time was right to launch a dedicated women's title rather than a supplement. In 1992 Northern and Shell launched a *Cosmo* style magazine with nude male photosets called *For Women.*

For Women's founding editor, Jonathan Richards, claims a conversation at a dinner party had convinced him that women wanted more than *Cosmo.* "I look at *Cosmo* and it promises everything and then fails to deliver."[70] The suggestion that the launch was based entirely on intuition would do N&S a disservice: its business is publishing and recognizing opportunities. The exploration of new areas of operation was a response to trends in publishing as a broad field but also to the particular problems faced by soft-core. The legitimate porn magazine market can be characterized by its relative stagnation, although falling sales of magazines yet rising profits for the major players are indications that producers have not stood idly by as sales drop. Northern and Shell embraced specialization: the company has become renowned for its niche publishing—titles targeted at particular tastes. The success of niche magazines such as *Big Ones, Asian Babes, Black and Blue, Big and Fat,* and *40+* indicates market dissatisfaction with the more conventional centerfold; they have the added bonus of being relatively cheap to produce. More important, they have been the publisher's successful response to the pressures of increasing competition from other media. For N&S titles such as *Big Ones International, New Talent,* and *Real Wives* have benefited the company: circulation figures are significantly lower than the sustained highs achieved in the 1970s by the "flagship" publications, but, because these magazines run on shoestring budgets and have a longer shelf life, they are profitable.[71] Produced by small editorial teams working on at least two other titles, these magazines also share copy, ideas, and photosets. Photographs are constantly recycled, and articles, interviews, and expensive editorial content are kept to an absolute minimum. Ironically, a public fracas has enveloped Richard Desmond just as he attempts to shrug off the porn king mantle. Former managing editor at N&S Deric Botham has accused Desmond of offering shoddy goods; in particular, Desmond stands accused of cheating punters by printing exactly the same photosets of one woman in two magazines under different names. Botham's outraged concern for the innocent consumer belies the long-standing tradition of recycling images. It is precisely this recycling that has made soft-core pay.

Magazine sales have also suffered from the increasing availability of new media forms, such as Internet sites, CD-ROM, and video, but publishers have responded with increased specialization and diversification into those and other markets. Magazine income is now supplemented by revenue from other sex media, in particular, sex phone lines, which offer the kinds of "bizarre" sexual activities expressly forbidden graphic depiction or mention in magazines under UK obscenity laws (e.g., anal sex, waterplay, bondage).[72] It is difficult to ascertain how far new developments have been responsible for the drop in circulation of the traditional top-shelf magazines; as each new technology comes along, however, the major players in the United Kingdom have been at the forefront of the exploitation of the sexual potentials of such technology. This suggests that continuing profitability is dependent upon being able to recognize the opportunities offered by technological advance and to expand the production base rapidly in order to adopt it.

N&S is a perfect example of the "capitalist porn-broker": the company is in the business because it is a business. As Nicholas Whittaker, former editor of *Fiesta* and *Razzle,* comments in his memoir, "The girlie-mag scene has changed over the years . . . sex has gone corporate. Northern & Shell have mags like *Penthouse, Forum, For Women,* but they're just part of a broad portfolio which includes respectable titles such as *OK Weekly* and *The Green Magazine.* You'll never see the bosses of N&S sashaying around Soho in fur coats, flashing gold rings. They aren't porn barons. Sex sells, and that's good enough reason for publishing sex magazines."[73] A former N&S employee has also commented on the business ethic at N&S and suggested that the company's working practices are reflected in a failure to produce "the sense of everybody's-doing-it celebratory fun" that other publishers achieve in their adult magazines.[74] N&S is not interested in breaking taboos but in maximizing profits. The company is still actively pursuing other areas of interest in mainstream media: they have already made the break into digital television and online publishing, and rumors currently abound regarding their intentions in radio broadcasting. Only 10 percent of the company's earnings now derive from pornography, although that is still a very significant one million pounds.[75] Significant or not, the adult titles are currently up for sale. With the recent purchase of Express Newspapers and the success of *OK!* Richard Desmond is now a serious newspaper and general interest magazine publisher keen to distance himself from the less respectable titles in his portfolio.

The Holy Grail of Respectability

Desmond's move toward respectability highlights the ways in which "culture" and dimensions of production are inextricably linked in my analysis of the British soft-core market. Northern and Shell is not the only UK company that has sought, and continues to seek, to operate in other market sectors: each of the main protagonists has managed to forge businesses in the more legitimate areas such as real estate, football club ownership, newspaper publishing, and lingerie manufacturing and sales. These more respectable areas of operation have cushioned the publishers during their bad times (entirely pragmatic and shrewd given the frequency with which some of them have been subject to costly prosecution). They are, of course, also attempts to reconstruct soft-core production culture around more creditable operations. By so doing, porn publishers in the United Kingdom have attempted to divert criticism and accusations of sleaze to recognition of their business acumen. Whereas the boom decades favored the classification of the top shelf as a site of sexual abundance, novelty, and deliberate attempts to shock, since the mid–1990s the emphasis has been on a more uneasy sexual hedonism. The reasons for this uneasiness lie in social and cultural changes, especially in attitudes towards women and sex. The real threat to top-shelf magazines has not come from the Internet, the law, or moral campaigners; these magazines have, in fact, been hit hardest by increasingly liberal attitudes to nudity. Ironically, the beneficiaries of liberalization in the 1990s have not been soft-core magazines but their rivals: the rug has really been pulled out from under publishers' feet by the arrival of respectable men's magazines. In the early 1970s, when *UK Penthouse* sold up to 300,000 issues per month, men's interests were inadequately catered to by the mainstream magazine industry. Hobby publications existed, but for those men who wanted "variety"—perhaps a mix of celebrity interviews, car reviews, and some sort of social/cultural commentary—there was little or no choice available. *Penthouse* and *Playboy,* with their mix of the "erotic" and "hard-hitting editorial," were able to appeal to a wide range of male readers and a whole host of mainstream advertisers. The advent in the late 1980s of men's magazines offering a very diverse mix of journalism, celebrity news and photographs, consumer goods, relationship discussions, and some sexual content without the attendant "dirty mac" label, has dealt the most decisive blow to the adult market. Soft-core titles no longer qualify for the title "men's magazine," having been "relegated" to the category "adult" or "pornographic." In 1995 they still accounted for a high proportion of the total sales of magazines aimed at a male readership (an estimated fifty-two million pounds of the total eighty-two million pounds in 1995, according to *KeyNote*).[76] But, given that magazines such as *FHM* and *Loaded* have broken the 500,000 sales barrier, those proportions are evidently changing. Industry insiders believe that there is little that can be done to reverse the downward trend in top-shelf sales:

> The money is in big quantities—you're hoping things will pick up. . . . The lad's magazines . . . they sell in big, big quantities. They've affected our trade. They're acceptable. Not many newsagents stock them [soft-core] any more. They're not as acceptable as they were. God knows why, cos the country's more liberal. But your danger is if the accountants take over you end up with a two page magazine at £20 . . . they say if we knock four pages out and put the price up by a pound we'll make a profit but they don't realize that it does affect your sales . . . it's a downward spiral. But even at value for money, they're not selling like they used to. What's changed over the thirty years? I suppose they're not so new, everything was new and exciting . . . then, we published pictures nobody had ever seen in magazines. We were courageous in our own way. We used to sell 150,000 copies of *Playbirds* and we printed 150,000 copies, we sold every copy. Now if you sell half of a print run you're lucky. We should have printed 500,000 but we didn't have the courage to print 500,000. We missed a big opportunity to make a lot more money than we did. If I'd known then what I know now I'd have printed vast copies and put the price up. We used to sell it for 75p but if I'd put the price up to £1, it wouldn't have affected sales, it was all new and exciting. I used to work on a break even

of a third returns but now you work on 60–70% to break even. It's a different ball game. [77]

Not only is the game different; the rules have changed. Popular culture conceptions of nudity and sexiness have shifted over the past three decades; Brian McNair has claimed that there is an increasing "pornification" of British culture employing the visual rhetorics of pornography.[78] Everyone, from Madonna to *Loaded,* is producing soft (sometimes hard) porn. As I have discussed, developments in soft-core magazine publishing have been limited by a range of regulatory practices, but other cultural industries such as mainstream magazines, production, and consumption have been less curtailed and have borrowed from soft-core in order to develop new vocabularies of sexual liberation and experimentation. Oversimplifying, I would suggest that celebrity women in men's magazines such as *FHM* and *Loaded* play a game with nudity and sexually provocative poses; they are able to escape censure because the magazines have managed a mix of sexual and non-sexual content that invites readers to treat sexual arousal as a game. These images, with their artistic elements (e.g., use of backgrounds, props, lighting, camera angles), manage to avoid the corpo-reality of the top shelf—it is all just a bit of fun and fantasy, not pornography per se. With the mantle of celebrity, these models are able to act out sexual self-empowerment and exploration free of the taint of exploitation that has dogged the top-shelf publications. In comparison, *Razzle, Men Only, Readers' Wives,* and *New Talent* are too cheap and somehow sleazy to be good, clean fun. The new men's magazines have a respectability that has long eluded the adult titles, and, with celebrity models more than happy to bare all, consumers no longer have to trawl the top shelf for a novelty nude. As sales drop, so do production values: *Fiesta* is currently the top-selling adult magazine with a decidedly down-market approach and audience. The social profile of *Penthouse* readers is also declining: in its heyday *Penthouse* had appealed to an ABC1 readership.[79] Since 1996 that readership is much more likely to be constituted by CDE males—their more affluent counterparts having moved to the respectable titles such as *Esquire.* Advertisers have followed and found in titles such as *Esquire, GQ,* and *FHM* the perfect vehicle for reaching high-earning male consumers: they no longer need to get into bed with porn publishers.[80]

Clearly, the top-shelf magazine has reached an all-time low: Richard Desmond has been seeking a buyer for his top-shelf titles since early 2001, and in 2003 David Sullivan handed over his magazine portfolio to his associates, the Gold brothers, who have yet to see any significant returns. Paul Raymond still seems to believe in the possibilities of the trade, although his considerable fortune clearly is not dependent upon magazines that achieve pre-tax profits of two million pounds. Indeed, while the company spokesman is upbeat about the future and the enviable position held by company titles—eight of the ten best-sellers are Raymond publications—their profits are not high and do nothing to suggest growth within the sector. The problems are manifold: although British attitudes to nudity have changed, they do not necessarily favor the kinds of nudity available in traditional soft-core, and legislation still exists that prevents significant development of the visual rhetorics of top-shelf magazines. New technologies and media formats have forged new ways of representing sexual activities. Moreover, in an age of stars it is simply not enough to bare flesh—there needs to be the extra frisson afforded by celebrity skin, and this, as I have already discussed, is not easily available to British soft-core publishers.

In an attempt to remain distinctive, top-shelf publications have embraced the Do It Yourself (DIY) aesthetic of *Readers' Wives,* a strategy with a double edge: although cheap to produce and easier to make returns on, such content confirms for many the supposedly innate sleaziness of pornography and contributes to its continuing slide. Sullivan, for one, has responded to the downturn in the sector's fortunes by embracing new technologies; his Web site www.free4internet.com (a gateway to porn sites around the world) has made significant profits, and another venture might actually contribute to an upturn in top-shelf fortunes. Since 2002 Sullivan has been publishing *Adult Sport,* an offshoot magazine of his Sport newspapers, "where stars go nude and topless!" and other titles such as *Sex Lives of the Rich and Famous.* Featuring paparazzi shots of celebrities in variously undignified poses—a favorite image is the accidental crotch shot—and recycled images or "grabs" from movies and "the photo-shoots they'd rather forget," *Adult Sport* belongs to the genre of gossip tabloid such as *National Enquirer.* In keeping with its Peeping Tom and budget aesthetic, the magazine retails at one pound and has spawned at least one imitator from the N&S stable, *Celebrity Adult Spy.* These publications are interesting precisely because they appear to draw on the same sense of sexual disenfranchisement evident in top-shelf publications of the 1970s. In the Oscar Awards special edition of *Adult Sport,* for example, the editor commented: "It's that time of year again folks, the Oscars, Hollywood's most glittering event and the time for all the leading ladies to put on their posh frocks. But here at *Adult Sport* we don't give a flying fuck about frocks, we like to have a look at what actresses keep under their skirts—and then print the pictures for all our lucky readers."[81]

Again, the specifics of textual formation and discursive strategies are beyond the scope of this essay, and indeed my focus on the production conditions of the top shelf leaves many questions unanswered, not least issues relating to readers' interpretations of the magazines and their contents. These are crucial areas of investigation, but all too often the details of the text have been foregrounded at the expense of research into the range of determinants affecting content and distribution. This exploration of soft-core magazine publishing cannot be considered definitive: because of the lack of archival material, it is a partial history and an imperfect investigation. It has, however, critically considered the relations between one area of soft-core production, legislation, and the cultural position of pornography in the United Kingdom. I have tried to show that soft-core has had a checkered history and that the analysis of top-shelf publications cannot simply attend to the text. The form and content of soft-core and the dynamics of the industry can only really be understood by investigating their place in a circuit of cultural production in which economics and culture are not held as two separate spheres.[82] The movements currently occurring in British attitudes to sexually explicit media will no doubt result in further shifts in organizational and production practices in the industry in order to maintain commercial viability. These transformations and trajectories of change need to be documented, analyzed, and understood alongside more extensive explorations of the textual features of girlie magazines before they adapt or disappear for good.

Notes

1. Regarding the pornographers, see essays in Catherine Itzin, ed., *Pornography: Women, Violence, and Civil Liberties* (Oxford: Oxford University Press, 1992); Andrea Dworkin, *Pornography: Men Possessing Women* (London: Women's Press, 1981); and, on victims, Itzin, *Pornography;* Diana E. H. Russell, ed., *Making Violence Sexy: Feminist Views on Pornography* (Buckingham: Open University Press, 1993).

2. Itzin, *Pornography;* Russell, *Making Violence Sexy;* Gail Dines, Robert Jenson, and Ann Russo, *Pornography: The Production and Consumption of Inequality* (London: Routledge, 1998).

3. One of the central tenets of moralistic and radical feminist discourses on pornography is that pornography proliferates faster than any other media form and that the content is increasingly violent; such claims are rarely substantiated with any evidence, but this lack of measurement seems not to matter—any sighting of pornographic materials makes it an object of concern.

4. Given the level of antagonism to pornography evident in discussions of the industry and its products, it is perhaps unsurprising that the activities of soft-core publishing are largely confined to private companies and that their accounts and activities are only understood in the vaguest terms by outsiders. It is very difficult to obtain market analysis of the soft-core industry, although this is beginning to change since Richard Desmond's Northern and Shell purchased Express Newspapers at the end of 2000. This essay can only be a partial history; the documentation required to offer a detailed and accurate picture of the UK soft-core magazine market is sadly lacking. I have interviewed existing and past members of staff at a number of magazines, and I was lucky enough to speak with David Sullivan, one of Britain's leading players. I am extremely grateful to all these people for their assistance. The outcomes of my discussions with them form the substance of this essay, alongside information gathered from published accounts of the magazine marketplace such as the *Keynote Report* (1995) and the trade publications *Campaign, Marketing,* and *Marketing Week.* These were most useful in providing background information to the mainstream magazine market. The soft-core magazine market was less easy to research, and here I have had to rely upon discussions in broadsheet newspapers and very occasional snippets in the financial and trade press. In addition there are a small number of book-length accounts of the porn industry: David Hebditch and Nick Anning, *Porn Gold: Inside the Pornography Business* (London: Faber, 1988); Mark Killick's account of David Sullivan's rise to the top in *The Sultan of Sleaze: The Story of David Sullivan's Sex and Media Empire* (London: Penguin, 1994); and Nicholas Whittaker, *Blue Period: Notes from a Life in the Titillation Trade* (London: Gollancz, 1997), an account of working for men's magazines. These cannot be considered incisive chronicles of the industry nor, indeed, can the outraged copy in the broadsheet newspapers that announced the purchase of Express Newspapers. An in-depth study of Britain's porn producers remains to be undertaken.

5. For readers unfamiliar with the British high street, the following explanations are of-

fered. Newsagents are small local shops dealing in newspapers and periodicals. In the past two decades many have expanded their stock to include the sales of essential food-stuffs such as milk and bread, but their primary trade remains the sale of printed materials. These stores often sell soft-core magazines displayed on the top shelf out of the reach of children and accidental browsing. Sex shops are premises licensed by local authorities under the 1982 Local Government Miscellaneous Provisions Act to sell, hire, exchange, lend, display or demonstrate "(a) sex articles; or (b) other things intended for use in connection with, or for the purpose of stimulating or encouraging (i) sexual activity; or (ii) acts of force or restraint associated with sexual activity." They are the only premises legally entitled to sell 18R videos and DVDs and "harder" soft-core magazines. For fuller explanation of the 18R classification, see Julian Petley's article "The Censor and the State, or Why *Makin' Whoopee!* Matters," http://www.melonfarmers.co.uk/brjp.htm (accessed 11 June 2001). Colin Manchester's *Entertainment Licensing Law and Practice,* 2d ed. (London: Butterworths, 1999) gives a detailed explanation of the provisions of the 1982 act.

6. "R18" is defined by the BBFC as follows: to be supplied only in licensed sex shops to adults of not less than eighteen years. The R18 category is a special and legally restricted classification primarily for explicit videos of consenting sex between adults. Such videos may be supplied to adults only in licensed sex shops, of which there are currently about ninety in the United Kingdom. R18 videos may not be supplied by mail order.

7. Some publishers are currently testing the boundaries of the acceptable in their magazines by using stills from 18R classified films showing vaginal and anal penetration; the police appear to be turning a blind eye, probably because juries no longer appear willing to find against scenes of consensual sexual activity between adults.

8. Although other parts of Europe sell glamour magazines on newsstands, it is generally accepted that British publications are too soft for European tastes. What constitutes soft-core in Britain would hardly qualify for the title "pornography" in most parts of the European Union and the United States.

9. Linda Williams, *Hardcore: Power, Pleasure and the "Frenzy of the Visible"* (London: Pandora, 1990), 29.

10. Williams, *Hardcore,* 29.

11. Dworkin, *Pornography;* Andrea Dworkin and Catherine MacKinnon, *Pornography and Civil Rights: A New Day for Women's Equality* (Minneapolis: Organizing against Pornography, 1988); Susan Kappeler, *The Pornography of Representation* (Cambridge: Polity Press, 1986).

12. Simon Hardy, *The Reader, the Author, His Woman and Her Lover: Soft-Core Pornography and Heterosexual Men* (London: Cassell, 1998), 52.

13. Galaxy (*Knave, Fiesta*); Paul Raymond Group (*Escort, Men Only, Mayfair*); Gold Star (*Rustler, Parade, LoveBirds*); and Northern and Shell (*Forum, For Women,* and mainstream gossip magazine *OK!*). David Sullivan's Conegate and Quietlynn publications ought to rank among the top producers, but he has recently sold his interests in publications such as *Whitehouse* and *LoveBirds* to Gold Star (owned by longtime business associates the Gold brothers). There are also a number of independents producing magazines for particular specialisms: Go-Go Publishing's *Cum* titles, Moondance's *Desire,* and the *Erotic Review* being the most mainstream, although as these are usually distributed via subscription they do not form a part of my discussion.

14. Joel Best, "The Social Control of Media Content," *Journal of Popular Culture* 14, no. 4 (March 1981): 611–617.

15. Avedon Carol, *Nudes, Prudes and Attitudes: Pornography and Censorship* (Cheltenham: New Clarendon Press, 1994), 127.

16. See, for example, I-Spy Productions' essay "Pornography and Capitalism: The UK Pornography Industry," in Itzin, *Pornography*.

17. In an article for the *Guardian* newspaper Julian Petley has offered an excellent exposition of the vagaries of British censorship laws, the current mess of conflicting criteria, and the attempts by Jack Straw and the Home Office to reinforce controls. An expanded version of the article is available on the MelonFarmers Web site: http://www.melonfarmers.co.uk/brjp.htm. The problems inherent in the provisions of these laws and the instability of the categories "obscene" and "indecent" have also been examined by various commentators, including Carol, *Nudes, Prudes and Attitudes;* Bill Thompson, *Soft-Core: Campaigns against Pornography in Britain and America* (London: Cassell, 1994); Laurence O'Toole, *Pornocopia: Porn, Sex, Technology and Desire* (New York and London: Serpent's Tail, 1998), for the anticensorship position; and, for the antipornography position, by Dworkin and MacKinnon, *Pornography and Civil Rights;* and Itzin, *Pornography.* All agree that the subjective terms are problematic, although the antipornography feminists would argue that the law could be used to decide on the acceptability of certain representations using the definitions of *harm*.

18. Leon Hunt, *British Low Culture: From Safari Suits to Sexploitation* (London: Routledge, 1998); O'Toole, *Pornocopia;* Eleni Skordaki, "The Production of Men's Magazines: Three Case Studies and a Sociological Analysis" (Ph.D. diss., London University, 1991); Thompson, *Soft-Core;* Whittaker, *Blue Period.*

19. Alex Spillus, "Who Makes the Profit?" *Independent on Sunday,* 21 April 1996, 4.

20. Spillus, "Who Makes the Profit," 4.

21. In 1996 Northern and Shell claimed a circulation figure of 1.5 million magazines per month, but its magazine profits have also dropped significantly (Company Report, 1996).

22. Hunt, *British Low Culture,* 2.

23. Stuart Hall, Chas Critcher, Tony Jefferson, John Clarke, and Brian Roberts, *Policing the Crisis: Mugging, the State and Law and Order* (London: Macmillan, 1978); Hunt, *British Low Culture,* 19.

24. Hunt, *British Low Culture,* 19.

25. Thompson, *Soft-Core,* 44.

26. Hunt, *British Low Culture;* Killick, *Sultan of Sleaze;* Thompson, *Soft-Core.*

27. Petley, "Censor and the State"; Thompson, *Soft-Core.*

28. Hunt, *British Low Culture,* 23.

29. For details of these prosecutions, see Paul Ferris, *Sex and the British: A Twentieth Century History* (London: Michael Joseph, 1993); Alan Travis, *Bound and Gagged: A Secret History of Obscenity in Britain* (London: Profile Books, 2000).

30. This central line of defense offered by the 1959 act that, far from being pornographic, a book, magazine, or film is a work of art and therefore open to the protection of the law was exploited by porn publishers, too, but took its own form. Pornography could be recuperated in the courtroom, "the defense of 'public good'—artistic, scientific or some other kind of merit which distinguished the meritorious from the exploitative . . . pornography . . . could be interpreted as being for the 'public good' by an astute counsel, as a series of therapeutic masturbation defenses proved" (Hunt, *British Low Culture,* 21). This stratagem could not last forever; by 1972 the *Longford Report* was calling for the closing of this loophole, and barrister John Mortimer, who

used the argument many times in his clients' defense, places its demise in 1977. See John Mortimer, *Clinging to the Wreckage* (London: Weidenfeld, 1982).

31. During the 1960s the "Permissive" label was most used by critics rather than "practitioners" and covered a range of activities and people. As Mary Whitehouse complained, the permissives were "pornocrats" or "the dogma-riddled lefties who see the undermining of morality as the prerequisite of take-over" (qtd. in Hunt, *British Low Culture,* 20).

32. Colin Manchester, *Sex Shops and the Law* (Dartmouth: Gower Publishing, 1986), 37.

33. For a full history, see B. Cox, M. Shirley, and M. Short, *The Fall of Scotland Yard* (London: Penguin Books, 1979).

34. Longford Committee Investigating Pornography, *Pornography: The Longford Report* (London: Coronet Books, 1972), 306–307.

35. Sullivan named the magazine after campaigner Mary Whitehouse, a leading figure in the religious and moral backlash against 1960s permissiveness. She died in 2001.

36. Hunt, *British Low Culture,* 130.

37. Hunt, *British Low Culture;* Thompson, *Soft-Core,* 1994; Mary Whitehouse, *Whatever Happened to Sex?* (London: Hodder and Stoughton, 1997).

38. O'Toole, *Pornocopia,* 133.

39. Thompson, *Soft-Core,* 30–31.

40. See, for example, Martin Barker, *A Haunt of Fears: The Strange History of the British Horror Comics Campaign* (London: Pluto Press, 1984); and his edited collection with Julian Petley, *Ill Effects: The Media/Violence Debate* (London: Routledge, 2000).

41. It was also linked to a more general crusade against the influence of the so-called Loonie Left in local authorities. For example, Rachel Thomson has described how the reform of sex education in schools in the late 1980s was driven as much by government desire for radical reform to the structure of education as it was by the interests of moral lobby groups, in "Moral Rhetoric and Public Health Pragmatism: The Recent Politics of Sex Education," *Feminist Review,* no. 48 (Autumn 1994): 47.

42. A feature of the *Sun* tabloid newspaper: photographs of a topless girl with shining eyes and smile that appear on page 3, hence its name. Many people have objected to the casual nudity of this feature in a daily newspaper. For an alternative reading of the meanings of page 3, see Patricia Holland, "The Page 3 Girl Speaks to Women Too!" *Screen* 24, no. 3 (1983), an extremely interesting and suggestive account.

43. There are many discussions of pornography's historical and contemporary role as scapegoat par excellence; see, for example, Walter Kendrick, *The Secret Museum: Pornography in Modern Culture* (New York: Viking, 1987); Laura Kipnis, *Bound and Gagged: Pornography and the Politics of Fantasy in America* (New York: Grove, 1996); Carol, *Nudes, Prudes and Attitudes;* and Lisa Z. Sigel, *Governing Pleasures: Pornography and Social Change in England, 1815–1914* (New Brunswick: Rutgers University Press, 2002).

44. O'Toole, *Pornocopia,* 133.

45. Both antiporn groups and UK porn publishers fear the "tide of filth" that would result from any relaxation of the current UK customs laws: the Continent produces a very different kind of sexually explicit material, which "benefits" from competition. That UK products would suffer is perhaps best indicated by the attempts by British publishers to take advantage of the new markets available in the glasnosted Eastern European states. The potential for reviving flagging sales at home appeared phenomenal, but Northern and Shell's foray into Poland in early 1992 with *Penthouse* failed dismally—the magazine closed in March of the same year, editorial director Paul

Ashford citing the lack of disposable income and no business ethic in Poland as the causes of the magazine's demise.

46. O'Toole, *Pornocopia,* 142.

47. My doctoral research into the production and consumption of *For Women* magazine indicates that the circulation of the magazine suffered precisely *because* it didn't show erections. Readers constantly made demands for more explicit shots, but the editorial team was unable to get around management at the parent company, Northern and Shell, or the distributors, W. H. Smith and John Menzies. For further discussion of this, see Clarissa Smith, "Pornography for Women or What They Don't Show You in Cosmo!" *Proceedings of the First Mapping the Magazine Conference,* Cardiff University, 26–27 June 2003, CD-ROM; "'They're Ordinary People, Not Aliens from the Planet Sex!': The Mundane Excitements of Pornography for Women," *Journal of Mundane Behavior* 3, no. 1 (February 2002); and "Fellas in Fully Frontal Frolics: Naked Men in *For Women* Magazine," *Paragraph* 26, nos. 1–2 (July 2003).

48. Smaller publishers find it very difficult to fight restrictions on their own. *Desire,* a magazine for men and women launched in 1994, ran into distribution difficulties over its images of couples. Unwilling to tone down the photosets to meet wholesalers' guidelines, the publishers chose the subscription and direct mailing route rather than mounting a legal challenge. David Sullivan, whose empire has not been hidebound to the same degree by considerations of "quality" and "artistic merit," has challenged the British courts and Customs and Excise on a number of occasions: using European law in 1986 to overturn a destruction order on "love dolls" and, more recently, beating the BBFC and Home Office minister Jack Straw over the classification of a number of films initially deemed too "hard" for an 18R rating; see Petley, "Censor and the State."

49. Bernard Williams, ed., *Obscenity and Film Censorship* (Cambridge: Cambridge University Press, 1981), 14–15.

50. It is here that the success of campaigns by feminist groups and Festival of Light can be seen. Arguments about the harmfulness of sexually explicit materials and the effects of the "permissive society" find a resonance with judicial and parliamentary attitudes toward sexually explicit materials. As both Ferris and Thompson have shown, British attitudes toward sex are so resolutely willing to think the worst that even consumer protection legislation is not accorded to porn's customers.

51. Skordaki, *Production of Men's Magazines,* 170.

52. Skordaki, *Production of Men's Magazines,* 181.

53. Skordaki, *Production of Men's Magazines,* 184ff.

54. Skordaki, *Production of Men's Magazines,* 186.

55. Skordaki, *Production of Men's Magazines,* 188.

56. Skordaki, *Production of Men's Magazines,* 199.

57. Skordaki also emphasizes the "interfering" role of the magazine owner; the costs of production and the limitations that are placed on content; and the need to provide novelty as well as continuity.

58. Skordaki, *Production of Men's Magazines,* 199.

59. Seymour Monthly Monitor, *Key Indicators on the UK Magazine Market,* no.16 (January 2001).

60. Distribution of "adult" magazines has also been affected by the "Off the Shelf" activities of the Campaign against Pornography.

61. O'Toole, *Pornocopia,* 143.

62. In 1981 the consumer magazine industry (some 2,434 titles) as a whole accounted for

7.8 percent of advertising spending; this figure dropped to 6.9 percent in 1991 (*Marketing,* 25 February 1993).

63. *Marketing,* 3 July 1986.
64. Stephen Driver and Andrew Gillespie, "Structural Change in the Cultural Industries: British Magazine Publishing in the 1980s," *Media, Culture and Society* 15 (1993): 187.
65. The Northern and Shell portfolio has also included *Chic, Digital Dreams,* and *Liverpool FC: The Official Magazine.* Portland Publishing, now Portland Holdings, has included *Asian Babes, Big and Fat, Big Ones, Black and Blue, Fifty Plus, Hottest Asian Babes, Real Wives, Readers' Wives, Thrills, Nude Wives, Amateur Video, Connect, Eros, Erotic Stories, For Men, For Women,* and *New Talent.* The company was also responsible for *Electric Blue* videos and a range of Web sites.
66. N&S could be described as a "me too" publisher, a term Brian Braithwaite, in *Women's Magazines: The First 300 Years* (London: Peter Owen, 1994), uses to describe how some publishers jump on the tailcoats of successful new formats. Certainly, N&S moved into gossip publications only after *Hello!* had done the groundwork; the same could be argued for its foray into gay magazines.
67. O'Connor, *Financial Times,* 20 July 2001, 8.
68. Driver and Gillespie, "Structural Change in the Cultural Industries," 199.
69. Jonathan Richards, letter, *Guardian,* 29 December 2000.
70. Interview, 13 January 1994.
71. Whereas other magazines have a limited life span of a month indicated by the date on the front cover, *Real Wives,* for example, gives only a volume number so that it can remain on display for months, if not years.
72. In 1987, 45 million calls were made to sex phone lines, generating thirty-five million pounds. Northern and Shell's phone lines accounted for one-third of the group's total profits in 1987 (I-Spy, "Pornography and Capitalism"). Following censure from British Telecom over content, however, the company sold the lines in 1988. Sex lines were also a benefit to publishers; David Sullivan suggests that it was advertising from these lines that kept many of the top-shelf titles afloat during the past six years.
73. Whittaker, *Blue Period: Notes from a Life in the Titillation Trade,* xx.
74. E-mail from Zak Jane Keir, former editor at Fantasy Publications, 13 November 2000.
75. D. Teather and O. Burkeman, *Guardian,* 23 November 2000.
76. KeyNote Report, *Men's Magazines* (Hampton: Key Note Ltd., 1995).
77. David Sullivan, interview with author, November 2002.
78. Brian McNair, *Striptease Culture: Sex, Media and the Democratisation of Desire* (London: Routledge, 2002); and *Mediated Sex* (London: Arnold, 1996).
79. The Joint Industry Commission on National Audience and Readership Surveys (JICNARS) employs demographic segmentations based on social class, defined by the occupation of the head of the household:
    A   Higher managerial, administrative, or professional;
    B   Intermediate managerial, administrative, or professional;
    C1   Supervisory or clerical;
    C2   Skilled manual workers;
    D   Semi- or unskilled workers;
    E   Casual workers, laborers, those on benefit.
80. Sean Nixon, *Hard Looks: Masculinities, Spectatorship and Contemporary Consumption* (London: UCL Press, 1996), details the "search for the holy grail," the high-spending male consumer, a quest that united manufacturers, advertising agencies, and magazine

publishers in the early 1980s and fueled the search for a winning magazine format for men.

81. *Adult Sport,* 10, no. 3, 29 March 2002.

82. Paul du Gay, *Production of Culture / Cultures of Production* (London: Open University Press / Sage, 1997).

Global Traffic in Pornography

The Hungarian Example

KATALIN SZOVERFY MILTER AND JOSEPH W. SLADE

According to Curt Moreck's *Sittenge-schichte des Kinos,* the first authoritative study of pornographic motion pictures, Budapest after the turn of the twentieth century was the principal source of the stag film, the precursor of today's triple-X video.[1] Stag films may have appeared as early as 1899, probably in France. Made in ten-minute lengths of black-and-white 35 mm film stock that fit on a single, easily smuggled reel, the silent stag depicted hard-core intercourse interspersed with raucous intertitles. Crude and demotic, clandestinely made and distributed stags seemed to confirm the historian Erwin Panofsky's contention that cinema itself had its origins in obscene folklore and pornographic art.[2] Although the total number shot did not exceed a few dozen per decade before World War II, classic stags persisted into the 1950s, then mutated into 8 mm shorts, theatrical features, and eventually VCR and DVD formats.

In 1910, said Moreck, Hungarians exported stags to other countries on the Continent. But Budapest's first film vogue did not last long: by the 1920s Hungary's stag filmmakers had been displaced by those of Argentina, Austria, France, and the United States. Now, a century later, erotic scenarios on cassette and DVD from Hungary again constitute a distinctive market niche and have resurrected a European eroticism eclipsed by American industrialization of sexual representation. Convinced that Budapest is now the "center of the porno world," filmmakers from across Europe have moved there to exploit the city's resources, even as domestic entrepreneurs have launched their own companies.[3] Nearly a quarter of all pornographic videos produced in Europe are made in and around Budapest, and most of the reigning Continental porn queens are Hungarian. Although history is instructive here, the success of "Budaporn" has less to do with a resurgence of *Mitteleuropean* decadence following the collapse of the Soviet Union than with the imperatives of globalization. Europeans are altering the content of pornography

173

and creating new icons of desire just as globalization is visibly reshaping pornographic industries by expanding demand, increasing production, consolidating distribution, and exploiting new locations.

Over the last decade cross-border traffic in hard-core video has soared, giving credence to the *Economist*'s 1998 prediction that pornography would become a standard component of the world's entertainment systems early in the twenty-first century.[4] Pornography has fueled Continental cable and satellite television growth since 1991, when *Variety* noted that European media had exhausted the world's stock of soft-core films and had begun exhibiting hard-core.[5] American systems were forced to follow suit. Long resistant to hard-core, staid Playboy Enterprises in 2001 purchased three explicit satellite sex services capable of reaching 100 million households; its stock price rose instantly.[6] Now American and European hotel chains routinely offer graphic movies on pay-per-view channels. The only bright spot on the otherwise dismal balance sheet of Vivendi, the troubled French media giant, is the revenue generated by porn features shown on its subsidiary, Canal Plus.[7] Even so, the sheer number of hard-core films (called *films de charme*) shown each month on French television (though after midnight) has provoked a backlash from conservatives.[8] Finland's Helsinki Television, a cable monopoly, only recently started charging for two late-night hard-core channels that had run for nearly ten years free to subscribers.[9] The Institute of Interdisciplinary Studies in Rome reported in 2001 that 37 percent of Italian women switched on porn channels during the day (not simply at night); the study predicted that female audiences for televised hard-core would increase by 10 percent over the following two years.[10]

Demand for home consumer VCR tapes and DVDs is especially strong in countries that still prohibit cable and over-the-air exhibition. Heightened circulation ended Britain's long-standing prohibitions against hard-core videotapes in 2000.[11] More than 300 adult stores have opened in South Africa,[12] and adult tapes and DVDs are available clandestinely in many other nations on the African continent. In June 2002 authorities in southern China seized 5.2 million pirated pornographic DVDs being unloaded in the port of Huizhou, though officials were motivated in part by the intellectual property protocols enforced by the World Trade Organization, to which China had been recently admitted.[13] In any case distributors such as Nanma operate in Hong Kong despite the colony's takeover by the Communists. Black market distribution of pornography in the Middle East is difficult to track, but robust demand is evident in that religiously conservative region as well.

Despite far from uniform laws and customs (e.g., in Italy production of porn is theoretically prohibited), erotic videos move freely among nations of the European Union. Partly to protect minors but just as obviously to protect the traffic in sexual materials for adults, the European Parliament in 2001 passed new guidelines for dealing with child pornography in the fifteen EU nations, including prison terms for those convicted of sexually exploiting children.[14] With only a few exceptions, European producers now follow the lead of their American counterparts by insisting on compliance with Section 2257 of the U.S. Code, which requires records proving the age of every performer. That legislation, though originally drawn by hostile political conservatives, has in effect stabilized the industry by defining legal adult content.[15] As a result, the Continental porn market is robust despite dislocations to be expected in the new economic bloc.

Demand has in fact increased the number of European porn producers, although they are still outnumbered by Americans. The European nations combined produce no more than twelve hundred porn videos per year (estimates differ), of which approximately three hundred come from Hungary.[16] By contrast, the United States turned out around eleven thousand soft- and hard-core videos in 2001; Vivid Video, for example, itself releases four features per week.[17] Japan probably produces more; some estimates place the number of cheap tapes as high as fourteen thousand per year.[18] Numbers are deceiving, however, because many poorly shot American and Japanese videos are highly fetishistic (as in Japanese bondage scenarios in which yards of ropes and knots obscure flesh) and thus attract limited numbers of consumers. Moreover, says a representative of Scala Agenturn, one of the largest European distributors, the general run of American videos is of such low technical quality that only about 10 percent is "saleable in Europe,"[19] and the percentage of exportable Japanese products is lower yet.

Some 150 American companies are now clustered in Chatsworth, California, dubbed "Silicone Valley." Of these, five or six (e.g., Vivid Video, Metro, VCA, and Evil Angel) vertically integrate production, postproduction, packaging, and distribution and thus control the lion's share of the market. European producers are scattered across the European Union, with studios located in France, Germany, Spain, the Netherlands, Sweden, and Denmark as well as Hungary and the Czech Republic, both of which joined the European Union in 2004. Unification has allowed producers to make use of peripatetic performers and technicians, to seek capital from banks of many nationalities, and to incorporate in countries with favorable tax rates and economic incentives.

Some countries are more receptive than others, of course, and the French experience is instructive. During the early 1970s France suddenly found itself inundated with American movies such as *Deep Throat* (1972) and *Behind the Green Door* (1972), whose immense box office successes threatened a corps of domestic producers (such as Jess Franco and Jean Rollin) that were just then shifting from traditional soft-core to more explicit features. In 1975 the French retaliated with Jean François Davy's *Exhibition,* a graphic documentary that opened at the New York Film Festival, and Danille Bellus's *Pussy Talk,* a tale of a loquacious vagina that did well at box offices around the world. The following year, however, confused by such developments, the French government adopted contradictory policies. On the one hand, the Giscard administration ended censorship of sexual films and attempted to protect the French porn industry by subjecting American imports to very high tariffs. On the other, responding to conservative pressure, it denied to domestic pornographers the government subsidies previously available to all filmmakers and imposed taxation on porn (but not legitimate) films as well.[20]

Demoralized, French porn producers all but ceded the field in the 1980s. Although more than two dozen French directors were still working in 1990, they maintained that the porn industry had declined even as it had subsidized French mainstream cinema during a long fallow period.[21] In 1991, as global demand heated up, director Michel Ricaud complained that the French industry lacked professionalism,[22] and so he began to shoot for foreign companies (he was killed in an accident shooting a Private Media feature in the Seychelles in 1997). When the General Agreement on Trade and Taxation (GATT) accords of 1993 relaxed some regulations and stimulated coproductions by foreign partners, Paris once again briefly held the lead in Europe—until Budapest took it away.

That happened in part because, although the French increased production, they did not push for greater distribution. As is the case with mainstream media conglomerates such as Time Warner and Bertelsmann, porn companies with global ambitions regard mastery of distribution as more crucial than increased production. In the United States a company's size, sometimes the result of early entrance into the market, sometimes the consequence of aggressive business practices, counts heavily where control of distribution is concerned. Just as the big six Hollywood studios have sewn up cineplexes in middle America, the half-dozen major U.S. porn studios can claim most of the shelves in video rental outlets and can deal from strength with cable and satellite channel managers. To ensure growth, some of the American market leaders have recapitalized though public stock offerings. Although Metro Video was delisted for financial irregularities, four other porn companies remain on the NASDAQ exchange, and others will no doubt follow soon.

The popularity of annual pornography trade fairs in Berlin, Barcelona, Cannes, and Budapest, during which naked starlets parade around drafty convention halls while buyers and sellers dicker, obscures similar jockeying for position in Europe. Here also size matters. The late Beate Uhse opened sex shops from Poland to Portugal to distribute videos shot in her own studios. By 1999, when Beate Uhse A.G. was first listed on the Frankfurt stock exchange (symbol: USE), it was ranked seventy-ninth among publicly traded German companies,[23] well ahead of other German porn majors ZBF Vertrieb and DBM Videovertrieb GMBH. Even so, DBM Videovertrieb GMBH, based in Wesel, Germany, also operates subsidiaries in Essen and Dusseldorf so as to reach neighboring countries more easily.[24] Private Media, the largest European producer, transferred its headquarters from Stockholm to Barcelona, in part because Spain is second among European nations, after Germany, in consumption of pornography and in part to reposition itself as a global distributor. Private now produces one hundred features a year, dubs them into ten languages, markets them directly to vendors in forty-four countries, has already been listed on the American NASDAQ exchange (symbol: PRVTMedia), and is actively seeking listings on European exchanges as well.[25] In 1998 Private made profits of 25 percent.[26]

Companies such as Globo (Milan), Scala Agenturn and Leisure Time (Netherlands), and TELSEV (France) also compete with Private, sometimes through interlocking arrangements with American distributors; films produced by Marc Dorcel (Paris), for example, are now distributed in the United States through Wicked Pictures. In 2001 Private Media repurchased its American distributor rights from Odyssey Group Video, its former partner, and created a wholly owned subsidiary, Private North America, so as more directly to enter the previously inhospitable largest market in the world. When *Forbes Global* called Private Media "One of the Top 20 Best Small Companies in the World," the trade journal *Adult Video News (AVN)* marveled at the speed with which Private had opened the way for European competition in America.[27] Not surprisingly, 20 percent of the first hardcore videos legalized in Britain in September 2000 were made by Private, which is determined to control as much of the market as possible.[28]

Control has become more of an issue as the Internet threatens to destabilize distribution. *Adult Video News* has also warned adult video outlets that high-speed delivery by broadband cable or wireless of porn-on-demand will probably shutter stores in the future.[29] Patterns of early consolidation are evident. According to *Wired* magazine: "Half of all adult sites gross less than $20,000 a year. Breaking in anywhere in the chain is tough. Going big is almost impossible" because giant Web sites and services already dominate traffic.[30] A University of Pennsylvania survey indicates that U.S. consumer traffic to porn Web sites has slowed as well.[31] That decline, says *Adult Video News,* challenges porn firms to target a "sweet spot for Internet growth" such as southeastern Europe's Bulgaria, Croatia, Romania, and Slovenia.[32] The lead of larger porn firms has increased as they have benefited from economic downturns by hiring laid-off dotcom workers. Vivid Video, for example, increased its online staff by 30 percent in 2001. As one job recruiting service noted, "What was once a behind-the-scenes old warehouse business is now becoming a mainstream business with the advent of the web."[33]

Europeans have taken note. In a bold move Private tried (and failed) to purchase Napster, the bankrupt company whose file-sharing protocols came under legal attack by American recording studios.[34] Like other porn firms, Private knows that distribution via the Internet will be key, and it knows that it can expect competition from legitimate video streaming firms such as RealNetworks.[35] Private's scenario is to create a new multi-channel porn universe in which adult customers can exchange (for a fee) vast quantities of hard-core around the globe using home computers. Its sophisticated Web site (www.private.com) is widely regarded as a commercial model; its interactive sector alone can handle more than a thousand clients at once.[36] Collapse of dotcom companies aside, it is still too early to predict distribution systems of the future, but pornographers will surely invent them, just as they invented the transaction technologies, pop-up and flash ads, video streaming, and innovations in virtual reality that more respectable commercial users of the Net have adopted.[37]

In the meantime traditional strategies have pushed pornographers to seek cheap labor and open new markets in tolerant countries. "Hungarians," a Private Media executive told *Forbes* magazine, "are the Brazilians of Europe,"[38] an indication that Europeans are following the lead of American porn firms. Like other American industries, Silicone Valley porn companies have transferred some operations to NAFTA countries. Brazil's lagging economy makes it receptive to pornography as a source of income, although friendly government policy could change under President Luis Ignacio Lula da Silva. Brazil's advanced television infrastructure provides both a supply of trained technicians and a wide range of video outlets. Despite the need to dub programs shot in Portuguese, Brazil already exports vast quantities of a quasi-pornographic genre, the soap opera, to a large Hispanic and world market. The country also boasts a modest indigenous hard-core porn tradition typified by directors such as "Coffin Joe," the pseudonym of José Mojica Maríns (*48 Hours of Hallucinatory Sex* [1986] and *Dr. Bartolomeu and the Sex Clinic* [2001]).

Moreover, Brazilian women attract directors because of their "natural" (i.e., non–surgically enhanced) multiracial beauty and willingness to perform extreme sexual acts. Rio and Ipanema, both plentiful sources of naked Carneval float riders, sinuous samba dancers, and raunchy nightclub performers, are good recruiting grounds. Supply exceeds demand, so that the going rate for eager women is $400 a scene as opposed to $1,000–1,500 (or more for stars) in Los Angeles.[39] Shooting on location requires only a hotel room, preferably one with a view of the Christ of the Andes statue for local Rio color, a secluded section of beach or woods, a few street scenes, or a nightclub at Carneval, where patrons are accustomed to seeing public intercourse. For these reasons John Stagliano[40] of Evil Angel Video set up a production subsidiary in São Paulo in 1991 and was quickly followed by other producers such as Al Borda, who launched the *Brazilian Beach Babes* series. Accusations that South American drug money has financed some videos,[41] while possibly accurate, have caused less alarm than fears that Brazilian performers transmit AIDS to American counterparts. Stagliano himself tested positive for HIV after having unprotected sex with a Brazilian transvestite. Perhaps sensitive to reports of AIDS in its sex industries, the Brazilian government passed legislation requiring that porn video box covers carry safe-sex messages advocating the use of condoms.[42]

Although one effect of increased production has been to elevate Brazilian images into global commodities, cynics might well characterize the process as cultural imperialism, since classic colonialism prescribes mining a colony for its raw materials then selling finished products back to it. Magazines and videos are openly displayed at kiosks everywhere in Brazilian cities, along with condoms, sexual appliances, and potions. As every major media conglomerate knows, the South American market for all forms of entertainment is itself vast, but, as *Adult Video News* notes, thirty-one million Latinos in the United States need ethnic pornography too.[43] Increasing ethnic porn has boosted sales and rentals. Looking at the 2001 nominations for the X-Rated Critics Organization (XRCO) Awards, one observer wryly remarked that half were for Brazilian videos, half for Hungarian.[44]

The Hungarian Example

Today European crews jostle their American counterparts shooting porn in South America, but in the late 1980s they needed fresh faces and economic advantages closer at hand. The collapse of the Soviet Union opened East Europe in 1989. Budapest in particular offered a unique combination of "camera-compatible women, laissez-faire government regulation, *fin-de-siècle* scenery, and low production costs."[45] Well before the demise of the Soviet Union, Hungary had begun experimenting with a mixed economy called "Goulash Capitalism" that by 1990 had incurred the largest foreign debt ($22 billion) in Eastern Europe.[46] Desperate need for hard currency made pornography attractive to the new government. Overestimating the financial rewards of pornography is common. In the United States, for example, Enron executives, panicked at the threat of exposure, approached Bob Guccione, publisher of *Penthouse,* with a scheme to distribute pornography as a way of bringing in quick cash. At the time, Guccione's General Media Communications, Inc., empire was sliding into bankruptcy, victim of the Internet, which distributes free the kind of graphic photos that had once made *Penthouse* so profitable.[47] In Hungary, however, the timing was perfect. Prior to 1989 the only way to get explicit magazines, videos, or sexual appliances was to smuggle them from Yugoslavia or the former West Germany. But, according to former foreign minister Géza Jeszenszky, "people hated the restrictions and rushed to obtain formerly forbidden fruits, including pornography."[48]

Sex magazines were first, starting with a joint domestic venture with *Penthouse* that primed demand for all-Hungarian publications.[49] Prerecorded telephone sex messages on answering machines, which require less investment than live conversations, followed.[50] The real money, however, began to flow in 1993, when the post-Soviet government ordered MAFILM, the state-run production facility, to rent its sound stages to foreign porn producers at bargain rates,[51] which had the additional benefit of providing work for film technicians sidelined by much-diminished Socialist cinema.

Christoph Clark claims to have been first. Perhaps the most popular male star in the French porn industry, Clark moved to Budapest in 1991.[52] Having worked with Marc Dorcel and Michel Renaud, Clark carried credentials sufficient to persuade Evil Angel's John Stagliano, the doyen of American porn filmmakers, to finance Clark's anal-themed video series, *Euro Angels,* for which the director uses Hungarian performers. Other producers followed. In 1993 Italian Rocco Siffredi shot the initial two installments of his series *True Anal Stories,* using models from Budapest's Nichols Talent Agency. Other directors soon made the trek: Luca Damiano, Silvio Bandinelli, Max Belocchio, Gianfranco Romagnoli, and Matera from Italy; Mario Pollack from Germany; Pierre Woodman from France. Lured by the buzz, Americans such as Patrick Collins, Scotty Fox, and many others also hurried to Hungary in 1993.

The capital thus generated percolated through the economy as rapidly as Lord Keynes might have wished. Local entrepreneurs such as Elisabeth King bought cameras, while others opened stores. Businessman Jozsef Temesi applied for a license to open a sex shop in Budapest in the early 1990s. Says Temesi: "Everybody knew that giving out permits to open sex shops was a 'bad thing,' but every politician was talking about opening the country toward the 'west,' so I guess they did not have a choice. Our product catalogs had to be approved by different government agencies. Imagine what happened! Some officials were just laughing, others were genuinely disgusted. Some of them even took the movies home to further examine them."[53]

Temesi opened Intim Center, complete with peep show booths, the first of a dozen sex shops now operating in the city. Temesi stocked nearly thirty Hungarian sex magazines, a wide range of vibrators and novelties, and roughly one thousand porn movies, 50 percent of them Hungarian produced. By 1995 Hungary had cornered the East European porn market.[54] Two years later, when Ildikó Strausz opened the Budapest Erotica Show, five thousand visitors showed up. By 1999 her trade fair drew sixteen thousand people to inspect products promoted by thirty-five exhibitors.[55]

With the industry solidly established, the Hungarian government took its cut by imposing a hefty special tax of 25 percent (in addition to normal taxation) on net revenues that total over one billion forints.[56] Unlike French porn filmmakers of the 1970s, however, those in Hungary grouse continuously about taxation but accept it as the cost of unfettered activity, albeit with the state as a silent partner now hooked on the money stream. Even with taxes, costs remain low enough to ensure profits, and every shoot, especially higher-budget foreign features, can pump money into the economy as producers rent equipment and locations and employ hairdressers, cosmeticians, porters, costumers, technicians, and so on. By virtually all accounts the porn industry is one of the most buoyant sectors of the Hungarian economy, and videos are one of its fastest-growing exports (no export license fee required).[57]

The legal climate was also favorable. Under the post-Soviet Hungarian constitution no laws forbade the making of pornography, nor did any statutes proscribe sodomy, bestiality, or acts regarded as perversities in the United States.[58] As traffic in pornography grew, the government did impose zoning ordinances similar to those in the United States which make it illegal to sell sexual materials within roughly two hundred yards of churches, schools, and medical institutions. Moreover, sexual materials displayed openly on newsstands or kiosks must be masked, so that explicit images are not visible. It is now illegal to shoot any porn movie when children are present, but for a time the child pornography laws contained loopholes that were occasionally exploited. For example, the law said that children over the age of fourteen could give "partial consent," which was translated to mean that, while two minors over the age of fifteen could be videotaped in intercourse with each other, a minor having intercourse with an adult could not, and at least one producer was prosecuted in such a case. Now that Hungary has been admitted into the European Union, former Minister Jeszenszky says that "we need to bring our laws [on child pornography] in line with those of Western Europe."[59]

According to recent legislation, prostitutes may now freely advertise their trade, which has been decriminalized. "If the state made prostitution legal," argues Ákos Borai, an official in the Ministry of Interior Affairs, "it cannot forbid advertising it."[60] Hungary also distinguishes between the exploitation of women in the "sex trade," a glaring social issue as Eastern European prostitutes flood the West,[61] and performance in media, a more respectable calling. In fact, the head of the Southeast European Cooperative Initiative, a Bucharest crime center dedicated to policing and reducing traffic in cross-border prostitution and sexual slavery, is headed by Hungary's Brigadier General Ferenc Bánfi.[62] Indeed, the Hungarian por-

nography industry, unlike its Russian counterpart, has been relatively free of organized crime. Partly because Russian mobsters consider pornography merely an
extension of the equally illegal prostitution they control, the mafia strangled a nascent video porn industry by demanding heavy payoffs for providing and "pro-
tecting" performers and locations, or so Private Media has reported.[63] In any case
the Russian mafia prefers to pirate foreign videos rather than make its own. (Low
per capita income in Russia is also a factor, since it forestalls a consumer base for
pornography.) The murder of porn actor Riny Rey (*Private Dancer* [1996]) in 1997
in Budapest seems not to have involved others in the industry.

Attempts to legalize the industry are in keeping with larger efforts to control the possible spread of AIDS without state intervention. In the United States,
partly because of pressure from performers, porn producers now often supply
condoms on the set, though in fact AIDS has claimed proportionately few lives in
the American industry, a circumstance considered important because porn videos
are often touted as a form of safe sex, given their tendency to encourage solitary
masturbation. (In April 2004 the American porn industry voluntarily called for a
multi-week moratorium on production when two performers tested positive for
HIV.) Because European producers—and Americans who shoot there—strive to
distinguish their product from American varieties by offering riskier unprotected
intercourse as a cachet, condoms in Hungarian porn are rare, and some commentators are concerned that so many of the performers come from villages where
education on the subject has been minimal.[64] Indeed, news that the Hungarian actress Caroline (aka Katalin) had tested positive for HIV in 1998 alarmed American producers who had employed her in Budapest.[65] Thus far, however, the spread
of AIDS in Hungary has fortunately been extremely slow. A United Nations agency
reported only 220 deaths from AIDS out of a total population of roughly 10 million. The report quotes György Berencsi, one of Hungary's leading virologists, to
the effect that, "if you test 5,000 people from high risk groups (such as prostitutes, prisoners, and people with other sexually transmitted diseases), one or two
(0.02%) would be HIV positive."[66] As in the United States, performers are required
to show producers and one another evidence of an HIV test no more than two weeks
old. According to director István Kovács, the performers in this small universe are
"taking care of themselves and each other."[67]

Needless to say, not all Hungarians are pleased that their country is now home
to Europe's largest porn industry, especially since some of them consider porn entrepreneurs as social degenerates preying on the young and clueless. Every few
weeks Hungarian television headlines some scandal of the sort involving a
housewife's mistakenly purchasing a triple-X cassette instead of a children's movie
or airs a complaint by another citizens' group. Despite zoning regulations, critics
fear that porn shops affect the quality of life, especially since they are often
thronged. One journalist calculated that 70 percent of peep show booths were occupied on an average weekday morning.[68] Production glut has put videos within
the reach of the bottom rung of the middle class. Domestic videos for home use
rent for as little as a U.S. dollar, while foreign cassettes fetch up to three in stores
such as the Intim Center; the former sell for four to eight dollars, the latter for

around twenty, but increasingly common pirated movies can be purchased for a dollar on the black market.[69] So far, Hungarian tastes run to heterosexual intercourse and commonplace fetishes (e.g., large breasts and penises, feet, corsets, high heels, and so on), as opposed to sadomasochism and bestiality; no one has commented on the size of the gay video market.[70] The Hungarian psychologist János Vizi suggests that domestic audiences embrace porn as a substitute for their own boring, uneventful sexual lives. Sexism is apparent in consumption, he notes; because males are more responsive to visual stimulation, male viewers far outnumber females, who can be repelled by scenes of intercourse without emotion.[71]

"Pornography is an industry for Hungary, not a tragedy," says Andràs Török, director of the Budapest Photography Museum (and former deputy minister of culture), who sees it as a partial solution to the country's still massive unemployment.[72] Nonetheless, the pornography industry often seems an unpleasant phase of the "shock therapy" that capitalism imposed on impoverished post-Soviet economies, justly condemned for its tawdriness, its exploitation of women and underclasses, and its stimulus of corruption, both petty and political. Whereas some former socialists applaud the "sexual revolution" fostered by porn, others condemn the "sexploitation" of the body's "labor value."[73] Critic Péter Esterházy, for example, thinks of pornography as claustrophobic. He suggests that pornography in Hungary is just as stifling to the imagination as was the country's formerly communist social structure; both pornography and communism promote "lies" about individuals and social institutions.[74] Feminists protest the commodification of women, though thus far analyses have concentrated more on subjects such as images in mainstream cinema, gender disparities, and economic inequities rather than pornography itself.[75] As is the case with trying to assess the social impact of industries from mining to automobile manufacturing, computing the effect of pornography on quality of life is both difficult and idiosyncratic.

Nonetheless, leaving aside objections that porn undermines morality, cheapens intimacy, and demeans women, many Hungarians are appalled that their cultural heritage is for sale and that porn seems woven into the fabric of life. Visiting a mineral bath or coffee shop, two of Budapest's signature pleasures, now carries the risk of a citizen's stumbling onto a naked couple being videotaped. General dismay greeted the news that one producer had bribed an official to permit him to shoot scenes in Budapest's venerable Benedictine-founded Toldy Ferenc High School, that another had gotten into the Szabò Ervin Municipal Library, and still a third had commandeered an army tank on active duty.[76] Italian producers Gianfranco Romagnoli and Steve Morelli have shot several epics, notably one on the spy Mata Hari, inside Festetics Palace (a national museum) near Lake Balaton, about sixty-two miles south of Budapest.[77] Producers seem determined to outdo Patrick Collins, owner of Elegant Angel, who paid off a transport official in order to shoot *Buttwoman Does Budapest* (1993) on the Number 18 tram as it wended its way through the affluent Taban Park neighborhood. Worse, Collins's wife, Tianna, appeared in most of the scenes and seemed to be inciting Hungarians to perform lewd acts in front of some of the city's star tourist attractions. Even where producers use only exteriors, Budapest's stunning cityscape functions as a character: cameras glide across at least one of the city's seven Danube bridges,[78] traverse the shopping streets, or register the Royal Palace, the domed Parliament building, the State Opera House, the Millennial Monument, or St. Stephen's Basilica, which now seem merely stops on a sex tour.

For all that, Hungary has reshaped the European porn video and made it instantly recognizable in a highly competitive world marketplace. This "branding" of a successful product is the result of creating new icons of desire, altering sexual content, and trademarking anal sex. Cynics might well observe that success has come on the backs—or relevant anatomical parts—of performers, and to a degree that is the case. As journalists often observe, actresses of Hungarian extraction outnumber those of all other nationalities in the European industry. Hungary has actually exported erotic entertainers since the 1920s, when its fiery dancers enlivened cabarets throughout Europe. Most famous of porn divas is Ilona Staller, known as "Cicciolina" (Cuddles). The daughter of an official in Hungary's communist Ministry of the Interior, Cicciolina began a modeling career in Italy in the 1970s. Eventually the star of more than three hundred porn cassettes, Cicciolina popularized herself through topless appearances on Italian TV in 1978, parlaying her notoriety into political candidacies first for Italy's Green Party, Lista del Sole, and then for Partito Radicale. In 1987 she won a seat in the Italian Parliament, after campaign whistle-stops at which she exposed her left breast to symbolize her ideological positions on environment, peace, drugs, and the death penalty.[79] After her portrait by Jeff Koons was exhibited at the 1990 Venice Biennale, she married the American pop artist, who painted or sculpted numerous versions of the two of them engaged in the anal intercourse that was her signature (they have since divorced). Retired since 1989 from porn, Staller in 2002 announced her intent to run for the Hungarian Parliament, a poorly timed move considering that Tamás Szecskö, a Socialist candidate, was forced to withdraw after revelations that he and his wife had appeared in a porn film.[80] Staller has garnered headlines more recently by claiming that she was once a spy for the Hungarian secret police,[81] by campaigning for AIDS education and treatment, and by offering to sleep with Saddam Hussein in the interests of world peace.[82] Her notoriety embodies an arch, almost mocking eroticism that many Europeans associate with her Hungarian roots.

Hungarian performers gravitated to Italy because of that country's adulation of porn celebrities. Erika Bella, Angelica Bella, and Simona Valli, all from Hungary, helped build the Italian industry.[83] The most successful is Anita Rinaldi (aka Anita Skultety, born in Dunaú jváros), a performer turned contract director for the European firm Xcel (distributed in the United States by Vivid Video) who, after reestablishing herself in Budapest, won the 2000 Best Director Award for *Planet Sexxx* at the annual American Erotic Film Awards. Rinaldi also owns Touch Me, a talent agency that casts porn videos as well as legitimate movies and television commercials. Other Budapest casting agencies include Blue Angel, Jordan's, Experience, and Exotic Model, all of which circulate catalogs with pictures of clients and a description of what each is willing to do. One agent, Sylvia Kerekes, handles 330 women and 7 men. Kerekes and Rinaldi adopt a hands-on approach, often appearing on the set to show their clients how to dress and to advise them on hygiene.[84] They can choose from a steady stream of wannabes. When journalists ask producers why they have set up shop in Budapest, the typical response is to point out the window to nubile girls parading by in high heels, micro-shorts, and transparent blouses.

As one might expect, the massive migration of pretty girls from the provinces to a city of severe economic disparities is itself irresistible to mainstream and porn scenarists alike. Typical of the former is Ágnes Incze's legitimate Hungarian film, *I Love Budapest* (2001). Incze's plot follows a country girl seeking a "grand life" in the metropolis, a goal, she is advised, that can be accomplished by "looking great" (e.g., wearing a tank top even in winter) and being liberal with blow jobs. In Incze's film magical realism rescues the heroine from a bleak factory and also from the lure of bars, drugs, and petty criminality of the city, but the director makes clear that the limited prospects for poorly educated young women elevate sex to a viable economic option.

A porn treatment of female flight from the countryside is the trilogy called *The Betrayal of Innocence* (1993) by the American Scotty Fox,[85] in which Marika, a farm girl, escapes her brutal stepfather only to fall prey to the corruption of Budapest. Marika works as a dancer in a live-sex club, becomes a prostitute, and services clients in the city's famous bathhouses. Each episode of *The Betrayal of Innocence* is clumsily structured and badly shot, even for Fox, never a polished director, who was working with a pickup local crew. One reviewer described the performers' hairstyles, costumes, and makeup as "fifties K-Mart."[86] The cheesiness was repellent; hapless performers who seemed genuinely vulnerable did not lure audiences. Fox's acne-scarred, clearly lower-class performers contrast sharply with the elegantly made-up women in today's upscale features, which layer Hungarian porn with ersatz glamour. Yet the hunger for style and excitement in both *I Love Budapest* and in Fox's incoherent trilogy is obviously a compelling force behind Hungary's transition to capitalism, and the dangers and rewards resonate with performers. For women otherwise trapped in factory or farm jobs, a short career in porn seems light, lucrative work with a lot of promise; power-dressed, armed with cell phones, recognized on the street, they can resemble at least for a time the many male entrepreneurs who pursue the capitalist mythos in Budapest today.

As Martina Mercedes says of what is still a barter economy: "If you model, you have to have sex with the agent, the booker and the photographer. In porn, I only have to have sex with one person, and I get paid for it."[87] Actresses such as Mercedes follow the lead of American performers such as Jenna Jameson, who is now worth millions. Given that Hungary's official minimum wage, in 2004, is less than three hundred dollars per month, and the average wage is only five hundred dollars a month, working in porn is a quick way to accumulate capital. A veteran such as Tünde Brust can make four hundred to a thousand dollars per scene: "With the money I earned, I bought a three-bedroom apartment. Later this year, I'm going to open a small grocery store, too."[88] Reliable native male actors, though less in demand, can also do well. Nick Lang (aka Attila), who entered the business in the early 1990s, has parlayed his salaries into "three cars and a house and a café, and a video rental business and [more]."[89] As is the case elsewhere, salaries vary enormously: appearing in a domestic Hungarian video may earn a performer only fifty dollars, while a well-heeled foreign entrepreneur can offer a major Hungarian starlet up to five thousand dollars a day.[90]

Performer advantage increases as the popularity of the more talented and photogenic performers forces European companies to embrace a studio star system. Like their American counterparts, Hungarian actresses strive to attract fans. Just as early American film producers resisted the star system until Carl Laemmle put Mary Pickford's name above his titles, European porn companies tried to keep performers interchangeable, identifying them in credits only by first names, in order to keep wages down. As Private Media's CEO Berthe Milton said at the beginning of the 1990s: "We always use new, fresh talent. . . . Normally we never use any talent more than three times. We never use porn stars."[91] Using a different strategy, German companies trademarked the names of stars such as Dolly Buster, Sarah Young, Teresa Orlowski, and Helen Duvall and still guard them as jealously as General Foods does the name Betty Crocker. When the original Helen Duvall (an economics graduate of Erasmus University) wanted to form her own production company, she had to relinquish the name; the actress who appears now is billed as the "new Helen Duvall."

In the United States, by contrast, Vivid Video shrewdly revived the old Hollywood studio system, placing a select group of Vivid Girls under exclusive contracts at guaranteed salaries and marshaling press agents to publicize stripping tours and TV appearances.[92] The rough capitalism in Hungary encourages free agency, so that at least some performers can make better deals for themselves, and one can chart an actress's rise by her name changes over time (see Kovi filmography in appendix). Even Private Media has accepted an inevitable truth, articulated by critic J. Morthland: to a far greater extent than with mainstream films, heterosexual viewers choose porn movies because they are sexually attracted to specific performers in them.[93] Starlets now travel to European ports via Private Media's own luxury yacht, actually a small liner with PRIVATE emblazoned on the side in six-foot letters. The ship doubles as a shooting location, and journalists are invited to come aboard to interview the latest stars.

Globalization dictates that stage names be easily recognizable to international audiences. Instead of Italian sobriquets, Hungarian divas these days choose French (Monique Covet), Swedish (Nikky Andresson, aka Nikki Anderson), or, increasingly, English names (Anita Black, Anita Blond, Wanda Curtis, Sophie Evans, Claudia Jackson, Elisabeth King, Bolivia Samsonite, Michelle Wild, Cassandra Wilde, Maya Gold, and so on). As is the case with celebrities in the legitimate movie and recording industries, stars of porn are products; in that respect the Jenna Jamesons and Nikky Andressons are no different than Britney Spears or Julia Roberts.

Names are only part of the branding required to build loyal global fans. For over a decade Hungarian performers have been renowned for beauty, sensuality, and a willingness to do anything on camera—a reputation again derived from Budapest's associations with lasciviousness. At one level semiotics is just fashion. Just as Russians in the old Soviet Union could instantly pick out American tourists on Nevsky Prospect by their bright clothing, polished shoes, even teeth, designer eyeglasses, coiffeured hair, and confident strides, so porn connoisseurs can quickly discern the "Magyar Look," a matrix of slightly swarthy skin, smoldering eyes and posture, sleek style, and provocative flair. American women are "overengineered," say Europeans, while Hungarians are "natural," that is, free of silicon, tattoos, and piercings. *Natural* is, of course, a relative term, especially since tattoos and piercings are beginning to surface on Hungarian bodies; if one's body is one's instrument, the urge to modify it must be powerful. Moreover, *natural* clearly no longer refers to the presence of pubic hair. The visual shorthand of globalized media has led to genital synecdoches, a process that mandates shaving or depiliating labia—and penises—and, for that matter, removing underarm hair, which used to be a European body marker. In any event promoters of the Magyar Look reject imperialistic American standards of beauty, turning away from both the scrubbed, nubile cheerleader image so beloved of *Playboy* readers and the torpedo-breasted blonde parodies who populate American porn videos. The intent is to enlarge the domain of eroticism to include the striking and the interesting rather than the predictably pretty, a campaign applauded in Europe.

The status of performers has been further complicated by mutations in format caused by globalization. Where mainstream movies are concerned, for example, globalization tends to privilege action narratives in which plot and dialogue are subordinated to frenetic events. Fights, weapons, and chase scenes across scenic countrysides and cityscapes require little or no dubbing into local languages, can be understood by anyone, and thus appeal across borders, whether shot in California, Germany, or Taiwan. For similar reasons American pornographers began around 1990 to emphasize "gonzo" formats that foreground virtuoso sexual performance in loosely connected sequences easily followed by export audiences. In a sense, of course, *all* hard-core videos lurch from orgasm to orgasm, just as Hollywood blockbusters career from explosion to explosion.[94] Porn professionals nonetheless categorize videos in the heterosexual market as gonzos or features.[95] So simple a division makes no room for varieties premised on fetishes from lingerie to lactation, bondage, or wrestling, a range that addresses tiers of marketing niches, but does employ a convenient yardstick: features embed the sex in traditional narrative, while gonzos do not. Performer recognition is crucial to the gonzo type. Scott Stein, a marketing director for Sin City Video, says that, while plot and a well-known director are marketable elements, "when you're dealing with more wall-to-wall or gonzo videos, really what you're pushing is the girl."[96] That fact sharpens competition between American and European performers.

More significantly, European producers have modified both the cheap gonzo format and the more expensive feature. Of the eleven thousand American porn videos made in 2001, only about two thousand were features, and these were mostly romantic or psychological dramas aimed primarily at women and couples. Private Media and its European rivals have chosen to develop polished features that are essentially action movies and to upgrade gonzo formats to look more like segmented features, thus adding a gloss that lures both home consumers and satellite TV suppliers.

Rocco Siffredi and Christoph Clark, for example, typically restructure gonzo sequences into a self-reflexive form that has found favor among American audiences, who just as readily embraced the "reality television" pioneered in Europe. Siffredi and Clark interact on screen with their camera crews, who treat the performers as athletes preparing for competition; males stroke their penises continuously to maintain erections, rather like football players doing warm-ups, while females apply lubricants to vaginas and anuses, like pole vaulters putting resin on their palms. Keeping everybody naked strips away some of the usual sexual hierarchies, since the only person with any visible "power" is the director, who is also a performer. Siffredi and Clark first run diagnostics, suggesting that a newcomer suck a penis to get a feel for it or probing vaginas and opening buttocks in a droll tour of flesh, using a vernacular invented for chatting about acts and positions. For most of the video, of course, the cameras focus on individual bodies as "hard" intercourse pushes physical limits. Clark's *Hardball* and *Eurogirls* series (installments of both series began in 1997) highlight sex on chairs, countertops, apartment balconies, and exercise machines, with bodies upside down, hanging from windowsills, hoisted onto trapezes, twisted into Kama Sutra poses, or reconfigured as heaps. For series such as *True Anal Stories* and *Rocco's Private Fantasies* Siffredi and two to four male colleagues will penetrate up to twenty women as the latter gather beside a pool or on the grounds of an estate to wait their turns; the result is less an orgy than a sexual track and field meet. Despite the rough sexual paces, says American director Veronica Hart, women enjoy working with Siffredi.[97] Both directors have won acclaim in the United States (Clark's *Eurogirls* won a series award from *AVN* in 2001), and their success has boosted European products.

Here group sex prevails, with female participants typically engaging in anal sex, double penetration (one penis in a vagina, one in an anus), and "airtights" (i.e., a double penetration plus fellatio of a third penis, so that all orifices are filled) and, in European versions still considered too extreme for the United States, double vaginal or double anal penetration, urination and bondage with penetration, and vaginal or anal fisting. Group sex is a response to the deliquescence of the story line, which leaves the narrative untethered. The "nasty" connotation of anal intercourse compensates for narrative slack, and enlisting the additional orifice heightens kinetic interest and foregrounds the individual performer. The Magyar Look is not enough: to radiate an identity, a naked Euro body must actually *do* something, and anal sex has become *the* Hungarian signature.

Because anal sex is virtually universal in Hungarian scenarios, audiences now assume that it will be present. "Shot in Budapest" is thus advertising shorthand for anal sex; when American video stores create a shelf section called "Hungarian," that is what the label usually means. Such stereotypes have their roots in folklore. Since at least the 1870s, consumers of erotica have attributed specific sexual tropes to particular nationalities. This tradition differs from familiar racial and ethnic syndromes that lump all Latins into Hispanic or all Asians into Oriental genres[98] by assigning tastes to nations: oral sex to the French (who gave their name to "French pictures"), flagellation to the English (the "English vice"), big breasts and big penises to the Americans, bondage to the Japanese, homosexuality to the Greeks and Italians, enormous dildos to the Germans, sacrilege to the Spanish. Bizarre, even silly, alleged national preferences constitute a form of niche marketing, a way of assigning identity to sexual representation.

However one thinks of anal sex, its prevalence suggests a maturation of pornography into a deconstructive, self-reflexive mode. In what is usually the penultimate phase of an anal sequence, the actress rides the male's penis in the position known in the trade as a "reverse cowgirl anal." Here the male disappears, reduced to the penis on which his partner posts. As she sits thus astride, the camera "reads" her entire dorsal side and face, emphasizing the depiliated labia around the vagina from which the penis is so clearly absent, a direct challenge to the immutability of gender. Whatever gender, and ethnic, instabilities seem evident here, few positions so convincingly demonstrate the corporeality—the materiality—of bodies themselves. In this position the actress's weight pushes her partner's penis deeper into her, though protocol calls for the actress to rock back from time to time, so that the male can withdraw to expose her empty anus (a shot called a "gaper"), a void of several inches that is itself highly symbolic. The penetration of so traditionally "secret" a place lends an authenticity to representation; hard-core porn in this regard achieves a degree of intimacy that mainstream cinema, for all its emotive range, rarely can. As Hungarian director István Kovács insists: "what [Hungarian performers] do on set is real. . . . [The filmed sex] has a quality to it that is real."[99] What is real, of course, is in the mind of the beholder, but certainly making sex "real" has been the goal of filmed hard-core pornography since its inception.

At the same time, nothing could illustrate so well as the Hungarian emphasis on anality Georges Bataille's thesis that Western eroticism is linked to nonreproductive sex. Bataille argues that eroticism, along with Western culture itself, has been divorced from natural cycles. By preserving and violating taboos, pornography affirms a sensuous artifice distanced from reproduction.[100] Similarly, a double penetration scene in which a Hungarian actress serves as the meat in a sandwich composed of two males and herself makes literal and visible Eve Kosovsky Sedgwick's argument that males bond across and through the bodies of females in Western literature and culture.[101] Moreover, according to Judith Butler, gender is performance, in the sense that performance calls gender into being, and in European porn performance is all.[102]

Hungarian performers seem comfortable with the female body's functioning as an axis for male satellites. Instead of reacting to anal sex as aggression, as American actresses sometimes do, Hungarian women accept a dramatic progression (oral, vaginal, anal, and oral again) of intercourse in which orifices are displayed and semiotically filled. The anality is oddly, even ironically, sanitized. Thanks to off-screen preparatory douches by actresses, penises are never withdrawn soiled, though the scatalogical implications are preserved and reaffirmed by a protocol called "ass to mouth," commonly rendered in industry parlance as an "ATM." Here penises move directly from anuses to female mouths for final fellatio and ejaculation. This deliberate breaking of taboo—not to mention invocations of the specter of AIDS—presumably heightens eroticism but also elevates the female, whose lips, brimming with semen, invariably smile directly into the lens to close the sequence, into an all-devouring figure.

So prevalent are the multiple penetrations of women that, if a dozen typical Hungarian videos were run on a bank of screens, the effect would resemble the temple sculpture friezes of India, whose erotic assemblages of figures depict female sexuality as cosmic force. But it is the anality that contributes most to the iconography. Because Europeans represent women as bent on capturing seed at all costs, the anal sequences refurbish the male fantasy of voracious females that has been somewhat attenuated by three decades of bland American porn. European anality thus provides an edge in a cut-throat market because it registers *as* fantasy. Such displays, artifice made plain (Bataille again), distinguish the Hungarian style. American divas are parodies of sexual attraction, unbelievable in their exaggerated, over-ballasted bodies. Hungarian divas may be natural, pretty women one might meet on the street, but the extreme sex pushes them beyond ordinariness.

Extreme acts are often uncomfortable, says a now-retired American actress, who is convinced that the European insistence on anal sex and multiple penetrations pushed American directors to include both more often in their videos. According to her, female performers rely on enemas, special lubricants, muscle control, and the professionalism of their male colleagues:

> It's mostly practice and blocking. The worst problem is when not everybody can find the same rhythm. And talking [on screen] about it: I could never say "Oh, honey, please fuck my tight little asshole" without breaking up. But once you get used to [double penetrations and airtights], they can be blessings in disguise. You have plenty to keep you busy, especially keeping the right parts pointed toward the camera, and you don't have to worry so much about projecting [as in acting], since there's always another dick to find a home for. Plus you get paid more for the scene. [An airtight] can also be a *little* bit of a turn-on, when you think about how you are actually doing something that is kind of hard to imagine. Everybody [on the set] jokes about it. I mean, nobody really fucks like that in real life.[103]

Although anal sex appeared sporadically and reticently in American porn in the past, including it accelerated only when European imports became common. Adding "foreign" tastes to American erotic repertoires does not always succeed. In the late1990s, for instance, American directors borrowed from the Japanese the *bukkake* scene, in which a dozen or so males masturbate as a group then, one by one, ejaculate over the body and face of an actress until semen puddles around her. Despite obvious economic advantages (unknown males who need only masturbate are cheap), *bukkake* videos have made only modest inroads, presumably because the fetishistic appeal of semen does not offset the subordination of women for most audiences. (In dramatic terms orgasms in most porn genres remain climaxes rather than the main events.) The greater staying power of anality, on the other hand, is evident not simply in porn videos by numerous American directors (e.g., John Leslie, John Stagliano, and Max Hardcore [Paul Little]) but also in the larger culture that they help shape.[104] The current American fascination with anality, manifest in such disparate media as "Sex and the City," HBO's hugely popular series, and "Pucker Up," the syndicated column by Tristan Taormino (novelist Thomas Pynchon's niece), owe a good deal to European influence.

Europeans have also transformed the porn feature into a higher-quality product. Here Private Media has raised the bar for other European companies by combining spectacular sex, spectacular locations, and spectacular special effects. Although its most ambitious venture to date is probably *The Uranus Experiment* (1999), an anal space opera that features intercourse in zero gravity, Private now routinely shoots Hungarian performers in venues more exotic than Budapest. Random examples include *Apocalypse Climax* (1997), a two-part takeoff on the mainstream Coppola film *Apocalyse Now,* shot in the Philippines; *The Fugitive* (1998), another trilogy and another takeoff but with a female fugitive in Venezuela; *Tatiana* (1999), yet another trilogy, a Hungarian historical drama; *Madness* (2000), a three-part murder mystery set in Brazil; *African Dreams* (1999), a sexual tour of animal parks in South Africa; *In the Arms of Evil* (2002), a vampire film that moves from Hungarian castles to South American resorts; and *Gladiator* (2002), two parts modeled on the Ridley Scott epic, with similar computer-generated Roman scenes. When Pierre Woodman shot hard-core scenes for his trilogy *The Pyramid* (1999), the pyramid of Cheops was in the frame, lifting his eroticism to a different plane.

Not everyone likes Private Media features. Critic Patrick Riley thinks that the gloss just barely masks overworked formulas, that the group sex and anality that are Private hallmarks have become tiresome, and that the company's imperialism has encouraged other producers to exploit new "hunting grounds" for talent.[105] But Private Media videos fly off the shelves in rental stores around the world. The company's globe-trotting is itself a bid for the international market, as is its reputation for quality. In addition to its stable of European directors (Antonio Adamo, Jean-Yves LeCastel, Frank Thring, Pierre Woodman), Private Media is now attracting high-profile Americans, most notably the accomplished Michael Ninn, who has released his *Perfect* (2002), a science fiction thriller, and *2Funky4U* (2002), an animated feature, through Private.

Private also began funding Hungarian István Kovács, better known as Kovi, whose career trajectory has been high and rapid. A former photojournalist who changed careers in 1992 after serious leg surgery, Kovi began shooting porn films for Helen Duvall, whose proprietary policies he found restrictive. Today he runs his own Budapest company, Luxx, located on the seedier Pest side of the Danube, and releases his films through various labels, including those of Private Media, to which he is attractive because of his ability to bring in a feature at low cost.[106] In 1998 Kovi claimed that he could make a ninety-minute video for seventeen thousand dollars, exclusive of his own fee, of course,[107] far less (it is rumored) than Pierre Woodman, long Private's lead director. Now, however, Kovi's penchant for travel has surely increased his budgets. Kovi shoots from twelve to fifteen features a year, drawing on a Budapest-based repertory company of approximately forty performers, some of whom travel with him to locations abroad. "We brainstorm together," he says.[108]

Although his rivals include perhaps a dozen Hungarians, as opposed to foreigners working in Budapest, Kovi is the country's premiere porn director and easily its most professional. Even so, domestic competition is fierce, especially among the three leading companies, Kovi's Luxx, Helena Video, and Fókusz Video, which together control about 95 percent of the domestic market. Recently, Kovi and Gábor Falussy, managing director for the company Lyss Ltd. and the Web site Erotika.hu, battled over Hungarian and Internet distribution rights to videos that Luxx Film has imported from abroad.[109] Local disputes are common. *Popo Magazin (Butt Magazine)* awarded Kovi the Hungarian porn Oscar in 2003, but he returned it when the magazine ran an article critical of him, as did his loyal divas, Michelle Wild and Maya Gold, who had been similarly honored.

Kovi's first efforts, such as *Stolen Glances* (1998), *Cuntry Club* (1998), *The Girl Takes a Ride* (1999), and *Lap Dance* (1999), all videographed in and around Budapest in nightclubs, city streets, and country fields, were fairly crude. Improving locations, seeking out the spectacular, improved his plots and his confidence. Americans first noticed his film *Lethal Information* (1999), an espionage caper involving a purloined computer disk, the recovery of which necessitated acts of seduction by a half-dozen female spies. These took place in warehouses, a speedboat, a jail, on a bridge, and beside a helicopter that landed for a tryst outside Budapest by its female pilot. In the two-episode *Indiana Mack* (2001) performers couple on jungle treks in South America, on trains racing across East Europe, on board a sailing ship in the Mediterranean, and underneath camels in the Moroccan desert. Kovi puts locations to maximum use. While he was in the desert to finish *Indiana Mack,* he shot additional footage to be edited into *Desert Camp Sex Exchange* (2001).

Since then, Kovi has shot sexual parodies of detective stories (*Intrigue and Pleasure* [2002], which twits *The Maltese Falcon*), television dramas (*Sex Slider* [2000]), domestic comedies (*Brides and Bitches* [2001], a funny take on *Father of the Bride*), horror movies (*Funky Fetish Horror Show* [2002], which lampoons teenage menace movies), romantic comedies (*Love Is in the Web* [2002], a rip-off of *You've Got Mail*), costume dramas (*Eternal Love* [2001]), techno-thrillers (*Computerized Sex Cravings* [2000]), and, of course, his own version of the country girl corrupted by Budapest tale (*Virginia's Story* [2000]), all of whose lightly plotted elements and action sequences are easily understood by viewers familiar with mainstream genres and with the originals that Kovi sends up. Parodying mainstream artifacts is a classic function of pornography but has additional advantages. Shooting so many features a year does not leave time for script development; it is much easier to rip off Hollywood. From time to time he also shoots vignettes, the upscale European version of a gonzo routine as a series of self-contained stories (in a typical example a chambermaid hides in a closet to spy on a couple, who, discovering the voyeur, pull her into the action). The American Adult Video Awards named him Best Foreign Director in 2001 for *The Splendor of Hell,* a vignette video. The following year Kovi won the more significant Best European Director award at Berlin's Venus Festival. In any case Kovi now ranks with Adamo and Woodman as a top European director.

Visually innovative, Kovi is often praised by porn critics for videos such as *Julia* (2000), in which he foregrounds a couple in front of a screen that depicts them in stunning reverse angle. He is proud of digital effects whose sophistication is unusual in the industry. In *DNA* (2002), for example, the protagonist and antagonist are the same woman, both played by Michelle Wild, who seamlessly appears to have intercourse with different males in the same room at the same time. The morphing effects in *Eternal Love* would be impressive in a mainstream film, all the more so because they were achieved on a low budget. His audio and dubbing excepted, Kovi's production values are among the highest in the global industry, partly because he can draw on Budapest's advanced recording, mixing, and postproduction studios.

Although it sounds odd to say so, what most distinguishes Kovi's porn is his visual depiction of sex. His videos embody careful planning, blocking, and setups of intercourse, as do most top-of-the-line European examples. American standards are lower. As Veronica Hart has observed, most American directors seem contemptuous of the sex that is their stock in trade; they "wander off the set during the fuck scenes," leaving the mechanics to the whim of the actors and camerapersons.[110] For Kovi sex is central, and he tries to make it interesting and erotic. Although he can save time and money by tweaking genres, he is careful never to subordinate the sex to plot, which is "realistic" only to the extent that it can tether fantasy. European sex scenes are far more demanding in terms of time and physical prowess than American, says actress Sylvia Saint (Silvia Tomcalova), a citizen of the Czech Republic, which is now catching the porn overflow from Hungary: "I prefer working in the States. Because in the USA they do not shoot hard sex like in Europe. They just do a couple of sex scenes and at a maximum you do anal. That's it. And they're much faster than the Europeans. A scene in L.A. usually takes up to four hours. In Europe sometimes one scene takes 20 hours."[111]

Preplanning enables Kovi to shoot his sex footage in three to four days. A large, jovial man, Kovi coaxes polished results from his company performers, all of whose contracts forbid drugs and alcoholism.[112] Kovi's female performers are carefully made up, and under his direction gaze seductively into the camera as they configure themselves into almost painterly poses. He has perfected this protocol, training actresses to coordinate their breathing with the motions of intercourse so that they appear to lunge toward the camera with every thrust of a penis. They smolder into the lens, not into the faces of their partners: licking lips, lifting chins, tilting heads, showing half-lidded eyes, evoking the ravishing, darkly voluptuous Magyar Look. Michelle Wild, Kovi's lead performer, excels at the technique: no matter where she is in a glut of bodies, her face is always visible to the camera.

Kovi's fellow Private Media director Frank Thring (himself Mel Gibson's costar in *Mad Max: Beyond Thunderdome*) uses Hungarians almost exclusively because they are "placid": sex, Thring says, is simply "no big deal" for them.[113] For the most talented, of course, sex—or its exuberant simulation—is a very big deal: Wild and Sophie Evans, to mention only two divas, easily persuade audiences that the most improbable act of intercourse, especially anal intercourse, is a splendid experience. Kovi helps the women develop followings by providing links on his Web site to theirs or featuring them until they can start their own sites. Luxx.hu currently carries dozens of photos of Michelle Wild, the expressive beauty that Kovi has nurtured into a diva, in poses that demonstrate amazing physical skill. Formerly a country girl, Wild is now recognized everywhere in Budapest, has launched a singing career there, recently won the "Best Tease" Award of 2003 at the U.S. Adult Video Awards, and, according to Kovi, is being wooed by Miklós Jancsó, the enfant terrible of mainstream Hungarian cinema (*The Red and the White* [1967]) to star in a new film. Pornography now, as always, refreshes mainstreams.

Kovi's success and that of European firms such as Private Media illustrate the potential of a two-way information flow that has been so often promised but so rarely delivered in the rhetoric of media convergence. If pundits rarely have pornography in mind when they sing the praises of globalization, it is telling that purveyors of the erotic should have chosen to challenge the American dominance of sexual imagery. Critics may deplore the commodification of sex, though it is clearly in keeping with a capitalism that Disneyfies family values and commercializes religion within a cultural arena that has expanded to worldwide proportions. Europeans now compete successfully because they have trespassed more boldly on the precincts of eroticism, reconceived its genres, and asserted the merits of different body types. Doubtless, other nationalities will displace the Hungarians. Already the Magyar Look is giving way to what might be called an "East European Look" as producers exploit Poland, the Czech Republic, and Croatia. Pornography is under no obligation to ensure proportional representation of particular ethnic or national groups; global markets will sort out erotic standards of beauty and desire.

In the end what may be the most salient aspect of pornographic videos is not that its bodies are inscribed with class, ethnicity, gender, and perhaps nationality but that our culture has chosen the body as a canvas in the first place. The popularity of pornographic videos—and the same came be said of an even greater volume of sports programming—is that it attests to the trust that audiences place in bodies as quotidian reality. For pornographers, despite their obvious manipulation of bodies, the intimacy of explicitly realized sex shores up essentialism. Against all odds, porn seems to say, bodies persist, for all of their commodification, as ultimately "undetermined" by the social and political upheavals that swirl about us. The worldwide appeal of Hungarian porn lends support to this paradox of representation: globalized capitalism would seem to free us from the weight of corporeality even as biological desire ensures that we remain entrapped by that corporeality. Or, and it amounts to the same thing, the message may be that ultimately consumers recognize and understand the spurious claims of marketing that would fashion the "material" aspects of sex and sexuality. As Franco Bernardi Bifo has observed of the rise of European porn performers: "The power of desire breaks down all borders, all traditional mights, all imaginary hierarchies. But this crumbling is not just a destruction, for new border lines and new hierarchies are taking shape."[114]

APPENDIX:
ISTVÁN KOVÁCS ("KOVI") VIDEOGRAPHY, ARRANGED BY U.S. RELEASE DATE

Except for examples otherwise noted, the following films (some are listed now at www.luxx.hu) have been released by Private Media, whose product lines include Private Gold, Private Video DeLuxe, Private Reality, Matador, Private Black Label, Pirate Video, and Pirate Fetish Machine. Private labels were distributed in the United States by Odyssey until 2001. As should be obvious from the credits, Kovi works with a repertory of performers whose names and English spellings change over time.

Features

Devil Deep Inside (Private Black Label 32, 2003). 95 min. Michelle Wild, Dike, Maya Gold, Tina Crystal, Black Diamond, Nikita, Simony Diamond, Csoky Ice, Mick Blue, Dieter von Stein, Lauro De Giotto.

Fetish Recall: Fact or Friction? (Pirate Fetish Machine 11, 2003). 106 min. Rita Faltoyano, Nikki Blond, Michelle Wild, Cameron Cruise, Maya Gold, Tina Crystal, Niki Bellucci, Tiffany, Csoky Ice, Mick Blue, Dieter von Stein, Lauro De Giotto.

Garden of Seduction (New Sensations, 2003). 93 min. Michelle Wild, Lucy, Katalin Kiraly, Maya Gold, Niki Bellucci, Kata Hilton, Emese, Renato, Csoky Ice, Mick Blue, Lauro De Giotto. Produced by Scott Taylor.

Sex Secrets of the Paparazzi (Private Black Label 28, 2003). 102 min. Dora Venter, Michelle Wild, Sandy Style, Sandra Ring, Bianca, Maya Gold, Nicky Black, Claudio Meloni, Bob Terminator, Nick Lang, Csoky Ice.

No Job No Blow (Pirate Fetish Machine 9, 2003). 108 min. Michelle Wild, Melinda Vecsey, Mandy Bright, Veronica Sinclair, Myli, Tchanka, Maya Gold, Leila, Steve Holmes, Csoky Ice, Mick Blue, Dieter von Stein.

Private Love Story (Private Black Label 27, 2002). 92 min. Dora Venter, Michelle Wild, Dorothy Black, Alissa, Mandy Bright, Sandra Ring, Patricia Diamond, Carmen White, Nick Lang, Steve Holmes, Csoky Ice, Mick Blue.

Fetish Academy (Pirate Fetish Machine 8, 2002). 91 min. Dina Pearl, Michelle Wild, Mandy Bright, Sandra Ring, Carmen White, Nicole, Irina, Laura Angel, Tina Crystal, Bob Terminator, Steve Holmes, Csoky Ice, Mick Blue, Dieter von Stein.

Love Is Blind (Private Black Label 26, 2002). 96 min. Sandra Iron, Carmen White, Patricia Diamond, Dora Venter, Michelle Wild, Dorothy Black, Mandy Bright, Alissa, Mick Blue, Steve Holmes, Csoky Ice, Nick Lang.

Love Is in the Web (Private Black Label 25, 2002). 99 min. Michelle Wild, Dorothy Black, Sandra Ring, Tiffany, Bianca, Carmen White, Vanessa Virgin, Angelica, Nick Lang, Leslie Taylor, Steve Holmes.

Fetish TV (Pirate Fetish Machine 7, 2002). 97 min. Mandy Bright, Karina, Linda, Veronica Carso, Bettina, Lisa Sparkle, Sandra Iron, Dora Venter, Patricia Diamond, Bailey, Tony DeSergio, Dieter von Stein, Csoky Ice.

Funky Fetish Horror Show (Pirate Fetish Machine 6, 2002). 107 min. Michelle Wild, Barbara, Judit, Nicolette, Myli, Lisa Sparkle, Carmen, Lolita, Sandra Iron, Steve Holmes, Csoky Ice, Dieter Von Stein, Leslie Taylor, Zolee.

Love Is in the Web (Private Black Label 25, 2002). 98 min. Michelle Wild, Tiffany, Angelica, Sandra Iron, Esther Virgin, Carmen White, Bianca, Steve Holmes, Leslie Taylor, Nick Lang.

DNA (Private Black Label 24, 2002). 100 min. Michelle Wild, Patricia Diamond, Melody Magic, Mandy Bright, Julia, Kyra, Myli, Claudio Meloni, Leslie Taylor, Steve Holmes, Tony DeSergio, Ian Scott, Steve Bailey.

Sex in a Frame (Pirate Fetish Machine 5, 2002). 109 min. Michelle Wild, Mandy Bright, Sandra Iron, Myli, Patricia R., Kyra, Nicolette, Carmen White, Veronica, Lolita, Steve Holmes, Ian Scott, Csoky Ice, Dieter von Stein.

Guns and Rough Sex (Private Black Label 23, 2002). 105 min. Michelle Wild, Bambi Dolce, Mandy Bright, Veronica Sinclair, Lisa, Steve Holmes, Nick Lang, Patricia Pallone, Adrienne Rouso.

Intrigue and Pleasure (Private Black Label 22, 2002). 130 min. Michelle Wild, Petra Short, Sylvia Dahl, Mandy Bright, Britnee, Chris Charming, Samantha, Mia, Steve Holmes.

The Sex Terminators (Pirate Fetish Machine 4, 2002). 109 min. Michelle Wild, Dina Pearl, Melinda Vecsey, Mandy Bright, Mili, Alice, Patricia Diamond, Franco Roccoforte, Claudio Villa, Csoky Ice, Leslie Taylor.

Fetish and Magic (Pirate Fetish Machine 3, 2002). 105 min. Michelle Wild, Dina Pearl, Katalyn, Mariana Claudet, Liza Anilo, Melinda Jersey, Veronica Sinclair, Steven Bailey, Claudio Villa, Csoky Ice, Dieter Von Stein, Leslie Taylor, Tony DeSergio, Alex Sandor, Simon Katalin, Rambo Man.

Fetish Obsession (Odyssey / Private Video Deluxe 16, 2002). 99 min. Michelle Wild, Mercedes, Dorothy Match, Sophie Angel, Britta, Vivi.

Lust Tango in Paris (Odyssey / Private Black Label 21, 2002). 131 min. Michelle Wild, Dora Venter, Mia Stone, Mercedes, Mandy, Christine Scott, Philippe Dean, Steve Holmes, Jan Scott, Pascal St. James, Sebastian Barrio.

Dominatrix Chess Gambit (Odyssey / Pirate Fetish Machine 2, 2001). 120 min. Michelle Wild, Dora Venter, Melinda, Nikki Montana, Britnee, Ginger, Jessica.

The Splendor of Hell (Odyssey / Private Video DeLuxe 14, 2001). 108 min. Monique Covet, Christina, Rita Faltoyano, Anita Paris, C. G. Summer, Angelica Bright, Chris Charming, Steve Holmes, Paul, Franco Roccoforte, Leslie Taylor. *AVN* Best Foreign Director Award, Best Foreign Vignette Tape Award, 2002.

Brides and Bitches (Odyssey / Private Black Label 20, 2001). 110 min. Dora Venter, Claudia Jackson, Maria, Michelle Wild, Rita Faltoyano, Judy Red, Betty Dark.

Eternal Love (Odyssey / Private Black Label 19, 2001). 94 min. Michelle Wild, Tony DeSergio, Claudia, Bambi Dolce, Lisa Pinelli, Petra Short, Melinda, Sheila Scott, Lauren Kiss, Nick Lang, Alberto Rey.

Eternal Ecstasy (Odyssey / Private Video Deluxe 15, 2001). 120 min. Michelle Wild, Sophie Evans, Tony Ribas.

Desert Camp Sex Exchange (Odyssey / Private Black Label 18, 2001) 92 min. Alexa Schiffer, C. G. Summer, Maria Ricci, Kristina Bella, Blond Panni, Stella Virgin, Chrystal.

Indiana Mack 2: Sex in the Desert (Odyssey / Private Black Label 17, 2001). 126 min. Dora Venter, Gariella Dion, Demi Blue, Roxanne, Alexa Schiffer, Blond Panni, Carmen Joy, Lauren Kiss, Nick Lang ("Indiana Mack"), Leslie Taylor, David Perry, Steve Holmes, Alex, Alex Mantegna.

Santo Domingo Connection (Odyssey / Private Black Label 16, 2001). 100 min. Dina Pearl, Monica Moore, Sheila Scott, Gili Sky, Judit, Maria, Sheila.

Indiana Mack: Sex in the Jungle (Odyssey / Private Video Label 15, 2001). 121 min. Dora Venter, Henriette Blond, Sheila Scott, Monique Vanda, Claudia Janson, Peggy Sue, Eva Black, Sharone, Leslie Taylor, Csoky Ice, Nick Lang ("Indiana Mack"), Freddy Dalton, Thomas Stone.

Colette's Kinky Desires (Odyssey / Pirate Fetish Machine 1, 2001). 113 min. Michelle Wild, Monica Moore, Sandra, Cleo, Christal, C. G. Summer, Franco Roccoforte, Leslie Taylor, Tony Ribas, Thomas Stone, Steve Holmes.

Erica (Odyssey / Private Black Label 14, 2000). 94 min. Monique Covet, Dorothy, Tamara N-Joy, Monica Moore, Cindy, Rita Faltoyano, Anita, Leslie Taylor, Nick Lang, Csoky Ice, Steve Holmes.

Sex Slider (Odyssey / Private Black Label 13, 2000). ? min. Nikki Andresson, Cassandra Wilde, Caroline, Dru Berrymore, David Perry.

Julia (Odyssey / Private Black Label 12, 2000). ? min. Maria, Mercedes, Adriana, Csila Star, Katy, Liz Petri, Sylvi Anderson, Nick Lang, Csoky, Leslie Taylor.

Virginia's Story (Odyssey / Private Black Label 11, 2000). ? min. Monica, Michelle, Kathy Divan, Dorothy, Virginia White, Fanny Blond, Antoanella, Caroline.

Computerized Sex Cravings (Odyssey / Private Black Label 10, 2000). 101 min. Genevievre, Amanda, Anita Black, Holly, Julia Taylor, Katja Love, Monica Moore, Silvia Bella, Alberto Rey, Csoky, Nick Lang.

Lethal Information (Odyssey / Private Gold 32, 1999). 107 min. Grety, Mary Eleniak, Diana, Leslie Taylor, Mina, Bolivia, Megan, Barbara, Wanda Curtis, Sophia Call, Timea, John Lenin, Nick Lang, Frank Gun, Mike Foster, David Perry.

Men in Fuck (Prime Video Productions / NuTech Digital, 1999). 87 min. Gabriela Blond, Frank Gun, Mike Foster, John Walton, Omar. Parody of *Men in Black*.

The Girl Takes a Ride (VCA Platinum Plus, 1999). 84 min. Mina, Vanessa, Leslie Taylor, Amanda Simon, Alexa, Dina Pearl, Laura Black, Zsolt Karlo, Frank Gun, Marki Mario.

Lap Dance (VCA Platinum Plus, 1999). 82 min. Nikita, Wendy Snipes, Alexa, Sheila Stone, Livi, Mina, Frank Gun, Nick Lang, Marki Mario, Mike Foster, Leslie Taylor.

Some Like It Hot (VCA Platinum Plus, 1999). 91 min. Anita Blond, Anita Dark, Pat, Evelyn, Claudia, Ani, Frank Mallone, Zenza Raggi, Bradon T., Reinhard.

Cuntry Club (Odyssey / Private Gold 33, 1998). 90 min. Estell, Chrissy, Nicole, Judi Bella, Grety, Ursula, Cyndy, Nick Lang, Frank Major, Valentino, John Walton, Jules.

Stolen Glances (Xcel Films, 1998). 64 min. Anita Blond, Judy, Sharone, John Walton, Frank Gun, John Lenin, Susy Hart, Roxanna Kitti, Ibolya Varga, Andrea Bella, Steve Hard.

Vignettes

Private Reality 15: Never Say No (Private Media, 2003). 84 min. Segments directed by Kovi, Jean-Yves LeCastel, and Puskin.

Private Reality 14: Girls of Desire (Private Media, 2003). ? min. Segments directed by Kovi and others.

Private Reality 13: Explosive Women (Private Media, 2003). 88 min. Segments directed by Kovi, Andrew Youngman, John Walton, and Dave Densen.

Private Reality 12: Dangerous Girls (Private Media, 2003). 87 min. Segments directed by Kovi, Jean-Yves LeCastel, Tom Herold, Little Al, and Xavi Dominguez.

Private Reality 10: Ladder of Love (Private Media, 2002). 80 min. Segments directed by Kovi, Jean-Yves LeCastel, Andrew Youngman, John Walton, and Gianfranco Romagnoli.

Private Reality 9: Do Not Disturb (We Are Having Fun) (Private Media, 2002). 72 min. Segments by Kovi, Andrew Youngman, John Walton, and Lucretia Del Toro.

Private Reality 8: Summer Love (Private Media, 2002). 79 min. Segments directed by Kovi, Gianfranco Romagnoli, Tom Herold, and Antonio Adamo.

Private Reality 7: Wild Adventures (Private Media, 2002). 97 min. Segments directed by Kovi, Antonio Adamo, Andrew Youngman, John Walton, and Little Al.

Private Reality 6: Dangerous Games (Private North America, 2002). 86 min. Segments directed by Kovi, John Walton, Andrew Youngman, Robby Blake, and Tom Herold.

Private Reality 5: Click Here to Enter (Private North America, 2002). 90 min. Segments directed by Kovi and Jean-Yves LeCastel.

Private Reality 4: Just Do It to Me (Private Media, 2002). 97 min. Segments directed by Kovi, Jean-Yves LeCastel, and Tom Herold.

Private Reality 3: From Behind Is OK (Private Media, 2002). 86 min. Segments directed by Kovi, Antonio Adamo, Jean-Yves LeCastel, Andrew Youngman, John Walton, Tom Herold, and Alessandro Del Mar.

Private Reality 2: Pure Pleasure (Private Media, 2002). 98 min. Segments directed by Kovi, Antonio Adamo, Jean-Yves LeCastel, Andrew Youngman.

Private Reality 1: Sexy Temptation (Private Media, 2001). 93 min. Segments by Kovi, Jean-Yves LeCastel, and others.

Private Odyssey I and II (Private Media, 2001). 95 and 96 min. Segments directed by Kovi, Jean-Yves LeCastel, Antonio Adamo, Pierre Woodman, Frank Thring, and others.

Private XXX 14: Cum with Me (Odyssey / Private Media, 2001). ? min. Segments directed by Kovi and others.

Private XXX 13: Sexual Heat (Odyssey / Private Media, 2001). 90 min. Segments directed by Kovi and others.

Private XXX 12: Sex, Lust and Videotapes (Odyssey / Private Media, 2001). 106 min. Segments directed by Kovi, Jean-Yves LeCastel, and François Clousot.

Private XXX 9 (Odyssey / Private Media, 2000). 86 min. Segments directed by Kovi, Antonio Adamo, Jean-Yves LeCastel, and Nick Cramer.

Private XXX 3 (Odyssey / Private Media, 1999). 109 min. Segments directed by Kovi, Frank Thring, and Pierre Woodman.

Triple X Files 12: Eat Up (Odyssey / Private Media, 1998). 94 min. Segments directed by Kovi, Frank Thring, Christoph Clark, Pierre Woodman, and John Millerman.

Triple X Files 11: Enjoy Jennifer (Odyssey / Private Media, 1998). 82 min. Segments directed by Kovi, Frank Thring, Christoph Clark, Pierre Woodman, and John Millerman.

Triple X Files 10: Memories (Odyssey / Private Media, 1998). 83 min. Segments directed by Kovi, John Millerman, and Christoph Clark.

Triple X Files 9: Hyapatia (Odyssey / Private Media, 1998). 92 min. Segments directed by Kovi, Christoph Clark, Arthus Milo, and Gabriel Zero.

Triple X Files 8: The Dungeon (Odyssey / Private Media, 1998). 84 min. Segments directed by Kovi, François Clousot, Christoph Clark, Pierre Woodman, and Scott Lucky.

Kovi has also made dozens of videos that have been distributed only in Hungary, usually advertised as made for Hungarians, in Hungarian, with Hungarian performers. The following translated titles are samples from the last few years.

> *The Garden of Lust* (Luxx, 2003)
> *Michelle and Sandra* (Luxx, 2002)
> *Playful Tongues* (Luxx, 2001)
> *Butt Mania* (Luxx, 2000)
> *Naughty Girls* (Luxx, 2000)
> *Six-Shooter* (Luxx, 2000)

Notes

1. Curt Moreck [Konrad Hammerling], *Sittengeschichte des Kinos* (Dresden: Paul Aretz Verlag, 1926), 175.
2. Erwin Panofsky, "Style and Medium in Moving Pictures," *Transition* 6 (1937): 121–123.
3. John Nadler, "'X' Marks the Spot," *Variety,* 9–15 October 1995, 40.
4. "The Sex Industry," *Economist* 346, 14–20 February 1998, 21–23.
5. Michael Williams, "Latenight Libido Rules Euro TV," *Variety,* 18 November 1991, 1, 52.
6. Playboy actually sold the Hot Network and Hot Zone channels to Vivid Video, which introduced hard-core, then resold them, along with Vivid TV, to Playboy for $92 million. See "The 25 Events That Shaped the First 25 Years of Video Porn," *Adult Video News* (August 2002), www.adultvideonews.com/cover/cover0802_01.html. Given the fast-changing nature of the pornography industry, this and the other sources drawn from the World Wide Web cited in this essay are often the most thorough, relevant, and timely.
7. Alan Cowell, "Vivendi Chief Gets an Earful from Unhappy Stockholders," *New York Times,* 25 April 2002, C1, 6.
8. Elaine Sciolino, "The French Spar over Sex: There's a Limit, No?" *New York Times,* 13 October 2002, A3.
9. "World Briefing—Finland: No More Free Pornography," *New York Times,* 6 December 2002, A8.

10. "Housewives One of Highest Pay-per-View Porn Consumers," *Ananova,* 29 July 2001, www.ananova.com/news/story (accessed 3 December 2001). Please note that *Ananova* articles are archived for only one year; each reference to *Ananova* is also cited by the date it was accessed.

11. The High Court decision was made on 18 May 2000.

12. "South Africa," LukeFord.com, 2002, www.lukeford.com/subjects/content/south_africa.html.

13. "Chinese Make Record Pornography Seizure, *Ananova,* 28 June 2002, www.ananova.com/news/story (accessed 10 October 2002).

14. "Crackdown Launched on Child Pornography 'Explosion,'" *Ananova,* 12 June 2001, www.ananova.com/news/story (accessed 3 December 2001).

15. Joseph W. Slade, "Inventing a Sexual Discourse: A Rhetorical Analysis of Adult Video Box Covers," in *Sexual Rhetoric: Media Perspectives on Sexuality, Gender, and Identity,* ed. Meta G. Carstarphen and Susan C. Zavoina (Westport, Conn.: Greenwood Press, 1999), 240–241.

16. In "'X' Marks the Spot," 40–41, Nadler put the number of videos shot in Hungary at 150; more recently, in "Blue Danube," *Nerve* 1, no. 1 (May–June): 46–53, 78, Natasha Singer accepted the figure of 300. All porn statistics are contentious. In 2001 *Forbes* magazine challenged the *New York Times'* estimate of the U.S. domestic market as generating between $10 and 14 billion, saying that the total was too high; see "In Face of Criticism, AVN Issues Strong Endorsement of Annual Statistics," *Adult Video News* (August 2001), www.www.adultvideonews.com/archives/200106/cover/cov0100.html.

17. "Vivid to Go IPO?" *Adult Video News* (September 2000), www.adultvideonews.com/bone/by0900_30.html.

18. Karl Taro Greenfield, *Speed Tribes: Days and Nights with Japan's Next Generation* (New York: HarperCollins, 1994), 88–89.

19. "World Porn," LukeFord.com, 2002, www.lukeford.com/subjects/content/world_porn.html.

20. Sophie Bordes and Daniel Serceau, "L'Irrésistible marginalisation du cinéma pornographique," *Érotisme et cinéma: Thèmes et variations,* ed. Daniel Serceau (Paris: Atlas L'Herminier, 1986), 155–172.

21. Antoine Rakovsky, "Le Brief apogée et long déclin du cinéma pornographique français," *Cinémaction: Les Dessous du Cinéma* (1991): 14–17; the volume also lists every French porn director working at the time.

22. Annabel MacGowan, "Euro-Report" (interview with Michel Ricaud)," *XXX Movie Illustrated: Adam Film World Guide* 6, no. 3 (November 1991): 36–41.

23. Wolfgang Saxon, "Beate Uhse, 81, Entrepreneur in the Business of Erotic Goods" (obituary), *New York Times,* 22 July 2001, 23.

24. Rüdiger Lautmann and Michael Schetsche, *Das Pornographierte Begehren* (Frankfurt: Campus Verlag, 1990), 19–20.

25. "Hardcore Porn Group Seeks European Listing," *Ananova,* 5 July 2001, www.ananova.com/news/story (accessed 3 December 2001). Originally founded by Berthe Milton Sr. in Stockholm in 1966, when pornography was legalized, Private Media exported the world's first full-color hard-core porn magazine and only later began shooting porn films. Milton moved the company (as Milcap Media) to Spain in 1985, branching into books, videos, DVDs, adult toys and fashions, condoms, and so on. It is now controlled by Berthe Milton Jr. through Fraserside Holdings, Ltd.

26. "Porn Goes Public," *Forbes,* 14 June 1999, www.forbes.com/global/1999/0614/0212060a.html.

27. "1993: The Private Revolution," "The 25 Events that Shaped the First 25 Years of Video Porn," *Adult Video News* (August 2002), www.adultvideonews.com/cover/cover0802_01.html.

28. Lattara to *rec.arts.movies.erotica* (rame.net) newsgroups, "Porn in the UK: UK R18 Videos under the New Guidelines," www.rame.net/library/lists/r18.html.

29. Mark Logan, "Whither Goes Thou, Adult? A Retailer's Guide to Preparing for the Twenty-first Century," *Adult Video News* (January 2000), www.adultvideonews.com/archives/200001/cover/cov0100.html; Connor Young, "Competing with Free Porn, Part One: Sizing Up the Competition, *AVN Online* (September 2002), www.avnonline.com/issues/200209/features/feat0902_02.shtml.

30. Edward Cone, "The Naked Truth: Welcome to the Real World of Internet Porn," *Wired* 10, no. 2 (February 2002): 100–103.

31. "Survey Shows Web Sex Losing Popularity," *Ananova,* 2 April 2002, www.ananova.com/news/story (accessed 10 October 2002).

32. Jack Morrison, "Challenge of Market Saturation: Revenue Down? Try Raising Prices and Expanding Overseas," *AVN Online* (September 2002), www.avnonline.com/issues/200209/features/feat0902_03.shtml.

33. "Dotcom Workers Flock to Porn Sites," *Ananova,* 12 June 2001, *www.ananova.com/news* story (accessed 3 December 2001).

34. "Private Media Group Offers to Buy Napster Trademark, URL," *AVN Online,* 12 September 2002, www.avnonline.com/issues/200209/pressreleases/091202–pr9.shtml; "Private Media Group Details Napster Strategy Adult P2P Development Objectives," *AVN Online,* 16 September 2002, www.avnonline.com/issues/200209/newsarchive/091702_pr1.shtml.

35. "Streaming Media: The End of TV—Again," *Wired* 10, no. 11 (November 2002): 50.

36. "Porn Goes Public."

37. See Joseph W. Slade, *Pornography in America* (Santa Barbara, Calif.: ABC-Clio, 2000), 115ff.; and Joseph W. Slade, "Electronic Media," *Pornography and Sexual Representation: A Reference Guide,* 3 vols. (Westport, Conn.: Greenwood Press, 2001), 2:701–748.

38. Richard C. Morais, "Porn on the Danube," *Forbes,* 14 June 1999, www.forbes.com/global/1999/0614/0212060s2.html.

39. Marc Medoff, "Brazilian Porn: The New XXX Frontier," *High Society* 27, no. 13, holiday issue (December 2002): 20–33.

40. Stagliano, perhaps the most flamboyant of American pornographers, is a key supporter of Republican Party think-tanks in this country; see Eric Schlosser, "The Business of Pornography," *U.S. News and World Report,* 10 February 1997, 42–50.

41. "Brazilian Porn's HIV Controversy," LukeFord.com, 4 May 2001, www.lukeford.com/subjects/content/AIDS.html.

42. "Brazil Puts Safe Sex Warnings on Erotic Videos," *Ananova,* 13 June 2001, www.ananova.com/news story (accessed 1 December 2001).

43. "Hispanic Heatwave: Porn's Rising Ethnic Sector," *Adult Video News* (November 2000), www.adultvideonews.com/archives/200011/cover/cover 1100_01.html.

44. "Brazilian Porn's HIV Controversy."

45. Singer, with photographs by Plachy, "Blue Danube," 49.

46. Matthew Brzezinski, *Casino Moscow: A Tale of Greed and Adventure on Capitalism's Wildest Frontier* (New York: Free Press, 2001), 36–39.

47. David Carr, "Cybersmut and Debt Undermine Penthouse," *New York Times,* 8 April 2002, C1, 9.

48. James Geary, with reporting by Simon Evans, "Sex, Lies, and Budapest," *Time Atlantic* 149, no. 12, 24 March 1997, 72.
49. Thomas Weyr, "Porn, Politics, and Paper," *Publishers' Weekly,* 12 January 1990, 21.
50. Gábor Vajda, "Zsuzsa in Hong Kong Wants to Talk to You: Phone Sex in Hungary Is Strictly a Pre-Recorded Affair, and So Far, an Unregulated One," *Budapest Week,* 7–13 October 1993, 5.
51. Nadler, "'X' Marks the Spot," 41.
52. Susie Mid-America, "Christoph Clark: Gentlemen Prefer Hard Anal" (interview), *Adult Video News* (February 1998), www.avn.com/html/avn/archives/98_02.
53. Zoltán Trencsényi, "Asszonyom, ezt tudnám nyújtani!" (Madame, This Is All I Can Provide for You!), *Népszabadság,* 11 November 1999, 9.
54. E. Fodor, "Budapest Európa pornófővárosa?" (Is Budapest the Porno Capital of Europe?), *Népszabadság,* 26 August 1995, 1.
55. Trencsényi, "Asszonyom, ezt tudnám nyújtani!"
56. Réka Bencsik, "Olcsó megoldàsok, tetemes haszonnal" (Cheap Solutions with Tremendous Profits), *Népszabadság,* 2 February 1999, 9.
57. Bencsik, "Olcsó megoldàsok, tetemes haszonnal," 9.
58. Bencsik, "Olcsó megoldàsok, tetemes haszonnal," 9.
59. Geary and Evans, "Sex, Lies, and Budapest."
60. F. Gy. A., "Ellenörzött szexhírdetesek" (Controlled Sex Ads), *Népszabadság,* 28 February 2001, 13.
61. Roger Cohen, "The Oldest Profession Seeks New Market in West Europe," *New York Times,* 19 September 2000, A1, 10.
62. David Binder, "European Operation against Sex Trade Bogs Down in Bosnia," *New York Times,* 20 October 2002, International sec., 10.
63. "Russians," LukeFord.com, www.lukeford.com/subjects/content/russians.html.
64. Nadler, "'X' Marks the Spot," 41.
65. "HIV," LukeFord.com, 11 May 1998, www.lukeford.com/archives/updates/980511.html.
66. United Nations AIDS Report, "Epidemiological Fact Sheet, 2002 Update," www.unaids.org/html/pub/publications/fact-sheets01/hungary_en_pdf.htm.
67. István Kovács, interviewed by Katalin Milter, Budapest, 18 December 2002.
68. Bencsik "Olcsò megoldàsok, tetemes haszonnal," 9.
69. Bencsik, "Olcsò megoldàsok, tetemes haszonnal," 9.
70. Bencsik, "Olcsò megoldàsok, tetemes haszonnal," 9.
71. See Mihály Aratò, *A Masik: NEM!?* (The Other: SEX!?) (Budapest: Grafit Kiado, 1997).
72. Singer, with photographs by Plachy, "Blue Danube," 46–53, 78.
73. Vajda, "Zsuzsa in Hong Kong Wants to Talk to You."
74. Péter Esterházy, *A Little Hungarian Pornography,* trans. Judith Söllösy (Evanston, Ill.: Northwestern University Press, 1997).
75. See Anikò Imre, ed., "Gender, Literature, and Film in Contemporary East Central European Culture" (special issue of CLCWeb: Comparative Literature and Culture: A WWWeb Journal [March 2001], http://clcwebjournal.lib.purdue.edu/clcweb01–1/imre01–1.html); Catherine Portuges, "Lovers and Workers: Screening the Body in Post-Communist Hungarian Cinema," in *Feminism and Pornography,* ed. Drucilla Cornell (New York: Oxford University Press, 2000), 575–586; Laura M. Dolby, "Pornography in Hungary: Ambiguity of the Female Image in a Time of Change," *Journal of Popular Culture* 29, no. 2 (Fall 1995): 119–128. For purposes of comparison with

the recent Russian experience, see also the essays in M. Levitt and A. Torporlov, eds., *Eros and Pornography in Russian Culture* (Moscow: Ladomir, 1999).

76. "Az Állam Hasznot Húz a Prostitúcióból," *Hetek* 3, no. 2, 20 March 1999, www.hetek.hu/index.php?ukk=4024.

77. See Singer, "Blue Danube," for photos of a crew working in a government office.

78. Or nine, depending on whether one counts the two railroad bridges.

79. Jean-Michel Caradec'h, "La Depute scandaleuse," *Paris Match,* 3 July 1987, 26–29; see also Riccardo Schicchi, *Cicciolina: Photos Riccardo Schicchi* (Cologne: Benedikt Taschen Verlag, 1992), 9–10.

80. On Staller, see "Porn Star Plans Hungary MP Bid," CNN.com, 27 January 2002, www.cnn.com/2002/WORLD/europe/01/27/hungary.poll/index.html; and on Szecskö, see "Would-Be Politician Withdraws after Porn Video Expose," *Ananova,* 27 July 2001, www.ananova.com/news/story (accessed 3 December 2001).

81. "Porn Star Says She Was a Communist Spy," *Columbus Dispatch,* 27 September 1999, 11A.

82. "Former Italian Porn Star Offers Herself to Saddam," *El Pereiodicoon* (Catalonia), 5 October 2002, www.ananova.com/news/story (accessed 10 October 2002).

83. Mona Pozzi has been virtually beatified by her fans following her early death from cancer, and Rocco Siffredi, the "Italian Stallion," is a national hero. Regarding the latter, see *Rock 'n' Roll Rocco I and II* (Arieta, Calif.: Evil Angel, 1997), two hardcore videos containing scenes in Rome, in which Siffredi is introduced onstage at a public concert; the crowd goes wild.

84. Morais, "Porn on the Danube"; Mark Kernes, "Anita Rinaldi and the Seven Dwarfs," *Adult Video News* (September 1998), www.adultvideonews.com/archives/199808/inner/invw.html.

85. (1) *The Awakening of Marika,* (2) *The Decadence,* and (3) *The Choice* (Chatsworth, Calif.: Coast to Coast Video, 1993).

86. Patrick Riley, *The X-Rated Videotape Guide V* (Amherst, N.Y.: Prometheus Books, 1995), 91.

87. Singer, "Blue Danube," 51.

88. Singer, "Blue Danube," 53.

89. Singer, "Blue Danube," 78. Obviously, not all performers do so well. The porn business, like its legitimate cinema counterpart, chews up would-be stars.

90. Bencsik, "Olcsó megoldàsok, tetemes haszonnal," 9.

91. "Private," LukeFord.com, n.d., www.lukeford.com/subjects/content/private.html.

92. "Branded Flesh," *Economist,* 12 August 1999, 56.

93. J. Morthland, "Porn Films: An In-Depth Report," *Take One* 4, no. 4 (March–April 1974): 11–17.

94. Linda Williams, following Richard Dyer, suggests that hard-core porn features resemble musical comedies punctuated by orgasms; see her book *Hard Core: Power, Pleasure, and the Frenzy of the "Visible"* (Berkeley: University of California Press, 1989), chap. 5.

95. Martin Amis, with photographs by Oliviero Toscani, "To Millions of American Men and Women, These Women Are Movie Stars," *Talk* 2, no. 5 (February 2001): 98–103, 133–135.

96. "New Girls (and Their Product) on the Block: Production Companies Employ Traditional and Innovative Creative Strategies to Market Fresh Faces to the Porn-Consuming Public," *Adult Video News* (October 2002), www.adultvideonews.com/cover/cover1002_01.html.

97. Hart, perhaps the most accomplished of all American porn performers, now produces (as Jane Hamilton) the videos of Michael Ninn and directs her own videos for VCA (telephone interview with Joseph W. Slade, 10 March 2001).

98. Obviously, Asian groups, to choose those examples, create their own subgenres. For instance, because pornography is illegal in Korea, it is being created mostly on the Internet, but Japanese porn is also quite different from, say, Thai porn. In the United States African-American and Hispanic-American entrepreneurs are quite deliberately inventing ethnic print and video porn in order to advance their versions of eroticism and sexual beauty into the mainstream; see Donald Suggs, "Hard Corps: A New Generation of People of Color Penetrates Porn's Mainstream," *Village Voice,* 21 October 1997, 39–40.

99. John Nadler and Emmanuelle Richard, "Hungary, the Hollywood of Porno," *Hungary Report* 1, no. 21, 24 August 1995, hungary-report@hungary.yak.net/

100. Georges Bataille, *Eroticism,* trans. from the French by Mary Dalwood (London: J. Calder, 1962); *Death and Sensuality: A Study of Eroticism and the Taboo* (New York: Ballantine Books, 1962); *Eroticism: Death and Sensuality,* trans. Mary Dalwood (1962; rpt., San Francisco: City Lights Books, 1986).

101. See Eve Kosofsky Sedgwick, *Between Men: English Literature and the Male Homosocial Desire* (New York: Columbia University Press, 1985).

102. See Judith Butler, *Bodies That Matter: On the Discursive Limits of Sex* (New York: Routledge, 1993); and *Gender Trouble: Feminism and the Subversion of Identity* (New York: Routledge, 1990).

103. A performer who insisted on anonymity, interviewed by Joseph Slade in New York, 20 June 2000, to be included in Slade's forthcoming *Shades of Blue: A History of the Stag Film.*

104. See Joseph W. Slade, "Flesh Need Not Be Mute: The Pornographic Videos of John Leslie," *Wide Angle* 19, no. 3 (July 1997): 114–148.

105. Patrick Riley, quoted in "Private," LukeFord.com, www.lukeford.com/subjects/content/private.html.

106. Kovi also has distribution agreements with Video Corporation of America and several German and Italian companies.

107. Morais, "Porn on the Danube."

108. István Kovács, interviewed by Katalin Milter, Budapest, 19 March 2001.

109. "Pornójogvita a magyar interneten," 21 February 2003, http:index.hu/tech/jog/porno0220; Luxx was previously associated with AZ Eroticcard.hu, which sold (for approximately one dollar) video clips that could be downloaded to cell phones.

110. Veronica Hart, telephone interview with Joseph W. Slade, 10 March 2001.

111. Clifford Cremer, "Sylvia Saint Profile," LukeFord.com, www.lukeford.com/stars/female/sylvia_saint.html/ (accessed 24 October 2002). Saint set herself a time limit of five years in the industry, during which time she became an anal specialist in dozens of films, saved her money, retired, married, and recently gave birth to her first child.

112. István Kovács, interviewed by Katalin Milter, Budapest, 20 October 2001.

113. Frank Thring, interviewed by Luke Ford, 21 February 2000, www.lukeford.com/archives/updates/000221.htm.

114. Franco Bernardi Bifo, preface, *Hard Set,* by Nicola Casamassima (Ferrara, Italy: Edizioni Trentini, 2000), 9.

Ideologies of the Second Coming in the Ukrainian Postcolonial Playground

Maryna Romanets

The postindependence period in Ukraine (since 1991) has become a time of liberation from different forms of totalitarian and colonial oppression, the systematized social repression of the body in the sterilized Soviet society, in which the domains of "pleasure" were prescribed and thoroughly sanitized by the state, being one of them. Having been implemented through militant moralism and prudery promoted by the state for its own political purposes, with Communist Party committees as sole custodians and caretakers of "a communism builder's moral code," this repression became epitomized during one of the first USSR-USA TV bridges at the dawn of Gorbachev's perestroika in the 1980s in an already proverbial vox populi declaration, "There is no sex in the USSR." This inhibition of the body has resulted in profound erosion, in the sphere of representations that constitute social identity, of any comfortable sense of the body. While theorizing the body in postcolonial terms, however, Homi K. Bhabha points out that "the body is always simultaneously inscribed in both the economy of pleasure and desire and the economy of discourse, domination and power."[1]

As a counterreaction to totalitarian constraints, after the breakup of the Soviet Union there occurred an astounding eruption and incorporation of sexually explicit imagery and iconography into diverse popular cultural forms. Along with these changes came the rise of a new social identity shaped in accordance with a changing societal structure in Ukraine. Therefore, an inquiry into the pornographication of Ukrainian mainstream might be instrumental in delineating some of the aspects of contemporary cultural production aimed at resisting imperializing systems and, thus, could become essential for further developments in Ukraine's postcolonial cultural politics. I intend here to examine a phenomenon, which has become pervasive in the West, in an essentially different context of a peripheral European culture that is experiencing manifold "posts"—postcolonial, postcommunist, post-totalitarian, and post-nuclear[2]—and for which some of these "posts" have already turned into "neos." Ukraine is also a society that is deeply disoriented by an overwhelming plethora of Western sexualized signs and images that have quite recently invaded its cultural space. This confusion is one of the constitutive dilemmas of contemporary culture in general. Western polyvalency of views on and conflicting attitudes toward pornography showcase the issue: it is considered to be an instrument of patriarchal oppression by antipornography feminists; it is not seen as homogeneously damaging and detrimental for women by pro-sex feminists; it is viewed as a site that is indicative of important changes in cultural climate by some "neutral" scholars; and it is completely dismissed as trash by others. Under Ukrainian conditions, however, this confusion is much more convoluted. The systems of codification of Western postmodern culture are often misread and misinterpreted in the process of their decoding by traditionally conservative, patriarchal, misogynistic, and almost premodern Ukrainian minds that are still under the cultural shock of the post-Soviet era. Ukrainians seem to be equally dazzled by a porno-spectacle that offers a radical discourse of permissiveness and repelled by it because it is conceived as alien to the Ukrainian national ethos and mentality by a certain segment of intellectuals.

While many Western champions of censorship seem to have capitulated before society's growing acceptance of titillation, the Ukrainian Parliament, on 20 November 2003, ratified Law No.1296-IV, which criminalizes, among other offensive practices, the manufacture and circulation of pornography and relegates the power to determine whether certain materials are pornographic to the newly formed National Expert Committee of Ukraine on the Defense of Public Morals.[3] The law appears to sum up lengthy and jumbled public and legislative debates on the issue, in the course of which, for instance, standard defining criteria of soft-core pornography—the representation of "the female sex organs as ultimate objects of male desire"[4]—mysteriously migrated to the sphere of "erotica," whereas *pornography* has come to denote what is usually associated with hard-core: sexual intercourse, featuring erection, penetration, and ejaculation. Unfortunately, the current legislative act does not clarify matters: its key concepts are vaguely defined and thus can be applied quite deliberately. On the one hand, they would offer weak protection against charges of pornography because what is assumed to be pornographic is not necessarily so but is, more often, a projection onto the images of the viewers' own repressions. On the other hand, this obscurity would allow one to find cracks in the pornography law in order to support such "international publishing projects" as the Ukrainian-Spanish-Czech magazine *Flash,* which is overflowing with pornographic subject matter categorized as legitimate erotica according to the earlier classification approved by the Cabinet of Ministers,[5] which evidently was used to formulate the new law.

It is not surprising that among all this verbal and visual mystification around formerly illicit cultural technology, combined with constant bombardment by images of unbridled sexual excess, an issue of *PiK* (P&C), one of the most reputable Ukrainian magazines on politics and culture, advertises *Playboy* on its back cover, while a quality television channel, *Novyi Kanal* (New Channel), features porn during late hours. Two top glamorous magazines, *Ieva* (Eve), for women, and *Lider* (Leader), for men, entertain their readership with glossy two-dimensional alternative sexualities confronting traditional heterosexual orientation with the dilemma of freedoms. *Lider,* quite conventionally, delights in parading provocative lesbian eroticism, whereas *Ieva* displays homosexual encounters between gorgeous males. The latter editorial choice might have appeared to represent, for the outsider, a radical step in questioning the traditional position of male sexuality and transgressing gender hierarchy (similar to the erotic appeal found in Western women's slash fiction that emasculates TV hard men). Besides, one can add another spin by bringing in the orthodox feminist notion that the act of viewing is masculine; thus, according to this prim doctrine, the female readership becomes either empowered by appropriating the authority of the gaze, a traditional male instrument of objectification, or, to push it farther, turns itself into transvestites, which explicitly signifies the erosion of gender roles and boundaries. I would suggest, however, that, keeping in mind intended reading audiences, everything is perfectly balanced and organically natural for Ukrainian sexual conventionality masquerading in fashionable discursive garments. Both scenarios, though transplanted into publications somewhat "alien" for the conceptual vocabulary of the genre, are structured on heterosexual binaries: men lust after women, while women lust after men. The refocalization that has taken place in Ukrainian society tends to be channeled toward almost occult compulsiveness about sex, for suggestive nudity in different degrees proliferates within advertising, popular fiction, TV commercials, and cinema.

Iurii Illienko's *Prayer for Hetman Mazepa* (2002), Ukraine's biggest-budget feature film since independence, which has proven to possess multiple explosive energies, provides an example of the obsessive desire to display culture's sexually repressed material as well as the weakening of the line between art and pornography. It faced a semiofficial ban in Russia, has become a weapon in political disputes at home, and has been persistently attacked for its excessive and brutal violence, nudity, and graphic representations of sexual scenes. Having chosen one of the most turbulent periods of Ukrainian history in which to set the film, Illienko focuses on the drama of Hetman Ivan Mazepa (1639–1709), the statesman, military leader, diplomat, patron of arts, polyglot, and poet whose confrontation with tyranny and intriguing amorous adventures inspired a wide array of works by European Romantic poets, painters, and musicians.

Illienko features Mazepa's ill-fated alliance with Charles XII (1682–1718) of Sweden against Peter I (1672–1725) of Muscovy in the Great Northern War (1700–1721), through which he sought the independence of the Ukrainian Hetman state. The defeat of Swedish and Ukrainian joint forces at the Battle of Poltava in 1709, with the subsequent bloody devastation of Baturyn (Mazepa's capital) by the Russian army, sealed Ukraine's fate by politically decapitating it and signified its submergence into a supranational, imperial community. For Ukrainians, Mazepa has become a symbol of resistance and national aspirations, for Russians an iconic traitor. Having been anathematized by the Russian Orthodox Church, Mazepa then was banned from official Soviet historiography, which enforced the celebration and glorification of the "reunification" of Ukraine with Russia. This glossed myth of unity was both actively promoted as the focal point of the period and relentlessly reduplicated in ideologically sanctioned heroic grand narratives. Illienko bends the straight line of imperial history into vicious circles to expose both its fictionality and the political dogma surrounding it. His work reveals the mechanisms of conversion whereby histories are erased but resurface as symptoms on the colonized body politic to be reread, reinterpreted, and rewritten.

A Prayer for Hetman Mazepa starts with the allegoric representation of the map of Europe as a female body, with Ukraine positioned, as the authorial commentary explains, in its "sweet womb that was desired by everyone and raped by everyone."[6] By superimposing an erotic space on the land, which becomes a double-valanced site for acquisition and penetration, Illienko persistently enacts the political and colonial suppression and subordination of Ukraine in violent sexual terms. The connections among conquest, colonization, and rape and the employment of a traditional Ukrainian poetic trope of a possessed and repossessed ruined maid run throughout the work. This essentialized female body, represented by obvious pornographic features with distinctively abusive connotations, becomes the site for the production and operation of power as well as the object of a double aggression to exterior malefactors and interior benefactors. To a certain degree woman here is also made to stand as a transparent medium, a homoerotic link connecting the colonizer and the colonized.

In this respect Illienko, alongside other Ukrainian mythmakers, seems to accept a definition of the colonized nations as essentially feminine races, in which femininity as a racial trait is linked with subordination to the "masculine" colonizer, which was current in Europe in the nineteenth century.[7] The attempts to challenge this widely spread colonial strategy based on the homology between sexual and political dominance, however, were undertaken by the nineteenth-century Ukrainian revivalists through the retrieval of Kozak (Cossack) heroic figures, which became a manifest symbol of Ukrainian masculinity and one of the central revivalist icons. *A Prayer,* while revitalizing the Kozak cult of courageous acts and masculine violence, carries on this tradition. Driven by the desire of representational revenge that is characteristic of masculinist anti-imperialist discourses in general, Illienko both fixes and destabilizes the inherited gendered power matrix by hybridizing the aggressive myth of both imperial and nationalist masculinities. His Ukraine—the symbolic mediator in the struggle between competing virilities—now appears as a submissive young maiden scarcely draped in white gauze, now as a threatening, controlling female in the harness and chains of sadomasochism (suggesting the old virgin/whore dichotomy), now as a monstrous executioner in a red leather apron, whose body is enormously exaggerated in scale.

In his phantasmagoric vision of Ukrainian history reflected through the hallucinations of the dying Mazepa, Illienko releases the destructive demons of chaos by bringing together various experiential layers that collapse into one another in the vortex of reality and mind, dream and reality, reality and fiction, past and present. The climactic scene in the string of pornographic symbology that infiltrates the film spotlights the obsessive seductress, who has been haunting Mazepa throughout his life, masturbating with her husband's decapitated head. The erotic triangle—Mazepa, his love/sex object, and her husband, who is also Mazepa's political rival—is brought into focus again, though with macabre overtones of quasi-chthonic rites.

The moment that stirred extremely hostile criticism in the Russian media and provoked the Russian Culture Ministry to consider banning *A Prayer,* declaring that it "could damage relations between Russian and Ukraine,"[8] is Illienko's representation of Peter I. An emblematic enlightened monarch of Russian history is transformed into "a sadist, a tyrant and a sodomite."[9] One of the most disturbing factors that, most likely, contributed to the wave of indignation in the generally homophobic Russian press is that Illienko forces Peter I out of the closet. Although the Russian czar is commonly profiled among distinguished homosexuals on Western gay Web sites and one of the first historical references to his homosexuality is found, as early as in 1698, in the evidence of a certain Captain Rigby tried in England,[10] the exposure must have been quite appalling for some Russians. A more subtle but strong undercurrent of both homosocial and homoerotic desire in the relationship between Mazepa and Peter, doppelgängers lusting and competing for power and domination, loving and hating each other, somehow went unnoticed.

Illienko's revisionist impulse teams art with sex and violence to produce one of the film's manifold shocks and to shake up historically amnesiac Ukrainian audiences. His transgressive porn infusions, however, were used, with a boomerang effect, against his devotees during the parliamentary election campaign in the spring of 2002. Because *A Prayer for Hetman Mazepa* received exceptionally generous funding from the government of Victor Iushchenko, TV channels hostile to the reform-oriented prime minister and his party repeatedly aired some of the most graphic and disturbing erotic scenes from the film "in a clear attempt to embarrass [Iushchenko's] supporters and discredit the bloc."[11]

Another case of pornography entering the Ukrainian political playground is much less refined than the nationwide broadcasting of Illienko's postmodern pornographication of history. In March 2002, while campaigning for the election for the Ukrainian Parliament, one of the candidates, a twenty-eight-year-old Olena Solod, decided to beat her opponents by stripping during a live TV show and exposing her Rubenesque figure in full view to add a bit of fun and color to an otherwise drab debate. Having become an instant celebrity, she is also said to have declared that, when she becomes a legislator, she will recruit two hundred male guards with specific physical characteristics: no less than 180 cm (5 ft., 11 in.) tall, with no less than 18 cm (7.5 in.) long penises.[12] Paradoxically, due to either the shock value of the political stripper's media performance and the crude, distasteful posters and photos featuring different angles of the neo-suffragist that were circulated among her constituency or to some other reasons (her program included legalization of prostitution and marijuana), public opinion polls indicated that at some point she was leading among other candidates in the city. She did not win then, but in the following fall she entered the race for a parliamentary seat again, having committed herself to a striptease show in the Parliament if she were to succeed. Solod's political ambitions, which also involved supporting her husband's aspiration to become the mayor of Zaporizhzhia by posing with him for a porn placard, are a dwarfish reflection of the impressive parliamentary career of La Cicciolina. The Italian porn star, who founded a "porno-political model agency," Diva Futura, became a parliamentary representative of the Radical Party in the 1987 general election in Italy.[13] Then she rose to another level of stardom by collaborating with Jeff Koons in his notorious show *Made in Heaven,* which operated within the conventional codes of pornographic representation and was first exhibited at the 1990 Vienna Biennale.

A similarly rampant pornotopia infests different Ukrainian Web sites regardless of their content, coming in different formats, smaller or larger, with banners or moving banners. Photographs of belles; endless streams of beauty pageant winners from different parts of the country; sexy queens by day, week, and month ranging from sweet loveliness to vamp types; and body art projects highlighting enchantresses in provocative postures are used for the sake of decoration. A female nude as a crowning adornment has become an almost indispensable element of Ukrainian Web design. Numerous entertainment guides include sections on escorts, personalized matching, and dating services, with galleries of available females on display for a male spectator. These bodies, acknowledged as potential objects of desire, are emblematic of conventional sex and gender roles. Being excluded from the erotics of exchange, they become a site to assert the sexuality of an active masculine user.

Specialized porn sites are designed in interactive regimes and offer a vast variety of sex games, from soft- to hard-core, "powerful sex blasts," sex simulators, assortments of stripteases, sex chats, sex forums, and video shops. Ukrainian cyber-pornography feeds on a visible segment of internationally recognized codes and has the appearance of its Western equivalents. It does not diverge from the supranational mainstream representing the commodifying power of sex, which becomes a consumer object, standardized, sleek, industrialized, polished, and flawless. The employed procedures of representation are based on canonical pornographic practices and on dominance-oriented strategies of objectification in which women are reduced to the parts of their bodies and assigned the role of voluntarily responsive objects. They are fetishizers in the most obvious manner by focusing on stripped erogenous zones—breasts, vagina, mouth—as the primary signifiers of womanliness and symbols of female sexuality. Through this mechanism of symbolic representation, with its mechanical objectification of signs in heterosexual pornography, woman, as Jane M. Ussher argues, turns into a hole to be penetrated.[14]

One of the sites bearing any kind of "national" specificity is Ukrainian Schoolgirls, which boasts of daily updates in its "exclusive content" featuring the "sexiest . . . amateur schoolgirls," whose authenticity is repeatedly emphasized visually and in the titles of its Web links: girls masturbate, girls hard-core, girls movies, sex stories, girls pics.[15] Ukrainian nymphets are dressed in typical Soviet brand school uniforms—dark brown dresses and white aprons commonly worn on ceremonial occasions—and red Young Pioneer ties,[16] which purposely position them in an age group under fourteen, although these sexual models look somewhat more mature than their age-designating outfits imply. To make the declaration of these implications even more explicit, "daddy's babes" congregate around a male pedo-phile figure old enough to both appreciate their perverted innocence and relate to defunct tokens of "a happy Young Pioneer childhood" of the Soviet regime. This transgression in several degrees—surpassing legally acceptable norms of the West-ern pornography industry, for example—is aimed at escalating excitement and sat-isfying more exotic tastes of a fantasy-ridden site's target clientele lacking in potency. The issue of the consumer becomes of interest here. In Ukraine, the coun-try with an abysmal swing between a thin stratum of fabulously rich and extremely impoverished "masses," the estimated number of computer users is 30 percent in urban areas (in rural districts this figure drops to 15 percent) of an approximate population of fifty million; moreover, the language of the site is English. Is this a sign of inevitable globalization or a trafficking in porn commodities packaged as a forbidden fruit through virtual reality, which replicates the ongoing transnational sexual slave marketing of Ukrainian women, who allegedly are willing to do more for less?[17]

Utilization, in a sexual setting, of insignias of the Soviet near-past by Ukrai-nian Schoolgirls is one of the facets of a tendency, both in visual art and litera-ture, that is characteristic of the post-Soviet cultural space in general. The dissident Sots-Art movement was the one to start playing with symbolic forms of totalitar-ian culture and placing their signs into a new context. The most successful were Vitalii Komar and Alex Melamid's parodies of the socialist realist aesthetic (e.g., "Stalin in the Mirrors" and "Stalin and the Muse"), which subversively illustrated Marxist-Leninist versions of reality. This dialogue with state-approved creative methodologies and imagistic systems, which took place in the 1980s, still goes on and tends to become a new prescriptive cliché itself. Although the Soviet state is obsolete, artists seem to be more comfortable with recycling its dead signifiers, which can be conveniently laced with an abundance of eroticism for a libertine ring and public appeal, than with looking for new art forms and ways of concep-tualizing them.

Ukrainian representation at the 2001 Venice Biennale, for example, contained a piece by Valentyn Rayevsky, *Blattopter BRD–1: Project Preventive Measures* (1999), an assemblage of military accessories, nudes, and cockroaches. The piece looks like a late-twentieth-century Soviet style version of the surrealist concept of the "mechanical bride," with all its sexist implications,[18] pollinated with one of the central totalitarian orthodoxies—glorification of military strength embodied in phallic tubes of martial equipment. At the same time, the artist adds an entic-ing touch to the installation by exploiting a vastly popular, in the closing decade of the last century, code of S-M sexual imagery by cladding his nudes in high leather boots, belts, and helmets. But this does not make them dominatrix figures who are ready to strike at any moment, nor does it articulate the artist's struggles over deep-seated beliefs concerning gender, power, sexuality, violence, and role-playing in society. Female flesh conflated with male machinery attends, rather, to the aphrodisiac delectation of the male beholder. What is interesting about Rayevsky's piece is that, having nothing to say, Rayevsky operates on the level of what is expected or recognizable as representative of "over there," in a land of

Western promise whose magnetizing attraction seems even to have strengthened after the fall of the iron curtain. *Blattopter* is played out in accordance with a demand-supply scenario that is generated by depleted, speculative, and manipulative desperate imagination, with Sots-Art as the only familiar operational mode that once used to be commercially successful in the West.

Another case of a peculiar cultural cross-breeding, in which new, "imported" subject matter is applied to well-rooted, familiar, and thus advantageous methodologies, is found in virtual pornographic fiction that infests the Web sites of various Ukrainian electronic libraries and is unobtrusively labeled as "erotica," "romance," or even "fiction about love." It seems to be symbiotically connected with the inherited socialist realist tradition and turns, quite unintentionally, into one of its most ardent proponents. I will focus on the erotica section of one such e-library, www.biglib.com.ua, which is fairly generic in reflecting the demand-supply correlation in the mass literature market. Its porn goods look very much like source guides and friendly manuals that both offer their readers sexual possibilities that are open to them and aspire to satisfy erotic curiosity of all possible types. The amount of detail provided depends on the author's enthusiasm and expertise in the area. This "pedagogic" bearing of the site is also indicated by the fact that, among the effusion of "creative" opuses, one finds incidental incursions of miscellaneous fragments from the *Kama Sutra,* Sade's *Philosophy in the Bedroom,* Oriental medieval erotic literature (I will abstain from commenting on the quality of translations), as well as solely pragmatic writings (e.g., "Sex in Human Life," "Art of Marriage," and "Man's Sexual Happiness"). No matter how paradoxical it sounds, such educational aspects of pornography may play a practical role in disseminating information concerning sexual issues in a country that missed the sexual revolution of the 1960s and 1970s; in which abortion has been the most effective, if not exclusive, means of birth control for decades; whose school curriculum does not include sexual education; and which occupies the fifth place in the world, after African countries, in the proliferation of AIDS.

Ukrainian electronic pornography attempts to traverse a new territory, but, very much like in the case of porn sites, it relates current sexual practices in a blatantly minimalistic manner. In this respect the well-developed Western pornographic tradition has become a source that provides signs, symbols, and signifiers for target postcolonial porno-mimicry. The indexes of time and place are mixed, representing both the familiar everyday life, marked by identifiable "realia" so that the readers can easily relate to what seems to happen next door, and the alien and exotic, to cater to the more romantic tastes of those who yearn for galvanizing adventures in faraway lands. Apartment buildings and summer houses that are indicative of native settings appear alongside Hawaiian bungalows, German family mansions, mysterious quasi-Gothic mansions in the manner of Stanley Kubrick's *Eyes Wide Shut* accommodating high-style orgies, and saloons of wrecked ships to remind the reader of the thrills and horrors of the *Titanic.* Sometimes this cosmopolitan chic reveals a crack, and an irresistible and gallant male, with impeccable manners, shows up in training pants for an elegantly served breakfast (those who are familiar with the Soviet and post-Soviet daily round will appreciate the detail). Setting is not the point here, however, and can be disposed of easily.

Predominantly anonymous authors (in this they are aligned with an authorial obscurity in pornography from the Victorian era; names would not mean anything anyway) compete in piling up descriptions of mechanical copulations, fetishistic, compulsive, and deeply pointless. Portrayal of an old-style heterosexual intercourse between two partners seems innocent and chaste in comparison. Sex parties usually involve a minimum of three players. If it happens to be a traditional duet disposition, it tends to be enriched by miscellaneous extras; for example, coitus with a gigantic soft cat in a heroine's dream, foreshadowing her sexual encounter with a human partner, becomes a helpful device. Group sex, fellatio, cunnilingus, anal penetration, lesbianism, onanism, masturbation, incest, rape, bestiality, defloration, necrophilia, pedophilia, prostitution, and homosexuality constitute staple ingredients of the texts and are mixed in various configurations according to the principle "the more, the better." All this is compressed into a short fiction format that does not allow for pensive poses or retardations; there is no time to stop—everything moves fast, as on an assembly belt, toward the end of the production line.

This fantasy world offers itself as reality, but its sexual scene structured on obsessional simulation turns out to be more real than the real itself. Women are invariably represented as incessantly craving sex; their bodies are reduced to unformed flesh, making them available in their degree-zero mode. Graphic depictions of women being penetrated from every imaginable angle, in every possible orifice, and in every conceivable posture of receptivity and access blur into one endless coitus perforated by near-hysterical cries, screams, moans, and groans as signals of utmost pleasure, delight, and ecstasy. Pornographic heroes, with larger-than-life-size penises, exhibit nondiminishing hardness for hours and are able to resume vigorous penetrative sex instantaneously after ejaculation an impressive number of times, preferably with different partners, as if challenging normal rules of physiology. It is in this contest with a reality that is persistently glossed that pornography draws on the operational modes of socialist realism. One can argue, thus, that any pornographic work is axiomatically based on such essentials and that socialist realism *is* pornography.

While analyzing the "discursive base" in the formation of socialist realist aesthetics, some scholars emphasize its obsession with realism and the imperative to supplant traditional objectivity with "an ultra- or supra-realism,"[19] starting with an ideal image to which the existing actuality has to be adapted and thus creating pure appearances that are, ironically, too real.[20] Such absorption of reality into hyperreality is also taking place in pornography. According to Jean Baudrillard, it signifies the end of illusion and imagination, for the sexual appears so close to the subject that it confounds itself: "One gives you so much . . . that you have nothing to add, that is to say, nothing to give in exchange. Absolute repression: by giving you *a little too much* one takes away everything."[21] Sexuality is not on display in pornography. Rather, pornography breaks down the sexual scene and foregrounds the obscene, representing desire in the absence of desire. Its simulacra of sexuality leave no place for weakness, failure, or inadequate performance. Male sperm flows in amounts sufficient for a modest flood, and female bodily fluids could constitute a sizable pool of lubricant for commercial use.

Both socialist realist and pornographic pulp, manifesting an era of excessive realism and hyperliteralism, display a clichéd unity of style and substance that reduces meaning to a set of imperatives devoid of any complex interplay. Both are fixated on the means of production, instead of on the production of meaning. Both are characterized by a monolithic predictability, for events depicted in them steadily follow prescribed patterns and develop in directions known in advance: for communism, in socialist realism emblematized in the shot of a rocket, thrust of an obelisk, eruption of an open-hearth steel furnace, and to orgasm; for pornography culminating in a symbolic cum shot. Similarly to socialist realism, which ritualistically reduplicates the central Soviet myths with their limited repertoire of master plots and narratives, Ukrainian pulp pornography also operates within a framework of well-rehearsed scenarios. It inviolably follows Gilles Deleuze's formulaic definition of the genre: "What is known as pornographic literature is a literature reduced to a few imperatives (do this, do that) followed by obscene descriptions."[22]

While assessing "the most realistic of realisms," with its ideologically derived, schematic features and authoritarian inflexibility, Andrei Sinyavsky contends that any attempt at psychological representation of the much-derided positive hero is "impossible, without falling into parody,"[23] for in this literature every implication is declared, every suggestion is declaimed, and everything is geared entirely toward "performance." The typical character, marching through an endless stream of Soviet literary productions, without major stylistic or structural alterations, has met his structural mirror image in a no less impressive typicality of a pornographic hero, newly emerging on the post-Soviet cultural horizon. Both are equally transparent, straightforward, and purposeful. Such regimes of representation are typical of contemporary Ukrainian porn, whose textual strategies strip its protagonists of any complexities by exposing their exclusively physical *jouissance,* constructing everything in full view, and putting it on display. Typologically, everything is centered around male erection and ejaculation. This is the world in which there is no more freedom or change than in a traditional production novel. The titles of the stories speak for themselves by unequivocally delineating their discursive space and conveying the laborious, reductive, and mechanical tedium of the genre—"Recollections of a Young Woman," "Betty's Diary," "Diary of a Boarding-School Girl," "Entertainment for Lolita," "A Virgin," "Defloration," "For the First Time," "Goddess of the Night," "Fallen Lady," "Witch Sabbath," "Desire," "Gratification of Desires," "Encounter with Phallus," "My Best Orgasm," "Orgasm to the Beat of the Train Wheels," "Fuck Me," "Swedish Threesome," and "Non-Swedish Triangle," to name only a few.

What is noteworthy is that these productions draw on an endless stream of weary myths and traditional misogynies. To construct titillating images of perilous sex, authors often resort to representations of sexually subservient females for whom humiliation is always infused with sexual pleasure and is an essential moment in escalating their sexual heat. These scenarios are a far cry from explorations of woman's masochistic desire to be dominated in the manner of Anne Rice's self-proclaimed "elegant sadomasochism,"[24] although they evidently draw on similar fantasies. In spite of the fact that many of these works describe situations of consensual captivity (not unlike numerous *Story of O* types of narrative), the brutality and aggression of heterosexual males are appalling, and, in this world of the pleasure slaves, women end up being displayed as nymphomaniacs whose rampant lust is aroused by progressive debasement and sexual assaults. This male violence is not something entirely unexpected, for it is immanent to socialist realism wrapped in the idea of heroism. It thus becomes a remedial instrument to compensate for man's sexual anxieties and fears, in porn, and for his sense of subordinate manliness, in sots-realism. Alongside misogyny, pornography also reflects the society's homophobic attitudes; for example, the collection *Volcano of Erotic Fantasies,* consisting of fourteen stories, includes only one with homosexual subject matter whose scene is laid on a dark night bus to make it less conspicuous.

Although registering some of the processes that take place in Ukrainian society, these works neither provoke public debate about sexuality and its representation nor contribute to it. I will further focus, however, on literary works that are sexually explicit enough to be discussed in the same terms as pornography but whose transgressive energies attend to various agenda: political, literary, national, and sexual, among others. They are loosely termed "pornorotic" to differentiate them from pornographic pulp. Before the breakup of the Soviet Union this type of literature was practically nonexistent in Ukraine. Taboo in the official socialist realist literary canon, it was also excluded from dissident literature, which was primarily preoccupied with political issues. As far back as in the 1920s, when Ukraine was experiencing a short wave of cultural renaissance, which turned into "Executed Risorgimento" after it fell to the Bolsheviks, Volodymyr Vynnychenko (1880–1951), the author of electrifying modernist prose, was accused of writing "pornography" because of his affirmation of sexuality that was opposed to the prevailing ascetic revolutionary ideal. He was among those literati who were breaking the code of self-censorship adopted by Soviet revolutionary writers in general. Because of his opposition to mainstream ideology and state politics, which included the "counterrevolutionary" streak, Vynnychenko—the first and the last Ukrainian pornographer of the Soviet era—ended up in exile in France, a rare gift of fortune because Ukrainian literature was virtually wiped out by Stalinist repressions.

With the body eliminated from the picture for the benefit of the soul for a lengthy period of time, Ukrainians seem to subscribe to the definition of a "spiritual" nation. In an ongoing postindependence dispute about Ukrainian national identity, matters of the flesh do not score too highly. In *The Theory of Ukrainian Love* (2002) Mykola Tomenko, while deliberating on ethno-psychological and sociocultural traditions of Ukrainianness and juxtaposing them to the expansion of mass culture that "is destroying cultural values and ethics of human relationships," states, "Ukrainians have never been cynics; that is why today's 'erotization' of nation through mass culture either from the East or from the West is not only antipolitical or anti-aesthetic: it is—unnatural."[25]

Whether one likes it or not, "unnatural erotization" is there. The recent proliferation of discourses concerned with sexuality in post-totalitarian Ukraine has both external and internal determinants. It is indicative partly of a literary vogue for "erotomaniac" fiction that has captured Western fin-de-siècle culture in the process of the recurrent contestation, rearticulation, and redefinition of gender norms, roles, and boundaries. This erotic heteroglossia in Ukrainian textual production is also partly geared toward revealing the fictionality of existing codes of morality. Here eroticism comes into play as a force that is capable of undermining certain hierarchical formations inherited from the previous authoritarian regime. I regard such new discursive practices as counterreactions to the repression of the sexual by the state and also to the ideological "kenosis" persistently promoted by socialist realist literature. By way of example a depressingly monotonous succession of "positive" characters in the Soviet literary canon, whose libido was channeled exclusively into the construction of communism, was conducive in establishing and fixing particular cultural stereotypes concerning sexuality and gender.

The discovery and investigation of the formerly untrodden ambivalent terrains of desiring bodies are being represented in a wide range of contemporary literary practices that are breaking political, social, and cultural injunctions to silence on the issues of sexuality. Being both one of the constitutive components of such works and the medium that most vociferously advocates free and diverse sexual self-expression, pornorotic literature questions the postulates of social structures that support and encourage negative attitudes to any form of sexuality. Through a representation of sexuality that makes its obscenity conspicuous, pornorotica violates conventional taboos. It thus releases repressed experiences and desires that can be instrumental in overcoming the consequences of oppressive orders, which neutralized and codified the body in the iconographic terms of a desexed socialist realism, in forging a new sexual identity utterly nonexistent under the Soviet hygienic moral code, and in disrupting the continuum of the inherited authoritarian tradition.

Oksana Zabuzhko, the most controversial contemporary Ukrainian writer so far, the "Ukrainian Sylvia Plath," who also authors a number of brilliant books in the area of cultural studies and philosophy, has opened a Pandora's box of dormant psychosexual and erotic explorations by her *Field Research in Ukrainian Sex* (1996). By releasing her findings into the contemporary literary scene in Ukraine, Zabuzhko unblocked the way for works ranging from blatant pornography to exquisitely structured texts-palimpsests. Her book became the first postindependence national best-seller and was translated into a number of European languages. Prior to its publication in 1996, a rough version of the novel, produced in Pittsburgh and distributed by the author among her friends, turned out to revive the Soviet era dissident *samvydav* (self-publishing) practices being photocopied and launched into circulation.

The controversial reception of Zabuzhko's novel, generated by the insulted virtue of (post)-Soviet neopuritans, can be compared on a miniature scale to a notoriety once surrounding D. H. Lawrence's *Lady Chatterley's Lover* (1928), Henry

Miller's *Tropic of Cancer* (Paris, mid–1930s; United States, 1961), and Vladimir Nabokov's *Lolita* (1955). Yet the intellectual infirmity of Zabuzhko's opponents and the absence of judicial laws and regulations (in the manner of Western commissions and reports on obscenity and pornography as well as pornography legislation debates), on the basis of which the author could have been charged with pornography and obscenity, saved her work from being censored and removed from bookstore and library shelves.

Field Research is the first explicitly erotic work to be written in Ukrainian literature by a woman who gained a voice to narrativize love. Zabuzhko's search for the power of self-articulation by positioning herself as an autonomous subject of erotic desire is presented through a fictionalized account of a real-life affair that blurs the margins between the genres of novel and life writing in its sophisticated manipulation of reality into fiction. At the same time, it is a discourse of what Freud calls "common unhappiness," the experience that informs women's writings and lives at large. In one of her interviews Zabuzhko speaks about complete self-identification of her Ukrainian women readers from the ages of twenty-five to sixty with her heroine and concludes: "it suddenly appears that you somewhat mystically apply sound not to your own words but to those of many thousands of specific living beings who suffered and largely remained silent, as if they did not exist at all: all that is not expressed in words very quickly sinks into oblivion. By giving voice to something, you allow it to exist."[26] Thus, her character's personal psychodrama becomes part of the wider societal scheme in imposition of control through discipline and punishment.

Field Research in Ukrainian Sex explores sadomasochistic intrigue, with all the accompanying nuances in understanding of sexual identity, bodily pleasure, and relationship of violence to subjectivity and society in the late twentieth century. By resorting to the representation of pain in her erotic explorations, Zabuzhko seemingly conforms to a century-old view that masochism is natural to the character of all women. In this framework masochism has become a central ideological construct in the production of a feminine stereotype that provides the conflicting playground for male fantasies, desires, and anxieties. On the one hand, Zabuzhko's protagonist appears to reenact obsessively the masochism in which the Soviet society has been so well schooled through the political technologies developed by the authoritarian state to exercise an absolute control over the bodies of its subjects. *Field Research* reveals the mechanisms that shape cultural models of domination and subordination that are projected onto heterosexual gender roles. The novel also presents a pattern both of the sexually codified violence to which many women are exposed and of the victimization toward which they seem to gravitate. Zabuzhko's text is instrumental in understanding "how domination is anchored in the hearts of the dominated," to use Jessica Benjamin's expression,[27] and why being a woman (and especially in Ukraine, as Zabuzhko's character emphasizes) automatically fixes positional roles.

The author sees the roots of women's subjugation not only in her society's misogyny but also in men's subservience under colonial and totalitarian rule, for imperialism subsumes the colonized into already existing gender relations. Under this condition the authoritarian oppressive systems are redirected against women in an exact duplication of both the colonizer's practices and a colonial scenario of mastery and submission. The protagonist explains her own compliance with the violence of her lover and with their abusive relationship in a context of sociocultural experiences collectively shared by that particular stratum of women who identify themselves as the Ukrainian subalternity as opposed to such an ideologically concocted and zealously promoted entity as the "Soviet people" into which all constitutive nations of the USSR were methodically homogenized: "We were brought up by guys who were fucked in every way from all sides . . . later we were screwed by the same kind of guys, and . . . in both cases they did to us the same thing that was done to them by those others, the *foreign* guys. And . . . we accepted them and loved them as they are, for not accepting them would mean taking the side of the others. . . . [T]hus the only choice we had and still have is between the victim and the torturer: between non-being and being-that-kills."[28]

On the other hand, Zabuzhko's protagonist does not invariably occupy one and the same subject position in the pain-seeking scenario. She shifts subject-object relations, thus destabilizing them, and moves freely along the axis of "submission-mastery." She alternates between becoming a laughing witch-dominatrix and exploring the depths of sexual submissiveness at the other end of the "whip." In this respect Zabuzhko desexualizes men and resexualizes women. She acts out her desires through the flows between aggression and passivity, pain and pleasure, domination and submission.

Having inherited the multilayered legacy that encompasses masochistic neuroticism of Soviet "injustice collectors,"[29] self-effacement of a canonical socialist realist hero in the name of communism, and a cult of suffering in the nineteenth-century literary tradition, Zabuzhko substantially infuses erotogenic masochistic practices with moral masochism. Being often concomitant with the desire to fabricate a different cultural order, moral masochism provides a drive for change. This drive, which acknowledges intensity, tensions, and contradictions of desire, channels Zabuzhko's text against repressive constructions of human subjects and of their gender and social relations. The representation of her erotic subjectivity invades the discursive territory previously officiated by neutered, sexless male practitioners of socialist realism who allowed women into their pantheon of unattainable virtues exclusively as satellite characters—reliable comrades, faithful friends, and chaste wives—to support assertive phallocentric masculine integrity.

Iurii Pokalchuk's sexual adventures and fantasies are played out on the opposite end of the spectrum from Zabuzhko's liberated sexuality. The strategies these authors employ in rethinking and rewriting the body could not be more different. Pokalchuk, an established prose writer and poet, literary scholar, and translator from many European languages, has engaged in writing Ukrainian foundational pornographic fiction. His project aims at filling one of the numerous gaping holes in Ukrainian literature, thus expanding its operational area as well as the functional zone of the Ukrainian language and contributing to the viability of both. On the one hand, the piquant subject matter of his collection of short stories *What Lies Beneath* (1998) has been inspired by political desire that is enhanced by a missionary drive to attract the largely russified Ukrainian reader to literature written in Ukrainian. This brings to mind another prominent writer of the Ukrainian "Executed Risorgimento," Mykola Khvyliovy (1899–1933), who once remarked that he would be confident in the survival of the Ukrainian language if it were to be spoken by thieves and prostitutes. I should mention in passing that Pokalchuk has succeeded here; his book, like Zabuzhko's novel, has been enjoying popularity among readership with various language preferences. On the other hand, the author experiments with pushing and manipulating the boundaries of the permissible in sexual representation.

Being well informed by current operational definitions of *pornography, What Lies Beneath* also tends to draw, to a noticeable degree, on the conventional compensatory male power fantasies and misogynist myths characteristic of the genre. The collection includes most of the hottest pornographic scenarios: conflation of rape with seduction, ano-rectal eroticism, group sex, incest, castration, prostitution, homoeroticism, and gang-banging. Sex scenes, however, do not completely subsume human relationships, for the author provides psychological motivations for his characters' actions. In "Evil" police hunt for a young girl because she has been transmitting venereal disease to men and boys whom she picks up along the highway. Insane, she runs away from home after being raped by her father, lives in the meadow, and has indiscriminate sex with strangers in exchange for food. This bleak story has two focal points, the girl herself, who is in a perpetual state of numbness, and a young doctor, in whose arms she ends her mad flight at the denouement. In another story, "The Prayer," a woman is paralyzed with fear when attacked in her own apartment by a teenager, who threatens to shoot her if she does not have sex with him and let it get filmed. Before leaving, the boy introduces himself as the son of the woman's lover. He is trying to prevent the ultimate collapse of his family, which has been drifting apart because of his father's illicit love affair, by getting discrediting pictures that, as he hopes, will induce his father to give up his extramarital relationship. Pokalchuk's pornoproduction also involves darker aspects of past and present, as in "The End," which narrates the protagonist's sexual maturation through numerous erotic exercises. In the conclusion he is sent by the author to die violently as a member of the Ukrainian student resistance battalion, all the fighters of which were castrated before execution by the Bolsheviks during the Russian occupation of Ukraine in the 1920s. In addition, Pokalchuk's sexual encounters are not entirely deprived of commitment, affection, understanding, passion, or even love ("Secondhand").

What Lies Beneath is lavishly adorned by erotica in visual art, starting with works by Michelangelo and Caravaggio, exposing homoerotic desire, evidently to provide an illustration to the only story that deals with gay subject matter. Interestingly enough, in this particular piece, under the suggestive title "The Azure Sun" (*blue* in Ukrainian is an equivalent for *gay*), as opposed to those that depict heterosexual relations, the author's regime of representation switches to understatements and avoidance of frank descriptions of sex. Pokalchuk's gallery of visual enticement stretches chronologically to include Eric Fischel's *Bad Boy* (1981), a painting of an adolescent boy voyeuristically viewing a woman's (his mother's) genitalia and naked body up close, which is said to have made the artist's career. This one is allocated to a story in which Pokalchuk ambitiously rewrites Sophocles' *Oedipus Rex*. But, if in Fischel's painting the perversion is implied in the voyeuristic transaction, the story actually narrates the incestuous relationship in shocking and superfluous detail. "Oedipus Was Born in Drohobych" (almost like Leopold von Sacher-Masoch's *Don Juan of Kolomyia*), which attaches itself to a well-known intertext and thus to an archetypal human condition, reads as an attempt at liberation either of repressed desires or from the chains of oedipal categories in Freudian theory.

Throughout history and across different cultural traditions writers, artists, poets, and philosophers have been looking for explications of an opaque "riddle of femininity." As if in a search for the clue to this mystery, Pokalchuk, in a number of stories, chooses a woman-centered type of sexual representation ("Madam," "The Way I Am . . . ," "Must," "What Lies Beneath"). Woman becomes here a director of the sexual scene and uses men to gratify her desires. Although by this Pokalchuk appears to reverse the socio-sexual conditions conventionally experienced by men and thus to question the male-defined eroticism of power, he falls into the pattern of many other masculinist discourses that explicitly draw the equation between "woman" and "sex" and fix its invariant meaning. The secret is demystified, revealed, unveiled, and thoroughly normalized when the writer conceptualizes the once enigmatic woman in a concise formula that does not imply any uncertainty of the feminine because, for him, the ultimate desire of every woman is to be laid. By means of such a frank pornographic orientation, he writes his Bildungsroman of sexuality that turns to some extent into a phallic declaration of potency and power. At some point it seems that repeated descriptions of sex are aimed at acting out the author's fantasies of sexual domination, some of them being profoundly suppressed adolescent erotic dreams.

Although some of Pokalchuk's male protagonists are teenagers, inexperienced virgins at the point of departure in their sexual explorations, they perfectly comply with prevailing porn scripts of erectility and verticality. His women are always responding ecstatically and orgasmically to multiple fuckings. The apotheosis of Pokalchuk's resourcefulness reveals itself in the following description of what could be loosely termed as lovemaking. Here the mechanistic assemblage of woman's sexual insatiability and her adolescent partners' utilization of varied sexual practices (vaginal, anal, and oral concomitantly) borders on the grotesque:

> she was lying on . . . [Slavko] with his penis in her anus . . . Kostyk lifted her legs up onto his shoulders and carefully entered her vagina, and now she groaned loudly because of new, unexpected, and previously not experienced before sensations; both penises were moving synchronically inside her, even more—now she was moving between both penises, feeling gigantic pleasure from both of them inside her . . . and when she felt . . . [Evhen's] penis on her lips, and then in her mouth, and then on her tongue, already thirsty, strong, desiring . . . they all wanted to explode and were now moving like a single strange human mechanism, like a machine, which

has not been invented yet by humankind and which might have given an individual the fullest pleasure.[30]

It is worthwhile mentioning that almost all of Pokalchuk's descriptions are focused on women—moreover, women in their thirties who initiate coitus with male teenagers. This is the rite of passage into manhood and the establishment of a masculine sexual identity designed by the author that ultimately undermines his assertion of male sexual mastery by stating its infantile basis explicitly.

Iurii Vynnychuk, "one of the groundbreakers of erotic genre in Ukrainian literature"[31] and the first editor of the erotic magazine *Hulvisa* (Lovelace) published in L'viv in the 1990s, consistently displays creative and whimsical anarchy by juggling different conventions, genres, canons, and cultural codes, new and old alike. Having been turned into a space to engage in an "epistemic dialogue" with a number of texts—literary, cinematic, and historical—his *Life in the Harem* (1996) demythologizes and demystifies the national saga of femininity through its pornographication and thus reveals its carefully suppressed and concealed sexual undercurrents. While dismantling Ukrainian domestic myth of femininity, Vynnychuk fabricates a pseudo-autobiographical manuscript of a historical figure—Roxolana, Nastia Lisovska (1505–1558), the most cherished concubine of Süleyman the Magnificent (1495–1566), who legally married the sultan and became the first really powerful woman in the Ottoman dynasty.

Roxolana was featured as one of the characters in William D'Avenant's (1606–1668) *Siege of Rhodes* (1656; pt. 2, 1659) and referred to by Francis Bacon (1561–1626) in "Of Empire" (*Essays* [1597–1625]), among others. The story of Roxolana, who was captured by the Ottoman vassals during their slave raid of Ukraine in 1520 and donated to the Imperial Harem by a nobleman who had bought her at a slave market and was greatly impressed by her knowledge of Greek and Latin,[32] has been nourishing the imaginations of Ukrainian writers, composers, and artists, who have been, throughout the last century, busily creating their male cult of an eminent Hurrem Sultan. Yet, as Zabuzhko observes, none of them focused on Nastia Lisovska's versatile and truly Renaissance personality as an outstanding diplomat, *intrigante,* benefactor, and reformist, comparable to her younger contemporary, Catherine de Medici (1519–1589). Instead, they were hypnotized by Süleyman and Roxolana's relationship and thus romantically fetishized her as an object of imperial desire. Such a symbolic role assigned to their female compatriot implicitly involves, among other things, the colonizer-colonized dichotomy. The fact that Roxolana's status as a love slave could generate the surge of patriotic feelings points toward Ukrainian males' acceptance of their own subservience in relationship to the Russian Empire.[33]

The escalation of this myth, which turned into virtual "roxolanomania,"[34] arrived at a new turn of the spiral with the twenty-six-part TV "serial monster" (1995–1996). Based, in the best-case scenario, on five pages of a fifty-year-old factual material,[35] this serial has summed up efforts of literary "roxolaniad," including Pavlo Zahrebelny's "historical epic" *Roxolana* (1986), to produce a bizarre crossbreed of romantic sexualized patriotism. It is ironic that such consistent attention to a certain aspect of Roxolana has managed to create a stereotype. For example, one of the businesses in Ukraine that deals with marriage, dating, and escort is called Roxolana Marriage and Travel.[36] Its services are featured on different Web sites advertising "Beautiful Ladies from Sevastopol, Crimea," evidently for foreign consumers (the language of the site is English). What adds an ironic twist to this enterprise is that during the Süleymanic period (1520–1566), which was the golden age of the Ottoman Empire embracing vast territory and diverse variety of peoples as the result of its successful military campaigns, Ukraine became a donor of concubines for Turkish harems, and one of the largest slave markets of the fifteenth and sixteenth centuries and on, which provided odalisques for harems in the Sublime Porte, was located in Caffa (now Feodosia, Crimea). Of course, the idea of trafficking is probably not the one that the agency intended to highlight; Roxolana figures here most likely as an exemplum of a success story and illustration of natural charms and attractions Ukraine can offer in terms of specific human resources.

This has become Vynnychuk's frame of reference for *Life in the Harem*. Using Roxolana, an iconic figure of Ukrainian femininity who has been admitted to the national pantheon of heroes, in the harem setting that she truly enjoys, Vynnychuk plays with the cult of cultural symbols in the most "unnatural" way. While writing his version of Roxolana's life and his own page of Ukrainian "imaginary history," he clearly articulates and develops those aspects of Roxolana's career that apparently captivated his predecessors and contemporaries but were carefully self-censored. The author brings the overtones of the previous intertexts to the extreme to produce an erotic manual and thus transgresses a "sacred boundary" of quality literature and its moral stance. In his attempt to provoke the reader to ponder how best to speak of lust and desire beyond cliché and using the idiom of "high" porn, he makes it even higher because his language is opulently stylized through transpositions of the Old Ukrainian lexis that simulates the authenticity of the sixteenth-century manuscript. At the beginning of Vynnychuk's text Roxolana explains: "I read writings about love recorded from Greek women, also from Saracen women but never have heard about *Rusynka* [medieval term for "Ukrainian"] writing such things. That is why, with my memory sound and my reason integral, I want to serve all those who find joy and delight in love, so that later on they refine lovemaking, without regarding it as licentiousness."[37]

Vynnychuk constructs Roxolana's narrative so that it resembles an array of texts by women writers who are supplying missing links in a feminine tradition as well as empowering themselves with voices to speak about taboo subjects. Roxolana's story becomes both an erotic confession of her personal experiences and a set of instructions in lovemaking for public use, utilizing the conventions of *Bahmane,* Turkish sixteenth-century erotic guides made popular in Europe in the nineteenth century. Nonetheless, Vynnychuk bases Roxolana's advice and descriptions on contemporary sexuality, without introducing too many picturesque details that would have been indicative of specifically Oriental sexual practices of the period.

Having laid the scene in the Imperial Harem of Süleyman the Magnificent, the author does not attempt at its representation as the locus of power in the Ottoman Empire, with an extremely organized system of administration and hierarchy; instead, he turns it into a lascivious sexual playground in which subordination is broken, and concubines, bored to death, delight in lesbianism and indulge in erotic games with eunuchs. Vynnychuk enacts sexuality as a ritual with highly elaborate codes in the place that has become one of the biggest mystifications of Orientalism, which mirrored Western psychosexual needs and provided the space on which to project fantasies of illicit eroticism. In this respect his fake memoir also draws on the nineteenth-century pornographic convention in the manner of *The Lustful Turk* (1828) and other "obscene novels obtainable at the seedier bookstalls of Paris, with their moustache-twirling Sultans and cowering slave-girls."[38] To appreciate the author's radical intertextuality, with its circularity of reference, one should be familiar with the descriptive systems, themes, social mythologies and histories, and other texts. Yet the reader who does not have this background and whose horizon of expectations is clear will enjoy universally recognizable codes, stylistic charm, irony, and grotesque nuances in Vynnychuk's dynamic prose.

Valerii Shevchuk, one of the most reputable grand men of letters in Ukrainian literature, has been trying to escape the confines of an ideologically approved method under the Soviet rule by turning to the golden age of Ukrainian baroque—the period prior to Russian colonization—both as a creative writer of exquisitely crafted novels and as an editor of Ukrainian baroque philosophers and poets. At the daybreak of independence, however, he, quite unexpectedly, published a novella, *Hunchback Zoia* (later included in the book *Snakewoman* [1998]), which signified his return from a claustrophobic ivory tower of the projective past to the present only to depart farther into and get lost in a newly discovered, and thus ambiguous, threatening, and confusing, zone of a volatile female sexuality that lures humanity into bestial pleasures.

By running counter to the iconic use of woman as a signifier of moral purity and sexual innocence promoted by socialist realists and cultural nationalists alike, Shevchuk creates his own version of eroticism, in which he swings to the opposite end of the spectrum in an implied dichotomy. I place it under the category of medieval pornorotica. His sexual tableau seems to exemplify what Camille Paglia contends to be an unchanging human sexual nature (in addition to the earlier reflections on pornography as a socially defined and unquestionably ideologically derived phenomenon): "In fact, pornography, which erupts into the open in periods of personal freedom, shows the dark truth about nature, concealed by the artifices of civilization. Pornography is about lust, our animal reality that will be never fully tamed by love. Lust is elemental, aggressive, asocial. Pornography allows us to explore our deepest, most forbidden selves."[39]

Shevchuk is deeply intimidated, however, by this elemental lust and makes it exclusively feminine. In *Hunchback Zoia* he plunges his male characters into delectable and tantalizing bondage with Zoia. She draws three young men into the whirlpool of sexual passion in a sheer amoral drive to reproduce, drains out their sexual energy, which they all naively try to protect by preventing their semen from getting into her gluttonous womb through interrupted coitus, and renders all of them impotent. The young men are infected by the same inextinguishable virus of the dread of and attraction to the feminine as their ancestors were hundreds of years ago, being susceptible to the same elemental bewitching female powers. This transhistoricity of sexuality is emphasized by a number of ancient female symbols used by the author. Zoia repeatedly mesmerizes her sexual victims with a gaze that is compared to that of a snake. Her blazing eyes, together with equally glaring conventional erotogenic areas—breasts and vagina—trigger the male protagonists' trancelike state, which makes them surrender to the cupidity of the flesh. As if dazzled by his discoveries in the sexual domain, the author summons Zoia's double, disguised as a fearsomely demonic Snakewoman in another novella. Here she is promoted to the status of the great goddess of fertility, repeatedly marked by the deity's sacred symbols—the snake, the tree, and the full moon. The protagonist's mating with the Snakewoman thus acquires a ritualistic dimension, that of ancient agricultural sacrificial rites.

In *Snakewoman* the temptress is also a phantom that possesses the omnivorous power and unleashes the forces of destructive Eros. She materializes from nowhere and mysteriously disappears as if in a phantasmagoric blurring of real and supernatural in the protagonist's quasi-masochistic fantasy. His haunting nightmare clearly manifests a mythic fear of woman; however, in his vulnerability to a pagan Ukrainian dominatrix there lurks an enticing attraction, which contains a perverse pleasure at being abused. Although Shevchuk's self-designated hermit, who runs away from urban life to a secluded place and gets lost in the woods, is completely confused about the borderline between the unconsciousness of sleep and the reality of reason, he seeks an encounter with an ominous woman. He is constantly anticipating it after seeing the Snakewoman earlier in the distance and is waiting for her. Shevchuk's seductress exudes the alluring and dangerous air of Nikolai Gogol's (Mykola Hohol) (1809–1852) Ukrainian witches, who are unsurpassable masters of suspense and are capable of transforming themselves from old hags into young enchantresses (*iarytnytsi*). Gogol's fascination with Ukrainian demonology and folklore, reflected in his descriptions of maddening witch races that provide an exhaustive account of magical metamorphoses in the roles of rider and ridden, abuser and victim,[40] appear to become one of the sources of unconscious intertextuality in the flowing of male desire for his compatriot in the late twentieth century.

Shevchuk's eclectic view of sexuality, which combines female paganism with male Christian asceticism, places his character's carnal experience with the pagan goddess of fertility in the framework of the Fall. Shevchuk stages his male character's personal existential fall against a solitary tranquillity of nature in a garden of Eden–type of setting, with the Snakewoman as a serpent of seduction. In this respect he is close to St. Augustine's reinterpretation of the Fall "as resulting in the betrayal of the will and reason to the tyranny of sexual desire."[41] Both Zoia and the Snakewoman become the devil's accomplices, well schooled in the hellish art of ligature that inhibits male sexual function by depriving "man of his virile member,"[42] according to the definition in the most comprehensive treatise on witches and witchcraft, *Malleus Maleficarum* (1486). By exercising one of the most feared powers in witch lore, both women become castrating females who terrify men by their *vagina dentata,* which swallows up and destroys the most elevated male possession. For Shevchuk's male characters woman's vagina becomes an infernal incinerator: "But just then she suddenly embraced me with her arms and legs; at this her depths flared and burnt me, and I exploded inside her, like a shell, scattered into a myriad of splinters of my flesh. Millions of splinters that were dispersed over a scorchingly hot field—and all my strength was drained."[43] The twin description from another novella, which also focuses on the climactic moment of ejaculation, uses the same operational mode in which the pleasures of seduction and lovemaking are substituted for sexual horror and torture, and the protagonist's second coming acquires apocalyptic dimensions: "And I felt that there, in hell where my rod was burning, volcano erupted shooting up a cloud of ashes, fire, and melted lava-fire. . . . And my flesh exploded for the second time, for the second time the earth was shaking, and my rod was burning in fire and scorching lava; the woman unlocked her embraces, and I fell out of them, like a nut from a green jacket, and tumbled helplessly on my back choking and dying."[44]

Shevchuk complements his paganism with Christian tenets, drawing on the classic statement in the notorious *Malleus Maleficarum* by two sixteenth-century clerics that "all witchcraft comes from carnal lust, which is in women insatiable . . . [;] summ[ing] up the widespread belief that women were by nature oversexed, wicked, and therefore dangerous to men."[45] Shevchuk's representation of relationships between men and women also embodies conventional ideas about the basic duality of the human condition; cultural orders (the masculine) are attempting to control and subordinate natural passions and desires (the feminine).

Les Podereviansky, whose *Hero of Our Time* (2000) has been wittily termed "porno-ethnography,"[46] is far from Shevchuk's existential dilemma. A visual artist and stage designer, Podereviansky has become a cult literary bad-boy in Kyiv as the author of short plays, which have been circulated in audio recordings for almost ten years. What started as Podereviansky's readings for a selected circle of his friends, just for fun, got disseminated among mass readers and listeners. Podereviansky is known even to those who have no idea about and no interest in Ukrainian literature. The fact that his works are made into musical remixes points toward Podereviansky's growing popularity. In addition, *The Hero of Our Time,* which includes twenty-three plays, has been published by the highly esteemed Kalvaria publishing house, which is indicative of its author's acceptance into Ukrainian literary mainstream. Although in his preface to the collection Ihor Lapinsky heralds Podereviansky as a prophet who has reflected the "apocalyptic faithlessness" of the time, the reader is recommended to place the book on a "secret shelf" alongside pornographic magazines and videos.[47]

His plays are extremely disturbing not only because of their violence— unmotivated murders, gluttony, alcoholism, defecation, fights, indiscriminate and unrestricted screwing—but also because of their aggressively obscene language, which is based on three strictly taboo words associated with copulation and their derivatives. The most shocking aspect of this linguistic choice is that this is a kind of language spoken by a considerable stratum of population in Ukraine. It has its own name, *surzhyk,* and is a mixture of Ukrainian and Russian whose in-betweenness bears sociocultural characteristics of an undereducated, uncultured, boorish, and vulgar populace. It has become a proper linguistic medium for the product of the most revolting sociopolitical experiment carried out by the Soviet regime—hybridized Soviet people—to reflect the derangement and idiocies of Soviet life. *Surzhyk* turns out to be equally adequate to represent an impotent and powerless individual in the face of the new order's absurdity. In fact, this is the language spoken by the president of Ukraine, Leonid Kuchma, former Communist Party functionary, as evidenced by the tapes recorded by one of his top security officers, which were passed on to Western mass media during an investigation of the president's involvement in the disappearance of Heorhy Gongadze, an "inconvenient" editor of an independent Ukrainian newspaper in 1999. This somehow adds to a general picture of Podereviansky's misanthropy.

Constructed from Soviet myths, Podereviansky's pieces feature their main themes and ideas; revolutionary romanticism, communist ideology, fraternity among Soviet nations, young pioneer childhood, Communist ideology, military and patriotic upbringing, strong family, and associations of artists and writers are all blended in his bizarre, macabre scenarios.[48] But it is socialist realism and its canon that are placed under the dramatist's merciless scrutiny. Podereviansky is playing down a corpus of works, produced by the Soviet school of writing, which was used as sociological material to mold the political mythology of the authoritarian state, as well as those from Russian prerevolutionary literature that constituted an integral part of school curriculum being thoroughly screened and ideologically sanctioned. The title of Podereviansky's collection, for example, replicates the title of Mikhail Lermontov's (1814–1841) canonical work published in 1840. One of the plays, *Pavlik Morozov,* complemented with the subtitle "Epic Tragedy," draws on a martyr figure of the period of Stalin's forceful, genocidal collectivization in the agricultural sector in the 1930s. Historical Pavlik Morozov (1918–1932) was killed, in Siberia, by his *kulak* grandfather (*kulaks* were prosperous individual farmers who resisted the collectivization campaign) for informing on his father to Stalin's secret police; Pavlik's commendable "political vigilance" (a key moment in Soviet propaganda) resulted in his father's arrest, conviction, and execution. Having been elevated to the status of a heroic symbol, he was forced upon young pioneers as a role model exemplifying the duty of law-abiding Soviet citizens to become informants even at the expense of family ties.

Podereviansky populates his "tragedy" with other real and fictional characters.[49] The name of Pavlik's mother, who is described as looking like a symbolic Motherland figure in propaganda posters, is Pelaheia Nylivna. It evokes the character of Maxim Gorky's (1868–1936) novel, *Mother* (1906), set during the first Russian Revolution of 1905 and featuring a religious woman who is converted to revolutionary ideals after her son's arrest as a political activist. Pavel Vlasov—Pelaheia Nylivna's illegitimate son, Pavlik's half-brother, and the degenerate ape-like antagonist in Podereviansky's play—alludes to the revolutionary protagonist in the same novel by Gorky. In addition, Maxim Gorky, who ended his literary career as the much celebrated spokesman for proletarian culture under Stalin's regime and the first head of the Writers' Union, formulated the central principles of socialist realism, which became a doctrine for future generations of Soviet writers.

There is also a blind prophet in Apollo's Temple, Mykola Ostrovsky, who instructs his followers in spiritual refinement and divine matters. Here Podereviansky summons the ghost of Nikolai (Mykola) Ostrovsky (1904–1936), another legendary figure in Soviet history. After having served in the Red Cavalry during the Civil War (1919–1922), Ostrovsky acted as a Red commissar, enthusiastically responding to the call of the Communist Party to participate in the epochal construction of a new society. Wounded several times, affected by typhus and polyarthritis that resulted in paralysis and blindness, he started to write his autobiographical novel, *How the Steel Was Tempered,* in 1930; it was awarded the Order of Lenin in 1935. This book was included into the Soviet literary canon and studied at schools. Mythologized as a paradigm of self-sacrifice, Ostrovsky became just another clichéd item in the propaganda discourse. Podereviansky places his prophet into a crystal coffin hung from the ceiling of the Apollo Temple in the middle of the Siberian taiga, on the marshes. Architecturally, the temple resembles a wooden shed on chicken legs, reminiscent both of folktales and *Ruslan and Liudmilla* (1820) by Aleksandr Pushkin (1799–1837), the greatest Russian poet and the founder of modern Russian literature, whose oeuvre was reductively interpreted for instructional needs of the "class-conscious" Soviet educational system. The crystal coffin is also borrowed from Pushkin's long poem, but, whereas in Pushkin it is a sleeping beautiful princess who lies there, Podereviansky provides it with a different occupant.

Podereviansky's characters also include General Vlasov, Pelaheia Nylivna's lover, Pavel Vlasov's father, and Canaris's secret agent. The text here draws on the historical general Andrei Vlasov (1900–1946), a Red Army officer who collaborated with Germans during the World War II, formed the Russian Liberation Army, which fought against the Stalinist regime, was tried and executed in 1946, and became an emblematic traitor. There are also two characters in absentia: Canaris, chief of the Abwerh in the Third Reich, the double of Admiral Wilhelm Canaris (1887–1945), chief of the Abwerh and the hidden hand of the Wehrmacht Resistance executed by Hitler; and Zeus, heavenly "leader and teacher" (a standard metonymic reference for both Lenin and Stalin). There also appear Alionushka and Ivanushka from the Russian fairy tale. Meek Alionushka is featured, however, as a mermaid cross-pollinated with a vampire, both aspects denoting the monstrous subconscious.

The "mythological" stratum of the play is represented by Menopause, a messenger of Gods; Sphynx, a winged, clawed monster with breasts and cunt; Bitch and Whore, bloodthirsty chimerae, goddesses of shit, flies, and menstruation; and Minerva's owl, which is turned into a huge fat bird, Filin (eagle-owl), general Vlasov's agent. The supporting cast consists of pioneers, *kulaks,* fascists, whores, apparitions, devils, dragons, and gorgons.

The scene is laid in a Siberian taiga during World War II, which parallels a favorite time frame of Soviet literature that indefatigably drew its inspiration from the "Great Patriotic War" to romanticize and lacquer it in heroic discourse. The atmosphere of the play is also supercharged with artificially staged "hunts" in Soviet history—for spies of the hostile bourgeois world as external evil agents and for "enemies of the people" as internal ones. Everybody in the play is drinking, whoring, and fighting. Pavlik, a *hitlerjugend*-looking hero, murders his father, mother, and the Sphinx and fucks the whores, the goddesses, Alionushka, and a white lamb, Ivanushka. In the final combat with his King Kong–shaped brother, Pavel Vlasov, Pavlik strikes a fatal blow but is tragically squashed by his rival's heavy corpse, which falls onto him. The death of the hero is hysterically lamented by Filin, echoing a famous Shakespearean scene at the battlefield from *Richard III* (1597).

In his absurdist play Podereviansky juxtaposes his anti-utopian nightmare to a utopian fantasy created by Soviet authors by tearing down the happy façade that camouflaged violence against individuals in the name of communism. Each play in the collection similarly rotates around the same type of absurdities, phobias, and crazed and senseless brutalities. Pornography is probably seen by Podereviansky as the most adequate mechanism to reflect on the calamitous aftermath of Soviet rule because it is another zone in which violence and culture overlap. His is an exceedingly masculinist discourse; its phallogocentrism is made absolute through the dissolution of any, even the most vague, standards of decency. Obscenity comprises the body of Podereviansky's language: substandard speech is not utilized as a kind of figurative language for the sake of expression, because his characters live in and through this language, which predetermines and structures their thinking and being. Obscenity also comprises the body of the plays' plots and the bodies of the characters. In his review of *The Hero of Our Time* Vadym Trinchiy mentions that Podereviansky's collection could have been called *Life of the Genitals*.[50] If the male reproductive organ could have gained a certain physical and intellectual autonomy, it would have acted as Podereviansky's characters do. The issue of keeping the psychosexual demons of the unconscious at bay, by which Shevchuk is so painfully tormented, is not something that Podereviansky would ever have considered. In his comediography of violence, the phallus par excellence invariably becomes the hero of our time.

My essay does not attempt to present a comprehensive survey of the Ukrainian "pornographic scene" but navigates the area in different directions in a contrapuntal manner. In addition, the works discussed here can be considered either pornographic and pornorotic or not, depending on the vantage point of the reader and foundations of moral strongholds he or she occupies. Yet they all display cases of what Deleuze calls "creative symptomatology"—not in terms of identifying health problems in society, or their absence, but in a broader view of "the world as a symptom, and the artist as symptomatologist."[51] All grow out of the culture that traditionally has been cultivating male supremacy and in which eroticism becomes violent and violence erotic in relations between women and men. All expose, if not confront, inherited totalitarian gender paradigms. All attempt to reject multiple repressive legacies and express a certain disillusionment with postindependence order. All emerge from the clash between the restrictions of the past and the dizzying choices of a newfound freedom. All demonstrate, to various degrees, disorientation in increasingly transnational cultural space. All enter into conflicting dialogues with imperial as well as their own cultural and literary myths. And, most significantly in the framework of this discussion, all chart the Ukrainian social, political, cultural, and sexual body through the infusion and conceptual displacement of pornographic discourse whose function is expanded, making it in part a means of shock therapy. By conducting her "field research in Ukrainian sex," Zabuzhko maps a liminal territory of Ukrainian sexuality to create her own corporeal cartography. Through her protagonist, who experiences erotic and spiritual catharsis, the writer engages in the project of cognitive liberation from the received tradition. Unlike Zabuzhko's body inscape, delineated by the immediacy of her erotic becomings, Pokalchuk's challenge to culturally enforced regimes of gender and sexuality does not extend much farther than his literary and political project to produce national pornography; as such, the book does its work, for at some moments it stirs, titillates, and gives rise to frissons of sexual pleasure, still remaining a fantasy of sexuality and sexual liberation that has yet to come of age. Shevchuk exposes his fundamental fear of the feminine, writing an archaic paradigm that is based on the unbridled indiscriminate lust of women who destroy and dehumanize men by making them vulnerable to the compulsive power of Eros and intertwining this ahistorical model with misogynistic attitudes to women in Christianity. He places his demonically pornographized women on the borderline between normal and anomalous sexuality. Vynnychuk's playful pastiche, in which he joins a male harem of Roxolana's admirers, is a deviant postcolonial endeavor wherein everything is turned upside down with postmodern zest and gusto. While reading, misreading, reassembling, and misinterpreting the system of hereditary and learned texts, rules, and figures in the corpus, he self-consciously lets the machinery show, thus demonstrating the fictitious and constructivist nature of any discourse, including the fanatically professed "objectivity" of socialist realism. Podereviansky's pornographic characters are creatures of brutal sexualized reality drawn on the paragons of socialist realist textual productions. His revisionist impulses are directed against this canon, which features imperious and spellbinding Major Texts. Unlike the works of Zabuzhko, Pokalchuk, Shevchuk, and Vynnychuk, his violent, satirical, absurdist plays do not represent an iconoclastic break from the Soviet epoch and from socialist realism as its ideological tool; instead, they signify the degeneration of both. Paradoxically, pornographic pulp that, as a developing genre, should in theory evince the farthest departure from representational modes of socialist realism, annexes and applies them in practice. Moreover, its rhetorical poverty, dreary naturalistic style, and tedious repetitiveness in plot patterns make it particularly vulnerable to the petrifying grip of the inherited socialist realist method. This testifies to the fact that in the sphere of culture, as Tejaswini Niranjana suggests, "decolonization is slowest in making an impact."[52]

Notes

1. Homi K. Bhabha, "The Other Question: Difference, Discrimination, and the Discourse of Colonialism," *Literature, Politics and Theory* (New York: Methuen, 1986), 150.

2. Oksana Zabuzhko, "Enters Fortinbras," *A Kingdom of Fallen Statues: Poems and Essays by Oksana Zabuzhko* (Toronto: Wellspring, 1996), 90.

3. Zakonodavstvo Ukrainy, Zakon vid 20.11.2003, no. 1296-IV, "Pro zakhyst suspilnoi morali," http://www.zakon.rada.gov.ua/cgi-bin/laws main.cgi?page=2user=o1y2003&sp=1.

4. Berkeley Kaite, *Pornography and Difference* (Bloomington: Indiana University Press, 1995), 37.

5. Ida Vors, "'Polunapriazhennyi orhan' vitchyznianoi presy, abo 'Kak zasadit Halie bez shchekotky,'" *PiK*, no. 44 (175) (2003), http://www.pic.com.ua/44–175/astyle/s5.htm.

6. Olha Briukhovetska, "Iak molytysia molotom, abo (De)konstruktsia mifiv," *Kino-Teatr* 2 (2003), http//www.ukma.kiev.ua/pub/KTM.

7. David Cairns and Shaun Richards, *Writing Ireland: Colonialism, Nationalism and Culture* (Manchester: Manchester University Press, 1988), 46–49.

8. "Russia Considers Banning Ukrainian Film," BBC World Service, 4 July, 2002, 16:57 GMT 17:57 UK, http://www.news.bbc.co.uk/1/world/europe/2094360.stm.

9. Ievhenia Mussuri, "Movie Miffs Moscow," *Kyiv Post,* 19 July 2002, http://www.thepost.kiev.ua/main/11497.

10. Alan Bray, *Homosexuality in Renaissance England* (London: Gay Men's Press, 1982), 98.

11. Mussuri, "Movie Miffs Moscow."

12. Pavel Hres, "V ukrainskii parlament lezut golyie baby," http://www.compromat.ru/main/kuchma/solod1.htm.

13. Brian McNair, *Mediated Sex: Pornography and Postmodern Culture* (London: Arnold, 1996), 142.

14. Jane M. Ussher, *Fantasies of Femininity: Reframing the Boundaries of Sex* (New Brunswick: Rutgers University Press, 1997), 158.

15. http://www.ukrainianschoolgirls.com/cgi-bin/click.cgi?supdiva.

16. The Young Pioneer League was a political organization created in the Soviet Union for the ideological upbringing of children from ten to fourteen years of age.

17. Victor Malarek, *The Natashas: The New Global Sex Trade* (Toronto: Viking Canada, 2003).

18. McNair, *Mediated Sex,* 140

19. Irina Gutkin, *The Cultural Origins of Socialist Realism* (Evanston, Ill.: Northwestern University Press, 1999), 4.

20. Abram Tertz [Andrei Sinyavsky], *The Trial Begins,* trans. Max Hayward, *On Socialist Realism,* trans. George Dennis (Berkeley: University of California Press, 1982), 200.

21. Jean Baudrillard, *Seduction,* trans. Brian Singer (New York: St. Martin's Press, 1990), 30.

22. Gilles Deleuze, "Coldness and Cruelty," trans. Jean McNeil, *Masochism* (New York: Zone Books, 1991), 17.

23. Tertz, *Trial Begins*, 213.

24. Katherine Ramsland, *The Roquelaure Reader: A Companion to Anne Rice's Erotica* (New York: Plume, 1996), x.

25. Mykola Tomenko, *Teoriia ukrainskoho kokhannia* (Kyiv: Mizhnarodnyi Turyzm, 2002), 11. All translations from Ukrainian are mine.

26. Oksana Zabuzhko, "Where There Are No Knights, a Robber Baron Will Turn Up," http://www.day.kiev.ua/DIGEST/1999/28/culture/cul–1.htm.

27. Jessica Benjamin, *The Bonds of Love: Psychoanalysis, Feminism, and the Problem of Domination* (New York: Pantheon, 1988), 5.

28. Oksana Zabuzhko, *Poliovi doslidzhennia z ukrainskoho seksu* (Kyiv: Zhoda, 1996), 140.

29. Daniel Rancour-Laferriere, *The Slave Soul of Russia: Moral Masochism and the Cult of Suffering* (New York: New York University Press, 1995), 2.

30. Iurii Pokalchuk, *Te, shcho na spodi* (L'viv: Kalvaria, 1998), 242.

31. *Potiah* 76, no. 1 (2002): 131.

32. Serhiy Makhun, "Slaves in the Sublime Porte: Slavic Factor at the Court of Suleiman I," http://www.day.kiev.ua/DIGEST/2002/01/culture/cu14.htm.

33. Oksana Zabuzhko, *Khroniky vid Fortinbrasa: Vybrana eseistyka 90-kh* (Kyiv: Fakt, 1999), 168.

34. Oleksandr Halenko, "Vytivky ukrainskoho oriientalizmu," *Krytyka,* no. 4.18 (1999): 12.

35. Halenko, "Vytivky ukrainskoho oriientalizmu," 13.

36. http://www.roxolana.hypermart.net/index2.htm.

37. Iurii Vynnychuk, *Zhytiie haremnoie* (L'viv: Piramida, 1996), 6.

38. Margaret Atwood, *Alias Grace* (Toronto: McClelland and Stewart, 1999), 442.

39. Camille Paglia, "The Return of Carry Nation," *Playboy* (October 1992): 37–38.

40. Nikolai Gogol, *Village Evenings near Dikanka, Mirgorod,* ed. and trans. Christopher English (Oxford: Oxford University Press, 1994), 376–377.

41. Bruce S. Thornton, *Eros: The Myth of Ancient Greek Sexuality* (Boulder: Westview Press, 1997), 214.

42. Charles Alva Hoyt, *Witchcraft,* 2d ed. (Carbondale: Southern Illinois University Press, 1989), 50–51.

43. Valerii Shevchuk, *Zhinka-zmiia* (L'viv: Klasyka, 1998), 87.

44. Shevchuk, *Zhinka-zmiia,* 173.

45. Anne Llewelynn Barstow, *Witchcraze: A New History of the European Witch Hunts* (San Francisco: Pandora, 1994), 135–136.

46. Vadym Trinchii, "Pro pornoetnohrafiiu," *Krytyka,* no. 5.43 (2001): 24.

47. Ihor Lapinsky, "Shcho neiasno? Vidvaha, nasnaha I zvytiaha Lesia Poderevianskoho," in *Heroi nashoho chasu* (L'viv: Kalvaria, 2000), 9.

48. Volodymyr Dibrova, "Prynts Hamlet Khamskoho povitu," *Krytyka,* no. 5.43 (2001): 26.

49. Les Poderevianksky, *Heroi nashoho chasu* (L'viv: Kalvaria, 2000), 133–134; subsequent references to character descriptions will be to these pages, which include the cast of characters.

50. Vadym Trinchii, "Pro pornoetnohrafiiu," 26.

51. Gilles Deleuze, *Essays Critical and Clinical,* trans. Daniel W. Smith and Michael A. Greco (Minneapolis: University of Minnesota Press, 1997), 178 n. 34.

52. Tejaswini Niranjana, *Citing Translation: History, Post-Structuralism, and the Colonial Context* (Berkeley: University of California Press, 1992), 4.

Stripping the Nation Bare

RUSSIAN PORNOGRAPHY AND THE INSISTENCE ON MEANING

ELIOT BORENSTEIN

Khrushchev Does Stalin

A Soviet primal scene for post-Soviet times:

Stalin moaned.

Khrushchev carefully unbuttoned his pants, pulled down his semi-transparent black shorts, freeing the leader's swarthy, straining phallus. Spitting on his fingers, the count [Khrushchev] began to tug tenderly at Stalin's nipple and moved his lips down the leader's body—to his blood-engorged phallus.

[. . .]

"Give me your ass, my sweet boy," Khrushchev commanded him softly, gripping Stalin firmly by the balls.

[. . .]

Khrushchev unbuttoned his own pants and took out his long, uneven penis with its bumpy head, its shiny skin tattooed with a pentacle. The count spat in his palm, lubricated Stalin's anus with his saliva, and, falling upon him from behind, started to thrust his penis softly into the leader.

[. . .]

The count's member went all the way into Stalin's anus. Squeezing the leader's balls with his left hand, the count took hold of his penis with his right hand and started to masturbate him slowly.

"You . . . what are . . . you . . . " Stalin lowed. "What's the nice man doing to the boy?"

"The nice man is fucking the boy in the ass," Khrushchev whispered
hotly.

Vladimir Sorokin, *Goluboe salo*[1]

Although it is impossible to know just how many readers have found themselves
sexually aroused by Vladimir Sorokin's description of oral and anal intercourse
between Soviet leaders, his novel *Blue Lard* (*Goluboe salo*)[2] has managed to elicit
the other response so often provoked by so-called pornography:[3] outrage and prosecution. In July 2002 a nationalist, pro-Putin youth group called "Moving Together"
filed a criminal complaint with the Moscow prosecutor against both the author
and his publisher and also organized a public demonstration that culminated in
flushing copies of the novel down a mock toilet. At press time the case was still
unresolved, leaving open the politically unlikely, but legally plausible, prospect of
the author's two-year imprisonment on pornography charges.[4]

Even a cursory examination of the facts reveals complications and contradictions, suggesting that the case is more a question of politics than morals. *Blue
Lard* had been published to some fanfare in 1999, almost three years before Moving Together took action: why wait so long for a spontaneous manifestation of moral
outrage? Although there are laws against pornography on the books and repeated
calls for a clamp-down, the Russian porn consumer can find products catering to
the standard varieties of hetero- and homoerotic taste on paper and video, expending
minimal effort if not minimal cash.[5] Why target Sorokin, an avant-garde author
with "high art" pretensions, rather than magazines and newspapers such as *Miss
X, Andrei* (a "men's magazine"),[6] or *Strip?* If pornography has such a negative impact on the morality of an entire nation's youth, why pin the blame on such a difficult novel? The impatient thrill-seeker has to wade through over 250 pages
peppered with obscure Chinese borrowings and futuristic cyber-slang before getting to the famous Kremlin buggery scene; one suspects that, if Stalin's anus were
as impenetrable as Sorokin's prose, the author probably would not be facing criminal charges. Moreover, Sorokin seems to revel in putting explicit sex scenes in
contexts that would ordinarily defy eroticism, beginning with the novel's name.
Even in a country where pork fat is considered a perfectly acceptable sandwich
ingredient, *Blue Lard* hardly seems like a title designed to arouse passions and
stir the blood.[7]

If *Blue Lard* is unabashedly explicit, the Sorokin Affair itself is suggestive
and evocative: its meaning must be teased out. The campaign against Sorokin can
only be understood in the context of the flowering of pornographic expression that
marked the first post-Soviet decade and in light of the culture's nervous attempts
to assimilate or reject it (or even, paradoxically, to do both at the same time). Politically, the Sorokin Affair looks like a step backward for a country that has only
recently emerged from a self-proclaimed dictatorship; from a Western point of view
charging a novelist with pornography seems almost quaint. In a multimedia age,
who cares what novelists are doing? But it is this very quaintness that immediately suggests one lesson to be drawn from the outcry over *Blue Lard:* in Russia
pornography is still a category of meaning and content, rather than simply form

and function. If the West has to be reminded by scholars that pornography grew out of satire during the European Enlightenment, Russia needs no such encouragement to make the connection between pornography and ideas. In Russia pornography *is* an idea.[8]

Pornography as Knowledge

In contemporary Russia pornography enjoys a peculiar status in that it is doubly ubiquitous: not only has the first post-Soviet decade been marked by a proliferation of pornographic texts and images on newsstands, televisions, and even shopping bags throughout the Russian Federation, but pornography seems all the more pervasive in that it is featured prominently in the standard litany of woes afflicting postcommunist society. Pornography in Russia cannot be accepted as a simple, straightforward phenomenon of supply and demand, or stimulus and response. Its widespread dissemination after years of prohibition automatically means that it will call attention to itself, becoming a topic of political and cultural debates. Yet the significance of Russian pornography should not be attributed to novelty alone; after ten years pornography has already become normalized, to the extent that it simultaneously occupies a discrete, commodified niche (stroke literature aimed primarily at heterosexual men), and has expanded to encompass nearly all aspects of cultural life (the pervasiveness of graphic sexual content in film, television, and popular fiction after years of puritanism suggests a culture that is being "pornographized" nearly to saturation). Both the proponents and opponents of pornography in Russia agree on one thing: pornography has meaning. This essay focuses on the way in which this meaning is constructed, by its critics as well as its practitioners.

Russian culture has traditionally privileged a conspiratorial epistemology (hoarding and restricting information) that leads to a dogged insistence on hidden meaning, symbolism, and interpretation; it is perhaps no accident that the discipline of semiotics was developed in a culture that is so self-consciously semioticized. Russian pornography partakes of this same model of knowledge, creating a system of signs that points to more than just sexual desire. To some extent Russian pornography shows a stronger connection to the classical porn of the Enlightenment era, in that it is overtly political and often can be linked to the satirical tradition. I argue, however, that Russian pornography's explicit engagement with ideology, which in part stems from the nation's own repressed pornographic tradition, is the result of particular post-Soviet anxieties. Pornography distills the ideological features that characterize contemporary Russian sexual discourse as a whole: oscillating between the extremes of utopian libertinism and crypto-fascist nationalism, Russian pornography allegorizes the culture's obsession with embattled masculinity, wounded national pride, and the country's perennially fraught relations with the West. It replicates and recapitulates the evolution of popular political attitudes from the heady days of the Soviet collapse to the disenchantment ten years after: early post-Soviet pornography explicitly aligned itself with liberal-democratic aspirations and a project of post-totalitarian liberation, but, more recently, pornographic/erotic publications have retrenched behind a reflexive nationalist discourse, often verging on crypto-fascism. And yet it is members of the "Right" and "Center Right" in Russia who also typically seek to repress pornography, and the few instances of selective prosecution have consistently targeted "liberal" authors and publications hostile to a nationalist ideology (hence, the Sorokin Affair). One cannot help but wonder: why should pornography be a battleground for Russia's soul?

Although pornography in Russia undeniably has a history reaching back hundreds of years, the Soviet era amounted to enough of a great break in porn tradition that the category of pornography has been largely reinvented in the perestroika and post-perestroika eras. This reinvention has hardly been from scratch, and, on the surface, Western models (from glossy magazines to grainy films) are clearly the most immediate source of inspiration,[9] and thus the Russian reader and viewer of pornography can be struck by a simultaneous shock of the new (explicit sexual representation had recently been almost unheard of) as well as a lingering sense of the second-hand (the first examples of post-Soviet pornography tended to look foreign/Western, even when they were not imported). Scholars in the West have long recognized that porn can provide unique insights about the specters that haunt a given culture. Laura Kipnis writes that "[a] culture's pornography becomes . . . a very precise map of that culture's borders," establishing "a detailed blueprint of the culture's anxieties, investments, contradictions."[10] Or, as Feona Attwood argues, pornography "functions as a 'melodrama' or 'allegory' for a given culture."[11] If pornography is routinely seen as a challenge to established norms even in times of stability, how much more threatening does it become to a country in a state of political, cultural, and economic upheaval? What is true for the West is even truer for Russia, where these anxieties are never far from the surface of the pornographic text: Russian pornography, whether its definition is limited to low-cultural men's magazines and films or stretched to include sexually explicit high art, is surprisingly self-conscious in its preoccupation with Russia's status as a nation and a culture. Indeed, I would argue that national concerns are part and parcel of Russian pornography *by definition:* the pleasure (and the danger) of Russian porn derives from the fact that eroticism and nationalism are offered up for consumption in a single package.

In part this results from the unusually compressed time frame of post-Soviet porn's development. Brian McNair has argued that the past two decades in the West have seen a "pornographication of the mainstream," in which imagery and themes that would once have been exclusively pornographic have trickled up into everyday culture,[12] but in Russia this process has been simultaneous with the (re)appearance of pornography as a distinct category. There is no time lag between the arrival of porn and the pornographication of the culture at large, rendering pornography a privileged locus for anxieties about cultural change. Pornography as a genre is distinguished from the rest of the mainstream not by its dogged focus on all things genital but by its unwavering focus on the sexually explicit as both an integral part of the nation's culture and as an allegory for it. It is this conflation of the sexual with the national that provides the true logic behind the selective campaigns against so-called pornography in the works of certain high-cultural figures:

where the antiporn crusaders at first look obtuse, they prove actually to be highly perceptive. Even if books such as *Blue Lard* have an entirely different readership from Russian *Playboy* clones, they are all constituent parts of the unique discourse that falls under the rubric of post-Soviet Russian "pornography": the depiction of sexualized bodies to explore a national idea.[13]

Russian Pornography before Perestroika

Only recently has pornography become an even vaguely legitimate object of study for Russianists, who have largely replicated the culture's own reticence on the subject. But something paradoxical happens to Russian pornography when it falls into academics' far-from-sweaty hands: the more it is studied, the more it recedes from view. While there is no doubt that sexual and scatological material has existed in Russia for centuries, recent studies have tended either to interpret pornography so broadly that the term threatens to lose all meaning or to frame it so narrowly as to virtually define it out of existence. Marcus Levitt and Andrei Toporkov's 1999 collection *Eros and Pornography in Russian Culture,* which contained the fruits of the first international conference on the subject, finds pornography in medieval folk woodcuts, nineteenth-century incantations, eighteenth-century bawdy songs, turn-of-the-century philosophy, and recent avant-garde fiction. In its admirable impulse toward eclecticism, the collection sees any text that deals with sexuality or uses foul language as fair game.[14] The very first contemporary scholarly study of pornography in Russia, a 1977 doctoral dissertation by William Hopkins, implicitly identifies one of the problems with discussing Russian pornography: so little of it appears to be designed for erotic appeal.[15] Rather, the early modern texts he discusses fall into the purview of pornography because of their use of forbidden language: it is as much the words as the actions described that are obscene. Thus, Hopkins eschews the term *pornography,* instead referring to the "genital semantic function," a phrase that accurately reflects the defining characteristics of the genre but which has problems of its own.[16] *Genital semantic function* takes the anerotic character of early modern Russian pornography to its extreme: resting awkwardly between philology and urology, the phrase seems designed to immunize the reader against any possible arousal. The pornographic texts in question are authored largely by reputable men of letters (Pushkin included), surrounding them with a literary aura that makes any attack on them seem tantamount to philistinism. Czarist-era censorship saw the struggle against pornography in moral and religious terms, conflating sexually explicit writings with blasphemy and godlessness.[17] As in much of Europe, pornography was a subset of obscenity.

In the West pornography as a category diverges from obscenity per se when it abandons literary and artistic pretensions and when blasphemy is no longer a relevant issue. In the United States pornography benefits from First Amendment protections and arguments based on artistic freedom, but it has been a long time since the public failed to distinguish between "highbrow" fiction with strong sexual content and mass-market stroke literature. In the visual arts it is another matter, but that is in part because prose is no longer the primary battleground for the souls of impressionable youth. In Russia a separate, "pornographic" sphere was only beginning to grow in the first decades before the Russian Revolution,[18] but the Soviet regime quickly drove pornography underground. Thus, in Soviet times pornography was at best a theoretical concept (the sort of thing found only in the decadent West) or, in a throwback to the previous century, a charge leveled at writers who broke with accepted standards of decorum (in terms of both content and lexicon). Either there was no pornography at all, or the lack of an approved place for pornography meant that any text with strong sexual content could be seen as pornographic.

With the onset of perestroika in the late 1980s and the concomitant wholesale lifting of taboos, sexual and lexical license became an integral, if unintended, part of glasnost. The term *pornography* was usually applied to a set of related, but discrete, phenomena: images of naked women (and occasionally men); soft-core, and later hardcore, films on videotape and broadcast television; sex scenes of varying degrees of explicitness in novels, stories, and newspapers; and the use of previously unprintable "obscene" language, or *mat* (forbidden words describing the human anatomy, sexual activity, and the rest of the physiological functions that Bakhtin so eloquently ascribes to the "lower bodily stratum"). Although conservative critics of the late 1980s and early 1990s often failed to distinguish between "literary" or "artistic" erotic representation and mass-market pornography, the phenomena that the word *pornography* was used to describe rather quickly sorted themselves out across the cultural spectrum. It was writers such as Sorokin and Viktor Erofeyev who first broke the taboos by using foul language and describing explicit sex in stories published in the highbrow journals, and a general softening of the linguistic etiquette eventually followed.[19] But fiction that has little or no artistic pretensions (in particular, the incredibly popular mystery and police novels), fiction that *is* oriented toward the mass reader, tends to avoid the extremes of Russian foul language—as does Russian mass-market pornography itself: when the contents of *Miss X* or *Andrei* are compared to those of their Western counterparts, the tameness of the language is striking.[20] Andrei Zorin notes that the avant-garde writers who broke linguistic taboos were motivated by an urge to be provocative and links this type of language with a kind of aggression.[21] Zorin's conclusion can be broadened: in Russian the most extremely obscene words (the equivalents of *fuck, cock,* and *cunt,* and all their endless Russian derivatives) belong to the performative category of sexualized aggression rather than sexuality per se. Moreover, the sheer ingenuity of Russian *mat,* which exploits every opportunity availed by the flexibility of a highly inflected language (several Russian jokes suggest that *mat* comes close to being a full-fledge part of speech), makes it appealing to avant-garde and postmodern writers interested in playing with linguistic potential. But, outside of the rarified heights of elite prose and the lower depths of street speech and locker rooms, obscene language can seem out of place. Even pornography designed to appeal to Russian men (who are presumed to be the most comfortable with *mat*) avoids these words entirely, since they apparently fall outside the category of the erotic altogether. No one fucks in Russian porn; they have sex, they "make love" (*zanimat'sia liubov'iu,* a hideous *calque* that puts sex on an equal syntactical footing with homework and business), or, when, desire completely overwhelms all lexical restraint, they screw (*trakhat'sia*).[22]

Both the postmodernists' overindulgence in obscene vocabulary and the pornographers' prim celebrations of sex are understandable and predictable consequences of the sudden relaxation of social controls in the last years of the 1980s. It was only fifteen years ago that a participant in a much-ballyhooed joint Soviet-American media event issued the famous (and famously misinterpreted) pronouncement that in the USSR "we have no sex."[23] The phrase became a veritable call to arms in the subsequent "sexual revolution" of the perestroika and Yeltsin eras, as if the entire culture industry were engaged in a nonstop, Stakhanovite effort to prove it wrong. Indeed, one of the unintended consequences of Gorbachev's policy of glasnost was that "openness" came to mean paying dogged attention to precisely those aspects of Soviet life that had previously been suppressed, and in the realm of culture that quickly came to mean sex and violence. There was no shortage of critics assailing the sexualization of Russian culture, but many of them were identified with the struggle against change in general, and in any case they were overwhelmed by the sheer quantity of erotic production.[24] After little more than a decade it is easy to forget how political and polemical this seemingly random sexual frankness was: to an even greater extent than during the so-called sexual revolution of the 1960s in the West, sexual openness was an explicit sign of personal and political freedom. The only thing more naked than the women plastered on so many publications and advertisements was the ideology behind it: a naive, largely masculine "liberation sexology" that identified sexual expression with democracy.

Pornopolitics: Sexing the Nation

In the post-Soviet years the proliferation of the naked female form in advertisements can certainly be seen as the function of the market; after all, nothing sells like sex. But, at least in the early years of new sexual freedoms, the market is not a sufficiently strong mechanism to explain the power of the nude. When small, short-lived publications such as *Baltiia,* a Russian-language tabloid from the late 1980s championing the cause of independence for Estonia, Latvia, and Lithuania, put a photo of a spread-eagled naked woman on its back cover (rather than on the front), the editors were making a clear connection between the "freedom" of sexual exposure and freedom from foreign domination. In the post-Soviet years similar images of supine female nudes could function as part of a discourse of national humiliation rather than pride, but *Baltiia*'s pin-up is doubly provocative, a declaration of independence on the part of the men who displayed her.[25] Not surprisingly, in most of the examples we will look at in this essay, the naked female form is a weapon of power in male hands; only the weapon's target will change over time.

The ties between sexual freedoms and political liberalization proved to be a marriage of convenience and a rather short-lived one at that. By the time the first issue of the Russian edition of *Playboy* appeared in 1995, its rhetoric of sexual revolution seemed decidedly dated. The editors wanted to have it both ways: to show that *Playboy* was more than a Johnny-come-lately, that it had always had a connection to Russia, but also to argue that *Playboy*'s Russian edition would further the cause of sexual liberation through its very existence. *Playboy,* we are told, was always a presence in the Soviet Union, at least in the lives of the Party elite: in an interview entitled "PLAYBOY in My Luggage" the personal translator to four Soviet leaders admits that he always brought copies of the magazine back with him from his foreign travels.[26] Artem Troitskii, the editor of the Russian edition, discusses the connection between Russia and *Playboy* as it unfolded over the decades, paying special attention to the representation of Russia on the magazine's pages. Troitskii begins his article by noting that Hugh Hefner began *Playboy* in 1953, the same year that Stalin died; elsewhere in the same issue Vasilii Aksenov states the connection more boldly: "The new age of the Twentieth Century proclaimed: 'The tyrant is dead, long live PLAYBOY!'"[27] Obliquely, *Playboy* takes credit for the relaxation of Russian mores, constantly insisting that the *Playboy* ethic of sexual freedom is the natural ally in the struggle against totalitarianism. Even as *Playboy* offers its reader the best that Western sex has to offer (including nude pictures of Ursula Andress, Bo Derek, Cindy Crawford, and Kim Basinger), it asserts its Russian pedigree. The parade of nude Western actresses is finally interrupted by a picture of Natalia Negoda, whom the magazine calls the "symbol of the Soviet 'sexual revolution'" because Negoda posed for the American *Playboy* back in 1989.[28]

In reality Russian pornography had already been staking its particular claims to sexual revolution, trying to strike a delicate balance between the needs for free expression and the demands of "good taste." Even liberal publications such as *Ogonek,* which, before the late 1990s, could normally be counted on to support any attempts at free expression, devoted a cover story in September 1995 to the dismal state of post-Soviet erotica, which had descended into vulgarity and violence.[29] When the first "Russian men's magazine," *Andrei,* appeared in 1991, the opening editorial argued for a "renaissance" of the long-suppressed Russian erotic tradition, which was so closely intertwined with "literature and art" and "high ideals": "*Andrei . . .* will fight against the psychology of 'slavish' sexuality—harsh, rude, hypocritical, blind." In other words, *Andrei* was arguing for an eroticism based on liberation, beauty, and morality, of which the intelligentsia could be proud: "The sexual revolution in our country is at a decisive stage. And *Andrei*'s mission is to stand against this 'revolutionary' vulgarity, which has started to appear on the newsstands as calendars, key chains, and postcards. If this elemental trend is not directed toward professionalism, toward beauty, under our conditions it can in the years to come become a monster the likes of which is undreamt of in the West."[30] By the time the eighth issue appeared, in 1997, the magazine's publisher, Aleksei Veitsler, had taken a more pessimistic view of the sexual revolution: "Our magazine began as a political action. It was the sexual revolution. The whole intelligentsia was with us—Aksenov, Nagibin, Voinovich. The best journalists and artists. But the sexual revolution ended; it was short and stormy, like the beauty of Russian women. Then came the fall. Then came the winter, with its orthodox tendencies, medieval hysteria. Some sort of fundamentalism. Not only here, but throughout the world. And now there's another struggle ahead."[31] The change in the ideological climate becomes clear when he is asked to describe his potential allies in this struggle: "All honest people. The miners, the army, the militia, and Cuba are with us. All the people who think progressively, but not those screw-ups who could create communism like they were supposed to, and who are now ruining capitalism."[32]

Clearly, something has changed in the politics and ideology of post-Soviet porn. Even *Andrei,* the most liberal of the men's magazines, has adopted a rhetoric of Russian boosterism that, while always present from the beginning, is now impossible to ignore. Certainly, the overall disenchantment with the West in general and the United States in particular that followed the early days of post-Soviet Russia explains a great deal. But pornography in general and men's magazines specifically proved to be a particularly sensitive barometer for the country's flagging enthusiasm for liberalism and growing infatuation with the discourse of nationalism, primarily because the question of national pride and humiliation in contemporary Russia is so thoroughly gendered. Without a doubt even a cursory glance at Russian porn confirms the almost ritualistic objectification and subordination of women, but, when the men who produce these words and images reflect on their work, it is the Russian male whom they present as weak and embattled. In the textual and visual two-dimensional world of the Russian pornographic magazine, Russian men see themselves as fighting back against national and sexual humiliation.

Magazines such as *Makhaon* and especially *Andrei* represent themselves as the veritable "rear-guard" of Russian manhood. From its very inception *Andrei* has staked out a specific territory on the map of Russian manhood. In its first issue in 1991 the editors write: "The first Russian journal for men . . . is essential today, for it is precisely men who need liberation from stressful aggression and lack of satisfaction more than anything. Their psychological freedom is a prerequisite for the emancipation of society from the crushing complexes of a distorted era."[33] *Andrei* has suffered more than its share of difficulties in the past decade and even ceased publication temporarily after most of its staff deserted for the now-defunct Russian edition of *Penthouse;* by the summer of 1997 it was only on its seventh issue, but its determination to fight for Russia's embattled masculinity has not wavered since its initial manifesto. Each issue contains articles detailing new aspects of the threat to Russian masculinity, printed under the rubric "The Rights of Men." Although the authors vary from issue to issue, the structure remains more or less constant: first, the writer decries the excesses of the "culture wars" in the West, then he exposes similar problems he sees in Russia. In 1995, in the sixth issue of *Andrei,* Viktor Erofeev wrote an essay for this section, under the name "The Flight of the Cloud in Trousers." The essay would be central to Erofeev's 1997 slim volume of essays called *Men,* supplying most of the material for the book's rather polemical blurb.[34] When printed in *Andrei,* Erofeev's article is preceded by a garish illustration of a monstrous female head with a woman's symbol hanging from her ear and a long, serpentine tongue sticking out of her mouth; the tongue is curled around the small, rigid figure of a faceless man, the helpless victim about to be swallowed up by this ravenous she-demon. The man's rigid pose could in itself almost be phallic, but the context deprives him of any of the prerogatives of traditional male power; not only does he look like a pawn from a chessboard, but, given that he seems to be staring directly into the eyes of the fishlike woman, he resembles the paralyzed victim of the gaze of the Gorgon.

After a rather typical diatribe against feminism and the controversy over sexual harassment in the West (which, Erofeev says, may culminate in the executions of former "fun-loving womanizers" for their past "crimes," "like former Trotskyites were shot in our country"), the author informs us that "man's fate in Russia looks different, but is no less dramatic." The Russian man is not merely embattled but has ceased to exist altogether: "That is, the concept has been retained in the language by inertia, out of mental laziness, but essentially, it's a phantom, a chimera, a specter, a myth." Erofeev's explanation centers around the idea that unites his work with the editorial missions of *Andrei* and *Makhaon:* "First and foremost, it's a question of consciousness." Although Erofeev is engaging in deliberate *épatage,* he is also arguing, in a sense, for men's consciousness-raising: "A man is a man when he thinks of himself as a man." Thanks to Soviet power (which Erofeev himself admits was instituted by male Russians), the Russian man has lost the honor and freedom that are the hallmarks of true manhood. Instead, the Russian man has been replaced by a "layer cake" made up of *chelovek* (person), *muzhik* (guy), and *muzh* (husband), all of which represent circumscribed, ultimately unfulfilling roles for the potential real man.[35]

Strictly speaking, there is nothing pornographic about Erofeev's essay. The topic and the argument are hardly new, as the burgeoning literature on the supposedly pathetic state of post-Soviet manhood attests. Erofeev's work is directed at his own contemporaries, middle-aged men who, with just the right amount of consciousness-raising, may be able to rise to the challenge of this chimerical model of male dignity. The choice of a forum for Erofeev's argument is, therefore, hardly accidental: what better way to get the attention of adult heterosexual men than by publishing one's works between pictures of airbrushed nudes with gravity-defying breasts? In the foreword to his story "The Life and Experience of Vova V." Vladimir Voinovich provides a similar justification for men's magazines and, perhaps, for his decision to publish in one: "*Andrei* is a magazine for men. All such magazines attract the reader with pictures of naked butts and pussies, race-cars and brand-name cigarettes. But the best of them sometimes alternate these pictures with rather serious texts."[36]

A similar claim is made by editor L. Konovalov in his opening editorial to the first 1997 issue of *Makhaon;* in part of his ongoing battle against the Russian government's attempts to limit the distribution of pornography, he rejects the "erotic" label for his magazine: "the arts and current-affairs magazine *Makhaon* is not an erotic publication." Instead, he writes, "the path of *Makhaon* lies in the affirmation of a sense of male self-worth."[37] Although the same essay also rejects sexual violence and sadism, some of the more vivid attempts at "affirming male self-worth" in *Makhaon* consist of articles and photomontages about masochistic women receiving the punishment they crave at the hands (indeed, at the feet) of potbellied, middle-aged men. *Makhaon*'s path to masculine pride seems to consist of a combination of female sexual submissiveness and extended rants on the evils of Russian "pseudo-democracy"; perhaps nowhere is this strategy better exemplified than by a full-page, color cartoon of a leather-clad Anatoly Chubais whipping a blindfolded blonde whose tattoo of a two-headed eagle and white, blue, and red sash suggest that she symbolizes Russia; with gritted teeth, handcuffed wrists, and pierced nipples, this woman turns her rear to the viewer as hundred dollar bills fall from her vagina into a box marked "Xerox," apparently in response to Chubais's not-so-tender mercies.[38]

Although *Makhaon* sees its greatest enemies among the leaders of Russia, it clearly has no love for the West. One article in the fourth issue (1995) blames the United States for the Chernobyl disaster, while Aleksandr Braterskii's piece "The Last Virgin in the USSR" describes the collapse of the Soviet Union in terms of seduction and rape, comparing the iron curtain to a hymen: "the people who deflowered the USSR wanted proof of her innocence—they wanted BLOOD."[39] In its disdain for both Russian democrats and Western culture, *Makhaon* is nothing if not consistent. *Andrei*'s attitude to the West is far more complicated, as the editors find themselves embracing certain Western values (consumerism and sexual freedom) while raging against Western competition. Erofeev's article hints at the specter that haunts Russian pornography: the specter of Western culture and Western men. If the Russian man is a thing of the past, the Russian woman is entirely real: "Woman consists of necessity. In Russia we have necessity by the ton. That is why Russia is feminine."[40] And, because she is aware that there are no men in Russia, she is so willing to leave the country and find real men abroad. Once again, this sexual threat is inextricably caught up with an economic one: the Russian man posited by *Andrei* laments the competition with Western men, while *Andrei* itself is haunted both by Russia's competition with American pop culture and by the magazine's own attempts to maintain its market share against the threat of men's magazines imported from the United States, particularly the Russian-language edition of *Playboy,* whose contents differ from the American version only slightly. When *Andrei* calls itself a "Russian magazine for men," the accent is on both "for men" and "Russian," in what seems to be a deliberate slap in the face to the Russian *Playboy.*

Even before *Playboy* appeared, *Andrei* had already begun to stress the Russianness of both its models and their settings. In the introduction to the fifth issue, in 1994, the editors lament that Russia has become a lawless, third-world country that is unable to withstand the onslaught of cheap foreign imports such as Snickers and Pepsi-Cola: "Upset? So are we. And that's why we work without days off, and that's why you have before you a new issue of the first Russian magazine for men, one of the few domestic products that isn't 'for export' and which is not an embarrassment."[41] In an editorial in the seventh issue the writers claim that, unlike the competition, their magazine is more respectful of Russian women: "*Andrei* puts our woman on a pedestal of admiration; unlike invader magazines, of which there are more and more in the kiosks, it does not present her in an unflattering and biased fashion next to foreign women in order that the 'house' model be MORE sexual and feminine. The invaders' task is simple: to prove that everything Western is better, more expensive, stronger—and also to turn our women into a cheap export that is ready for anything."[42] Not only does the magazine that once identified itself with the allegedly Western values of freedom and democracy now take on an overtly nationalistic tone, but its vocabulary deliberately evokes the rhetoric of war: Western magazines, like Western armies, are "invaders" on a hostile mission of conquest.[43]

Although the pictures, stories, and ads in *Andrei* portray a free-spending, luxurious lifestyle available only to the wealthiest of "New Russians," the magazine's implicit nationalism makes itself known throughout. If the letters to the editor are to be believed, the readership has responded to *Andrei*'s pro-Russian boosterism. In the best tradition of Soviet-era collective letters, a group of officers from the Baltic Fleet in Tallinn wrote to *Andrei* in 1995 in the sixth issue, thanking the magazine for mentioning the three hundredth anniversary of the Russian fleet: "You really are our magazine. Even our national pride, to some extent. Although we've been places and seen many different men's magazines, *Andrei* is nicer and closer to the heart of our Soviet man."[44] The officers' letter is so full of patriotic fervor that it would be easy to forget that they are writing about a pornographic magazine rather than, say, the launching of a space shuttle; the anachronistic reference to "our Soviet man" by a group of Russian military personnel based in newly independent Estonia only heightens the identification of *Andrei* with a nostalgia for Russian greatness.

The officers' nationalistic enthusiasm for an erotic magazine seems excessive only when removed from context; the issue that prompted their letter (no. 5 [1994]) featured a special photospread dedicated to the three hundredth anniversary of the Russian navy. "The Battleship Marina" consists of pictures of a female model wearing only a sailor's cap (with the word *Andrei* on it) as she writhes against the heavy artillery of a gunboat. Aleksei Veitsler's photos and text deliberately invoke Eisenstein's *Battleship Potemkin,* only here the film's agitprop message and homoerotic aesthetics are replaced by the none-too-subtle conventions of the heterosexual pin-up: whereas Eisenstein's camera lingers on the bodies of Russian sailors, Veitsler's camera interposes a naked woman between the handsome, semi-nude men. Alluding to the incident that sparks the uprising in Eisenstein's film, Veitsler describes the tense scene on a ship in 1905, when the shipmen of the *Potemkin* are ready to kill one another over rotten meat: "But here we'd be better off with Professor Freud instead of the student Ulianov [Lenin]." If only, Veitsler writes, the model Marina Pavlova were on that ship, she would have shouted, "Who wants to try some of my meat?!"[45] Veitsler's fantasy montage climaxes in an imitation of early Soviet propaganda, with a picture of a fully clothed Pavlova, on the shoulders of three of the sailors, raising the Russian flag rather than the banner of revolution. The text makes the utopianism of this scene explicit:

> And everything turned topsy-turvy, like in a fairy tale.
> And the screen was lit in color.
> And it's as if a wave washed off the red from the flag over the ship.

And there was no decades-long gale.
And the Crimea is ours.
And the fleet is Russian.
Only the riveted battleship has a new name.[46]

Such declarations could not have come at a more politically sensitive time. The much-trumpeted anniversary of the Russian navy took place against the backdrop of heightened tensions between Russia and Ukraine over the status of the Black Sea Fleet and potential Russian claims on the Crimean Peninsula. If the 1994 *Andrei* was in part a special issue for Russian sailors, it neatly combined sexual and political fantasy, one in which the all-male world of the battleship is mediated by the willing body of a desirable woman and the coveted Crimea need not be shared with anyone.

Magazines such as *Andrei,* whose basic economic task is to sell sexual images of Russian women to Russian men, ultimately return to some of the fundamental questions of sexual discourse in Russia today: how are sex and the marketplace to be reconciled? If sexual metaphors characterize the "free exchange of goods and ideas" between Russia and the West (the source of both the marketplace in general and the very genres of pornography and soft-core titillation such as the monthly newspaper *SPID-Info*), how can the anxieties provoked by the commercialization of sex (the incursions on privacy, the threat of foreign wealth and potency) be allayed? *Andrei* points the way by thematizing the anxieties themselves, continually revisiting them in a lighthearted manner. The seventh issue of *Andrei* includes a feature that incorporates exotic locales while turning the threat of the "export" of Russian women into the stuff of comedy: a blonde model is photographed in various locales (and various stages of undress) in Cairo and the Egyptian desert, under the heading "One hundred camels for a Russian girl." Capitalist exchange is replaced by Eastern barter, and the Russians girl's price, for once, is anything but practical ("We sent . . . the camels on their way to friend in Tashkent. Will they get there?").[47] The photo spread depends on a sense of mutual exoticism as well as a broad parody of cross-cultural kitsch; in the corner of a full-page photo of the naked Russian woman on a camel is a fully clothed Arab woman on a tractor. The contrast between the "backwards" camel and the "progressive" tractor is a cliché of Soviet Socialist Realist tales of the struggle to civilize the nomads of Central Asia, but, whereas the USSR brought communism, *Andrei* pretends to bring the example of sexual liberation. The caption reads: "The magazine for men was welcomed by a few emancipated women of the East. Out of solidarity with our struggle for the beauty of the body, one of them even climbed up onto a tractor—the symbol of progress."[48] The Eastern locale allows Russia to take on a missionary role familiar from the days of communist internationalism, at the same time displacing cross-cultural anxieties by turning Russia into the source of sexual "export." Here Russia gets to be the West, raising the sexual question in a mysterious, repressed East.

The implicit ideological agenda of *Andrei* is to compensate for the trauma of the nation's fall from the status of a world power, especially to the extent that this humiliation might be felt by the individual Russian man. The demons of the recent past are to be exorcised through sex. Hence, a two-page spread in the seventh issue features semi-nude women in SS costumes against the backdrop of the Chernobyl nuclear power plant, thus reinterpreting a national tragedy in terms of sadomasochistic games. The cover feature for the third issue, from 1992, is a woman holding an automatic assault weapon and a grenade as she poses clad in nothing but an army helmet and dog tags; this section, entitled "Conversion," addresses the shock and dislocation entailed by the process of refitting the country's huge military-industrial complex for a new market economy. Aleksei Veitsler, the section's author, supplies the reader with photographs of the naked and busty Natalia Sergeeva, purported to be an officer in the Russian army. A life in the army has not prevented her from retaining the "traits of a real woman." Unequaled with both the rifle and the frying pan, Natalia realizes that it is time for her to leave the army. Her decision combines the personal and the political in that she recognizes the exigencies of a post–Cold War world while heeding the sound of her biological clock ("I want to have a family").[49] In the final photo Natalia stands on the beach with her back turned to the camera. The text reads: "Sergeant of the Guard Natasha emerges from the boiling iron of war like Aphrodite from the foam. . . . Transfigured and waiting for happiness. Keep her photograph, like they keep souvenirs made from the shells of intercontinental missiles. As a memento of conversion."[50] Here conversion becomes something beautiful and divine, involving both transfiguration and the birth of new life. At the same time, the attributes of military might (guns, camouflage fatigues, and army boots) are transformed into sexual paraphernalia. In the new world the military yields to the pornographic.

A similar process takes place in a truly bizarre section of the seventh issue, published under the title "Chechnia: What the Soldiers Aren't Saying." Here pictures of Russian soldiers fighting, eating, and sleeping in Chechnya are framed by the erotic images of their fantasies, such as Eastern women in leather fetish garb, wielding whips. A pimply faced Russian soldier stares vacantly at his food, and the photograph is surrounded by images of naked women caressing phallic-shaped breads. The photos are accompanied by a prose poem about the unexpressed desires of the Russian soldier; in the final two pages the men are shown firing weapons, while the poem describes their eventual return to their "next-door girls with their firm behinds, whom they will have this way and that way, without extraneous words, upon their return; then [these girls] will bear them children."[51] The naked woman whose picture accompanies this text is now far less threatening than the previous models; her expression and her demeanor really do suggest the "girl next door," while the gun she holds is merely a plastic toy. The Russian soldier is thus shown to be dreaming of returning to a world in which war is the stuff of fantasy, while women are the reality, even as the magazine's reader has both war and sex offered up to him as erotic stimulant.

Andrei's world of male power and Russian pride thus manages to transfigure the site of the country's greatest post-Soviet humiliation into a source of ultimately reassuring erotic fantasy: in what might be considered a postmodern reinterpretation of the biblical injunction on swords and plowshares, the phallic rifle wielded by the young Russian soldier with such uncertainty is transformed into a long, pink, plastic sex toy caressed by a nubile Russian beauty. Although the Chechen is perceived as an internal enemy, the implicit connection made by *Andrei* between men at war and men's erotic magazines suggests the specific function that such journals hope to perform in the post-Soviet imaginary: to rally the flagging spirits of Russian men, who are surrounded by hostile forces on all sides.

Screwing with Russian Culture

The initial flirtation between pornography and liberalism, replaced by a much stronger union between pornography and nationalism, has resulted in ever stranger bedfellows, with the country's most prominent "erotic" publications staking out a paradoxical position in the post-Soviet culture wars: the rhetoric, imagery, and ideology are strongly reminiscent of the cultural conservatives who so routinely condemn them. Just as Russian pornography eschews the vulgarity of *mat* in favor of high-flown language and appeals to the sublime, it has assumed the mantle of guardian of the Russian cultural heritage. Although its pervasive *bricolage* and mixing of genres make contemporary Russian pornography a postmodern phenomenon, its ideology is postmodernism's polar opposite. The contrast between the ethos of postmodernism and the long-standing Russian cult of culture could not be more pronounced, and practitioners of postmodernism are often portrayed by their ideological opponents as amoral cynics who revel in the decline of everything that made Russia great. Whereas Russian pornography joins the cultural conservatives in continuing to put the national cultural heritage on a pedestal, the postmodernists continually undercut any reverential attitude toward art, literature, or the Russian "national idea." Thus, in Russia, the term *postmodernist* is used as often to describe a particular artist's or writer's attitude toward culture as to characterize his or her artistic technique.

This cultural divide is crucial to any understanding of the highly selective campaigns against pornography in the post-Gorbachev era. After Yeltsin's government used military force to remove the opposition from the country's legislature in October 1993, the Press Ministry closed down several newspapers that allegedly advocated "fascism" but admitted that one of the publications targeted was guilty of something entirely different: a Latvian-based, Russian-language newspaper called *Eshche:*

> As concerns the newspaper *Eshche,* which was in no way involved in the violence in early October, it was openly seeking to deprive its readers of any moral footing. Activity of this kind and calls for the destruction of any morals and morality are deemed to be no less dangerous for society than the calls for restoring the Communist Party of the Soviet Union.
>
> Aggressive amorality with its degrading influence is no less a danger to society than fascism, and we intend to carry on a consistent and tough struggle against it.[52]

The story of *Eshche* is particularly instructive, for it illustrates the way in which post-Soviet Russia has treated pornography as both a political and cultural threat. The publisher of *Eshche,* Aleksei Kostin, was arrested on 6 October 1993 on pornography charges, only to be released three days later. The prosecutor then proceeded to accumulate further evidence against Kostin and the paper, arresting the publisher once again on 4 February 1994.[53] The newspaper was subjected to several assessments by "experts," who determined that *Eshche* was indeed pornographic (as opposed to erotic). The case foundered in legal limbo for over a year (as did the publisher—he remained in prison the whole time, in violation of Russian procedural law), never resulting in prosecution. The newspaper itself emerged none the worse for wear, garnering the support of many outspoken liberals and even upgrading its production values to include color photos as well as black-and-white.

From the beginning *Eshche* was an odd choice for pornography charges, since dozens of graphic, hard-core publications were already circulating throughout the Russian Federation without resistance. On the other hand, the prosecutors clearly recognized that *Eshche* was different from most of its competition, and it was this difference that rendered the newspaper so odious. If the mainstream men's magazines peddle an amalgam of eroticism and nationalism, *Eshche,* which its defenders, such as Zugar Gareev, call a "postmodern phenomenon,"[54] counters with a parodic, nostalgic transnationalism, comically proclaiming that the former USSR is a "Common Erotic Space" (a parody of then-current phrases such as a "Common Cultural Space" or a "Common Ruble Space"). Yet even as it has little use for discussions of Russian national identity, *Eshche* is far from cosmopolitan in its outlook; instead, it defines its audience in terms of mentality and shared experience rather than ethnic or national makeup. *Eshche* presents a sexual vision as seen through an entirely (post-)Soviet lens. Its erotic adventurers are truck drivers and collective farm workers, and its stories about sexual experimentation in other countries are told from the point of view of the bemused former Soviet sex tourist. Dmitrii Stakhov sees the newspaper as a catalog of a "dying breed": the "Soviet people." He writes: *"Eshche* is a mirror for Soviet man. 'Both you and your intimate manifestations are open to the gaze of another. Look at yourself!' *Eshche* seems to be calling. 'You are still Soviet in a no-longer-Soviet world.'"[55] Stakhov's interpretation of the newspaper has an added appeal, one that Stakhov himself does not make explicit: the very title of *Eshche* (which could mean both "still" and "more") would then combine Stakhov's idea of the Soviet who is "still Soviet" with the more obvious sexual connotation of "more" (i.e., one can never get enough).

Eshche hardly fits in with the leaden seriousness of the other publications targeted immediately after the 1993 October events (such as the national chauvinist mouthpiece *Den'* (the *Day*), which was quickly reborn with a bit of temporal sleight-of-hand as *Zavtra* (*Tomorrow*), but its not-yet-fashionable nostalgia for Soviet kitsch did lend it some superficial resemblance to "Red-Brown" publications. The evaluations made by the "experts" point to a different reason for the official hostility to *Eshche:* it had a distinct "cleverness and subtleness" that they found troublesome.[56] As the committee of experts noted repeatedly, *Eshche* includes a surprisingly wide range of materials, "artistic works with explicit bedroom scenes," letters from readers, "pornographic" photographs ("when the camera records the minute details of the sexual act or the sexual organs prepared for the sexual act"), and explicit advertisements for sex toys. The experts were concerned about the "consistency" of the publication's "cultural level." As one of the experts noted, popular newspapers such as *Mister Iks* were "simple" pornographic works, never attempting to rise from a "low" cultural level, while *Eshche* used pornographic pictures to illustrate artistic texts.[57] Goldschmidt is quick to point out the absurdity of such an evaluation: "*Playboy* would be prosecutable because it could be argued that the text was a trick to get people to open up the centerfold . . . , but a book describing itself openly as a guidebook to child molestation would not be actionable because it did not attempt to hide its intentions."[58] I would argue, however, that the absurdity of the experts' evaluation is quite revealing and is, in fact, in tune with the anxieties that certain forms of pornography provoke in Russia today. *Eshche* violates the established boundaries between high and low, and therefore is as potentially disruptive to the reigning cultural discourse as the overtly fascist *Den'*, if for different reasons. The men's magazines also mix genres and bring together high and low, but they compensate for their *bricolage* by ensuring that even their centerfolds are put in the service of patriotism and traditional cultural values. *Eshche* lures the reader with explicit sexual photographs, only to undermine his value system with its playful postmodernism and unfailing irreverence.

In today's Russia sexually explicit materials that are easily identifiable as pornography or erotica tend to reinforce the cultural hierarchy, attempting to instill a sense of national pride as well as sexual arousal. Moreover, their artistic pretenses may be an attempt to raise the publications from the gutter, but in the final analysis these men's magazines know their place: their appeal to cultural traditions does not contaminate high culture because these publications are so clearly "low." A cultural conservative who consumes Russian pornography may be "lowering himself," but, if he does open up the magazine, he sees his own worldview largely confirmed. Indeed, the fetishization of the classics in Russian glossy men's magazines creates the illusion that the hegemony of high culture remains intact in the post-Soviet era: pornography may be a social evil, but at least the pornographers are still quoting Pushkin. Far more threatening, then, is "high art" that refuses to accept the boundaries between high and low and that sees the indulgence in sexually explicit material as part of an artistic agenda and therefore potentially admissible into the cultural canon. High culture elevates porn while remaining unsullied, but pornography, it seems, can leave high culture permanently stained.

By 2002, when Moving Together began its crusade for Russian literary purity, Sorokin had been merrily flouting cultural strictures for two decades, with stories of sadomasochism and the entire bouquet of "philias," from necro- to pedo-, more often than not involving figures who were supposed to command respect (e.g., Party members, Komsomol leaders, and government officials). If that were not enough, Sorokin routinely compares literature to a "narcotic," something habit forming and presumably harmful, rather than uplifting and redemptive. When *Blue*

Lard appeared in 1999, it attracted a fair amount of attention and mixed reviews, but nothing the novel contained could come as a surprise to anyone familiar with his work. It was, however, his first full-length novel in several years, which meant that, unlike his previous, Soviet-era works, it was initially released to the mass market, rather than printed in a journal, published in an obscure collection, or left to languish in samizdat. With the benefit of hindsight, the publication of *Blue Lard* now looks like the last gasp of the Yeltsin era, when the outcry against such a novel would have come largely from marginalized extremists. Since then, some of these extremists are no longer marginalized: Alexander Prokhanov, editor of the notoriously racist and anti-Semitic newspaper *Zavtra,* is now an award-winning novelist with at least some veneer of respectability,[59] while Yeltsin's replacement by Vladimir Putin has given cultural conservatives a figure to rally around *within* the government, rather than outside it. Putin himself has remained largely above the fray, but his firm, quasi-authoritarian attitude has made him an attractive figure for what the West would call the "radical Right." When seen as a text for the nascent Putin era (a reading that would be perversely anachronistic were it not for the current anti-Sorokin campaign), *Blue Lard* appears far more transgressive than it did when it was first published. Putin's harsher rhetoric, KGB past, and overall firm demeanor have clearly been a balm to those in Russia longing for the "firm hand" of a true leader, but the firmest hand in *Blue Lard* is busy tickling the leader's testicles rather than bringing order to the country. As Gary Shteyngart points out, perhaps the biggest offense to nostalgic nationalists is that Stalin is a Bottom rather than a Top.[60]

Sorokin's approach to culture and politics is antithetical to the unrelenting earnestness of Moving Together, a group that looks back wistfully to the days when the Communist Youth League provided the nation's young people with both a set of clear and unwavering values and an array of wholesome activities to occupy their time. By contrast, Sorokin is not satisfied with merely tipping over the culture's sacred cows; he has to violate their every orifice. For Moving Together it is a matter of saving the country's youth from a dangerous infection. As their leader, Vasily Yakimenko, puts it: "Out of fifteen words, here are nine profanities. In Russia, literature has always given people answers that they can't find in everyday life. When a young person is just discovering literature and they read Sorokin's vulgarity, it's like showing them a porno film. After Sorokin, they'll think Chekhov is boring and uninteresting."[61] Yakimenko is ascribing to all Russian literature a pedagogical role that Sorokin explicitly rejects (and perhaps it is no accident that so many of the teachers in Sorokin's works turn pedagogy into pederasty—both moralists and pedophiles make a fetish of children). Thus, *Blue Lard* is actually more harmful to children than a hard-core sex film, since young people are presumably not likely to see *The Cherry Orchard* and *Debbie Does Dallas* as equivalent works of culture consumption. The urge to protect children from contamination is expressed even more forcefully by the proverbial "man on the street" at an anti-Sorokin rally in June 2002: "We would like Sorokin's books in [the] future to be recognized as containing pornography and sold only in plastic covers, like pornographic magazines, in special establishments. We would like the culture minister finally to take some kind of measures against writers like this. . . . Finally, we do not want the kind of society that tolerates this kind of thing."[62] What he wants, of course, is entirely utopian, since it presumes that contemporary Russia really does enforce rules on pornography's distribution and keep sexually explicit materials wrapped safely in plastic.

Indeed, even most of Sorokin's defenders are careful to dissociate themselves from his work, repeating the mantra that they dislike *Blue Lard* but defend the author's right to publish. Oleg Mironov, Russia's human rights ombudsman, spoke out against Sorokin's prosecution but was critical of "foul language and pornography in the arts: "Writers should speak of the reasonable and the eternal instead of cursing and describing improper scenes."[63] In other words, they should behave more like the publishers of *Andre, Makhaon,* and even *Playboy,* whose conservative cultural program and persistent nationalism are far more palatable than the disruptive pornographic imagination of Vladimir Sorokin or the irreverence and irony of *Eshche.* Post-Soviet Russia is remarkably comfortable with the conflation of the sexual and the national, with the unspoken notion that Russia's current dilemma and ultimate fate can be conceptualized in sexual terms, but only when both sexuality and the "Russian idea" are taken seriously, when each remains on its pedestal. When seen in this light, Russian pornography displays a distinct resemblance to political propaganda, a phenomenon the country has had far more time to assimilate: the target audience must be provoked to the proper response (sexual arousal and ideological agitation, respectively). The dominant, nationalist pornography in contemporary Russia attempts to combine these two goals, to produce the very phenomenon that postmodernists would so easily ridicule: excitement that is both sexual and ideological, a proud and patriotic erection.

Notes

1. Vladimir Sorokin, *Goluboe salo: Roman* (Moscow: Ad Marginem, 1999), 257–258. All translations from this and all other Russian texts are my own, unless otherwise noted.
2. The particular word for "blue" in Sorokin's title (*goluboi*) is also a slang term for "gay man." Western press reports also cite the novel's title as *Gay Lard, Blue Fat, Blue Back-Fat, Sky-Blue Bacon* and *Sky-Blue Pork Fat.*
3. Setting aside the lively scholarly and political debates on the nature of "pornography" (and its even more enigmatic cousin, the "erotic"), I will use the term to describe audiovisual and textual materials foregrounding explicit sexual content. More to the point, I will apply the term *pornography* to the texts that tend to be referred to as such by Russian polemicists: for the purposes of the present study it is pornography if enough Russians call it pornography. No value judgment is implied. Hence, Sorokin's works are discussed in this essay not because I feel they should be considered pornography but because enough powerful and influential people *call* it pornography. The Sorokin Affair is creating and altering the discourse of and about Russian pornography, regardless of whether or not Sorokin's novels and stories are pornographic.
4. For a detailed, English-language overview of the Sorokin Affair, see Jamey Gambrell, "Russia's New Vigilantes," *New York Review of Books,* 16 January 2003, 40–43.
5. Although prices have fluctuated greatly over the years, a pornographic videocassette tends to cost at least as much as a monthly subway pass and possibly much more. The

cheapest of the erotic newspapers cost little more than their mainstream counterparts (the equivalent of a loaf or two of bread), while a single issue of a glossy "men's magazine" costs the equivalent of two or three hardback books.

6. Although the Russian terms *muzhskoi zhurnal* and *zhurnal dlia muzhchin* (men's magazine) can designate general "men's interest" magazines such as the Russian editions of *Men's Health* and *Soldier of Fortune,* they are also often used to designate upscale, soft-core pornography.

7. With characteristic bluntness Sorokin has made this very argument in the press: "Pornography is a concrete genre. Its chief goal is to cause a reader's erection. I have never pursued that goal" ("Russian Writer Blasts Pro-Kremlin Critics," United Press International, 29 June 2002).

8. Indeed, one prominent Russian literary figure, Kornei Chukovsky, would even assert at the turn of the twentieth century that the connection between pornography and ideas was unique to Russia: "Russian pornography is not plain pornography such as the French or Germans produce, but pornography with ideas" (as cited in Laura Engelstein, *The Keys to Happiness: Sex and the Search for Modernity in Fin-de-Siècle Russia* [Ithaca: Cornell University Press, 1992], 386). Chukovsky made this claim in his review of one of prerevolutionary Russia's most notorious pornographic novels, Mikhail Artsybashev's *Sanin,* a work that shocked its readers with its presentation of cynical, sex- and death-obsessed young provincials rather than with any explicit sexual descriptions.

9. There has also been a resurgence in interest in prerevolutionary pornography and erotica, as evidence by Andrei Balabanov's award-winning 1999 film *Freaks and Men,* a cinematically beautiful reconstruction of a late-nineteenth-century pornographic photography studio.

10. Laura Kipnis, *Bound and Gagged: Pornography and the Politics of Fantasy in America* (New York: Grove Press, 1996), 164.

11. Feona Attwood, "Reading Porn: The Paradigm Shift in Pornography Research," *Sexualities* 5, no. 1 (2002): 91–105.

12. Brian McNair, *Mediated Sex: Pornography and Postmodern Culture* (London: Arnold, 1996), 24.

13. The question of a "national idea" has been a vexing issue for both the government and the media since the Soviet collapse. According to a popular school of thought based on readings and misreadings of Nikolai Berdyaev's 1946 *The Russian Idea* (Herndon, Va.: Lindisfarne, 1992), Russia has always been guided by some form of a dominant "idea" that both unites the nation and defines its mission. After the October Revolution, Bolshevism filled this role, but, with Soviet ideology largely discredited, many in Russia now feel that the country needs a new "idea" or "ideology" to replace it. Although an ideological void might seem like a less pressing matter than unemployment or rampant crime, the need for a national idea figures prominently in the post-Soviet press and in opinion polls. In 1996 Boris Yeltsin even put together a government commission to develop a new national idea, although the commissions' findings were greeted lukewarmly (Kathleen E. Smith, *Mythmaking in the New Russia: Politics and Memory during the Yeltsin Era* [Ithaca: Cornell University Press, 2002], 158–172).

14. M. Levitt and A. Toporkov, eds., *Eros and Pornography in Russian Culture* (Moscow: Ladomir, 1999). In the interests of full disclosure I should note that I was one of the book's contributors.

15. William Hopkins, "The Development of Pornographic Literature in Eighteenth- and Early-Nineteenth-Century Russia" (Ph.D. diss., Indiana University, 1977).

16. Hopkins, "Development of Pornographic Literature," ix.

17. Paul W. Goldschmidt, *Pornography and Democratization: Legislating Obscenity in Post-Communist Russia* (Boulder: Westview, 1999), 90–91.

18. Engelstein, *Keys to Happiness,* 359–386.

19. For a discussion of the function of explicit anatomical vocabulary in contemporary Russian fiction, see Helena Goscilo, "Body Talk in Current Fiction: Speaking Parts and (W)holes," in *Russian Culture in Transition: Selected Papers of the Working Group for the Study of Contemporary Russian Culture, 1990–1991,* ed. Gregory Freidin, Stanford Slavic Studies 7 (Palo Alto: Stanford University Press, 1993), 145–177.

20. Helena Goscilo notes the "slippage into euphemism and periphrasis" in hard-core pornographic publications, an approach to language she calls "canonical rhetoric within soft porn." Goscilo advances a number of convincing explanations for the alternation between coy evasion and clinical vocabulary in Russian pornography, including the need to educate unenlightened readers about anatomy and sexual function (Goscilo, *Dehexing Sex: Russian Womanhood during and after Glasnost* [Ann Arbor: University of Michigan Press, 1996], 157).

21. Andrei Zorin, "Legalizatsiia obstsennoi leksiki i ee kul'turnye posledstviia," in Freidin, *Russian Culture in Transition,* 139.

22. For a more extended discussion of linguistic reticence in contemporary Russian discourse, see Eliot Borenstein, "About That: Deploying and Deploring Sex in Postsoviet Russia," *Studies in Twentieth Century Literature* 24, no. 1 (2000): 52–62.

23. Because of the ambiguity of the Russian word *seks,* this phrase can be read somewhat more sympathetically than it usually is (Borenstein, "About That," 53–54).

24. It is worth noting that pornography in particular and overt sexuality in general were usually prominent features in a standard conservative laundry list of social ills, signifying the total breakdown of social standards. As the perestroika era receded, jeremiads on the decline of morality could be found in publications and broadcasts throughout the political spectrum. In 1993 the liberal *Nezavisimaia Gazeta* (Independent Newspaper) printed an op-ed piece by Valentin Aleksandrov, complaining that "plaster casts of reproductive organs are displayed for sale on Novyi Arbat and the central squares right under the nose of the Moscow mayor's office" (8). Setting aside the Freudian and Gogolian implications of his words, Aleksandrov's screed seems to suggest that the problem is almost carnivalesque in its reversal of the metaphorical bodily hierarchy: penises, whether they are human, plastic, or symbolic, must be kept far from the centers of power (phallic though these institutions may be).

25. Even after the Soviet collapse, the Baltics would still serve as a foreign (but not too foreign) locus for the pornographic. *Eshche,* an erotic publication that was singled out for particular harsh sanctions by the Russian authorities in the early 1990s, is published in Latvia, where pornography is subject to less regulation.

26. Aleksandr Lipnitskii, "Viktor Sukhodrev: PLAYBOY v moem bagazhe," *Playboy* 1 (1995): 97.

27. A. K. Troitskii, "Rossiia v pleiboiskom prishchure," *Playboy* 1 (1995): 94; Vasilii Aksenov, "Matushka-Rus' i igrivye synochki," *Playboy* 1 (1995): 56.

28. Troitskii, "Rossiia v pleiboiskom prishchure," 33.

29. *Ogonek* 39 (September 1995): 41.

30. *Andrei* 1 (1991): 4.

31. *Andrei* 8 (1997), 39.

32. *Andrei* 8 (1997): 39.

33. *Andrei* 1 (1991): 3.
34. Other essays were originally printed in *Playboy,* in which Erofeev started publishing his essays not long after his work in *Andrei* appeared.
35. Viktor Erofeev, "Polet oblaka v shtanakh," *Andrei* 6(1995): 46.
36. Vladimir Voinovich, "Zhizn' i perezhivaniia Vovy V," *Andrei* 6 (1995): 22.
37. L. Konovalov, "Ot redaktsii," *Makhaon* 1 (1997): 1.
38. *Makhaon* 8 (1997): 4.
39. Aleksandr Bratersky, "Poslednii devstvennik SSSR," *Makhaon* 4 (1995): 24.
40. Erofeev, "Polet oblaka v shtanakh," 46.
41. "Intermediia," *Andrei* 5 (1994): 2.
42. *Andrei* 7 (1997): 2.
43. Such military rhetoric is also used by Erofeev throughout his article in issue 6; for example, when he explains that the successful wife gives his husband the illusion of conquest, she herself will be the true victor: "Then it will end up like 50 years ago: the USSR wins, but it's Germany that celebrates" (Erofeev, "Polet oblaka v shtanakh," 46).
44. "Natsional'naia gordost'," *Andrei* 6 (1995): 4.
45. Aleksei Veitsler, "Bronenosets Marina," *Andrei* 5 (1994): 6.
46. Veitsler, "Bronenosets," 15.
47. Aleksei Veitsler, "Sto verbliudov za russkuiu baryshnui," *Andrei* 7 (1995): 50.
48. Veitsler, "Sto verbliudov za russkuiu baryshnui," 49.
49. Aleksei Veitsler, "Konversiia," *Andrei* 3 (1992): 82.
50. Veitsler, "Konversiia," 89.
51. Aleksandr Anin et al., "Chechnia: o chem molchat soldaty," *Andrei* 7 (1995): 92.
52. Itar Tass, 14 October 1993, in FBIS-SOV–93–198, 15 October 1993, 30, as qtd. in Goldschmidt, *Pornography and Democratization,* 145.
53. My presentation of the facts of the *Eshche* case is based on Goldschmidt, *Pornography and Democratization,* 178–182. Goldschmidt notes that the arrest of the publisher rather than the editor was an unusual move and was contrary to Russia's press law. But the editor, Aleksandr Linderman, lived in Riga and had no intention of traveling to Moscow to be arrested. Kostin's detention was apparently intended to force Linderman to turn himself in (178).
54. "Erotika i vlast': kto kogo…," *Ogonek,* 17–18 May 1994, 13.
55. "Erotika i vlast': kto kogo…," *Ogonek,* 14.
56. Goldschmidt, *Pornography and Democratization,* 179.
57. Goldschmidt, *Pornography and Democratization,* 180–181.
58. Goldschmidt, *Pornography and Democratization,* 182.
59. He also shares a publisher with Sorokin: both his novels *Gospodin Geksogen* and *Blue Lard* were printed by Ad Marginem. Among the many conspiracy theories advanced to explain the Sorokin Affair (from a cheap publicity ploy to sell more books to a plot by Putin's enemies to make him look bad) is the hypothesis that the Kremlin is using Moving Together's anti-Sorokin campaign as a way to punish Ad Marginem for publishing *Gospodin Geksogen,* which asserted that the 1999 Moscow apartment bombings were all part of a plot to bring Putin to power (Mikhail Zolotonosov, "Kul'tura: Drova izdatel'skoi topki," *Moskovskie Novosti,* 12 March 2003, 26).
60. Gary Shteyngart, "Letter from Russia—Teen Spirit: On the Rise of Post-Soviet Youth," *New Yorker,* 10 March 2003, 46.
61. Lawrence Sheets and John Ydstie, "Dispute in Russia over a Book by Vladimir Sorokin

and Whether or Not It Is the Dissemination of Pornography," "All Things Considered," National Public Radio, 8 August 2002.

62. "Pro-Putin Youth Group Takes Stand against 'Pornographic' Modern Russian Novel," BBC Worldwide Monitoring, Ekho Mosvy Radio, 27 June 2002.

63. Steve Gutterman, "Russian Police Investigate Prominent Writer on Pornography Charge," Associated Press, 11 July 2002.

Walking on the Wild Side

SHEMALE INTERNET PORNOGRAPHY

JOHN PHILLIPS

Academic interest in representations of sex in film, television, and print media now has a relatively long history and, indeed, has attained a measure of respectability that it may not have possessed as recently as the early 1990s. Numerous studies have been published to date, many by gay and feminist scholars, on the nature and effects of such representations, particularly in so-called pornography. Very little attention, however, has been focused by scholars on the Internet, perhaps because it is still a relatively new medium but, above all, I think, because, in spite of the recent expansion of cultural studies in universities and the readiness of researchers in that area to analyze any and all social and cultural objects, including those from popular culture, the Internet remains an unordered and chaotic space, Internet material defying definition, challenging conventional categories of authorship, genre, and form. Such a space can appear daunting, its contents lacking the specificity required for critical investigation. Internet sites have increasingly appeared in the bibliographies of our students, despite warnings that most of their content is unauthoritative and unreliable. It is understandable, then, that many in the academic community would seek to avoid any contact with the Internet, even as an object of study in itself. The view is often heard expressed among colleagues—and in many respects it is a legitimate one—that Internet material is unoriginal and unexciting in both form and content and thus unworthy of critical interest. What little attention has been devoted to Internet pornography concentrates on images of men and/or women who can, broadly speaking, be described as "straight" or gay, engaged in activities associated with these binary sexual identities. The few who have turned their critical gaze to Internet porn have shown little if any interest in Internet sites representing transsexuals.[1] As far as I know, the only critic to date to have devoted any serious effort to the subject of transgender in pornography is Laura Kipnis, whose work is of undoubted value and insight, but her focus is pictorials and personal ads in transvestite magazines,[2] rather than transsexual, or "tranny," porn on the Internet, and she is less interested in transvestites as pornographic objects than as subjects that transgress stereotyped norms.[3] Much of Kipnis's work is nevertheless of relevance to the study of transsexual porn, and I shall refer to it from time to time here.

The male-to-female transsexual porn object is a relatively recent phenomenon. Indeed, opportunities for both men and women to transform their bodies in any kind of permanent fashion have been available only since the early twentieth century, while the World Wide Web that has enabled the dissemination of transsexual pornography across the world in ways unthinkable in the past has existed for a much shorter period of time. It would seem helpful to proceed by first sketching the history of the two technologies that have made possible the creation of this new and powerful pornographic object.[4]

The Internet is the hardware base (computers and connections between them as well as the software that make communication possible) upon which the World Wide Web is built. The host computers are owned and run by a variety of different institutions, including government agencies, businesses, universities, and other organizations. There is, therefore, no single organism that owns or controls the Internet, which is partly why it is practically impossible to regulate. The history of the Internet dates back to the 1940s, when the U.S. military was interested in creating a communication technology that would survive nuclear war, but the commercial and informational potential of the Internet was not realized until the growth of the personal computer in the 1990s.

Concern about the dissemination of pornographic images on the Net arose in the mid–1990s. In the summer of 1995 *Time* magazine printed a story about the threat of "cyberporn," which claimed that the Internet was dominated by pornography. Although the article and the research behind it were subsequently discredited, the allegations led to attempts to control the Internet in the United States through legislation.[5] As a result, the Communications Decency Act was introduced, but, following challenges by civil rights groups, the act was eventually thrown out as unconstitutional.

It is undeniable that many forms of pornography are easily accessible on the Internet, but the nature of sites accessed and numbers of "hits" are extremely difficult to quantify because such information derives from those who own and manage the sites themselves and who therefore have a vested interest in artificially inflating access figures. It is also not possible to count the number of times files are downloaded because the Net only measures how many people are given the opportunity to download, not how many actually do so.[6] Yet, on the basis of claims made by porn sites themselves and of an impressionistic evaluation of the ever burgeoning numbers of tranny sites as evidenced by results thrown up by search engines, "shemale" Internet pornography can be said to be a significant and growing phenomenon. As with all forms of pornography, the rapid growth of Internet technology in the space of just a few years has itself led to a similarly rapid growth in such material.[7] And, because anyone with a personal computer can access any site on the World Wide Web, this pornography knows no national or ethnic frontiers and is genuinely universal.

The Internet, then, has only been accessible to public use for little more than a decade. By contrast, Western culture has a long history of cross-dressing. Ancient Greek and Roman writers refer to young men who wanted to live their lives as women. The influence of Christianity led sex change to be viewed as a taboo (and therefore eroticized) activity. The *Malleus Maleficarum* (The Witches' Hammer), for example, associated sex change with satanism. For the early medieval church cross-dressing was nothing less than a heresy, although there are many medieval accounts of cross-dressed female saints. Joan of Arc was actually burned for the heresy of wearing men's clothes. There is much evidence, too, of the medieval and Renaissance male cross-dresser, especially among male prostitutes and actors. From the Restoration onward, much more documentary evidence exists of transgender behavior: for instance, in the Netherlands between 1550 and 1839, 119 women are known to have lived as men.[8]

There is also evidence during this period of men who lived as women. Stephen Whittle quotes evidence of a cross-dressing culture developing in the latter half of the seventeenth century alongside the "gay" scene in London taverns. These taverns became known as "molly houses" (*molly* was originally a term for a female prostitute and, like the word *queen,* became a term for the effeminate male homosexual). The image of the "molly" gave rise to a distinctive homosexual culture.[9]

In 1885 the Criminal Law (Amendment) Act made all homosexual behavior illegal in the United Kingdom, and cross-dressers became easy targets for the police because they were associated in the public mind with the homosexual subculture. This law led some members of the medical establishment to campaign to change the view of homosexuality from that of a crime to that of an illness that might be cured, and, in response, a whole new medical field developed: sexology. Sexologists such as Richard von Krafft-Ebing (the first to take a special interest in the sexual impulses of individuals) discovered through extensive case study that homosexuals were not always the same but were, in fact, diverse in history, practices, and desires.[10] After Krafft-Ebing, the German scientist Magnus Hirschfeld was the next most influential voice in sexology. It was Hirschfeld who in the early years of the twentieth century finally separated transgendered behavior from homosexuality, allowing the medical profession to regard the former as treatable.

Until the end of the nineteenth century those who felt trapped in the wrong body, then, could do no more than cross-dress, living their lives in some cases as a member of the other sex. The rupture between cross-dressing and transsexuality came with the development of new medical technologies. Transsexuality, the quest to transform the bodily characteristics of sex via hormones and surgery, originated about a hundred years ago, following the discovery by scientists in the late nineteenth century of sex hormones, identifying them as male or female. In the early twentieth century it became possible to isolate the specific effects of "male" and "female" hormones. By the 1910s European scientists had begun to publicize their attempts to transform the sex of animals, and by the 1920s some doctors, mostly in Germany, had agreed to alter the bodies of a few patients who longed to change their sex. It was not until after World War II, however, that the issue of sex change was seriously addressed in the United States, and in 1949 Dr David O. Cauldwell, an American psychiatrist, was the first to use the word *transsexual* to refer to people who sought to change their sex. By the end of the 1950s there was already a clear scientific distinction between "hermaphrodites," or people who had both male and female gonads, "transsexuals," whose gender identities did not correspond with their physical sex, and "homosexuals," who were sexually attracted to their own sex but had no desire to change sex. Although some surgery and hormone treatment had been practiced since the 1920s, then, it was not until the postwar period that new advances in plastic surgery and the invention of synthetic hormones made sex change more freely available.

The first widely publicized case of male-to-female (MTF) sex change occurred in 1953. Christine Jorgensen, a former American GI, returned from Denmark, where she had undergone the first of several operations as part of what became known as gender reassignment, and, given her film star looks (she was blonde, beautiful, and chic) and gift for self-publicity, she quickly became a media sensation. In what was probably the first public demonstration of erotic interest in a transsexual, there was clearly a large measure of titillation in the media coverage of Jorgensen's case. Her experience blazed a trail for others, however, and, thanks to the media publicity, almost at once her psychiatrist in Denmark, Dr. Christian Hamburger, started receiving requests from others for advice and treatment, leading in 1953 to the publication of a paper, "The Desire for Change of Sex as Shown by Personal Letters from 465 Men and Women."[11] The medical profession suddenly realized that large numbers of people wished to change their biological sex and gender role, and clinics were set up, first in New York and San Francisco, then gradually in many other Western cities, to respond to this demand. When the endocrinologist Harry Benjamin published the first major textbook on the subject in 1966, gender reassignment was still the subject of extensive social stigma both publicly and in the medical world.[12] Nearly forty years later, some of the stigma remains, but most now accept that transsexuals should be allowed access to hormone therapy and surgical reassignment.

With the assistance of female hormones and sometimes surgical intervention, then, male-to-female transsexuals have for some time been able to acquire breasts, to flesh out their hips and buttocks into a more rounded feminine shape, and to get rid of facial and bodily hair so that their skin acquires a more feminine smoothness, although it is only over the past decade that Internet technology has afforded such individuals (and the pornographers who exploit them) the means to transform themselves into valuable erotic objects. The "pre-op" transsexuals that make up the overwhelming majority of transsexual models represented in Internet pornography, however, have retained their male genitals, greatly enhancing their erotic appeal (see later discussion).[13] In fact, the opportunities for mass exposure and therefore high levels of remuneration that the Internet and, in some cases, prostitution provide are arguably the main incentive for many young and attractive pre-op MTF transsexuals to remain pre-op, although the expense of reassignment surgery may also prove a deterrent. Whatever the reasons for the preponderance of pre-op MTF transsexuals, it is the latter's uncertain or ambiguous status that has been found by some to be politically problematic.

What troubles gays about transsexuals is that their very existence threatens the notion of fixed and specific sexual orientations. As Leo Bersani observes, "It is not possible to be gay-affirmative, or politically effective as gays, if gayness has no specificity."[14] Although little has been written about porn images of transsexuality, we are bound to assume that they would receive the same negative reception from the gay community as transgendered persons have done in the "real" world and for similar reasons. Judith Butler's argument against fixed and unambiguous gender identity that implicitly favors transgender without referring to it explicitly, has itself been criticized on these grounds: "As an assault on *any* coherent identity, it forecloses the possibility of a gay or lesbian specificity (erasing along the way the very discipline—gay and lesbian studies—within which the assault is made): resistance to the heterosexual matrix is reduced to more or less naughty imitations of that matrix."[15] Moreover, as Kipnis observes, feminists have often expressed resentment that the transvestite male—and the same might surely be said of the male-to-female transsexual—may play at being a woman while retaining all the privileges of male power, as symbolized by the phallus; hence, some feminist theorists of gender are highly suspicious of transgender, fearing that transgendered males in particular are producing negative caricatures of femininity and are fundamentally hostile to women.[16]

More crucially in the context of this pornography, the phallic focus that the pre-op transsexual simultaneously embodies and invites keeps both viewing subject and viewed object trapped in a phallicist economy that is politically unacceptable to those feminist and lesbian groups seeking to transcend phallogocentrism to achieve what Judith Butler calls a "postgenital sexuality."[17] The photosets of transsexual pornography are typically constructed around a number of binary oppositions that reinforce and reflect the male-female binarism of heterosexist culture.

All of this helps to explain why this form of pornography has remained virtually invisible to those researching the representations of sexuality and gender in pornographic media. Antipornography feminists such as Andrea Dworkin and Catherine MacKinnon, for example, whose main aim is to show the abuse and degradation of women represented in pornography produced by and for heterosexual men or lesbian and gay commentators whose interest understandably lies principally in pornographic material aimed at their own communities have shown little or no interest in transsexual pornography.[18] In either case this pornography defies the categorization and definition that their arguments demand. What is often called "shemale" or "tranny" porn in the trade disrupts some common assumptions about what porn is, especially, the antiporn feminist view that porn represents the graphic sexual abuse of women for the pleasures of heterosexual men, and yet, as we shall see later, the abusive rhetoric accompanying shemale porn is comparable to that found in more mainstream porn sites depicting biological women.

There is little doubt, on the other hand, that transsexual pornography defies the conventional categories of gender classification. The bodies portrayed in tranny porn sites appear to belong to at least three gender categories, from transvestite males, to pre-op male-to-female transsexuals with breasts and penises, to "post-op" transsexuals with breasts and vaginas. Some are depicted as engaging in sex acts with men, some with women, some with both.

The critical neglect of this subject is psychologically rather than politically motivated. This brand of pornography is disturbing because, unlike any other, it undermines and disrupts the viewer's (and that includes the critic's) sense of his or her own sexual identity. Indeed, tranny porn puts sexual and gender identity into question more powerfully than any other form of pornography. Academic neglect of the subject is no doubt also linked to suspiciousness of transgender in culture generally, to the extent that in Anglo-Saxon countries it can only be approached from the safe distance of humor; thus, popular culture is full of male-to-female cross-dressers, designed to provoke laughter: as Kipnis observes, films from *Some Like It Hot* to *Tootsie* to *Mrs. Doubtfire* reveal a nervous but excited interest in cross-dressing: "There's clearly a vast cultural anxiety around cross-dressing, co-existing with an equally vast fascination about the transgression of the codes of proper dress for the proper sex."[19] The same might be said to apply to the "dame" figure in the traditional British pantomime and to the burlesque travesties of farce. The more recent popular successes of self-mocking gay presenters on UK television suggest that such figures represent a similarly safe means of neutralizing the anxiety provoked by both homosexuality and transgender while indulging a morbid fascination for it.

For these reasons alone, Queer Theorists ought to take transsexual pornography far more seriously than they have done hitherto.[20] In its emphasis on the constructedness of gender and sexuality and its drive to escape the binarism of fixed heterosexual or homosexual positions, Queer Theory seems perfectly suited to the analysis of transsexual pornography and its effects. If, as Luce Irigaray claims, woman is the sex that is not one, the pre-op transsexual is the sex that is both, an overdetermined gender cluster that, Janus-like, faces simultaneously into the masculine and the feminine.[21]

This essay will, accordingly, draw upon some of Queer Theory's fundamental notions, together with a number of familiar psychoanalytical concepts, in an attempt to fill the critical gap identified here. In exploring the modes and metaphors of shemale pornography on the Internet, I will focus on the construction of the viewer within the pornography itself as male. This is not, of course, to exclude the possibility of women viewing this pornography, but my concern here is with the visual and verbal imagery (the photosets and their accompanying verbal text) that explicitly target heterosexual men.[22] These culturally constructed images will be seen to have little to do with any transgender or transsexual reality but essentially to be fantasy products, chemically, surgically, and fictively designed to appeal to largely unconscious desires. Analysis of the nature of these desires will suggest that the attractions of this pornography are, above all, attributable to its transgressive character, inviting a repositioning and redefinition of sexual desire in the light of the appeal of shemale pornography and transsexual prostitutes to heterosexual males.

Most Internet shemale porn shows cross-dressed men and pre-op transsexuals, always referred to as "she," often in lingerie and various states of undress to begin with (some are fully clothed; others may be naked but hide their genitals between their legs initially), but the photosets usually follow the pattern of a strip-tease, quickly leading to the uncovering of the penis, which may at first be flaccid and then may become erect. Some sites show stills from movies depicting "cum shots" or ejaculation as a finale. This gradual unveiling of the phallus and its capabilities is sometimes playfully depicted as a pleasant surprise for the male viewer, who may be represented in the scenario as an unsuspecting "straight guy" who is tricked or enticed into sexual relations with a tranny. The following, for instance, is not untypical: "Could you believe that she has balls? We send out hot shemales to pick up unexpecting [*sic*] guys. Of course the guys don't know they are shemales! How will they react? Visit *Tranny Surprise.*"

By the same token the verbal rhetoric of many sites often appeals to the "bi-curious," though heterosexually identified, male viewer: "Are you curious about shemales?" "Why not try the best of both worlds?" This rhetoric sometimes appears to exaggerate the masculinity of its target customer by positioning him as a violent "macho" man. In the following accompanying text to be found in *LadyboyGuide,* for instance, the customer is implicitly invited to identify with the aggressive male lover of a passive transsexual: "Wang is completely obedient and complied to my every command without a word. Even when I ripped her ass open, she just turned her head to look behind her and then beamed at me, wide eyes [*sic*]." Other sites seek to position the prospective customer as a solidly (and reassuringly) "normal," upright and, by implication, heterosexual male:

> Looking for something different to fulfill your fantasies?
>
> This is an exclusive opportunity to spend time with a gorgeous, feminine, "shemale."
>
> It's time to put all those taboos aside.
>
> Your secret desires are shared by many, healthy, upscale, professional men, just like you, who are interested in meeting a Sexy Pre-Op Transsexual. (Internet ad for transsexual escort)

The models are frequently engaged in sex, alone or with others: other men, other transsexuals, and even women. Some photos have a sadomasochistic character (e.g., displaying leather corsets, whips, and/or face masks), and other types of fantasy scenarios are enacted, featuring the leather-clad dominatrix or the flirtatious schoolgirl. Facial expressions range through all familiar female stereotypes: raunchy, innocent, ecstatic, the starlet, the slut, the shy virgin, the "good ol' girl," and so on. Whatever the variations, however, the phallus is always the central and final focus of this pornography, represented as the most powerful term in the binary oppositions that help to frame and define it. The visual focus in these images frequently switches from female clothing to male genitals, from breasts to penis, from stereotypical female physical qualities such as pretty features, smooth and hairless skin, girlishly long hair, and hourglass curves to the aggressive masculinity of large testicles and rampant erection. Indeed, it is largely from these contrastive juxta-positions that the shemale's erotic power stems. The rhetoric of accompanying ver-bal commentaries is frequently structured around a similar binarism, as the following examples taken from different shemale Internet sites clearly demon-strates: "Want a woman but still ache for a man? Come to *Transsexuals*. We can make your fantasy come to life!"; "These women each have a package in their panties." Moreover, the very names of many of these sites foreground this binarism: "Shemales," "Chicks with Dicks," "Girls with Balls," "HeGirls," "Transgirl," "Pretty Girls with Big Dicks." From the perspective of a progressive gender poli-tics, some might argue that the positioning of the male viewer as a "curious het-erosexual" reinforces homophobia by implying the undesirability of the homosexual position.[23]

On the other hand, this privileging of the heterosexist model is, one might say, inevitable. As Butler has recognized in relation to the lesbian body, it is per-haps not possible for the transsexual body to be constructed entirely outside the heterosexuality it might at the same time be said to subvert.[24] In pornography, in particular, both the gay and lesbian and the transsexual body are constructed by discourses dominant in society as a whole that privilege masculinity and phallo-centrism. In a more obvious way than the gay or lesbian, however, the shemale constructs herself through hormone treatment and surgery, and it might be argued that the shemale to that extent escapes hegemonic cultural discourses (which may be said nowadays to include socially acceptable concepts of gayness) to achieve a measure of autonomy and self-definition. Moreover, the shemale image in fact func-tions more as a threat to the dominant heterosexist culture by doing the very thing that some gay activists and commentators find politically undesirable: that is, by undermining concepts of fixed sexual and gender identity and transgressing the boundaries that conventionally demarcate sexual desire.

I might begin to argue this case by emphasizing the paradoxes that emerge from my analysis in the preceding section: the marrying of the feminine and the masculine; the construction of the viewing position as straight, yet the focus be-ing on the penis; the disregard for conventional sexual and gender roles (especially in photosets depicting more than one transsexual, either alone or with one or two males or biological females; here the shemales may engage in sex with each other, with the males or biological females, or with all three). Before attempting to ex-plain male heterosexual desire for the transsexual object, I shall briefly suggest why, on balance, the paradoxes of transsexual pornography might be considered politically subversive and so must surely serve the cause of a nonnormative ap-proach to the crucial issues of identity politics.

In spite of the difficulty of escaping the binary matrix of conventional sexual and gender roles, Butler's analysis of gender helps us to see how the transsexual object disrupts this binarism in one important respect: by appealing to a "*trans-itional*" category of sexual orientation somewhere between the hetero and the homo. This is a new category, not synonymous with bisexuality, a sexual category created by new hormonal drugs but also by its very representation in pornographic images and in the language created to describe and define them. As for the word *shemale,* it may be seen less as a word that privileges the masculine than as a linguistic oxymoron that simultaneously reflects but, by its very impossibility, challenges binary thinking, collapsing the divide between the masculine and the feminine. It is in this sense that pre-op transsexuality can be viewed positively as "queer," in that it is at odds with all norms, whether of a dominant heterosexuality or a gay/lesbian identity. If this form of porn is simultaneously exciting and disturbing, it is in part because the phallic woman that the transsexual represents challenges the fixity of our own sexual identities.

Queer Theory derives much of its thinking from poststructuralist ideas of identity as decentered and unstable, in particular from Jacques Lacan's model of the subject as structured by the unconscious, from Jacques Derrida's deconstruction of binary concepts, and, of course, from Michel Foucault's model of subjectivity as the product of discourses. Strongly influenced by poststructuralist views of human subjectivity as shifting and contextual, Butler concludes that gender "does not denote a substantive being, but a relative point of convergence among culturally and historically specific sets of relations."[25] Echoing Simone de Beauvoir's famous maxim, Butler claims that sexual and gender identities are a "doing" not a "being" (Butler refers directly to Beauvoir's oft-quoted claim that one is not born but, rather, *becomes* a woman).[26] There is no reason to assume, Butler argues, that genders should remain as two, and she questions the immutable character of sex: may it not, after all, be as culturally constructed as gender?[27] There is, therefore, no such thing as a specific female identity.

Butler is also indebted to the work of Monique Wittig, who maintains that not only gender and sex are cultural constructs but that the body itself is never just a given, that, like notions of masculinity and femininity, it is also constructed. Butler follows Wittig in acknowledging that this construction is primarily linguistic: "That penis, vagina, breasts, and so forth, are *named* sexual parts is both a restriction of the erogenous body to those parts and a fragmentation of the body as a whole."[28]

In her 1999 preface to *Gender Trouble* Butler specifically relates this linguistic construction to the case of the transsexual: "What about the notion, suggested by Kate Bornstein, that a transsexual cannot be described by the noun of 'woman' or 'man,' but must be approached through active verbs that attest to the constant transformation which 'is' the new identity or, indeed, the 'in-between-ness' that puts the being of gendered identity into question?"[29] Here, at last, Butler acknowledges the transitional nature of the transsexual, implicitly recognizing the latter's place outside conventional sex and gender categories and therefore the threat she represents to the heterosexist hegemony: "Butler emphasizes the dangers for the social system of 'permeable bodily boundaries.' . . . Any activity or condition that exposes the permeability of bodily boundaries will simultaneously expose the factitious nature of sexual differences as they are postulated within the heterosexual matrix."[30] In focusing upon the construction of the transsexual in language alone, however, Butler misses an opportunity to exploit the case of the transsexual as an example par excellence of her theory of gender as performativity. In *Gender Trouble* Butler adopted Foucault's argument that "sexuality" is the product of discourses and extended it to include gender, which she viewed as a performative effect: "gender proves to be performative—that is, constituting the identity it is purported to be. In this sense, gender is always a doing."[31] Borrowing the logic of Nietzsche's claim that "there is no 'being' behind doing," that the subject does not preexist the deed, or, as Nietzsche puts it, that the "doer" is merely a fiction added to the deed—the deed is everything,[32] she then applied this notion to gender: "There is no gender identity behind the expressions of gender; . . . identity is performatively constituted by the very 'expressions' that are said to be its results."[33] Drag, she argued, exposes this performativity of gender well: "In imitating gender, drag implicitly reveals the imitative structure of gender itself—as well as its contingency."[34]

While the theatricality of the drag queen clearly lends itself to an illustration of performativity, if writing this work now, Butler might well have referred to the transsexual to explain the Nietzschean idea of gender identity as a "doing," for, while the former merely "puts on" the external trappings of an exaggerated and seemingly parodic femininity, the latter *becomes* a woman in the sense first established by Beauvoir and elaborated by Butler. Moreover, in spite of Butler's purely linguistic analysis, the transsexual's bodily construction does not take place in language alone: through medical intervention the transsexual is able to give Beauvoir's famous maxim a literal and physical reality.

Because of the literal *becoming* of the male-to-female pre-op transsexual, then, it seems that this figure disrupts the hegemony of what Butler calls "compulsory heterosexuality"[35] and transcends the binary system of gender imposed by it far more effectively than the drag artist or the gay man or woman. For what are we to call the "pre-op tranny"?—no longer just a "he" and not yet quite a "she," the "chick with a dick" hovers confusingly and in many cases indefinitely between the masculine and the feminine.[36] When Wittig wrote of the lesbian as "the only concept I know of which is beyond the categories of sex," one can only conclude that this assertion was born more of ignorance or personal prejudice than of detached objectivity.[37]

The shemale also serves Butler's arguments against the normative regulation of sexual and gender identities by undermining the presupposition of a causal relationship between gender and sexual desire: as mentioned earlier, shemale pornography displays transsexuals engaging in sex acts with men, women, and other transsexuals (anal penetration but also fellatio and cunnilingus). It is now received wisdom that, because a man wants to be a woman, this does not mean that (s)he sexually desires only men, so that a male-to-female transsexual may think of herself and behave as a lesbian. More than any other identity category, the shemale represents the possibility of the liberation of both gender and desire from binary or fixed norms. The transgressivity of the transsexual is therefore politically progressive, but it also, as we shall now see, plays a significant role in the tranny's success as a pornographic object of male desire.

Wanting It All

The vast majority of transsexuals appearing on Internet porn sites are "passable" women, and, indeed, when judged according to conventional Western criteria of feminine beauty, many are stunningly attractive. We are a long way from the ludicrous caricature of woman that is the pantomime dame or the outrageously attired drag queen. The pre-op transsexual model is typically young (between eighteen and thirty), girlishly pretty, slim but curvaceous, with a smooth, toned, and often tanned skin. In some exceptional cases the model has worked in the mainstream glamour industry, passing herself off successfully (and very profitably) as a biological female. Many sites depict European and American shemales, both black and white, but Asian "ladyboys" and Brazilian transsexuals appear to have a particularly high profile.[38] Clearly, it would be beyond the scope of this study to account for the varying sexual tastes and preferences of individual viewers with regard to differences of race and color. What follows, therefore, is an attempt to analyze the generalities of attraction to shemales. Accordingly, my analysis will be principally inspired by psychoanalytic theory, which presupposes the existence of universal unconscious desires transcending ethnic and racial differences.

The shemale appeals directly to two fundamental aspects of male sexual desire: promiscuity and the search for novelty. All of the elements of the shemale's attraction for heterosexual males fall, therefore, into either or both of these overlapping categories.

If shemale porn is a popular form of Internet porn, as indicated at the outset, it is probably because the shemale represents and reflects back to the male viewer the polymorphous perversity of his own desire. The transsexual, then, combines the attractions of femininity with the promiscuity and sexual availability of the masculine. The stereotypical sexual voracity of men is thus transplanted, as it were, into women, conventionally perceived as passive and slow to awaken.

One might say, in fact, that the shemale unconsciously represents the masculinization and colonization of the foreign land, the dark continent that, for Freud, is woman. If the pre-op Internet shemale has acquired through hormones and surgery the physical shape of a woman to match the mental and psychological attributes of femininity that she doubtless already possessed, she is also represented as retaining enough physical, psychological, and symbolic traits of male sexuality to be identifiably same as well as excitingly other. "Woman" is thus tamed; the inaccessible, unapproachable, and ultimately incomprehensible feminine is made ever available and totally comprehensible thanks to the reassuring presence of the indispensable and omnipotent phallus. The shemale can pleasure a man better than any woman, the rhetoric has it, since she combines all the attractions of femininity with a unique understanding of the male body that only another male can possess. Shemale Internet sites often attempt to exploit this stereotyped view that only another "man" knows what really turns a man on: "These shemales can suck you off better than your wife."[39]

At the same time, as with many porn images of biological women, the shemale offers an opportunity to express a powerful unconscious frustration with the maddeningly coquettish female object of male desire. The metaphorical language of shemale porn expresses degradation of the feminine as part of a process of erotic overfeminization and, at the same time, a settling of scores with the desired but castrating woman who exploits her sexual power over men. Terms such as *sluts, whores,* and *bitches* are used in many sites to describe the transsexual models depicted. In this perspective the shemale image is, therefore, vulnerable to analysis as the simultaneous expression of desire and hatred for the feminine, just like any other pornographic image that represents women as a potential object of male violence or contempt. Feminists might well argue here that the transsexual is, in this sense, an unconscious substitute for all women, a male effigy of the feminine that can be burned at the phallic stake. At the same time, the transsexual's ambivalent gender status suggests that the motivations for this verbal and sometimes physical violence are more complex: in the transsexual scenario the abuse is more ironic than serious, aimed at enhancing the erotic power of the shemale by emphasizing her sexual appetites and drawing attention to her "femaleness," albeit in ostensibly negative terms.

Both erection and, above all, ejaculation are as ubiquitous in straight as in shemale pornography, which perhaps suggests that the motivation for such displays in the straight scenario is less the satisfaction of the viewer's homoerotic desires than of a more complex unconscious need. This question might seem less clear-cut in the case of shemale porn, in that the viewer of this phallus-centered pornography may arguably be responding to latent homosexual urges. On the other hand, homosexuals are, after all, sexually attracted to attributes of masculinity (muscular physique, body hair, Adam's apple) of which even the pre-op transsexual model has rid herself. In case the male "heterosexual" viewer does harbor homophobic anxiety about his own sexuality, this is neutralized by the model's excessive femininity, as exhibited in her bodily postures, facial expressions, and figure-hugging clothes.

If the pre-op transsexual is vastly more popular among Internet spectators than post-ops, then, it must be because the continued presence of the male genitals serves a more complex function than the simple satisfaction of homosexual or even bisexual urges. Drawing upon the Freudian theory of castration anxiety in all males, Linda Williams offers an explanation for the importance of what in the porn industry is known as the "money-shot," that is, the fully visible ejaculation of semen. Williams sees the money-shot, an essential component of every hard-core movie, as a fetishistic figure of female lack, reassuring men, calming their castration fears.[40] All fetishes are, for Freud, a substitute for the phallus that the female has lost and, as such, a means of assuaging male castration anxiety.[41] In this sense desire for the shemale may be said to be, at least partly, fetishistic in nature. Moreover, for Freud a fetish "saves the fetishist from being a homosexual by endowing women with the characteristic that makes them tolerable as sexual objects."[42]

The male's unconscious fear of castration gives rise to a need for visual evidence of "intactness" with which the male viewer unconsciously identifies, and in the shemale scenario this evidence is not merely peripheral, as in heterosexual porn, but occupies center stage, where Irigaray's "nothing to see" of the woman is filled by the "look-at-me-ness" of the male erection.[43] The fearsome threat of the vagina *dentata* has in the shemale been replaced by the reassuring familiarity of the phallus. In the unconscious perspective identified by Freud, then, the transsexual is not a man, chemically equipped with the attributes of a woman, but a woman to whom the lost penis has been restored.[44] Hence, the constant focus in transsexual porn on the penis, its size, power, and availability, both active and passive (e.g., "Imagine being fucked by your girlfriend!"; "These bitches love being sucked dry"). At the same time, the male viewer may somewhat paradoxically be made to feel inferior by the well-endowed transsexuals he encounters, and, indeed, this sense of sexual inferiority is often encouraged by accompanying verbal messages—for example, "Her dick is bigger than yours." Indeed, some photosets are actually accompanied by advertisements for penis enlargement pills.

Linked to the need for visual signs of intactness is perhaps the satisfaction of a desire to see visual evidence of the other's arousal. Such a desire is not limited to twenty-first-century visual pornography: Peter Cryle identifies it in the emphasis on erection and discharge to be found in erotic fiction of eighteenth-century France. The commonplace that women are known to dissimulate, faking orgasm in particular to please their male partners, leads the men in these novels and the male readers whom they represent to require verification of female pleasure: "A woman's desire is manifest in her erect clitoris, available for examination in a way that is parallel, if quantitatively inferior to a man's. . . . What climactic eroticism needs and desires is proof. It finds this proof readily in the bodies of men, and exacts it in kind from the bodies of women."[45]

In the most literal of senses, then, the shemale porn consumer "wants it all": the feminine *and* the masculine, the breasts *and* the penis, visible and incontrovertible signs of *jouissance* from the uncastrated woman. The penis plays a crucial role in the arousal of the spectator—not necessarily because the latter is actually homosexual but because of the shocking and simultaneously exciting contrast it represents. The juxtaposition (all-important in visual porn) of an ideally huge erection with equally huge breasts (archetype of the feminine) and with girlish prettiness and shapeliness incarnates an impossible fantasy of sexual totality that offers the male viewer complete sexual satisfaction, not simply because the transsexual image contains the attributes of both sexes but because, as already noted, the viewer is offered in fantasy the sexual skills of another "male." From a psychoanalytic point of view this demand for total satisfaction is the expression of an unconscious yearning for the lost maternal phallus and an unconscious desire to return to preoedipal unity with the mother. Collapsing both sameness and difference, the shemale represents the prelapsarian fantasy of the original undivided being, a utopian state that Monique Wittig nevertheless sees gender as destroying: "Gender is an ontological impossibility because it tries to accomplish the division of Being. But Being as being is not divided."[46] For Joyce McDougall, similarly, the fantasy of the hermaphrodite, as old as the cultural history of mankind, is linked to a primordial desire to abolish the difference that separates self from other:

> I want to maintain here that the hermaphroditic ideal has its roots in the
> ideal of a unity of child with maternal breast. The search for an ideal state

in which lack does not exist proves that the breast is already lost, that is, already perceived as being the essence of an Other. Thus, the bisexual illusion in all its manifestations is constructed upon the ramparts of sexual difference, but its underlying basis is located in the primordial relationship, in the still present desire to abolish this separation from the Other, to deny this impossible alterity.[47]

McDougall argues that the desire to be the other sex while retaining one's own sexuality is a universal unconscious desire.[48] Desire for the transsexual, then (McDougall was writing well before the advent of the hormone treatment that has to a large extent made possible the transsexual's "becoming" in the late twentieth and twenty-first centuries), is perhaps a displaced fantasy desire to *be* transsexual oneself, to regain that lost state of undifferentiation that we all enjoyed in the mother's womb.[49] The transsexual's penis and breasts that the viewer wants to suck and so literally introject are all maternal objects, the former being an unconscious metaphorical displacement for the mother's lost phallus as well as a third nipple from which milk can be made to flow, a symbolic union and absorption of material sustenance, maternal love and sexual sensations that have their origins in the physical stimulations of the uterus.

As both male and female, the shemale in Lacanian terms both *has* and *is* the phallus. In Lacan's rereading of Freud's oedipal phase, the male infant goes from *being* the phallus that the mother lacks to *having* the phallus by identifying with the father. The pre-op shemale clearly still has the phallus (not because she still possesses a penis—the phallus is more a signifier than a real object—but because, as a biological man, she retains male authority and power, or what Lacan calls "The Law of the Father").[50] But at the same time, in feminizing herself, in transforming herself into an erotic object of male desire, she again *becomes* the phallus that (s)he was in the preoedipal phase, when, as an infant, (s)he tried to identify with the phallus as the mother's object of desire. In a Lacanian perspective this is precisely what the fetishist and, in particular, the transvestite does, and in this respect the pre-op transsexual is vulnerable to the same analysis. Quoting Lacan, Bice Benvenuto and Roger Kennedy provide a clear and concise summary of this process:

> The infant's main means of obtaining satisfaction is by identifying himself with the mother's object of desire—his desire is then the desire of the Other. To please her, to keep her love (or so he thinks) he must at one level *be* the phallus. He informs the mother that he can make up to her what she lacks, and he will be, as it were, the "metonymy" of the phallus, replacing the desired phallus by himself. It is around this lure that the fetishist articulates his relation to his fetishistic objects (such as bits of clothing, shoes, etc.) which are symbols of the woman's phallus in so far as it is absent, and with which he identifies. The transvestite identifies with the phallus as hidden under the mother's clothes—he identifies with a woman who has a hidden phallus.

According to Lacan, the perversions seem to play a never-ending imaginary game, where the phallus is neither completely present nor absent: "The whole problem of the perversions consists in conceiving how the child, in his relation to the mother, a relation constituted in analysis not by his vital dependence on her, but by his dependence on her love, that is to say, by the desire for her desire, identifies himself with the imaginary object of this desire, in so far as the mother herself symbolizes it in the phallus."[51]

In her own commentary on Lacanian psychoanalysis and its relation to gender, Butler stresses the link between being the phallus and the desire to rediscover a pregendered existence when self and (m)other were inseparable: "To be the Phallus is to 'embody' the Phallus as the place to which it penetrates, but also to signify the promise of a return to the preindividuated jouissance that characterizes the undifferentiated relation to the mother."[52] To desire (s)he who both is and has the phallus is therefore to identify simultaneously with the masculine and the feminine positions as described by Lacan, an impossible situation symbolic of an unconscious yearning to become again the unsexed fetus, to be reunited with the mother in the fullness of the womb before gender differentiation occurred.[53] If, as we saw earlier, the "mother's" penis is superior in size to that of the awestruck "infant" viewer, this is as it should be in the hierarchy of the mother-child dyad.

Desiring the shemale may, then, after all, be an unconscious substitute for desiring the mother. In this respect the shemale is a perfect representation of the phallic mother fantasy that counters male castration anxiety. The photosets of shemale sites appear typically to play a game with the viewer, as we have already seen, teasing him with a gradual striptease leading to a sudden and shocking unveiling of the phallus, as the beautiful "girl" with feminine curves and soft skin is dramatically revealed to be genitally and often priapically male.[54] This game is, of course, known by all to be a pretense, the kind of ritualistic repetition that Freud identifies as an unconscious meaningful ritual. We recall that in the repetition of childhood play Freud saw the symbolic reenactment of the painful separation of infant from mother and that in this separation Lacan sees the origins of desire.[55] This is the *fort! da!* game, which both Freud and Lacan link with the origins of language, the latter identifying language itself as a substitute for the lost object of the mother's body.[56] This game of repetition crucially provides the child, and for Freud the agent of any creative activity, with the means of mastering a potentially painful memory. This is ultimately the role of all objects, but it is a function fulfilled perfectly by the Internet Web site, over which the viewer has the illusion of total control and to which he returns again and again.

The Shock of the New

If this *fort! da!* game compels the viewing subject to repeat it endlessly in the unconscious hope of making the lost maternal object present again, it is because it is paradoxically novel and exciting each and every time it is played. The play between the hidden and the visible that constitutes desire's enigmatic object and the shock of discovery are therefore central components of the metaphors of shemale porn. A comparison might usefully be drawn here with Roland Barthes's *S/Z,* which breaks down a short story by Balzac entitled "Sarrasine" into small narrative units and proceeds to analyze them in terms of a number of codes.[57] The Balzac story is especially relevant to our purposes in its main theme, which concerns a young man's passion for an opera singer he thinks to be a woman but who is in fact a castrato. Barthes's "enigmatic" code, served by any phrase or sentence that helps to create mystery or enigma and so excite the reader's curiosity, may be applied to the first images in the shemale photoset. It is by adroitly manipulating this code in "Sarrasine" that Balzac is able to suggest to the reader (as to the eponymous hero) that La Zambinella is a woman while simultaneously hinting that the opposite might in fact be the case. Like Balzac's hero, the reader is intended to be shocked, and yet, at the same time, he is curiously excited by the eventual discovery of the truth, which, we are given to believe, he may unconsciously have guessed at all along. Similarly, the shemale photoset initially performs not just the illusion of femininity but the suspension of disbelief by third parties, whether visually present in the images or implied in accompanying verbal text. This performance, as already indicated, leads to a final revelation of the phallus, which any males present in the images appear to find shocking . . . and arousing. Yet, as in the Balzac story, rendered even more erotic by Barthes's own gradual and teasing unveiling, the reader/viewer plays a game with himself, a willing accomplice in an erotic game of hide-and-seek. The finale is always shocking, but the shock was expected right from the start. And if, like Balzac's Sarrasine, we discover that the object of our desire is not what we thought it was, then we are compelled to acknowledge that we are not who we thought we were.

This pleasant half-expected shock—a sense of that "familiar strangeness" that Freud identifies as associated with repetition and the repression of desires in the unconscious—derives much of its erotic impact from the revelation of contrastive juxtapositions.[58] We saw earlier how an emphasis on such binary oppositions might be considered politically regressive, and yet an essential element of the shemale's erotic power stems from them: for example, breasts/balls, chicks/dicks, pretty girl / raging erection, smooth skin / stiff prick. These oxymorons create an uncertainty that is both reassuring and troubling, generating a thrill of pleasure in perversity, the sense of infringing on those social and sexual taboos that defend both collective and individual identities, though without any associated moral or ethical guilt. They also help to generate an arousing sense of the transgression of limits defined by our culture. For Foucault transgression is precisely the experience of such limits, outside of any ethical considerations: "It is likely that transgression has its entire space in the line it crosses."[59] More than any other, the pre-op transsexual inhabits this line between genders, and desire for the transsexual object is, therefore, a unique example of Foucault's concept of transgression as a liminal activity.

In conclusion it seems important to reiterate that, by its very nature, the Internet is a fantasy realm and that Internet pornography belongs, maybe more than any other pornographic medium, to fantasy alone. The vast majority of those who look at shemale images are unlikely, after all, to have any real contact with transsexuals. Fantasy allows the subject to free itself of sexual and gender identities in a manner that would prove difficult or impossible in the real world. By challenging received ideas concerning the nature of sexual desire and its relationship with fixed gender positions, these "chicks with dicks" might in the end be shown to have rendered a vital service to the cause of an ongoing sexual and gender revolution. Far from being peripheral to contemporary debates about the representation of sexuality, transsexual pornography is of direct relevance, on a political and philosophical level, to the interests of all working in the field. Provocative, disturbing, even repulsive for some, the fantasy images that we have been considering are clearly not high art, but they are complex cultural phenomena that deserve far more critical attention.

Notes

1. Laurence O'Toole's recent detailed survey of pornographic media in *Pornocopia: Porn, Sex, Technology, and Desire* (London: Serpent's Tail, 1998), for example, makes no mention at all of transsexuals or pornography in which they are represented.

2. The term *transvestite* refers to men who dress in women's clothing, while the term *male-to-female transsexual* denotes men who have physically changed their primary or secondary sexual characteristics through hormones or surgery—typically, men who have grown breasts through hormones or implants but still have penises, that is, "pre-op" transsexuals. "Post-op" male-to-female (MTF) transsexuals have undergone an irreversible operation to remove their penis and testicles and construct labia and a vagina. According to psychologists working in the field, the difference between transvestites and MTF transsexuals is that transvestites see themselves as men and want to be men, albeit men dressed occasionally as women, whereas MTF transsexuals actually want to be women, but this distinction is far from clear-cut. "Female-to-male" (FTM) transsexuals are not found in Internet or any other kind of pornography and are therefore not discussed here.

3. Laura Kipnis is one of the very few academic commentators on pornography centering on transgendered subjects. See, for example, her essay "She-Male Fantasies and the Aesthetics of Pornography," in *Dirty Looks: Women, Pornography, Power,* ed. Pamela Church Gibson and Roma Gibson (London: BFI Publishing, 1994), 124–143. Much of the material in this essay is recycled in chapter 2 of her excellent book, *Bound and Gagged: Pornography and the Politics of Fantasy in America* (New York: Grove Press, 1996).

4. For the history of the Internet, see Mac Bride, *The Internet* (London: Teach Yourself Books, 2001); John Naughton, *A Brief History of the Future: The Origins of the Internet* (Phoenix, 1999); and Tim Berners-Lee, *Weaving the Web: The Past, Present and Future of the World Wide Web* (London: Texere, 2000). For the history of cross-dressing and transsexuality, I am indebted to the following sources: Joanne Meyerowitz, *How Sex Changed: A History of Transsexuality in the United States* (Cambridge, Mass.: Harvard University Press, 2002), 1–50; and Stephen Whittle, *The Transgender Debate: The Crisis Surrounding Gender Identity* (Reading, Eng.: South Street Press, 2000), 33–42.

5. Marty Rimm, "Marketing Pornography on the Information Superhighway," research carried out at Carnegie-Mellon University, *Georgetown Law Journal* 83 (June 1995):

1849–1934. See Naughton, *Brief History of the Future,* 32–33: "Critics pointed out that many of Rimm's statistics—for example, his claim that 83.5 per cent of the images stored on the Usenet newsgroups are pornographic—were nonsensical. Two acknowledged experts from Vanderbilt University, Donna Hoffman and Thomas Novak, maintained that pornographic files represent less than one half of 1 per cent of all messages posted on the internet."

6. See Naughton, *Brief History of the Future,* 33.

7. As Naughton points out, the Net does not require the consumer to cross a "shame" threshold when accessing pornography, since this can be done in the privacy of one's own home, and so the exponential rise in the consumption of porn on the Net is completely unfettered by any fear of moral or ethical stigmatization. This reveals some unpalatable truths about human nature, which is perhaps why the issue of Internet porn provokes such heated responses. Naughton, *Brief History of the Future,* 34–35.

8. See Whittle, *Transgender Debate,* 35.

9. In eighteenth-century England feminine men and masculine women, known as mollies and tommies, respectively, were regarded as third and fourth genders: see Randolph Trumbach, "London's Sapphists: From Three Sexes to Four Genders in the Making of Modern Culture," in *Bodyguards: The Cultural Politics of Gender Ambiguity,* ed. Julia Epstein and Kristina Straub (New York: Routledge, 1991), 112–113; see also Rictor Norton, *Mother Clap's Molly House* (London: GMP Publishers, 1992).

10. See Richard von Krafft-Ebing, *Psychopathia Sexualis* (1877; rpt., London: Velvet Publications, 1997).

11. See Meyerowitz, *How Sex Changed,* 40.

12. Harry Benjamin, *The Transsexual Phenomenon* (New York: Julian Press, 1966). *Endocrinology* is defined as "a new science that attempted to locate the essence of sex, gender, and sexuality in the secretions of the gonads" (Meyerowitz, *How Sex Changed,* 16).

13. Some images on these sites represent post-op transsexuals, but they are a very small minority.

14. Leo Bersani, *Homos* (Cambridge, Mass.: Harvard University Press, 1995), 61.

15. Bersani, *Homos,* 48.

16. See Kipnis, *Bound and Gagged,* 88.

17. See Judith Butler, *Gender Trouble. Feminism and the Subversion of Identity* (1990; rpt., New York: Routledge, 1999), 39; *phallicist* and *phallogocentrism* are terms derived from Freudian psychoanalysis and Derridean poststructuralism and designate the male orientation in the linguistic and cultural expressions of the West.

18. Among works by antipornography feminist campaigners, see, for instance, Andrea Dworkin, *Pornography: Men Possessing Women* (London: Women's Press, 1981); and Catherine MacKinnon, *Only Words* (London: HarperCollins, 1994). An excellent example of writing in this area by lesbian and gay critics is the collection of essays entitled *Gay Signatures: Gay and Lesbian Theory, Fiction and Film in France, 1945–1995,* ed. A. Hughes, O. Heathcote, and J. Williams (Oxford: Berg, 1998).

19. Kipnis, *Bound and Gagged,* 90–91.

20. Although Judith Butler does not refer to transsexuals in any detail in her seminal work on Queer Theory, *Gender Trouble,* she declares in her 1999 preface to the book that, were she to rewrite it "under present circumstances," she would include in it a discussion of transgender and intersexuality (preface to the 1999 ed., xxvi). Indeed, she has devoted a recent, if brief, essay to the subject: see afterword to "Transgender in Latin America: Persons, Practices and Meanings," a special issue of the journal *Sexualities* 5, no. 3 (1998).

21. See Luce Irigaray, *This Sex Which Is Not One* (Ithaca: Cornell University Press, 1985).
22. I shall restrict my analysis here to the still images posted on Web sites, leaving aside the more complex investigation of she-male movies that can either be purchased or downloaded from the Internet.
23. All of this confirms the power of norms to resist resignification. As Bersani points out, "resignification cannot destroy; it merely presents to the dominant culture spectacles of politically impotent disrespect," and, referring specifically to Judith Butler's positive view of drag as exemplifying the performativity of gender: "These mimetic activities are too closely imbricated in the norms they continue" (*Homos,* 51).
24. In conceding this, Butler is at odds with Monique Wittig's view of lesbianism's politically subversive potential; see Bersani, *Homos,* 47.
25. Butler, *Gender Trouble,* 15.
26. See Butler, *Gender Trouble,* 43.
27. Butler, *Gender Trouble,* 10.
28. Butler, *Gender Trouble,* 146.
29. Butler, *Gender Trouble,* xi.
30. Bersani, *Homos,* 46–47.
31. Butler, *Gender Trouble,* 33. Butler refers to Foucault's work on the hermaphrodite Herculine Barbin as demonstrating the inadequacy of conventional medico-legal discourse to account for the sexual practices of such people: "Herculine is not an 'identity,' but the sexual impossibility of an identity. . . . The linguistic conventions that produce intelligible gendered selves find their limit in Herculine precisely because she/he occasions a convergence and disorganization of the rules that govern sex/gender/desire" (31).
32. Friedrich Nietzsche, *On the Genealogy of Morals,* qtd. in Butler, *Gender Trouble,* 31.
33. Nietzsche, *On the Genealogy of Morals,* qtd. in Butler, *Gender Trouble,* 31.
34. Butler, *Gender Trouble,* 175.
35. See Butler, *Gender Trouble,* 24.
36. Because of the enormously profitable careers enjoyed by many pre-op transsexuals in the porn and prostitution business, surgery to remove the male genitals is frequently indefinitely postponed.
37. Qtd. by Butler, *Gender Trouble,* 26.
38. In this context the term *Asian* is used in its North American sense to denote natives of Far Eastern countries, and not those from the Indian subcontinent. Thailand, in particular, has a well-known reputation for transsexuals.
39. Similarly, lesbians often claim that another woman is more skillful than any man in pleasuring a woman.
40. Linda Williams, *Hard Core: Power, Pleasure, and the Frenzy of the Visible* (London: Pandora Press, 1990), 116.
41. See Sigmund Freud, "Fetishism" (1927), in *Pelican Freud Library,* vol. 7: *On Sexuality* (London: Pelican Books, 1984), 345–357.
42. Freud, *On Sexuality,* 7:353.
43. "L'horreur du rien-à-voir de la femme"; see Luce Irigaray, "Ce corps qui n'en est pas un," in *Ce sexe qui n'en est pas un* (Paris: Minuit, 1977); Eng. trans., *This Sex Which Is Not One.*
44. I am, of course, referring to Freud's well-known theory of the oedipal phase, during which the infant male views his mother/sister as castrated and fears a similar fate at the hands of his father.
45. Peter Cryle, *The Telling of the Act: Sexuality as Narrative in Eighteenth- and Nineteenth-Century France* (London: Associated University Presses, 2001), 154–157.

46. Monique Wittig, *Straight Mind,* 81, qtd. by Bersani, *Homos,* 189 n. 19.

47. Joyce McDougall, "L'Idéal hermaphrodite et ses avatars," *Bisexualité et différence des sexes, publié sous la direction de J.-B. Pontalis,* 409–431 (Paris: Éditions Gallimard, 1973), 410–411; my trans.

48. McDougall, "L'Idéal hermaphrodite et ses avatars," 417.

49. See McDougall, "L'Idéal hermaphrodite et ses avatars," 413–414. The collection in which McDougall's essay appeared is dated 1973.

50. As indicated earlier, this is also one of the reasons for gay and feminist hostility to transsexuals.

51. Bice Benvenuto and Roger Kennedy, *The Works of Jacques Lacan: An Introduction* (London: Free Association Books, 1986), 132–133, quoting Jacques Lacan, *Écrits* (Paris: Seuil, 1966), 197–198.

52. Butler, *Gender Trouble,* 203 n. 13.

53. The psychoanalyst Louise Kaplan argues that the transvestite also desires a position beyond sexual difference. For Kaplan perversions are not just sexual pathologies; they are pathologies of gender role identity. What they represent is an inability to conform completely to the gender conventions and gender stereotypes of the dominant social order (see Louise J. Kaplan, *Female Perversions: The Temptations of Emma Bovary* [New York: Anchor Books, 1992], 9). Kaplan believes that transvestites are attracted to elaborate, theatrical forms of feminine display as a way of denying sexual difference.

54. This striptease, of course, also occurs at the level of each individual image as it gradually unfolds upon the computer screen from thumbnail to full-size picture. This happy coincidence, resulting from the nature of Internet technology itself, adds to the provocative effect of such images upon the viewer.

55. See Jacques Lacan, "The Seminar on 'The Purloined Letter,'" *Écrits,* 46.

56. See Lacan, *Écrits,* 319.

57. See Roland Barthes, *S/Z* (Paris: Seuil, 1970); trans. Richard Miller (New York: Hill and Wang, 1975).

58. See Sigmund Freud, "The Uncanny" (1919), *The Pelican Freud Library,* vol. 14: *Art and Literature* (London: Pelican Books, 1984), 335–376.

59. See Michel Foucault, "Préface à la transgression," *Critique* 195–196 (1963): 751–769.

CONTRIBUTORS

ELIOT BORENSTEIN is an associate professor and chair of Russian and Slavic studies at New York University. He is the author of *Men without Women: Masculinity
and Revolution in Russian Fiction, 1917–1929* (2000) and the editor and
cotranslator of Mark Lipovetsky's *Russian Postmodernist Fiction: Dialogue with
Chaos* (1999). He is currently completing a book entitled "Made in Russia (tm):
Popular Culture and National Identity after 1991."

COLETTE COLLIGAN is an assistant professor of English at Simon Fraser University,
Canada. She is currently completing a book on obscenity entitled "Trafficking
Smut: Obscenity, Media, and Globalisation in the Nineteenth Century." She has
published essays on nineteenth-century literature and culture in *Nineteenth-Century
Contexts, Victorian Review,* and *Dickens Studies Annual.*

SARAH LEONARD is an assistant professor of history at Simmons College in Boston, Massachusetts. She is currently at work on a book that examines the creation,
enforcement, and meaning of secular obscenity law in nineteenth-century Germany.
During the 2002–2003 academic year she was a Mellon Postdoctoral Fellow at
the University of Pennsylvania and a participant in the Penn Humanities Forum's
"Year of the Book."

KATALIN SZOVERFY MILTER is currently a doctoral student at Ohio University's School
of Telecommunications. She has previously earned B.Ed. and M.A. degrees in English from Eotvos Lorant University in Budapest, Hungary, and an M.A. degree
in Communications from Ohio University. She has worked as an interpreter, teacher,
and conference manager in Europe and in the United States. Her research area is
the use of the Internet and technology in education.

JOHN PHILLIPS is the author of *Nathalie Sarraute: Metaphor, Fairy-Tale, and the
Feminine of the Text* (1994), *Forbidden Fictions: Pornography and Censorship in*

Twentieth-Century French Literature (1999), and *Sade: The Libertine Novels* (2001) and coeditor, with Gaëtan Brulotte, of "The Encyclopedia of Erotic Literature." He is a professor of French literature and culture at London Metropolitan University.

MARYNA ROMANETS teaches in the Department of English at the University of Northern British Columbia (Canada). She has published articles on contemporary British, Irish, and Ukrainian literatures, focusing on the issues of representation and gender, politics, and language; intertextual relations; as well as the mechanisms of textual production and translation theory and praxis in Britain, Canada, France, Russia, Sweden, Ukraine, and the United States. She is currently completing the book "Displaced Subjects, Anamorphosic Texts, Reconfigured Visions: Improvised Traditions in Contemporary Irish and Ukrainian Women's Literature" and working on a project on "The Postcolonial Syndrome: Pornography in the Speculum of Socialist Realism."

LISA Z. SIGEL is the author of *Governing Pleasures: Pornography and Social Change in England, 1815–1914* (2002) and numerous articles on the history of pornography, sexuality, and the body. She is currently focusing on the circulation of sexual meanings for a book entitled "Narratives of Love and Perversity during the Interwar Years." She is a visiting assistant professor of history at DePaul University.

JOSEPH W. SLADE has held National Endowment for the Humanities, Hagley Museum, and Gannett Fellowships and has taught at Long Island University, New York University, the University of Chicago, and Ohio University, where he is director of graduate study in the School of Telecommunications and codirector of the Central Region Humanities Center. A literary critic turned historian of technology, he has written more than sixty articles on literature, culture, technology, and film. Among his books are *Thomas Pynchon* (1974 and 1990), *Beyond the Two Cultures: Essays on Science, Literature, and Technology,* edited with Judith Y. Lee (1990), *Pornography in America* (2000), and *Pornography and Sexual Representation: A Reference Guide,* 3 vols. (2001). He is coeditor of *A Cultural Atlas of the Midwest* (2004) and is working on two other books, "Shades of Blue: A History of the Stag Film" and "Lethal Maxims," a biography of the father and son who invented the machine gun and the silencer.

CLARISSA SMITH is a senior lecturer in media and cultural studies at the University of Sunderland. She has written a number of articles on women's consumption of sexually explicit materials and is researching and writing a project provisionally entitled "Women, Pornography, and Sex Toys: From Oppression to the Jelly Rabbit."

ANNIE STORA-LAMARRE is author of *L'Enfer de la IIIe Republique: Censeurs et pornographes, 1881–1914* (1990) and editor of *Incontournable morale: Annales littéraire de Franche-Comté* (1999), *Archives de la peur: Les Populations à risque de la Franche-Comté au XIXe siècle, Annales littéraires de Franche-Comté* (2000), and *La Cité charnelle du droit: Annales littéraires de Franche-Comté* (2002). She is a professor of contemporary history at the University of Franche-Comté.

INDEX

abolition, 67–99
Africa, 14, 68
AIDS (Acquired Immune Deficiency Syndrome), 126, 137, 178, 181, 212
Alloula, Malek, 14, 95n20
America, *see* United States of America
Amsterdam, 117. *See also* Netherlands
Anderson, Nancy F., 116, 122n21
antipornography: Andrea Dworkin and, 127, 135, 137–138, 168n17, 259, 272n18; Bill Thompson and, 152, 168n17; Catherine MacKinnnon and, 127, 168n17, 259; feminism and, 5, 15, 135, 153–154, 166n3, 168n17, 170n50, 182, 207, 259; in France, 129; leagues, 58, 61, 129, 249; Mary Whitehouse and, 152, 169nn31, 35; Moving Together and, 233, 248, 249; National Vigilance Association (NVA) and, 63, 88, 98n57, 102, 116; in Russia, 236, 249, 252n24; in the U.K., 126–127, 146, 169n45; in the U.S., 16, 127, 137
Argentina, 173
Armstrong, Nancy, 104
ars erotica, 139
Austria, 173

Bailey, Victor, 100
Bataille, Georges, 91, 126, 133–134, 139, 188, 189
Baudrillard, Jean, 213
Beauvoir, Simone de, 263

Bending, Lucy, 93n8
Best, Joel, 149
bestiality, 85, 182, 213
Bhabha, Homi K., 205
Bibliothèque Nationale, 4, 48, 132. *See also* l'Enfer de la Bibliothèque Nationale
Blackburn, Sheila, 100
Brazil, 177–178, 190, 265
Britain, *see* United Kingdom
British Museum, 4
Brussels, 117
Budapest, *see under* Hungary
Butler, Judith, 188, 259, 262, 263–264, 272n20

capitalism, 20, 185. *See also* consumer culture
censorship, 9, 12, 14, 15, 16, 21, 27, 33, 49, 58–59, 60–64, 116, 125, 127–130, 140, 153–156, 169n170, 175, 233, 253n53
Central America, 14
child pornography, 51, 133, 174, 180, 210–211
children: and childhood, 116; and incest, 12–13, 100–124
China, 174
citizenship, 23, 31, 37, 41
class, 4, 37, 101–102, 104, 171n79. *See also* middle class; working class
colonies, 52

consumer culture: and mass markets, 148, 193, 236, 244; and pornography, 12–13, 15, 17, 22
contraception, 57, 63, 89
Corbin, Alain, 51
Czech Republic, 175

Darnton, Robert, 5, 104, 127, 142nn15, 17
Davidoff, Leonore, 116
Davis, Tracy, 92n3
Deism, 32
Deleuze, Gilles, 214, 228
democracy, 12, 44, 54, 55, 57, 238
Denmark, 4, 151, 175, 258
Derrida, Jacques, 263
deviance, 3, 23
Driver, Stephen, 159
Duchet, Claude, 50

Electra complex, 119, 120. *See also* Freud, Sigmund
l'Enfer de la Bibliothèque Nationale, 4, 48–53, 64, 142n24
England, *see* United Kingdom
Englisch, Paul, 42, 45–46n14
Enlightenment, the, 5, 8, 9, 25n21, 30, 31
erotica: definitions of, 6–7, 206; and the Internet, 212, 219; vs. pornography, 6–7
Europe, 4, 5, 54, 173, 189

Favret, Mary, 70, 94n15
feminism, 16, 57, 135, 138, 241, 259. *See also* antipornography: feminism and
film: Erwin Panofsky and, 173; history of pornographic, 173; pornographic, 5, 251n9; racialism and, 14
Findlen, Paula, 7, 29
Finland, 9, 174
Fisch, Audrey, 68, 72, 93n4
flagellation: as English, 71, 78, 79, 81; as "the English vice" 13, 67, 69, 89, 91, 187; theories of, 69, 91. *See also* flogging
flogging, 67, 68; and Whipping Act of 1862, 68, 93n8; whipping, masochism, and race, 13, 22, 67–99. *See also* flagellation
Foreman, P. Gabrielle, 78

Foucault, Michel, 3, 6, 81, 134, 137, 145n83, 263–264, 270, 273n31
France: in eighteenth century, 20, 267; French Revolution, 10, 46n16, 128, 131; laws regarding pornography, 63, 127; Paris, 83, 106, 117, 125, 127, 142n11, 176; and pornography, 9, 15, 16, 17, 31, 51, 62, 88, 125, 128, 173, 175; Third Republic, 4, 48, 52–53, 64; in twentieth century, 125
Frantz, David, 7
Freud, Sigmund, 3, 69, 91, 92n3, 116, 117, 118–119, 124nn79, 82, 131, 133, 139, 243, 266, 267, 268–269, 270, 273n44

gallant literature, 32, 51
Garfield, Deborah, 78
Germany: Berlin, 27; Biedermeier period, 29; Munich, 38–39; Napoleonic Wars and, 29, 32, 33; National Socialist (Nazi) Party in, 15; and pornography, 9, 10, 15, 27–47, 62, 175; Revolution of 1848, 27, 29, 37, 41; West Germany, 15, 179
Gibson, Ian, 67, 69, 92n3
Gillespie, Andrew, 159
globalization: effects of, 206; Europe and North America's role in, 54; and pornography, 18, 19, 21, 83, 90, 173–204, 211
Gordon, Linda, 101
Goujon, Jean-Paul, 133
Great Britain, *see* United Kingdom

Hall, Catherine, 116
Halttunen, Karen, 68
Hardy, Simon, 148
Hart, Lynda, 91
Heath, Stephen, 133
Hegel, Georg Wilhelm Friedrich, 91
Heller, Tamar, 92n3, 94n14
heterosexuality, 3, 20, 21, 23, 79–81, 207, 261
Hoff, Joan, 2
homosexuality: and erotica, 3, 131, 136, 144n71, 145n75; and homoerotic desires, 79–80, 114, 208, 219, 257, 258, 259; and homophobia, 115, 215, 262; and pornography, 21, 22–23, 52, 78, 81, 137, 139, 213

Hungary: "Budaporn," 173; Budapest, 18, 173; "Goulash capitalism" and, 179; and pornography, 18, 19, 21, 173–204
Hunt, Lynn, 5, 8, 22, 30, 104, 150, 151, 152
Hyam, Ronald, 95n21

illustrations, pornographic, 76
immorality, 12, 32, 45, 58, 61, 101, 127. *See also* morality
incest: laws against, 100, 102–103; legal definitions of, 100; and the National Society for the Prevention of Cruelty to Children (NSPCC), 102–103; and the National Vigilance Association (NVA), 102, 116; pornographic novels of, 104–113; pornographic themes of, 112; and pornography, 13, 74, 100–124, 158, 213, 219–220
indecency, 41, 127. *See also* obscenity
industrialization, 12, 51–52, 64
Italy: pornographic stars in, 183; and pornography, 4, 174

Jackson, Louise, 101, 115
Johnson Commission (1970), 2

Kendrick, Walter, 92n3
Kipnis, Laura, 3, 235, 255–256, 259, 260, 271n3
Kovács, István (Kovi), 190–192, 194–199
Krafft-Ebing, Richard von, 102, 117, 257

Lacan, Jacques, 263, 268–269
Lansbury, Coral, 92n3, 94n14, 98n53
Legman, Gershon, 83
Lindemann, Mary, 104

Magyar Look, 18, 186, 187, 192–193. *See also* Hungary
Malthusianism/neo-Malthusianism, *see* contraception
Marcus, Steven, 69, 92n3, 124n82
masochism, 90, 140, 217–218. *See also* sadism
Masson, Jeffrey, 118
McCalman, Iain, 5, 69, 92n3, 93n9
McClaren, Angus, 115
McDougall, Joyce, 267–268

Meese Commission (1986), 2
Mendes, Peter, 76, 83–84, 92n3, 98n56
Middle East, 174
middle class, 4, 31, 34, 36, 44, 100, 101, 104, 114, 120
Miller, Henry, 48
Miller Test, of obscenity, 127
modernity, 30
morality, 22, 28, 30, 49, 52–54, 57, 59, 104, 153, 166n3, 182, 223, 244. *See also* immorality
morals legislation, *see* obscenity

nationalism, 12, 52
Nead, Lynda, 92n3
Nelson, James, 92n3
Netherlands, 9, 15, 50, 175, 257
Netz, Robert, 127
Nichols, Charles, 95n20

obscenity: definitions of, 6, 10–11, 28–29, 33, 37, 48, 53, 55, 62, 93n9, 126, 142n22, 149, 168n17, 206, 236; democracy and, 44; in France, 127; in Germany, 10–11, 28, 33, 37, 41, 44, 45n12; laws, 10–11, 37, 41, 89, 94n15; in the U.K., 63, 67, 126–127, 149, 154–155, 161; in the U.S., 89, 127
O'Toole, Laurence, 152, 154, 159, 168n17, 271n1

Pauvert, Jean-Jacques, 130, 131, 132
Pease, Alison, 93nn3, 9
pedophilia, 141, 213. *See also* child pornography
Petley, Julian, 166–167n5, 168n17
photography, 62, 89, 117, 148, 161, 164
Playboy, 15, 18, 20, 149, 150, 151, 163, 186, 206, 238–239, 242, 250
pornography: audience for, 53, 114 (*see also* women: as audience for pornography); beliefs about, 2, 234; crime and, 58; definitions of, 6–8, 93n9, 94n16, 126, 141n3, 142n22, 149, 167n8, 206, 219, 234, 236–237, 250n3; distribution patterns of, 114, 116–117, 150–152, 158, 161, 173–204, 256; divorce and, 56–57; on DVD, 173, 174; economics of, 1, 2, 16, 17, 18, 26n40, 114, 146,

pornography (*continued*)
149, 158, 162–166, 166n4, 175, 176,
179, 180, 181, 200n16, 244, 250–
251n5; education and, 59, 139, 169n4,
212; effects of, 56, 58; effects on
children of, 140, 249; ethnic, 178,
204n98; hard-core, 174, 237; impact of,
234; international trade and, 116–117,
173–204; and the Internet, 21, 22, 147,
161, 165, 177, 210, 212, 255–274, 271–
272nn5, 7, 274n54; laws regarding, 16,
27, 56, 58–59, 61, 63, 100, 130, 149,
151, 152, 155, 168n30, 174, 180, 206,
233, 256, 257; legalization of, 16, 17,
18, 21, 147, 200n25; letters to magazines, 157; as literature, 19, 32–45,
125–145, 216–229; magazines, 157,
207, 239; and national identity, 4, 234,
235, 242, 250, 251nn8, 13; pay-per-
view, 174; and politics, 10, 12, 20, 29,
37, 40–41, 44, 59, 100, 104, 183, 209,
232–234, 244; and pornographers, 117;
postcards, 14, 22, 62, 95n21; printers
of, 33; producers of, 147, 154, 175; and
religion, 31, 38, 46n16, 60, 126, 129;
scholarship and, 1, 4, 6, 14, 24n7,
45n14, 70, 92n3, 236, 251n6, 255; and
social change, 12, 29, 36, 53–54, 140;
sociologists and, 55–56; soft-core, 146,
157, 163, 164, 206, 237; technology
and, 2, 11, 14, 18, 21, 53, 147, 153, 161,
165, 171n72, 177, 256; and trade fairs,
176, 180; and urban space, 54
postcolonial world, 6, 205–231
Presley, John Woodrow, 92n3
prostitution, 8, 87, 180, 213
publishers, 11, 16, 26n40, 31, 33, 41,
46n17, 49–50, 55, 60, 69, 73–74, 76,
78, 81, 83, 116–117, 127, 130, 146–
149, 152, 153, 155–159, 167n7,
168n30, 252n53
pulp novels, 22

racialism: in Europe, 14, 52; incest and,
108; and pornography, 12–13, 83, 84–
85; in slave-flogging pornography, 75,
82; and themes in pornography, 67–99;
theories of, 52; in U.K., 75; and
violence, 82

Réage, Pauline, 16, 90, 135–136, 139
Renaissance, 8, 257
Richardson, Michael, 134
Russia: and the Cold War, 20; homophobia
in, 209; and pornography, 4, 9, 16, 18,
19, 20, 52–53, 181, 207, 232–254;
Russian Revolution, 237; Soviet Union,
178, 205, 211; Young Pioneers in, 210–
211, 230n16
Rutherford, Jonathon, 115

Sacher-Masoch, Leopold von, 16, 91,
99n69, 117. *See also* masochism
Sade, Marquis de, 89, 91, 99n69, 104, 125,
126, 129, 131, 132, 134, 135, 139, 212.
See also sadism
sadism: and the Marquis de Sade, 89; and
pornography, 13, 17; and sadomasochism, 17, 91, 211
sadomasochism, 147, 182, 217. *See also*
sadism
Sánchez-Eppler, Karen, 78, 82, 95n20
Scandinavia, 16
Scheick, William, 92n3
Scotland, 9, 102. *See also* United Kingdom
sexual identities: fetishistic, 175; heterosexual, 79; homosexual, 3, 21, 52, 139;
lesbian, 51, 74, 133, 139, 207; and
national identities, 12, 20, 88, 90, 186–
188, 210; queer, 137, 260; and
pornography, 3, 22, 69, 216, 262–264;
transsexual, 21, 22, 255, 260, 262
sexual violence, 13, 68, 74
Sigel, Lisa Z., 92n3, 93n9, 94n15, 97n41
Sinyavsky, Andrei, 214
Skordaki, Eleni, 157–158, 170n57
slavery: economics of, 68; and homoerotic
desires, 71, 82; images of, 76; narratives of, 71–73, 87; and pornography,
67–99; and punishment or torture,
92n1; in U.S., 71
socialism, 49
social welfare, 102
Sontag, Susan, 126, 134
Sorokin, Vladimir, 20, 23, 233, 248,
253n59
Sorokin Affair, *see* Sorokin, Vladimir
South Africa, 174
South America, 68, 178

Soviet Union, *see* Russia
Spain, 9, 175, 200n25
Stalin, Joseph, 5, 211, 226, 232–233, 249
Steedman, Carolyn, 124n79
Stevenson, David, 9
Suleiman, Susan, 134
Sweden, 4, 151, 175
Switzerland, 60

Thomson, Rachel, 169n41
transsexuals: definitions and terms regarding, 271n2; images of, 21, 22, 255–274; medical technologies and, 257–259; theories regarding, 274n53. *See also* sexual identities

Ukraine, 18, 19, 20, 205–231, 244
United Kingdom: and abolition, 67; British Adult Publications Association (BAPA), 156–157; British Board of Film Certification (BBFC), 147, 167n6; Edwardian, 100, 112, 114; eighteenth century, 272n9; flagellation and, 73; high streets and newsagents in, 166–167n5; Home Office, 102, 121n13, 168; laws regarding pornography, 63, 149, 151, 257; London, 117; Page 3 Girl, 153, 169n42; politics, 25n24; and pornography, 5, 10, 15, 17, 19, 21, 53, 127, 174; Postal Office, 117; sadomasochistic literature and, 52; Victorian, 91, 100, 101, 104, 113, 114
United States of America: California, 175; Civil War, 68, 85–86; incest in, 103; laws regarding pornography in, 256; low quality of pornography in, 175; and pornography, 15, 16, 23, 59, 83–84, 90, 98n46, 127, 151, 173, 181, 185, 236, 242, 256; slavery in, 71, 77, 81, 85, 87; Victorian, 78
unzüchtige Schriften, 28, 29

venereal disease, 102
video: actors/actresses/stars in, 18, 178, 179, 183–185; directors, 190–192; as industry, 180; pornographic, 18, 22, 147, 148, 149, 156, 161, 173, 190–192, 193; production, 181; working conditions in, 178, 192

Waugh, Thomas, 3, 6, 15
West Indies, 84, 96n23, 108
Wilde, Oscar, 114
Williams, Linda, 5, 148, 266
Williams Committee (1981), 155
Wittig, Monique, 263, 264, 267
Wohl, Anthony, 101
Wolff, Larry, 118
Wolfram, Sybil, 121n16
women: as audience for pornography, 30, 138–139, 140, 154, 161, 182, 207, 217, 220; cult of domesticity and, 45; effects of reading pornography on, 56; as femmes fatales, 51; fictionalized authorship of, 113, 123n49, 135; as flogged slaves, 73, 90; hypersexualized, 12, 158; images of, 12, 152, 186, 210; New Women, 115; as nymphomaniacs, 158, 213; obstacles to creating pornography for, 51; pornography by, 135–136, 138, 139, 217; status of, 35–34, 41, 43, 45, 51; as symbols of moral purity, 223; violence against, 115; as white slaves, 89–90
Wood, Marcus, 70, 94n16
working class, 4, 55, 58–59, 101, 103, 120, 152
World War I, 15; interwar years, 26n37
World War II, 15, 258

Yellin, Jean Fagan, 77–78, 95n20
Yugoslavia, 4, 179